PHILANTHROPY IN AMERICA

POLITICS AND SOCIETY IN TWENTIETH-CENTURY AMERICA

Series Editors

William Chafe, Gary Gerstle, Linda Gordon, and Julian Zelizer

A list of titles in this series appears at the back of the book

PHILANTHROPY IN AMERICA

★ ★ ★ A HISTORY ★ ★ ★

OLIVIER ZUNZ

Princeton University Press ★ Princeton and Oxford

Published by Princeton University Press, 41 William Street,
Princeton, New Jersey 08540
In the United Kingdom: Princeton University Press, 6 Oxford Street,
Woodstock, Oxfordshire OX20 1TW
press.princeton.edu

Library of Congress Cataloging-in-Publication Data

Zunz, Olivier.
Philanthropy in America : a history / Olivier Zunz.
p. cm. — (Politics and society in twentieth-century America)
Includes bibliographical references and index.
ISBN 978-0-691-12836-8 (hardcover : alk. paper)
1. Charities—United States—History. 2. Nonprofit organizations—
United States—History. 3. Humanitarianism—United States—History.
4. Endowments—United States—History. I. Title.
HV91.Z86 2012   361.70973—dc23
2011017479

British Library Cataloging-in-Publication Data is available

This book has been composed in Minion Pro and Univers

Printed on acid-free paper. ∞

Printed in the United States of America

1 3 5 7 9 10 8 6 4 2

To the memory of my friend Stephen Innes (1946–2005)

CONTENTS

ACKNOWLEDGMENTS

My heartfelt thanks go first to an extraordinary group of dedicated people at the Ford Foundation. Barry Gaberman, Susan Berresford, Christopher Harris, and Alan Divack recognized in the early formulation of this book my ambition of telling philanthropy's contribution to American democracy and helped turn the idea into reality. I am grateful also for the support I received from the W. K. Kellogg Foundation and the Charles Stewart Mott Foundation. The Hagley Museum and Library made it possible for me early in the research to spend a summer exploring the Pew Charitable Trusts' records in the Soda House on the banks of the Brandywine.

At the University of Virginia, my long-time academic home, my colleagues on the committee that oversees the Bankard Fund for the Study of Political Economy have shown much confidence in this project and provided funds over several years. So has the Institute for Advanced Study in Culture, the haven for scholars that James Davison Hunter has so ably created.

Very talented students have taken an active role in this work. They have helped research and interpret the appropriate sources. I feel privileged to have worked so closely over the years with Andrew J. F. Morris, Derek Hoff, Christopher Loomis, Christopher Nichols, and Daniel Holt, while they were earning their doctorates in history at UVA. Jordan Berman and Brent Cebul also have aided the research.

At my second academic home, the École des Hautes Études en Sciences Sociales in Paris, I have tried out every idea for this book during my annual presentations to the American history seminar run by Pap NDiaye, Cécile Vidal, and François Weil at the Centre d'Études Nord-Américaines.

Sustained exchanges with Kim Gould Ashizawa, Arnaldo Bagnasco, Dwight Burlingame, David Hammack, Steven Heydemann, Richard John, Stanley N. Katz, Ira Katznelson, James Loeffler, Holly Cowan Shulman, Nancy Summers, Francis X. Sutton, Thomas Troyer, Joshua Yates, and Philip Zelikow have improved the work dramatically. Julian Bond has shared with me family papers from the days his father Horace Mann Bond worked for the Rosenwald Fund. Flavio Brugnoli, Piero Gastaldi, and Mario Gioannini at the Compagnia di San Paolo in Turin have followed this research with a sustained interest in the American experience.

At Princeton University Press, Brigitta van Rheinberg not only recognized this book early on as one she wanted to publish, but also provided excellent advice on the manuscript. So have two anonymous readers for the Press. Eva Jaunzems has contributed her remarkable copyediting skills.

I owe a very special thanks to three long-time close friends. Nicolas Barreyre, Arthur Goldhammer, and Charlie Feigenoff have taken much of their valuable time to review my manuscript in minute detail and have encouraged me to reformulate my ideas as often as needed.

Christine, our children Emmanuel and Sophie, Sophie's husband James, and our two splendid grandchildren Henry and Lila have shown much patience with me, each in their own way, as I have completed this work.

It is customary but also appropriate to add that deficiencies that remain are my own.

Olivier Zunz
Charlottesville, Virginia
Spring 2011

PHILANTHROPY IN AMERICA

INTRODUCTION

"To spend money is easy, to spend it well is hard," wrote economist Wesley Mitchell in the pages of the *American Economic Review* in 1912, elaborating on the "backward art of spending money" that character-ized most Americans.[1] Mitchell contrasted the American consumer's "ignorance" with the big industrialist's efficient expenditure based upon accumulated empirical knowledge. As the founding director of the Na-tional Bureau of Economic Research, a think tank the newly created Commonwealth Fund bankrolled in 1919, Mitchell soon became the beneficiary of another kind of expenditure that reflected the exploratory habit of mind of some contemporary industrialists and other Americans of means.[2] They were investing large sums in new philanthropic founda-tions and endowments designed to foster social progress in which they believed.

Andrew Carnegie, who conducted large-scale philanthropy with the same obsession with which he streamlined steel operations, remem-bered late in his life the day when he "resolved to stop accumulating" and began "the infinitely more serious and difficult task" of what he termed "wise distribution."[3] Certainly, he wanted everybody to know that he had reached his decision to become a philanthropist as a mat-ter of duty. In his own words, he was following a "gospel of wealth" that obligated him to return to society what he had taken, but he was deter-mined to do so by following the same intelligent managerial principles that had made him a rich man. Carnegie's approach to philanthropy gained currency. Over the course of the next century, philanthropists and their advisers followed in Carnegie's footsteps, perfecting the art of spending money for the common good.

Carnegie and his peers clearly felt exhilaration at putting their fortunes to work for large causes at home and abroad. They enjoyed

1

the exercise of power entailed in building entirely new philanthropic institutions—most notably the general-purpose foundation—and underwriting important experiments in higher education, science, and medicine. Their innovation was to conceive of philanthropic funding as yet another financial investment and to use the skills they had acquired in business to minimize the risk of their speculations, and to vastly enlarge the scope of their charitable giving. Traditional charitable givers had more modest goals and did not expect much in return for their generosity. What may have been true of the traditional giver, however, was no longer true of the modern philanthropic funder. American philanthropy would be a capitalist venture in social betterment, not an act of kindness as understood in Christianity.

Carnegie and other wealthy industrialists, however, were not the only ones who invested in the greater good. Philanthropic practice grew ever more inclusive after the turn of the century as new forms of giving attracted donations from millions of Americans of modest means. At his new economic institute, Mitchell measured the ways in which Americans spent their income, and that included contributing to the new mass philanthropy. Community chests, community foundations, and national health organizations such as the American Cancer Society superseded America's tradition of small-scale, local associations with national, mass appeals aimed at tackling increasingly ambitious causes like curing major diseases or pressing for social reform.

The rise in disposable income among the middle and working classes dramatically increased the number of Americans who could join in such causes. Speaking of the comparatively high wages skilled workers were receiving in American industry, German economist Werner Sombart famously wrote in 1906 that "all Socialist utopias came to nothing on roast beef and apple pie."[4] Sombart opened a long debate as to whether high wages had killed class consciousness in America. Whether they had or not, Americans were clearly ready to contribute a portion of their "roast beef and apple pie" to promote the social good. By the 1950s, mass philanthropy was so well integrated into everyday life in the United States that one could identify the season by the door-to-door collection in progress—winter and spring for health agencies and the Red Cross, fall for community chests. A large part of the American population understood that their small gifts cumulatively enhanced the life of the nation and in turn their own.

In this book, I tell the story of the convergence of big-money philanthropy and mass giving that has sustained civil society initiatives over a long twentieth century. From Andrew Carnegie to Bill Gates, and from ordinary people who purchased Christmas seals to fight tuberculosis to those who wear pink ribbons to battle breast cancer, the nation has come to view philanthropy as both a quintessential part of being American and another means of achieving major objectives. Foundations originating in large private fortunes have collaborated with institutions of mass philanthropy in promoting scientific research, supporting educational institutions, and fighting for human rights. Together they have forged a philanthropic sector that donors, beneficiaries, and the state recognize as a critical source of ideas as well as of funding.

American philanthropists' most important innovation, made possible by the multiplication of large fortunes in the late nineteenth century, was to envision an unlimited agenda of works, in which participants redefined goals as circumstances changed. In partnership with reformers, philanthropists no longer confined themselves to narrowly defined causes, as both tradition and the existing legal framework of charity required. They promoted instead nothing less than "the well-being of mankind," a phrase that came to be increasingly used in foundation charters and bequests. Mass philanthropy added size to the scope of this new and uniquely American open-ended philanthropy—the outcome of a silent but major legal revolution that I detail in this book.

Throughout the nineteenth century, the influence of philanthropy over public affairs had been limited by the "dead hand" of the donor—the legal obligation for trustees to follow strictures only because they were the donor's wishes. Julius Rosenwald, the man who built Sears, Roebuck and devoted his fortune to building thousands of elementary schools for African-Americans in the South in the early twentieth century, made just that point in an article in the *Atlantic Monthly* in 1929. Rosenwald produced a long list of trusts that had become quickly irrelevant because they were narrowly defined. As an example, he pointed to a trust set up to ensure that the female students at Bryn Mawr College be sufficiently nourished. The donor had created a fund to provide the young women with a baked potato at every meal, but when Rosenwald wrote young women were worried more about overindulgence than malnutrition.[5] Rosenwald himself expressed his strong opposition to the dead hand by putting a time limit on the large fund he had created for his philanthropic ventures. Others have chosen to design trust instruments more creatively, making it possible for trustees to update goals according to shifting conditions. Their foundations would be able to tackle new problems as they emerged rather than being tied to the original wishes of the founder or the letter of an outdated charter.

The more ambitious the philanthropic projects, the more inextricably they became linked with national affairs. Politicians and regulators, confronted by a myriad of innovations and by the leverage philanthropists applied, formalized the federal government's recognition of philanthropic institutions as public assets through its revenue acts. After Congress ratified the Sixteenth Amendment instituting the income tax in 1913, the Treasury Department created a single category in the tax code for exempting philanthropies, whether originating in big money, mass appeals, or communities. Tax exemption has not only nurtured philanthropy in society, it has entrenched it. Equally important, it encourages an otherwise very diverse group of institutions that have dispersed and/or solicited private funds for the public good to work together, in essence fostering a nonprofit sector of groups with similar interests and privileges.

The nonprofit sector is the outcome of this unique encounter between philanthropy and the state. It is a hybrid capitalist creation that operates tax free so long as profits are reinvested in the common good. Otherwise, it retains many of the characteristics of for-profit enterprises. For instance, funds that remain in endowment are managed according to market principles, though revenues are designated for the support of beneficiaries rather than for the profit of stockholders. Over its history, the nonprofit sector has become a distinct and pervasive part of the American political economy. Taken together, its funding from four principal sources—annual gifts including monies solicited through fund-raising campaigns, returns on a variety of endowments, net in-come earned in performing not-for-profit functions, and government subsidies, all tax exempt—is today comparable to that of the Pentagon.[6]

Despite the continued recognition of philanthropy as a public asset, its history has been contentious. Philanthropists have invested their re-sources in the greater American fight over the definition of the common good. They have taken sides in all the partisan encounters that have di-vided our society and have strategically intervened in essential debates on citizenship, opportunity, and rights.

The federal government, however, has been eager to encourage the creation of philanthropic resources only to the extent that it could si-multaneously prevent their application to the political process and preserve the prerogatives of the executive and legislative branches. The most commonly heard rationale for keeping philanthropy at bay, or for proscribing some of its activities, is that the state cannot subsidize through tax exemption philanthropic lobbying of politicians and po-litical campaigns that not only would impinge upon its own functions but also would give an unfair advantage to some. Courts and govern-ment officials have therefore built an often arbitrary divide between a political-neutral field of "education," which they allow to philanthropy, and political "action," which is off limits. How Americans have managed this theoretical divide over the course of the twentieth century is a big part of the history I am about to tell.

Thus philanthropists were allowed to finance schools for African-American children in the South but were subject to a host of legal hur-dles when they attempted to desegregate them, assist in voter registra-tion, or otherwise help minorities fight for their civil rights. Nonprofits regularly ran up against this barrier. Even when they tried hard to avoid political controversy, philanthropists have not easily separated their good works or even theoretically value-neutral science from the larger political context surrounding them. As a result, they have campaigned for changes in the law.

In recounting ideological confrontations, court battles, and institu-tional reorganizations aimed at applying large private resources to the common good, I retrace systematically the ways in which nonprofit and government sectors have joined forces and competed with one another. I pay special attention to how different administrations have used regulation of nonprofits as strategy in partisan battles over larger social issues. I see not the uninterrupted growth of a leviathan but a dynamic succession of experiments in government–civil society cooperation. Different administrations have attempted dissimilar ways of constructing a mixed political economy of giving. Herbert Hoover tried to integrate a self-financing nonprofit sector into a well-defined federal chain of command, first in the "associative state" of his years as secretary of commerce, then in his attempt as president to contain the Great Depression. President Roosevelt and his "relief czar" Harry Hopkins took a completely different approach, insisting on full autonomy for the federal government to distribute its own resources across the country and to that end excluded philanthropy from New Deal federal-state relations. In the Great Society, President Johnson created an original fusion of private and public funds to deliver social services to the poor, many of which emerged from philanthropic pilot programs. His mixed political economy of giving has survived even the recent challenges of what President George W. Bush called "compassionate conservatism."

Philanthropists and government officials have cooperated more readily when working together on international rather than domestic affairs. Private funding of humanitarian rescue operations and development work has remained throughout most of the century an adjunct of American diplomacy, especially in war zones, and during the long Cold War with the Soviet Union. While deep conflicts between conservatives and liberals at home have often faded in the larger terrain of the Pax Americana, there have been very significant exceptions when philanthropic organizations have shown enough autonomy to alter the course of foreign policy. Most recently, American philanthropic organizations were instrumental in generating global means of economic development and humanitarian intervention. They took the lead in combining state and private resources in global funds to provide indispensable resources of food, medicine, and agricultural implements directly to populations in need around the globe. By setting the terms of its partnership with state and international organizations, philanthropy is today funding a global civil society.

The book you are about to read is therefore a history of how and why philanthropy has mattered in the American century. I ask whether philanthropy, despite some openly conservative manifestations, should be understood as part of the American progressive tradition. I show how philanthropic institutions have contributed enormously to democratic society without ever achieving an uncontested place within the political system. Most importantly, I show how Americans of all classes have invested enormous energy in philanthropy, and how the resulting network of foundations and community institutions has enlarged American democracy.

CHAPTER 1

"For the Improvement of Mankind"

In the span of two generations following the Civil War, an unprecedented number of Americans became rich and powerful enough to shape community and national affairs by themselves. In the 1870s, there were just 100 millionaires in the United States. During the next twenty years, more people made more money more rapidly than ever before in history, and they made very large gifts to society. In 1892, the *New York Tribune* counted 4,047 millionaires.[1] By 1916, there were over 40,000, and at least two of these millionaires, John D. Rockefeller, Sr., and Henry Ford (the second having contributed much to the expanding wealth of the first), counted their fortunes in billions.

That many of these men—in some instances, their widows—opted to give much of their newly acquired money away was to have major consequences for the way Americans manage a host of important endeavors. Reinvesting large fortunes in philanthropic institutions depended on establishing long-term alliances between the rich and reformers. These partnerships diverted unprecedented sums of private money to the service of a modernizing, universalizing program of human progress. Instead of limiting their activities to pre-established purposes, as mandated by the rules governing charitable contributions, they advanced an open-ended program of works for the improvement of mankind.

The philanthropic projects were acts of generosity and hubris on a scale never before entertained. The new rich felt free to both envision and fashion the common good, and they did so. Until then, it had been unimaginable that some Americans could be wealthy enough to build, almost entirely by themselves, a complete university and have it compete effectively with older schools that had acquired size and strength over generations. And yet, this is what Johns Hopkins did in Baltimore, Ezra Cornell in Ithaca, Leland Stanford in Palo Alto, and John D. Rockefeller in Chicago.[2] In fact, the University of Chicago was just the first in a series of prestigious institutions of research and policymaking that the oil magnate bankrolled, including the China Medical Board, the Rockefeller Sanitary Commission, the General Education Board, the Rockefeller Institute for Medical Research, the Laura Spelman Memorial, and the Rockefeller Foundation.[3] Wealthy Americans built scores of new libraries, museums, and hospitals across the nation, often in tandem with local groups, and continued to make multiple gifts to existing institutions.

This direct conversion of massive capitalist wealth into public assets, under the guidance of the wealthy themselves and their wise advisors, was a most significant new development in late-nineteenth-century America. With their gifts, the new rich expanded the realm of civil society. What made their philanthropy historically distinctive is that they conceived of it very broadly.

The institutional innovations and programs of the new philanthropy were big enough to be widely recognized early on as a new force in "civilization," to borrow Daniel Coit Gilman's characterization of the phenomenon. Gilman, a founding member of the American Social Science Association (1865), the first president of the Johns Hopkins University (1876), and perhaps the original academic entrepreneur, explained it well in "Five Great Gifts," a 1907 *Outlook* magazine article.[4] Having sought out philanthropists at a time when their numbers were growing rapidly, he was in a good position to assess their work. Gilman emphasized that the scale of the new gifts and the ambition behind them put them in a category altogether distinct from traditional investments in local welfare institutions.

Gilman underscored the new philanthropy's insistence on long-term solutions to social problems instead of temporary relief for the destitute. High among its goals was the search for root causes.[5] Gilman also identified philanthropy's two most important programs of the early years. The first was building a national structure for scientific research in higher education, an agenda that ultimately would help transform the

United States into a major power.[6] Here Gilman highlighted not only John D. Rockefeller's endowments but also Andrew Carnegie's several institutions of research and Mrs. Olivia Sage's gift creating the foundation she named after her deceased husband Russell Sage (a railroad financier who had no interest in giving his fortune away but made his widow the richest American woman). Gilman explained that the new money was used not only to support all kinds of investigations but also to secularize American higher education by allowing research and teaching programs to break loose from sectarian religious control.

Gilman then identified rebuilding the American South after the Civil War—especially educating the freemen—as philanthropy's second big project. The South offered a unique field of application for philanthropy's scientific and educational mission as well as its policymaking agenda in agricultural reform and public health. George Peabody, a wealthy Baltimore merchant who lived in London, initiated this project in 1867 with his Fund for Southern Education, often considered the first modern foundation.[7] The Peabody Fund was the first of a long series of philanthropic investments in the region (including the Slater Fund in 1882, the Rockefeller General Education Board in 1902, and the Julius Rosenwald Fund in 1917).

When Gilman pointed out that the new philanthropy was "national" in scope instead of "provincial or local," and that the managers of the new philanthropy—those reformers entrusted with simultaneously formulating and executing the grand charge of their philanthropic patrons—could not be "suspected of personal, sectional, political, or denominational prejudices," he was claiming for philanthropy an instrumental role in promoting national unification in Reconstruction and beyond.

Charity had been for the needy; philanthropy was to be for mankind. Philanthropists, however, could not have done this by themselves. The much-heralded shift from charity to philanthropy could not have happened without a partnership between the rich, who had made their careers as organizational wizards, and the various progressive elites of the academic world, local governments, the judiciary, and emerging professional associations. Together these interests figured out how to put the new money to work for science, education, and public health. They recognized that heretofore-unavailable private fortunes constituted an important public resource for social progress. From the East Coast and Midwestern centers of capitalist development, the alliance spread to the South.

The Southern philanthropic drive would eventually set the stage for an even larger reform effort across national boundaries. A harbinger of things to come, post-Reconstruction philanthropy in the U.S. South would serve as a pattern for lifting parts of Latin America, Asia, and Africa out of poverty, disease, and ignorance and bringing relief to war-torn Europe. That it became in some instances easier to export modernizing ideas abroad (or to accept failure) than to operate in the Southern United States in opposition to Jim Crow is only one of the tough realities of the story I am about to tell.

The Rich and Reformers Join Forces to Change the Law of Charity

Some important obstacles had to be overcome before this progressive vision could be realized and many large fortunes put to use for the public good. This was especially true if a gift came as a bequest. The law of charity traditionally protected heirs by limiting bequests to narrowly defined causes. As reformers with ambitious agendas increasingly came to vie with heirs as the beneficiaries of large fortunes, it became imperative for the reformers to revisit the law of inheritance and the administration of trusts. Only in the best of circumstances, as in the harmony between the elder and younger Rockefellers, did heirs contribute to the creation of big philanthropies. The reverse was more common, and the heirs had the law on their side.

In order for a bequest to withstand a challenge from heirs or competing interests, the trust instruments normally had to state in quite specific terms how the money was to be used, identify trustees clearly (often through incorporation), and provide for a class of beneficiaries.[8]

Heirs who were looking forward to becoming rich and who were upset when this did not happen, often challenged the gifts—and the less specific the gifts, the easier the challenge.

These entrenched legal precedents dated back to the founding of the nation and beyond. Although American states had abolished British laws as soon as their post-revolutionary legislatures met, the 1601 British Statute of Charitable Uses continued to carry weight in American courts because it listed acceptable purposes for gifts: for relief of the indigent, medical care, learning, religion, and objects of general public utility.[9] In their desire to encourage philanthropy, British ecclesiastical and chancery courts had used the statute to ensure that charitable trusts were carefully defined, as did state equity courts in the United States. Judges had recourse to another precedent in British law to keep trusts active in the event that the donor's initial intent was lost with the passage of time or the designated categories of beneficiaries disappeared. In such cases, the old legal doctrine of *cy-près* (stay as close as possible to the donor's wishes) provided guidance for the courts to redefine trusts and maintain them.

In the court of law, the ambitious new philanthropists placed themselves in opposition to the centuries-old charitable practice of carefully delimiting purpose and beneficiary. They did not want to feel constrained in their giving. They conceived of their largesse as open-ended so that it might achieve the greatest impact on society. The sheer increase in size and scope of their donations, as well as the number of such cases, eventually forced courts—and legislatures when it became imperative to rewrite the law—to recognize the new philanthropy's lofty potential for society. Because legal requirements that limited gifts to specific purposes impaired the conversion of vast fortunes into programs to serve such broad concepts as the common good, donors and prospective beneficiaries fought to remove them.

The British had faced a similar challenge before the Americans. Historian W. K. Jordan has shown in his masterful work on Tudor philanthropy that the taxation powers given British communities for poor relief were meant to be used as a last resort only if charity failed to provide the needed funds.[10] As a result, the British chancery courts accommodated most charitable bequests meeting the minimal requirements of the definition in the Statute of Charitable Uses, whether administered by an incorporated body (governed by a charter) or not, when heirs challenged them.

In the United States, interpretation of the British precedents varied widely. In New England, a strong associational life encouraged donations of all sorts. With church disestablishment and the budding of the benevolent empire of bible, tract, and missionary societies, Sunday schools, educational institutions, and charities, New England (and Midwestern states, which were populated by New Englanders) showed an inclination to permit most bequests. In Massachusetts, for example, few donations to charitable and educational establishments were effectively challenged by heirs, no matter how vague. For instance, all donations to Harvard were protected as a matter of course. In an 1865 case, the Massachusetts Supreme Court upheld a charitable bequest with instructions to the executors to apply the gift to "the furtherance and promotion of the cause of piety and good morals."[11] Other states were stricter. In Virginia, heirs who challenged bequests to church and charity for vagueness resorted quite effectively to common-law restrictions and requirements of incorporation to block donations. Courts often felt compelled to side with them.[12]

The real battleground for open-endedness was New York, the state with the largest number of new fortunes—and thus, potentially, a major springboard for the new philanthropy—but where the Constitution of 1846 had abolished the chancery courts in an effort to unify the court system and systematize incorporation law. This created a new legal environment for donors and some confusion. Though New York had repealed the 1601 Elizabethan Statute along with all other English laws in 1788, for the first half of the nineteenth century the state's chancery courts largely upheld disputed charitable trusts as long as they conformed to the general categories in the statute. Under the 1846 constitution, New York courts continued to enforce charitable trusts for a while, but by the 1860s judges were prohibiting grants to charitable trusts they deemed too vague in favor of charitable corporations to which the state granted clearly worded charters.[13] From the judges' standpoint, the reform spared them from the guesswork of engaging in *cy-près* should the trust become obsolete. They could instead stick to the letter of the charter.

New York judges who promoted this reform reflected concern with the negative impact of large gifts on economic expansion—especially mortmain, or the transfer of land to charitable organizations for perpetual ownership. Worried that land-rich churches restricted the amount of land in circulation and stifled the market, they made their views heard in the 1848 general incorporation statute for charities that limited the value of the assets a charitable corporation could hold. New York State thus contained the growth of civil society institutions until the tide turned in the 1880s, when it became clear to the state's legislators and judges alike that the public had much to gain from the philanthropic redistribution of new wealth.

A significant trial of how large a gift could be came in 1881, when a bequest to Cornell caused the University to exceed the asset limit it had been allowed under its 1865 charter. The benefactor, Jennie Fiske, donated her fortune to Cornell to further the library and construction program her father, John McGraw, a close friend of Ezra Cornell, had started a few years earlier. The challenge to the gift was much talked about as the plaintiff was none other than Jennie Fiske's husband, Willard Fiske, a Cornell faculty member.[14] Realizing that legal restrictions stood in the way of educational expansion, the legislature promptly produced a new university charter without asset limitation. But the 1882 charter modification could not be applied retroactively, and the university lost the Fiske donation on appeal in 1888. More profound changes were in the offing.

The real test case of open-endedness came when Samuel Tilden in his 1884 will earmarked his own fortune—earned as a corporate attorney—to create a free public library in New York City.[15] Tilden was a popular figure, and so was his cause. The New York governor had won the popular vote in the presidential election of 1876 only to lose to Republican Rutherford B. Hayes by one vote in the electoral commission.[16] A leading swallowtail Democrat—as the gentlemanly Democrats were once called because of their preference for wearing frock coats—Tilden fought his own party's crooked welfare system with its exchange of alms for votes. As an attorney and Democratic Party leader, he successfully brought down Boss Tweed and the corrupt ring that controlled New York City. With his own money, he wanted to build a library for the city, as Ben Franklin had done in Philadelphia. Libraries were a favorite project of railroad magnates and other industrialists in late-nineteenth-century America, most famously Andrew Carnegie.

Tilden's nephews and nieces (he had no children) challenged the will on technical grounds. The governor had provided quite generously for each family member, so the challenge was unexpected. But the nephews and nieces, very much in debt, had been looking forward for some time to becoming rich, and they used every legal avenue open to them.

In his essay on great gifts, Gilman praised Tilden for his high-minded testament. Carnegie, however, chided Tilden for not having built his library during his lifetime. Carnegie argued that all Tilden and other philanthropists had to do to bypass legal limitations on bequests was to follow his example and give their money away while alive.[17] But that did not go to the root of the problem. The long-term obstacle to large-scale open-ended philanthropy was an obsolete legal framework.[18]

New York law required that donations be made to corporate bodies with a recognized charter. Accordingly, the nephews and nieces asserted that the Tilden bequest was illegal because the new library had yet to be incorporated. Moreover, some of the bequest language was surprisingly vague. If, for some reason, the trustees of the estate failed to create the new library, the bequest specified that the money would then go to another worthy public cause of their choosing, provided it was lofty enough to be for the "benefit of mankind." That too violated the law, based on British precedents of specificity. The challengers had the upper hand, and the Supreme Court of New York had no choice but to side with them, though reluctantly. The heirs won in 1888. Here was a large open-ended gift that could not survive a court challenge, at least not immediately.

Still the tide was turning towards open-ended bequests. Tilden's heirs faced the active opposition of reformers, as did those who challenged other large bequests. Over time the reformers won more cases as the gifts' potential for social betterment grew more manifest. Although Tilden's nephews and nieces were initially successful, they had not counted on the determination of Andrew Green, Tilden's law partner and lifelong associate. Green would later become famous for orchestrating the consolidation of the five boroughs into greater New York in 1898, but at that moment, all he wanted for New York was to save the Tilden trust to form the New York Public Library. Although he could not, under state law, overcome the rights of Tilden's heirs, he could seek delays in paying them. Green reached a settlement with one of Tilden's heirs and used the portion of the will he had thus recovered to work out a partnership with New York's Astor and Lenox libraries. The Tilden trustees opened the New York Public Library in 1895, and Green lobbied the legislature to change the law.

The most important outcome for the future of philanthropy is that New York State did exactly that in 1893 with a special act of the legislature known as the Tilden Act.[19] The new law not only restored the charitable trust as a legal instrument of philanthropy in New York State to make it easier to give money, but also made it possible to leave a bequest undefined and to put the trustees in charge of redefining its goals for each generation. New York legislators in effect transferred the power of *cy-près* from the judge to the trustee. The new legal framework would make it possible for successive generations of trustees to alter the donor's plan in response to society's needs.[20] It removed a longstanding objection to philanthropy and endowments in general, that is, the binding of one generation by another, a drawback that Jefferson had lamented already in the early years of the nation.

With philanthropy covering an ever-broadening field, courts around the country no longer struck down vague bequests so long as they could prove charitable intent, as a Pennsylvania Supreme Court case, *In re Knight's Estate*, shows. Heirs challenged a gift in 1894 to a so-called religious organization by the name of the Friendship Liberal League.[21] To many observers it was unclear what the organization advocated or believed in. It was a church only to the extent that William James, had he known about the organization, might have given it that designation among the many types of churches he listed in his *Varieties of Religious Experience* (1902). One witness testified that "the league was not intended to propagate any ideas religious or otherwise," but on cross-examination he gave it a more militant character. He said that "it was opposed to all isms." Another witness testified that the object of the league was "the investigation of truth," and that "a Christian or infidel would be alike eligible to membership." In the end it was good enough for the judge "to know that the league is in effect their church; and that its services are intended to give expression to their peculiar views about religion, and in some way to aid in the social, intellectual and moral elevation of themselves and others." The ruling contained a broad definition of charity, "to refer to something done or given for the benefit of our fellows or the public." The Supreme Court of California affirmed a similarly broad principle of open-endedness in giving when stating in 1890 that "the enforcement of charitable uses . . . must expand with the advancement of civilization" and "new charitable uses must be established."[22]

New York's legislative action in the Tilden case was thus part of a broader shift in American law. Maryland had passed a similar law in 1888, guaranteeing that no devise for charitable use would be voided for uncertainty of beneficiaries. In 1907, Michigan enacted a statute that basically copied the 1893 Tilden Act. Virginia passed its version in 1914.[23] Soon enough states had similar statutes to make open-ended philanthropy for the good of mankind the law of the land. Officials of the Rockefeller Foundation must have felt an awkward sense of being Americans when the British Treasury in the mid-1920s denied the foundation a tax exemption for returns on British investments on the grounds that the "well-being of mankind" was not a recognized charitable purpose in England.[24] American philanthropy had by then found its unique identity.

The Rich and Reformers Agree to Systematize Welfare

The Tilden Act was the first major victory of the fledgling partnership between the rich and reformers. As a greater array of projects became possible, the alliance gained much strength from the long-standing and virtually universal dissatisfaction in late-nineteenth-century America with the distribution of alms to the poor. Not only was charity unpopular, but the ineffectiveness of the existing patchwork of poor houses and outdoor relief was widely deplored.[25]

Reformers around the country had been for some time looking for ways to rethink the welfare system. The new wealth promised the means for reform, even if it meant reducing funds available to charity. Americans believed they could eliminate welfare almost completely by identifying and addressing the root causes of social evils. The American Social Science Association, which emerged in the 1860s in part from the Massachusetts Board of Charities, was a group of elite Protestant scholars and reformers—Gilman was a charter member and Tilden a leading figure—who saw social science investigation and social service reform as the most urgent routes toward eventually alleviating and even doing away with industrial poverty.

Most charity workers were well aware of the pauperizing tendencies of almsgiving, even as they disagreed with the unalloyed Social Darwinism that Carnegie indulged in his pronouncements. From the Charity Organization Society's office in New York City, its tough-minded founder Josephine Shaw Lowell was designing a so-called "scientific" system for the coordination of charities to prevent the duplication of aid to New York City's poor, while at the same time taking a stand against abuses perpetrated by capitalists against workers in the workplace.[26] It was important to her to do both. But when a downturn in the economy or personal misfortune led immigrants to seek alms, they expressed their distrust of the charity system by being selective takers whenever they could. Many immigrants sought welfare in their own ethnic associations of mutual help more often than in Protestant charitable institutions, which they perceived to be instruments of assimilation and social control.[27] Southern blacks knew that applications for help only added justification for their disenfranchisement.

The rich, however, endorsed Lowell's efficiency drive because it was consistent with their own desire for a shield from solicitors. Big givers were daily besieged by individual appeals for help which they did not have time to read, let alone answer. Baptist minister Frederick Gates, who enjoined John D. Rockefeller, Sr., to give his money away or "it will crush you and your children, and your children's children," testified that the elder Rockefeller was "hounded" like a "wild animal" by supplicants.[28] Mrs. Sage received 20,000 letters asking for money within six months of her announcement that she would turn her late husband's fortune over to charitable causes.[29] Pursued doggedly by supplicants but determined to tackle larger social problems, philanthropists turned to reformers in academic, professional, and religious circles. If big-money philanthropy were to be effective, individual cases had to be somehow aggregated, and a few general principles of giving defined.

Initially for a measure of personal relief, Rockefeller, who remained a pious Baptist, channeled his giving through the American Baptist Education Society, of which Reverend Gates was executive secretary. Rockefeller wanted both a buffer to protect him from the incessant solicitations and an organization that could deal with these requests in some enlightened way. He kept his distance from charities even in his own Cleveland and made a forceful case for sound business principles in his giving. Trusting Gates turned out to be an important decision. Gates sought to define the broad missions but to leave the organizational details to grantees or, in his own words, to engage in "wholesale" philanthropy, not "retail." Mrs. Sage, while continuing to respond to many different sorts of appeals, turned to attorney Robert de Forest, Josephine Shaw Lowell's close associate who became president of the New York Charity Organization Society in 1887. Her goal was for de Forest to fund programs of social work and by extension the study of social issues in the foundation she established in New York City in 1907.[30]

Thus developing and formulating general ideas for the new philanthropy became another project of the progressive generation and the purpose of multiple, if often controversial, deals between the rich and reformers across the country. Much common ground was found in the recognition that the large newly available philanthropic resources should not go directly to the poor. Instead these resources were to be treated as public assets, making it possible to address large questions of social organization. Most reformers were nonsectarian Protestants who embraced universal values to reach across fragmented American communities. They were looking for comprehensive approaches. As they realized the potential of big donations for their scientific and educational projects, they sought association with the philanthropic moguls.

Although some of the wealthy were eager to use their fortunes to transform society and reformers needed funds to support their causes, working together was a balancing act. Of resentment and mutual avoidance there was plenty. The philanthropists were the titans of industry who caused the very afflictions that reformers sought to undo. As antitrust suits made the headlines, muckrakers frequently denounced those who gave money away as hypocrites and their philanthropies as fronts to distract the public from illegal corporate strategies. But at the same time, as historians have often underscored, many progressive reformers who stood for industrial regulation—work safety and collective bargaining—could find little common ground with the labor movement whose language and strategies they did not share. This facilitated their rapprochement with philanthropists.

Workers for their part stood their ground whether in bread-and-butter unionism or in American socialism. They did not believe that what they needed first were libraries. In the 1890s, many communities, invoking recent memories of the tough labor lockouts the company had practiced, were reluctant to accept Carnegie libraries. Twenty of the forty-six solicited towns in Pennsylvania turned down the offer by voting against allocating the required share of matching funds.[31]

Suspicion of the new philanthropy was not limited to labor circles. Missionaries had their qualms too. Social Gospel minister Washington Gladden denounced "tainted money" and kept the controversy alive for years, especially after the Congressional Board of Foreign Missions accepted John D. Rockefeller's large gift in 1905.

Politicians paid close attention to the cumulative effect of these denunciations. President Theodore Roosevelt warned his attorney general Charles-Joseph Bonaparte in 1908 that the "representatives of predatory wealth" were "by gifts to colleges and universities . . . occasionally able to subsidize in their own interest some head of an educational body."[32] Congress had given national recognition to several Carnegie and Rockefeller philanthropies by granting them their charters. Senator Nelson Aldrich (R-R.I.), John D. Rockefeller, Jr.'s father-in-law, had engineered a charter for the Rockefeller General Education Board in 1902, to support its work in education, agricultural productivity, and public health throughout the country, especially in the South. But such national sponsorship became increasingly hard to secure. The well-publicized antitrust suit and court-ordered breakup of Standard Oil, beginning in 1910, made it politically impossible for Congress to grant a charter to the proposed Rockefeller Foundation.[33] The foundation was denounced instead as a "Trojan Horse" ready to undo democracy. U.S. Attorney General George W. Wickersham criticized it as "an indefinite scheme for perpetuating vast wealth," believing it to be "entirely inconsistent with the public interest." Attorney Frank Walsh, whom President Wilson had appointed chair of the U.S. Commission on Industrial Relations, and who was pro-labor, denounced the Rockefeller family's "huge philanthropic trusts as a menace to the welfare of society."[34] The Rockefellers therefore ended up in 1913 applying for a charter in New York State, where their foundation was welcome. The labor violence that erupted in Rockefeller-owned Colorado coalfields and culminated in 1914 in the disastrous Ludlow Massacre led to added denunciations.[35]

Deep-seated hostilities endured through the years no matter how much good work was done. Senator Robert La Follette, who had been sitting by Walsh's side at the Industrial Commission, pursued the battle in his own state of Wisconsin. His unabated animosity against foundations took posthumous effect in 1925 when the Regents of the University of Wisconsin adopted a much disputed resolution forbidding the state university from accepting gifts from foundations (the measure was rescinded in 1930).[36]

Listen to such voices, and it would seem that philanthropic institutions could not contribute much good to society. But history has shown that enough wealthy Americans and reformers, including reformers who were critical of the industrialists' labor and economic practices, found ways to achieve détente and to further a larger social agenda that benefitted millions.

The Philanthropic Foundation: A Success Story?

The advent of open-ended philanthropy generated an intense period of institutional creativity at the turn of the twentieth century. The most important outcome was the "foundation" as a new kind of institution designed to administer large philanthropic resources to various communities of recipients. The general-purpose foundation was a genuine American invention, a direct outcome of the greater range of options the new rich and associated reformers could rely on for adapting philanthropy to society's changing needs and contributing to public policy. Twenty-seven foundations were in operation by 1915.[37] There were over 200 by 1930. Although many remained charitable trusts supporting traditional causes, the leading ones, in the words of Frederick Keppel, second president of the Carnegie Corporation, were dedicated to the search for "truth."[38]

Foundations were the offspring of the turn-of-the-century legal changes reformers had fought for. Legal distinctions between giving during one's lifetime or in one's will were a thing of the past. Mission statements that would have been struck down by courts a few years earlier became commonplace. Mrs. Sage enjoined her new foundation "to take up the larger and more difficult problems" of the day (1907). In an early draft for the charter of the Rockefeller Foundation, Reverend Gates stated as its goal "the promotion of any and all of the elements of human progress" (1910). The final resolution, only slightly more concrete, was "to promote the well-being of mankind throughout the world" (1913). Almost all of the Carnegie institutions were designed "to encourage, in the broadest and most liberal manner, investigation, research, and discovery, and the application of knowledge to the improvement of mankind." Simon Guggenheim added "the appreciation of beauty" to this list of broad goals. In creating the foundation dedicated in 1925 to the memory of his son John Simon, he wanted maximum flexibility because no one could "foresee the future."[39] The programs were presumably universal, benefiting all, at least in principle, without distinction of color, race, or creed.

There was a fair amount of experimentation in management methods. Foundation priorities often reflected the philanthropists' personal interests. So long as Carnegie remained at the helm of his charities, his pet projects were funded first. Church organs were a whim, but thousands of churches got them. Community libraries became an obsessive priority. Simplified spelling was not so surprising a wish from a former telegraph operator who saw in the idea a way to accelerate the adoption of English as the lingua franca and thereby to help the peace movement, to which he was devoting a large percentage of his gifts.[40] Carnegie, Olivia Sage, and other big philanthropists also responded to a number of the traditional appeals emanating from the many organizations of civil society.

The modern American university, a latecomer to the world of knowledge, owes an enormous debt to the new philanthropy. Philanthropic investment in education and science under the guidance of academic leaders like Gilman was heavy. Philanthropists found in educators and scientists grantees who could put the new money to work for both credible and important goals. The idea was not simply to expand the number or size of academic institutions, but to create an educational establishment that was ecumenical and open to science rather than denominational in outlook. In this endeavor, the two early giants of large-scale philanthropy, the Rockefeller and Carnegie organizations, played a critical role in secularizing American higher education. As foundations, they used their newly acquired leverage quite effectively to keep religion and science distinct and separate.

Henry Pritchett, former president of MIT, advised Carnegie to support science. Because an attempt by the Cleveland administration and the National Academy of Sciences to establish a research university in the nation's capital had failed, Carnegie and Pritchett established the Carnegie Institution of Washington (1902) with research departments in experimental evolution, marine biology, history, economics, and sociology, soon expanded to include astronomy, geophysics, and botany.[41] Congress granted the charter. President Roosevelt was among the trustees, as were the president of the senate, the speaker of the house, the secretary of the Smithsonian Institution, and the president of the National

Academy of Sciences. Gilman, a logical choice, was elected the institution's first president; Robert Woodward, dean of the College of Science at Columbia University and editor of *Science,* the second.

Carnegie and Pritchett were reluctant to support existing institutions of higher education so long as they remained controlled by religious denominations but, from their base at the Carnegie Foundation for the Advancement of Teaching, they devised a means of forcing American colleges to eliminate those religious requirements that stood in the way of scientific education. The need for faculty pensions, which Carnegie had recognized as a Cornell trustee in the 1890s, when the faculty was earning less than white-collar workers at Carnegie Steel, became the instrument for implementing the change. Establishing pension systems was in the air in the business world and in insurance circles, and much needed in academia, as Pritchett informed Carnegie.

The masterful strategy was to make the eligibility of faculty to receive a pension paid for by the Carnegie Foundation for the Advancement of Teaching dependent on the college removing from its charter denominational requirements (such as requiring trustees, officers, faculty or students to belong to any specified sect or imposing any theological test). In other words, the Carnegie Foundation successfully turned pensions into tools of secularization. Colleges around the country complied one after the other, even if the move was vocally resisted at Methodist Northwestern, Presbyterian Princeton, and Baptist Brown. Initially, the pension program included only private institutions, but with faculty members threatening to leave such public universities as Wisconsin, Illinois, and Minnesota for private colleges, Carnegie extended the program to them in 1908. In 1917, it became the Teachers Insurance and Annuity Association, the parent company of the plan most university professors currently use.[42]

Under the umbrella of their now very broad mission statements, foundations took on the job of reforming entire fields of education. With the Rockefeller Institute for Medical Research in 1901, Gates and Rockefeller had created a model institution for medical research. The decision to build an institute independent of a university had been difficult, especially as it involved a painful break with the University of

Chicago, when it had become clear that the University trustees wanted to join forces with the local Rush College of Medicine. Not trusting that the arrangement would generate a "temple of science," the Rockefellers invested their money elsewhere.[43] Pathologist William H. Welch of Johns Hopkins served as the Rockefeller Institute's first director before installing his student Simon Flexner in that position.

A few years later, the Carnegie Foundation for the Advancement of Teaching hired Simon Flexner's brother Abraham to investigate medical schools. The resulting report, which Flexner blandly entitled *Medical Education in the United States and Canada* (1910), crystallized for a generation what the new medical education should be, that is, taught by a full-time faculty totally free from constraints not directly related to the educational mission.[44] Abraham then moved over to the Rockefeller General Education Board and put much of the vast resources now at his disposal behind Welch, who, back at Hopkins, had become instrumental in leading doctors towards accepting full-time faculty positions.[45] The deal to fund Hopkins was struck in 1913.

Two years later, the General Education Board funded a school of hygiene and public health, also at Hopkins and also under Welch's guidance. The General Education Board turned down a proposal from Harvard, which was unwilling to adopt radical changes in medical education. The story of a foundation stimulating competitors and selecting winners sounds all too familiar today, but it was new then. Rockefeller's seriousness in reforming medical education was underscored when Harvard's former president Charles Eliot was unable to secure the money for his own university despite using his seat on the General Education Board to lobby on its behalf. The Flexner brothers were Jews, and thus an irate Harvard dean could not help but denounce Abraham as "circumcised alike in pecker and intellect."[46] But Flexner eventually prevailed in implementing his views on medical education in the country at large.

Another characteristic of the new foundations was their recruiting of experts to conduct in-house investigations as well as to promote different educational and professional programs. Abraham Flexner is best known for his pioneering inquiry into medical education. Mary Richmond's 1917 *Social Diagnosis* was a landmark of social work from the Russell Sage Foundation. Foundation managers developed connections with the larger world of expertise from which they could recruit, and on which they could always call. Already in the 1920s, the term "philanthropoid" came to be used in the foundation world to designate "those who give away the money of others" in the matrix of teaching, research, and policymaking.[47]

This role only grew in the 1920s and 1930s. Funders and recipients learned how to work together. Even the foundations' detractors, like sociologist Eduard C. Lindeman, who in the 1920s kept exposing them in the muckraking tradition, now granted them the status of a new "cultural phenomenon."[48] Grantees still bothered by tainted money overcame their reluctance. By then, foundations provided about 7 percent of annual giving (it is about 12 percent today), but by concentrating their giving they made their influence felt in the world of knowledge and public policy well beyond this seemingly small percentage.

While the new foundations carried out their agendas, potential recipients actively sought out philanthropic resources in any form. As Gilman correctly saw it, this impulse was especially strong in academic entrepreneurs like him. In dealing with donors, university presidents feared that faculty radicalism might upset donors and stymie funding. But despite a few highly publicized contests over academic freedom at Wisconsin, Stanford, and a few other universities, the influx of big-philanthropy money into academia only grew throughout the twentieth century and fostered the scientific project.[49]

A "Temple of Science"

The rich and reformers forged together a secular, scientific, and professional academic establishment for the country at large that dramatically enhanced Americans' ability to generate new knowledge. The early history of the University of Chicago illustrates the ways in which the new philanthropy emancipated academic life from its sectarian straitjacket and introduced a new scientific ethos to the country.

Of all the major academic projects launched in the late nineteenth century, Chicago stands out as a seminal philanthropic enterprise that almost instantly outgrew its local and sectarian origins to become emblematic of the more liberal Protestant perspective that would be the hallmark of the new American philanthropy at its most effective. The rich funders supported educational reformers within an institution turning more ostensibly liberal.

Rockefeller had decided early on to channel his philanthropic gifts through the American Baptist Education Society to shield himself from the constant stream of supplicants. On behalf of the society, Gates, who had reached the conclusion that Midwestern Baptist students were in dire need of a good educational institution, proposed to rebuild at Chicago an existing Baptist school, which had closed its doors after the Chicago fire.[50]

As a Baptist minister, Gates did not plan a secular institution, but as he explained it twenty years later to the younger Rockefeller, he believed "sectarianism" was bad not only for science; it was also "the curse of religion."[51] William Rainey Harper, who became the university's first president, also wanted a center of higher education uninhibited by denominational requirements. Although a biblical scholar and ordained Baptist minister once associated with the original Baptist University at Chicago, Harper agreed to leave Yale only after he was given free rein to build a first-class university, that is, one where he could recruit the best minds irrespective of their religious affiliations and even beliefs. Thomas Goodspeed and Henry Morehouse, the other two ministers among the founders, were more conservative. Although Rockefeller supported several small Baptist schools (Denison College in Ohio, Spelman College for African-Americans in Georgia), which remained genuinely Baptist, he had a different vision for Chicago. He gave a free hand to Gates and Harper, who tested the donor several times on the issue of orthodoxy.

Here was a gift to a religious denomination—the Baptists—that was used to create an institution that immediately shrugged off its denominational requirements. The very same Baptist ministers who sought the money and founded the school simultaneously led its secularization. Educators at Chicago, backed as they were by a large donor who, in his

own words, admired "scientific men" who "arrive at some helpful contribution to the sum of human knowledge," could afford independence
from the parochial outlook of parishioners.[52] The ministers placed advancing knowledge ahead of sectarian loyalty.

Controversy over Chicago's religious liberalism lingered in Baptist
circles in the 1890s. Augustus Strong, a Baptist minister who had been
very close to Rockefeller in Cleveland, and whose son had married
Rockefeller's daughter, led the charge against Harper.[53] Strong tried to
derail the Chicago project by accusing Harper, as a biblical scholar, of
being lax in textual interpretation. Strong's motives, however, were not
entirely pure; he was seeking Rockefeller money for a university in New
York under his own control. But as a result of this controversy, Harper
was forced to teach his biblical classes outside the Divinity School at
Chicago. Ultimately the Divinity School itself became a liberal center
for the scientific study of religion. After a few years, the only remnant
of denominational orthodoxy at Chicago was the requirement that the
university president be a Baptist (which eventually led its acting president, psychologist James Angell, to depart in 1919 to head the National
Research Council); that requirement would ultimately be abolished as
well. The only time when Harper seems to have yielded to Baptist grassroots pressure was in limiting the number of African-American students, thus avoiding alienating Southern applicants.

Leaving the sectarian origins of the university behind was necessary also for very practical reasons. Even though the initial Rockefeller gift was very generous, it was a matching grant. The university
grew by attracting other donations, most often in the form of bequests
from prominent Chicago families. Looking to the community for help,
the ministers quickly ran through their Baptist donors. Disestablishment was partly a matter of necessity to gain the support of the larger
community.

Although the object of their donations was local, many of these donors framed their gifts in the universal language of the new American
philanthropy. Some were quite explicit in supporting the ambitious scientific scope of the project. Martin A. Ryerson, heir to a local fortune,

president and treasurer of the University's Board of Trustees, and benefactor of the physics program, encouraged "the cultivation of science for
its own sake." Real estate developer Helen Culver explicitly directed her
gift for biology "to be used in perpetuity for the benefit of humanity,"
using the language increasingly heard in the halls of philanthropy in the
1890s.[54] Representing the William B. Ogden estate gift for a school of
science, Andrew Green, who had fought the Tilden heirs in New York,
made the gift to the university on the condition that "admission to the
proposed school of students and professors alike" be made "without reference to their particular religious beliefs."[55] This ethos, a hallmark of
the Rockefeller charities under John D. Rockefeller, Jr.'s leadership, was
what the Baptist ministers who led the school wanted in the first place,
and it enabled the University of Chicago to emerge as one of the centers
of American Protestant liberalism.

The spirit of the pact between the rich and reformers was perhaps
best expressed in the personality of its most prominent member. As
heir to the largest American fortune, John D. Rockefeller, Jr., had suffered a deep personal crisis and depression in 1904 when he came to
realize that he was not cut out for the family business. He responded
by steeling his resolve, abandoning corporate directorships and, with
his father's encouragement, devoting his life entirely to philanthropy.
Although he had no inclination towards any kind of radicalism, Rockefeller was deeply influenced by the progressive Social Gospel view of
political economy taught by his professors at Brown University and also
espoused by Frederick Gates. He felt a deep sense of purpose and was
steeped in the enlightened duty of the rich to help mankind. With the
family philanthropies invested in medicine, education, and the natural
sciences, he pushed for "scientific progress carried out under God's inspiration" in secular circumstances.[56]

Rockefeller promoted the union between the rich and reformers,
which had emerged in science, technology and expert knowledge, and
culminated in the new American academic environment. Conversely,
despite genuine reservations about a rise in inequality that sprang from
the very economic concentration that bankrolled the new philanthropy,

the larger reform milieu formed a partnership with big-money philanthropy that permitted both to grow. That Rockefeller could hold his ground in Congressional testimony in defense of the open shop after the 1914 Ludlow Massacre was in no small part a reflection of the progressive movement's own difficulty with labor. Participants in philanthropy advocated bypassing the autonomy of subcultures. But it remained to be seen whether a program of universal progress, which managed to flourish despite its lack of affiliation with the labor movement, could be exported to the American South, where the deep-seated conflicts of race relations directly interfered, and to the larger world.

Exporting Northern Philanthropy to the American South

The South was a major test of the philanthropic program's exportability outside its initial milieu. As Daniel Coit Gilman explained in his essay, developing a modernizing program for the improvement of rural life in the U.S. South appeared early on the philanthropic agenda. The big idea was a three-pronged educational campaign aimed at ending illiteracy, improving public health, and boosting agricultural productivity.[57] But every program philanthropists launched was hampered by a fundamental inequity between blacks and whites seemingly so intractable that they never addressed it head on. This avoidance, however reasonable, exerted its toll. The Northern alliance of wealth and educational reform could not spread easily in the South, where resistance to measures that benefited African-Americans severely tested philanthropic effectiveness. As philanthropists eventually realized, any long-term positive outcome depended on turning the recipients themselves into agents of change, and this entailed the collaboration of local churches (the very institutions that philanthropists felt were obstacles to progress elsewhere) as well as state and local governments.

The compromises the philanthropists reached among themselves and with the local actors show clearly two contradictory trends that would come to characterize American philanthropy in the twentieth century: the real limits of its application when it came to issues of social justice, and at the same time its role in helping launch social justice movements that took on lives of their own.

What Northern philanthropy could do was vital for emancipation as federal investment in Southern education receded before a tide of white supremacy. With the white South fearing that federal funds might take the Negro "beyond himself," Congress failed to pass the common school bill that New Hampshire Senator Henry Blair proposed in 1884.[58] Only through land transfers indirectly benefiting the industrial schools of Hampton and Tuskegee did the federal government continue to play a small role in the freemen's education.

John D. Rockefeller, Jr., had meant to call the General Education Board the Negro Education Board.[59] To him, the Southern drive was yet another way to renew his parents' commitment to the education of the freemen. His mother, Laura Spelman, had been raised by abolitionists. At the request of its two founders, the older Rockefellers had expanded the Atlanta Baptist Female Seminary, which was renamed Spelman College in 1884; they then founded Morehouse College, also in Atlanta, this time for African-American boys, and named it after Rockefeller American Baptist Education Society associate Henry Morehouse.

Baltimore merchant George Peabody had also pioneered educational efforts. He made his initial donation for education in the Southern states in 1867. At the time, the Freedmen's Bureau, which W.E.B. Du Bois called "the most extraordinary and far-reaching institution of social uplift that America has ever attempted," heavily invested its resources in education.[60] The bureau focused on establishing missionary schools for newly freed slaves. When the bureau ceased its operation in 1871, Peabody Trustees, including President Rutherford Hayes, Chief Justice Morrison Waite, and Secretary of State William Evarts, were anxious to appease white Southerners, many of whom were illiterates who resented the education Northern missionaries were dispensing to African-Americans. The first Peabody general agent, Barnas Sears, had served on the Massachusetts Board of Education. Instead of missionary schools limited to African-Americans, he promoted state systems

of public education such as Horace Mann had developed in Massachusetts, theoretically capable of serving all pupils, and he began the strategy of using Peabody funds to stimulate their creation.

In pursuing appeasement, Sears made a point early on of funding
white schools almost exclusively. Reporting on the fund's appropriation
in Montgomery, Alabama, in 1881, after Sears's death, his daughter justified the policy. She observed that while during the previous year over
one hundred white children had been denied admission to an "over-
crowded building," the New York Missionary Society "has erected a
handsome brick building exclusively for the colored race, and the white
citizens of the city have to endure this painful contrast."[61]

Sears did not leave African-Americans completely out. He appointed several former Freedmen's Bureau commissioners as Peabody
agents and distributed only 6.5 percent of his funds towards "Negro
education" during the twelve years of his administration. Freemen received a small boost in the face of declining missionary involvement
and the federal government's disengagement from the region when, in
1882, New England manufacturer John Slater established a new fund
(over which former President Hayes also presided) entirely dedicated
to their education.[62]

When he became general agent for both the Peabody and Slater
funds, Southern educator and former Confederate officer J.L.M. Curry
pursued Sears's idea of building state educational systems with the potential for educating the entire population. A Harvard Law School graduate, also impressed by Massachusetts policy, Curry allocated Peabody
and Slater funds in such a way as to stimulate local politicians to match
them with tax revenues for public education.

The strategy of public education in the American South slowly grew
from this initially modest philanthropic incentive. How to translate a
project for fostering public education based on a strategy of public-fund
allocation into significant gains for African-American communities
was the huge challenge Northern agents set for themselves by appeasing
whites. While genuinely attempting to help the freemen, they irrevers-
ibly allied themselves with Jim Crow. Only through persistently exploit-

ing a few cracks in the system could philanthropic agents hope to plant seeds of social justice.

Over a hundred concerned white educators and civic leaders from both North and South met in Capon Springs, West Virginia in 1898 to discuss the state of Southern education. This conference and successive ones (John D. Rockefeller, Jr., and his associate, Baptist minister Wallace Buttrick, attended in 1901) led to the creation of the Southern Education Board. The leader of the Board was Robert C. Ogden, a partner in John Wanamaker's Department Store and the director of its New York operations, who also presided over the Hampton Institute Board of Trustees. For several years Ogden took Northern philanthropists on well-publicized railway tours of the South to visit black and white schools. George Foster Peabody (a New York investment banker from Georgia, unrelated to the benefactor of the Peabody Fund) was essential in funding the Southern Education Board in its early days. The board mobilized the energies of both Frederick Gates and John D. Rockefeller, Jr., who, in turn, launched the General Education Board. Long Island Railroad President William H. Baldwin, whom others trusted to invest their money "wisely" in the South, became its first president.[63]

For the moment, Northern philanthropists and their Southern allies worked with a theory of race relations predicated on a vision of an organic society they claimed they shared. University of Tennessee President Charles Dabney argued that we should consider "the human race" as "an organism" and "the Negro as a man."[64] Curry stressed the danger of an alternate course because "We are bound, hand and foot, to the lowest stratum of society. If the Negroes remain as co-occupants of the land and co-citizens of the States, and we do not lift them up, they will drag us down to industrial bankruptcy, social degradation, and political corruption."[65] Booker T. Washington echoed: "The Negro can afford to be wronged; the white man cannot afford to wrong him."[66]

The philanthropists developed a theory that the best hope for the freemen was an educational strategy they misleadingly labeled "universal." In practice, this meant educating white Southerners first. As University of Virginia president Edwin Alderman rationalized it, education for whites would make them more tolerant of blacks. If "knowledge and not prejudice will guide his conduct," Alderman wrote, the education of one white man "is worth more to the black man himself than the education of ten Negroes."[67]

In proceeding with "universal education," the philanthropists saw society clearly divided between a superior and an inferior race. "There cannot be any question about that," General Education Board director Wallace Buttrick told a group of Tennessee school superintendents.[68] Curry concurred: "History demonstrates that the Caucasian will rule. . . . White supremacy does not mean hostility to the negro, but friendship for him." To white Southerners stuck with "primitive people" in their midst, the most appropriate way to go about educating these people was to recognize this basic fact of life.[69]

Dabney summed up the connection between primitiveness and industrial education in arguing that "the negro is a child-race, at least two-thousand years behind the Anglo-Saxon in its development, and like all other races it must work out its own salvation by practicing the industrial arts, and becoming independent and self supporting."[70] Curry admired the methods of industrial education that General Samuel C. Armstrong (the son of missionaries in Hawaii, and the former commander of U.S. Colored Troops in the Union Army) had developed at Hampton. Armstrong's teaching had deeply impressed the young Booker T. Washington during his years at the normal school. Curry now pressured Washington on behalf of the Slater Fund to expand these methods into an educational creed for the black South rather than the more traditional curriculum Freedmen's Bureau-supported Northern missionaries had advocated. Baldwin in turn advised Washington that the Rockefellers could be major donors at Tuskegee, adding to the resources already provided by Andrew Carnegie and other donors.[71]

It is important to note that philanthropists and reformers alike were genuine in their desire for improvement in race relations and should not be confused with the hardline Jim Crow biological racists to whom they conceded race inequality. Although the philanthropists approved of the principle of segregation—the law of the land since *Plessy*—and had no real vision for an alternative to it, they were clear-headed that mass education, even industrial education, would eventually overturn the status quo in American race relations. They welcomed that fact and promoted the idea that educated people needed opportunities in a more tolerant society. "Unless the colored race is to be removed from the country, how," Baldwin asked, "can we educate millions of them and keep them so separate and apart?"[72] Baldwin also knew that much of the Jim Crow legislation was due to "fear on the part of the ignorant white people that the Negro will get on top."[73]

W.E.B. Du Bois, who converted to Marxism later in life, accused Baldwin of having been interested merely in training a docile black labor force "to break the power of the trade unions." Historians have often echoed his indictment and applied it broadly.[74] But the available evidence supports it only partly. Unlike other railroad executives, Baldwin was open to collective bargaining—although he remained a defender of the open shop. Like John D. Rockefeller, Jr., Baldwin was a supporter of a moderate progressive regulatory movement. Baldwin's commitment to the South as "his greatest opportunity for good work" was sincere enough to make a deep impression on Chicago philanthropist and Sears, Roebuck leader Julius Rosenwald, who devoted his fortune to black education.[75] Inspired also by Booker T. Washington, Rosenwald sought to establish a black school in every Southern county. It was as an American Jew that Rosenwald, addressing a black audience at Hampton in 1911, denounced "race prejudice" as "destructive"; "it offers nothing but a hopeless warfare and a blank pessimism."[76]

The northern philanthropists, Rosenwald among them, persisted in working with the state in an attempt to expand black education from within bureaucratic systems committed to Jim Crow, which they had no means or inclination to challenge directly. The General Education Board and the Slater Fund created county training schools, basically elementary schools with an emphasis on training African-Americans for agriculture or domestic service. These schools epitomized the unequal hybrid system that private foundations and Southern state bureaucracies were developing. The General Education Board funded operations partially, but insisted that the buildings be state-owned and that the state, county, or district tax itself at least $750 annually to support the schools. According to one estimate, for blacks age fifteen to nineteen, these training schools (which covered the basics of an elementary education) were the sole source for education in 293 of 912 counties in fifteen Southern states. By 1929, there were 368 county training schools, with Slater and the General Education Board giving $135,866 in that year for their support and public funds another $1,888,852.[77]

Despite the leverage, the results were limited. On the one hand schooling for blacks increased and literacy improved. On the other, the inequality between spending for whites and blacks worsened dramatically within state systems. In 1890, Alabama's expenditures per white pupil were 18.4 percent greater than those for black pupils. By 1911, the figure had risen to 459 percent![78]

Philanthropists and educational reformers sincerely believed that education would eventually lead to civil rights. In this conviction, they differed from the biological racists who implemented Jim Crow. But they had faith in official pronouncements that held little promise. Charles Brantley Aycock, governor of North Carolina from 1901 to 1905 and a leader of the universal education movement, proclaimed his support for disenfranchisement, but with the proviso that blacks should have the means to regain suffrage through education. He supported in good conscience this anachronistic version of liberalism—a Southern version of the selective franchise of nineteenth-century Europe—at a time when Northern Democratic machines were naturalizing millions of illiterate immigrants to America and giving them alms to turn them into loyal Democratic voters. Even African-American victims put the best face on disenfranchisement by openly harboring the hope that education would eventually ensure access to the polls. Booker T. Washington told the Louisiana disfranchising convention: "In the degree that you close the ballot box against the ignorant, you open the school house."[79] Disenfranchisement significantly undermined the philanthropists' work. With blacks excluded from politics, reformers in state systems of education could not find the political support to serve them with tax money. Education for the freemen became a never-to-be-lifted prerequisite to political rights.[80]

Under these tough circumstances, philanthropists understood that the best they could hope for was to turn African-American communities into active partners in their own education. Even if the philanthropic alliance between the rich and reformers in state departments of education failed to overcome white supremacists, it could still help Southern African-American communities help themselves.

In practice, the General Education Board allocated no more than 10 percent of its expenditures between 1902 and 1918 to Negro education.[81] Because philanthropic support could never replace proper state appropriations, its strategy was to provide promoters of African-American education within the state systems access to funds protected from political oversight. It was then up to these sympathetic insiders on the ground to foster an educational creed in the poorest and most discriminated-against communities.

The General Education Board thus helped to establish and directly funded dedicated supervisors of Negro schools (who were initially white) within state departments of education. By 1920, all Southern states had such a position. Wycliffe Rose, the University of Tennessee educator who became head of the General Education Board after administering the Rockefeller Sanitary Commission and heading the International Health Division of the Rockefeller Foundation, expanded this cooperation with state departments of education in the 1920s by funding additional supervisors of rural black schools.[82] The initial means of intervention were again quite modest for a region as big as the South, but in the end they grew and added educational opportunities from within.

Thus Jackson Davis, the superintendent of schools in Henrico County, Virginia, began a program of visitations to black rural schools by black supervisory teachers. Davis used monies given the Southern Education Board in 1905 by Anna Jeanes, a wealthy Philadelphian, for the express purpose of black education (upon her death a year later, a separate Jeanes Fund was created). Davis's idea for supervising teachers came from the work of Virginia Randolph, a black teacher in his district.[83] She was so effective that he sent her around to improve the quality of other schools and to raise local awareness of them. Some black teachers resisted the supervision. Reformers like Davis did all they could to encourage communities to cooperate and invest energy in the program—for example by making all preachers honorary members of the teacher's association, an important recognition of the significance of local churches in educational pursuits.[84] The General Education Board began paying Davis's salary in 1910. Davis later reported: "I have never come in contact with any finer character than some of the Jeanes teachers. They have gone back into the back country, worked under all sorts of hardships, have traveled in all kinds of conveyances and walked oftentimes in all sorts of weather. They have been patient with the people in their ignorance and prejudices. They succeeded in organizing the people into school community associations and bringing to bear the united sentiment of the community in favor of better school buildings, longer terms and more practical work in the schools by introducing simple industries. The school ceased to be known as the 'public free school,' contemptuous accent on the 'free,' but became 'our' school, and the new buildings that were put up represented real sacrifice and devotion. The schools lost their isolation. They became tied up with the life of the people. Now this began to create a demand for a different kind of teaching. People began to appreciate the schools more and to send their children more regularly and to contribute to the lengthening of the term."[85] Davis remembered that poor black people building their local schools themselves, no matter how unassuming, and doing so without public assistance save for the teacher's modest salary, "discovered themselves as a community and no one could see their pride of achievement without being aware of its deep significance."[86] By 1939, the Jeanes Fund had placed African American supervising industrial teachers—known as the "Jeanes Teachers"—in at least 505 counties in thirteen states. Jeanes teachers also sometimes acted as assistants to county superintendents.

Davis devoted a lifetime to establishing such linkages in the South, working from the inside to improve black education within the framework of white supremacy.[87] He was convinced that "the South cannot be forced against its will."[88] If it were, the work would fail just like that done during Reconstruction. All that could be done within his lifetime, he was convinced, was to plant seeds of social justice by means of a tough community-by-community strategy of empowering the victims. Like Booker T. Washington, he was willing to accept disenfranchisement now in return for participation later.

The idea of empowering victims was taken to a regional scale by Julius Rosenwald, who had rapidly emerged as the greatest giver to the cause of Southern black education. By the end of his life in 1932, Rosenwald had helped construct 5,357 school buildings in the black South. As much as 40 percent of all black children enrolled in school in that year attended Rosenwald schools. Unlike the General Education Board, the Rosenwald Fund, under the able leadership of former Rockefeller employee Edwin Embree, demanded that communities, in addition to local governments, cost-share for each school.[89] As a result, black families increasingly contributed to this hybrid system of educational funding. This is a major achievement not to be overlooked. Poor blacks were willing to endure much sacrifice to educate the children. As Booker T. Washington had advised early on, the community contributed to the cost of lumber and bricks. Sears, Roebuck & Company provided window sashes, doors, nails, screws, paint, and blinds at the lowest possible cost.[90] Much labor was contributed by the community.

Horace Mann Bond, a young black intellectual trained by Robert Park and Franklin Frazier at the University of Chicago in the 1930s, who worked while a doctoral student for the Rosenwald Fund in Louisiana, estimated that of the $28 million it cost to build these schools, black families had contributed almost 17 percent. More often than not, communities themselves organized and raised the money internally and then applied to the Rosenwald fund. Some of the money they borrowed.[91] Community investment leveraged contributions from Rosenwald and, in some cases, led to a general appropriation from tax funds. This was heroic work carried out under the constant threat of white violence. Bond, who witnessed the aftermath of a lynching, reported he was always afraid he "might do something that would bring harm or suspicion directed at the Negroes with whom I dealt." His wife Julia thought the community was "at the mercy of whatever impulse may come over these white people."[92]

The attempt to have communities of recipients directly seek resources from the state is rich in lessons. For the next half century, most
African-Americans would receive their education from a hybrid network of religious schools, state elementary schools built with a mix of
state, philanthropic, and African-American money, some high schools,
and a handful of colleges that philanthropists supported. Martin Luther King, Jr.'s maternal grandmother and mother were both educated
at Spelman. Martin Luther King, Sr., made his way to Morehouse after
much self-schooling and, following a long courtship, married Alberta
Williams, whose father ministered to the elite Ebenezer Baptist Church.
Their son, Martin, Jr., would follow him to Morehouse.[93] That modest
black educational institutions eventually produced America's greatest
civil rights leaders is the culmination of an important story many times
tragically sidetracked yet at the heart of the American philanthropic
movement. These educational institutions trained a generation of leaders who exposed national failures while using their schools, in conjunc-
tion with their churches, to launch a civil rights revolution.

Embracing the Humanitarian Movement

Philanthropy's Southern educational strategy was directed partly towards schooling the freemen. Philanthropists also financed improvements in farm productivity and public health, the other two big issues
that defined Federal Progressive-era public policy for the economic improvement of the South. They then turned these Southern economic
projects into an international humanitarian movement for global health
and development.

In 1908 President Theodore Roosevelt had turned to the Russell Sage
Foundation to fund his Country Life Commission, aimed at improving
life on the farm. At the same time, the Rockefeller General Education
Board's farm demonstration program, under agriculturalist Seaman
Knapp's leadership, became part of a national system of agricultural
extension agencies carried on through the state agricultural colleges.
The program led to the 1914 Smith-Lever Act, the federal legislation

that greatly expanded farm demonstration for soil conservation and increased yield with matching federal-state grants, and the 1917 Smith-Hughes Act, which created a Federal Board of Vocational Education.[94]

It was as part of this wave of reforms that plans were first formulated at a meeting of the Southern Education Board for the organization of the Rockefeller Sanitary Commission for the eradication of hookworm disease in the American South. Easily transmitted through the skin, the disease affected primarily those who walked barefoot on the contaminated soil around unsanitary latrines. As one of its effects was to sap energy, the disease reinforced the stereotyping of the poor as lazy. It was soon discovered that whites were actually more susceptible than blacks to catching the obstinate parasite.[95] The program to fight it began in Virginia in 1910 under the direction of Tennessee educator Wycliffe Rose, whose objective was to create state-funded boards of health partly overlapping with the new state educational systems he had had a hand in fostering. School buildings housed the dispensaries where, by 1914, one million patients had been examined. Rose launched a vast educational campaign as well as research on vaccination. But progress in killing hookworm and raising life expectancy was not easily measured as the bureaucratic-educational-philanthropic coalition had again to overcome much local resistance to outside interference in Southern lives.[96]

In extending their reach abroad, philanthropists exported their Southern work. The Rockefellers hoped to make their agenda of public health and farm productivity a pattern for the world.[97] The International Health Commission they created in 1913 was a direct outcome of the Southern Sanitary Commission and its efforts to fight hookworm. Wycliffe Rose, who had led the hookworm campaign, became its head, and many of the same personnel were involved in both programs. From Virginia, the program moved to Egypt, then to Ceylon; and beginning in 1917 to Brazil, to Mexico, and the Andes. It included research on other diseases such as malaria and yellow fever as well. From Virginia to the Andes, it was the same effort at stemming hunger and disease, built on a new scientific foundation. Some participants in the program were in fact more interested in conducting scientific research than in establishing lasting health and educational structures abroad, but the two worked in tandem.

Carnegie was not interested in these issues. He extended his church organ and library programs to the British Isles, and he funded the peace movement in France and Germany, but global war soon stood in his way.[98] The Rockefellers and their associates, however, wanted to eradicate disease and improve agricultural yield where they could. They meant to ignore national boundaries as much as possible. They pursued goals applicable in peace and war, in free and occupied lands. They did not even feel seriously challenged by initial American claims of neutrality in the Great War but did join the American war effort in 1917. In war-torn Europe, the philanthropists said, the battle against the flu epidemic and "germs" became part of a larger war against Germans. Indeed almost half of the 116,516 American casualties in the Great War died of the flu. Rockefeller's International Health Commission intensified its medical work in France, again under the leadership of the ubiquitous Wycliffe Rose, who managed to overcome French bureaucratic rules. The British Empire was another matter. In British Guiana, Rockefeller officials became disgusted with the lack of cooperation from imperial institutions running "an empire on the cheap."[99] In parts of India, and in Ceylon, local planters, interested only in their own protection against hookworm and the sanitation of their own grounds, refused to collaborate in the larger pursuit of public health.

No matter the difficulty, starting with their efforts to build educational institutions and address racial disparities in the South, philanthropists put science to the service of humanitarianism. Their commitment would be long lasting and integrated into the larger American civilizing mission. While lingering division over "tainted money" became irrelevant, failure in the American South mattered if American philanthropists were to promote an American example. Early philanthropic efforts pointed to a still familiar dilemma of American influence in the world—that of projecting abroad American solutions that had not yet reached fruition at home and were not easily applicable to local conditions far away. British planters in India and Ceylon could readily point to persisting American racism to dismiss the philanthropists' efforts, and they did. The moral dilemma would haunt Americans throughout the century: "What is your right to give lessons if you can't put your own house in order?"

Philanthropy's goals and its rhetoric were universal; its practice, however, was often shaped by opportunities and regressive ideologies. In the American South, philanthropists had become complicit with structures of inequality in order to achieve some of their goals. But the persistent application of large financial resources for the good of mankind—with tangible results like the American research university or modern medicine—gave the philanthropic movement a moral integrity that even its fierce detractors have never been able to deny and from which many have benefitted.

CHAPTER 2

The Coming of Mass Philanthropy

Turning large fortunes into public assets for the good of mankind was a huge project. But what gave philanthropy even more of a central place in modern American life was the simultaneous creation of a people's philanthropy—or mass philanthropy—that engaged the large American middle and working classes in their own welfare.

Philanthropy would not be a democratic value if it remained the domain of the wealthy. Only when the rest of the population aligned its old welfare institutions and charitable habits to the systematic search for the common good would philanthropy become a national commitment. One requirement for effective mass giving was the creation of a culture of giving, where making contributions in response to mass appeals would become routine. Another was the ability to reach everyone. National fundraising campaigns like the March of Dimes canvassed the entire population in large and small cities alike, while local do-good associations federated into community chests across the country. The managers for these new charities worked out a division of labor between new charity professionals and legions of volunteers. Together, they devoted mass campaigns to the open-ended scientific program of foundations as well as to the traditional goals of local charities.

There had been dramatic occasions in America when fundraisers had bypassed the church and lodge, where appeals were normally made, to collect money more widely. American communities improvised fundraising campaigns across the country for great humanitarian causes. The U.S. Sanitary Commission collected its funds for the wounded of the Civil War. In Virginia City, Mark Twain famously described how the money was raised: "If the town would only wait an hour, an office would be ready, books opened, and the Commission prepared to receive contributions" from "the clamorous multitude."[1] After the Civil War, several tragedies abroad generated special campaigns such as auctions, benefits, theatricals, concerts, and entertainments to help the victims, as when rescuing the starving Irish in the late 1870s or mobilizing against the massacres of Armenians in the mid 1890s.[2]

But it was the Progressives' promotion of "collective responsibility," as Theodore Roosevelt put it, that set American mass philanthropy on its course.[3] The leaders of the new mass philanthropy—promoters of the public health movement, heads of federated community institutions, social workers, and reformers—discovered early in the century, in social worker Lilian Brandt's words, "large subterranean pools of benevolence" upon which they drew.[4] The difficult part was to tap those pools. They spent much energy on finding ways to accomplish this, and their efforts were rewarded—though what they marketed was not a consumer good but a cause in need.

The Idea of Mass Philanthropy

Institutionalizing mass philanthropy began in earnest in the public health movement—specifically in the fight against tuberculosis—at the turn of the twentieth century. The fundraising techniques developed during this era made it possible to envision a drastic change in the giving habits of Americans.

Americans normally contributed to local charities. In his 1906 book on the need for a living wage, Father John Ryan, who would become an important Catholic supporter of the New Deal, reported on workers' giving habits. He based his analysis on a survey (conducted for the Bureau of Labor) of 2,132 families with an average annual income of $687 and an average size of 5.7 persons. Workers gave 1.5 percent of their annual income to their church for church maintenance as well as charitable causes. They gave another 1.8 percent to labor and other voluntary associations, though in most cases this was a form of insurance. Many of the contributions went to ethnic organizations with burial benefits.

They gave an additional 0.4 percent for informal charity, unmediated by church or lodge, to help friends and neighbors in distress.[5] Working-class budgets collected by the U.S. Bureau of Labor Statistics confirm these figures.

Thrift was also an important part of ordinary Americans' lives. The Charity Organization Society volunteers, as well as the new crop of professionally trained social workers encouraged all people of modest means to save money as much as they could. They valued thrift as both a means of personal improvement and a minimum safety net. Social worker Mary Wilcox Brown reported in *The Development of Thrift* (1899) on success in inculcating frugality in the laboring classes via cooperative savings, building and loan associations, and people's banks.[6] Margaret Byington reported on the effort workers made to save in her contribution to the 1908 Pittsburgh survey of working-class life.[7] While expressing some reservations about the pitfalls of excessive saving, Father Ryan shared the same conviction. Noting that workers paid almost 1 percent of their income for property insurance, up to 3 percent for life insurance, and up to another 3.25 percent for sickness and death benefits to a combination of fraternal associations and insurance companies, he expressed the hope that they would eliminate insurance and death benefits spending through savings.[8]

Now a tuberculosis association was proposing an entirely new formula to donor and beneficiary alike: Make giving a form of safety net against broader threats. Invest some money for the common good as well as your own in a philanthropy devoted to eradicating a major cause of impairment and death.

With the germ theory of disease as their scientific grounding, reformers supported an intense educational campaign against tuberculosis. The Census Bureau estimated in 1908 that tuberculosis alone accounted for 11 percent of all American deaths—and one quarter of New York City children were affected.[9] Only pneumonia was worse. But as President Theodore Roosevelt's Committee of 100 on National Health described it succinctly in 1908, "the weak and spasmodic efforts of charity" were not effective to respond to the scourge of tuberculosis.[10]

The campaign against it was slow to pick up. In 1892—ten years after German bacteriologist Robert Koch had identified the tuberculosis bacillus—Dr. Laurence L. Flick, a recovered American patient who had become a physician, started the Pennsylvania Society for the Prevention of Tuberculosis, the first group dedicated to fighting the disease. For eight more years, the Pennsylvania society remained the only such organization in America, with fewer than one hundred members. A second society formed in Toledo in 1900. In 1903, Dr. S. Adolphus Knopf founded a third association in New York.

The National Association for the Study and Prevention of Tuberculosis was finally launched in 1908 after Knopf asked the New York City Charity Organization Society to sponsor a Committee on the Prevention of Tuberculosis.[11] Edward Devine, Charity Organization Society secretary, and Lillian Wald, founder of the Henry Street Settlement House in the Lower East Side, were instrumental in launching the national organization. Separately, the New York State Charities Aid Association set up a Committee on the Prevention of Tuberculosis in 1907.

But the alliance between the rich and reformers, which had worked so well in higher education (chapter 1), did not immediately materialize in public health. Despite the commitment by progressive reformers and the worthiness of their goals, no big donor emerged to take the lead in funding the eradication of tuberculosis. In fact, no large philanthropist had yet targeted any specific disease at the time the National Association for the Study and Prevention of Tuberculosis was created. It would be another two years before the Rockefellers began their battle against hookworm in the American South in 1910.

The concept of mass fundraising to fight tuberculosis reached the United States by chance. The Danish-born immigrant Jacob Riis, well known as a pioneer photographer of tenement life and campaigner to clean up the slums, had seen six brothers die of tuberculosis. In 1904, he received a Christmas letter from Copenhagen bearing a peculiar seal in addition to the traditional postage stamp.[12] A Danish postal official had had the idea, embraced by his government, of selling the seals to raise money to build a local hospital for children with tuberculosis. Three years after Riis received the remarkable letter, construction of the hospital near Copenhagen was complete. Riis told the story of this highly successful "penny subscription" in *Outlook*, urging the duplication of this type of fundraising in the U.S. He pointed to the fact that "no millionaire" had come forth "to endow" the fight against tuberculosis and went on to say that "no millionaire" was "wanted," that the job would be "far better done by the people themselves." Riis added: "Five years of that sort of campaigning, and we ought to be on the home-stretch."[13]

The seal idea was picked up by a young member of the editorial board of *Outlook*, Emily Bissell, who, as secretary of the Delaware Red Cross, wanted to join a physician cousin in supporting a tuberculosis sanitarium in Delaware.[14] Bissell convinced the Red Cross to sell the seals at Christmas time to benefit the National Association for the Study and Prevention of Tuberculosis. Teaming up with the Red Cross, an increasingly important player in the management of natural disasters, was an important step. The Red Cross would later take the lead in developing volunteerism and fundraising during World War I, but it committed itself at this moment only to the sale of Christmas seals for the tuberculosis society. It made them available in post offices around the country, a location ordinary Americans could easily get to (for the same reason, the federal government would install postal savings banks in 1911).[15] At Bissell's local Wilmington post office, where the first seals were sold, the Red Cross displayed a promotion sign: "These stamps do not carry any kind of mail but any kind of mail will carry them."[16]

Here was the original impulse for this successful early-twentieth-century mass-fundraising effort. The 1908 seals campaign, which raised $135,000, provided ample encouragement to repeat such appeals. In his landmark *History of Fundraising*, Scott Cutlip described the seals campaign as a turning point in the acceptance of mass philanthropy by the American population. Within just eight years, by 1916, the sale receipts topped the $1 million mark. By the mid-1960s, a mailing of 40 million letters brought in $26 million.[17]

The idea originated in Denmark, but as Riis put it, "Denmark is a small country." America, in contrast, was a vast nation that had not only a tradition of charitable giving, but also large organizational capabilities, and so it is no surprise that it was in the United States that the potential of the seals campaign was realized. Such a broadening of philanthropy through a close attention to raising money in the population at large was a project for the age of mass marketing.

One innovation led to another. Charles de Forest (radio pioneer Lee de Forest's brother), who ran the seals campaign for the National Association for the Study and Prevention of Tuberculosis, had the idea of expanding the market for the stamps by using children as "crusaders" in their neighborhoods in 1915.[18] In 1919, the National Education Association recommended that every elementary school in the country use the crusade-style of health education promotion. The better the children performed health chores like washing hands and brushing teeth, the higher their rank as "crusaders" in the Modern Health Crusade. There were three million "crusaders" in the U.S. in 1919.[19]

This is how, presented with a new idea, the tuberculosis association began to compete for the small amounts of cash that social workers had heretofore wanted American workers to put into savings accounts.[20] While big money philanthropy had required some key legal changes before it could take off, fundraising in the mass necessitated a change in financial strategy on the part of working-class families. Ordinary Americans were asked to reallocate small sums they would have saved for personal use in hard times as gifts to large organizations for the collective good. This was an important conceptual transformation, which took time to mature. People of small means had to learn how to balance thrift and gift, and even to view them as complementary behaviors. In the end, they came to think of mass philanthropy as a form of public thrift.[21]

With its lead in mass fundraising, the National Association for the Study and Prevention of Tuberculosis stimulated many of the other institutions in the matrix of giving to join in fighting the white plague. One indirect result of these alliances was that participants saw how they could use mass philanthropy for their own ends.

The new general-purpose foundations (see chapter 1), with their commitment to solving large social dysfunctions by addressing their root causes, finally developed complementary programs. Homer Folks, the commissioner of public charities in New York, who sat on both the Charity Organization Society committee and the board of the National Association for the Study and Prevention of Tuberculosis, was responsible for establishing the first municipal hospital for tuberculosis in New York City. He turned to the Russell Sage Foundation, where he had the ear of first director John Glenn, a social worker from Baltimore, for administrative funding of the national association. John D. Rockefeller, Sr., personally contributed as well.[22] The Rockefeller charities, having by then targeted hookworm in the South, joined the tuberculosis fight by initiating a vast operation in war-ravaged France. Other big donors, who had been initially missed, contributed to the crusade against the disease. Railroad magnate James J. Hill gave $100,000 for research to New York doctor and health officer Hermann M. Biggs, who was caring for Hill's wife.[23] Henry Phipps, Carnegie's old friend from very early railroad days, helped Dr. Flick establish the Tuberculosis Institute in Philadelphia, essentially a research laboratory. The Russell Sage Foundation and Anson Phelps Stokes (who gave to African-Americans in the South) helped bankroll the Saranac Sanitarium in New York's Adirondacks.[24]

Other funding partners in the fight against tuberculosis came from business, labor, and government. Life insurance companies naturally invested in reducing mortality among their customers, and these definitely included the working classes. Metropolitan Life paid for a major study of tuberculosis in Framingham, Massachusetts, and underwrote a large educational campaign.[25] The Modern Woodmen of America funded a sanitarium in Denver, which opened in 1908 and housed many patients through the 1920s. The Woodmen taxed its members across America to pay for the sanitarium and even used it as a selling point to attract new members. State boards of charities and local governments sponsored traveling exhibits and educational campaigns.[26] In New York State, thanks to Folks's efforts, reporting tuberculosis cases became law in 1908. The Board of Health was reorganized in 1913 and professionalized with the provision, pushed for by Biggs and Rockefeller Institute director Simon Flexner, that health workers could be hired from anywhere in the country, thus freeing the board from local political appointees. Other states followed suit. Among the reformers, Baptist minister and leader of the Social Gospel movement Walter Rauschenbusch wrote a prayer for the "Tuberculosis Sunday" services held in churches and schools.[27]

The first campaigns were notable for eliciting support from a spectrum of groups and for establishing the first tentative links among diverse charities, hospitals, churches, ethnic associations and fraternal organizations in a common philanthropic movement. Mass philanthropy was the engine of a national collaboration that would only grow in the twentieth century to sustain long-term battles against other life-threatening diseases. Between 1904 and 1916, the number of dispensaries and clinics for tuberculosis multiplied from 18 to 455. During the same years, local voluntary associations invested in the campaign jumped from 18 to 1,324.[28] Edward T. Devine pointed out in *Charities* that the association made itself "of direct practical value in legislation, in the education of the public, and in bringing about a coordination of philanthropic, medical and educational agencies for the conquest of the great scourge."[29] Funds raised to fight the disease were critical to opening sanitariums.[30]

The large fundraising mobilization around a single cause and the recruiting of volunteer crusaders was the great change. In 1905, no more than 5,000 Americans were actively working on the prevention of tuberculosis. By 1915, the "army," as the National Association for the Study and Prevention of Tuberculosis liked to call all engaged in active campaigns, numbered up to 500,000 people at certain times of the year, including children busy selling seals.[31] The campaigns naturally rested on—but also went well beyond—the existing institutions of lodge and church to broaden their appeals. A growing number of Americans responded to these pleas by absorbing the expenses as part of the regular family budget. A "people's philanthropy" had emerged, based on the abstract concept of reciprocity between giver and recipient.

At the same time, community leaders across the country experimented with federated fundraising drives to pool resources for community work. They wanted not only to increase overall participation in funding social welfare, but also to apply more professional methods of accounting and spending to a multitude of parochial concerns. Different charities broadened their appeals locally by launching a community chest movement of cooperating with others in fundraising. In federating, chest leaders wanted to free themselves from depending on the very wealthy as well as to bypass the identity politics of neighborhoods and parishes and the mutual avoidance of the lodges. They were attuned to the collective possibilities of a "metropolitan community," as sociologist Roderick McKenzie called it, one that included a city and its suburbs, where size and diversity would be assets in fundraising drives.[32] The principle that prevailed in the tuberculosis campaign—small financial investments in the collective welfare by as many people as possible—appealed to them.

In joining a community chest, local social service agencies combined their individual fundraising campaigns into one and subjected themselves to a common procedure for parceling out the money raised. The Charity Organization Society had heretofore promoted cooperation among charities as a means of efficiency—to avoid duplication of aid to the poor. The new federating effort in raising money, although not free from elite influences, had a different inspiration and purpose altogether. The idea was, as a social worker explained it in *The Survey*, to turn the entire community into "an entity possessing a conscience and a will."[33]

There were a few early attempts to federate fundraising. In Denver, Colorado, Protestant, Catholic, and Jewish leaders had launched a common fundraising drive in 1887 (wishing to replicate a similar campaign in Liverpool, England), but it brought only modest returns.[34] More successful financial federations took hold in Jewish communities. United Jewish Charities were established in Boston (1895), Cincinnati (1896), Chicago (1900), Philadelphia, Detroit, and Cleveland (1904). A broader interfaith Federation of Allied Charities was successfully established in Elmira, NY, in 1910.[35]

It was in John D. Rockefeller's hometown of Cleveland, albeit without his help, that the community chest movement began in earnest. At the time, no more than 4 percent of American urban households could be counted on to give to welfare/social-work agencies. Half of 1 percent—the classic progenitors of "noblesse oblige"—contributed

96 percent of all collected funds. To find more donors, the Cleveland Chamber of Commerce launched the Federation for Charity and Philanthropy in April 1913, after five years of study.[36] Under the chamber's impulse, the chest retained a distinctly Protestant leadership. Social workers active in the local efforts of the Americanization movement that spread across the industrial belt contributed not to a philanthropic melting pot but to a significant pooling of fundraising resources across ethnic and religious boundaries.

The *New York Times* noted the big idea: the campaign promised donors they would be spared from multiple solicitations. They would be "immune from the separate appeals of the institutions represented." In tune with the wider philanthropic spirit of attacking large problems, the new Cleveland federation proposed to spend part of the money for "broad social and philanthropic education."[37] "A broadly based constituent board" made up of leaders of major community groups governed the chest and made a commitment to sound money management.[38] This finally moved Rockefeller, who was an advocate of federating in corporate affairs, to send a pledge larger than all his previous gifts to the separate charities. Rockefeller believed "the spirit of combination and cooperation" would "eventually prevail in the art of giving," just as it had in business, much of it under his managerial wizardry.[39]

In these years, social work was becoming more than a calling left to volunteers. It was turning into a profession, one that would help overcome social fragmentation in communities. As social workers became concerned with setting terms of membership in their new profession, they committed to learning how to fund their activities.[40] Carnegie Foundation for the Advancement of Teaching reformer Abraham Flexner believed social workers could not claim professional status, for they knew no special skills. But social workers were anxious to acquire just such skills, fundraising among them.[41] In 1898, the New York Charity Organization Society launched a six-week summer school in "philanthropy" and began developing a social-work curriculum. Other cities followed suit. This was the beginning of specialized schools of social work and social-work departments in colleges, and in 1917 the National Conference of Charities and Correction changed its hoary name to the

"National Conference of Social Work." In the early years, social workers adhered to the Charity Organization Society emphasis on cooperation and central registrations to coordinate local relief, family service, and other welfare agencies, even as they worked on a more personal understanding of welfare recipients. They now developed mechanisms of fundraising with the help of Chambers of Commerce across the country in responding to the many requests for funds.

It was perhaps not entirely an accident of history that the same Clevelanders who pushed for federation in fundraising created the following year another long-lasting new philanthropic institution—the community foundation—this time distinct from the Federation for Charity and Philanthropy, to raise money from middle-class and modestly wealthy Americans rather than the masses. In 1914, a local banker and attorney by the name of Frederick Harris Goff (whose wife was among the initial trustees of the chest) pioneered the idea of the community foundation. Goff, who had represented the street railways in their tense negotiations with Cleveland mayor Tom Johnson, was a skillful broker. As a former attorney turned banker with a wide network of acquaintances, he frequently advised clients at many different levels of wealth on how to write their wills. Noting a lack of creative philanthropic ideas in these wills after the immediate family was provided for, he suggested gifts to community institutions for community-wide welfare. Once again, the bequest language reflected the larger transformation impulse embedded in the foundations set up by much wealthier Americans. Goff's clients promoted the "well-being of mankind" but targeted their gifts to local needs.[42]

Goff was inspired by Arthur Hobhouse's *The Dead Hand: Addresses on the Subjects of Endowments and Settlements of Property* (1880), a collection of papers the British judge and charity commission member had read before the Social Science Association. In the margins of the book, Goff, who was familiar with the recent legal changes regulating giving, noted the need to keep philanthropic funds free from obsolete donor intent. Hobhouse made the point that endowments should be free from the "grip of the dead hand" and overseen by a "living and reasonable owner of property."[43] To that end, Goff proposed a turnover of community foundation trustees to keep them attuned to the needs around them. The community foundation would keep its investment and distribution arms separate. Affiliated banks would manage the funds. New civic leaders who held positions of trust in the community and had reputations for probity would be periodically chosen to distribute the money earned by the funds.

Goff emphasized the community foundation concept as a means of democratizing philanthropy. In his program for open-ended gifts, he was obviously following transformations pioneered by the large foundations, but politically he kept away from them. Called to testify in Congress before the 1915 Walsh Commission, which excoriated the Rockefellers, Goff had a chance to place community foundations in a democratic context. He insisted that disbursement was entirely in the hands not of a self-perpetuating board but of a "committee of citizens" regularly renewed. Eager to distance himself from the very wealthy, Goff also insisted that the community trust "lacking the resources of Rockefellers, is especially open to poor people with enough idealism about small amounts of philanthropy to want these to be kept useful as the years go by."[44] This was good copy and also powerful. The idea took off, and other community foundations soon sprang up.

In the long run, the two mechanisms—the community chest and the community foundation—led to distinct outcomes. The chest movement eventually became the United Way, with affiliates in many American communities. With the Combined Federal Campaign entrusted to its national organization, it has become a very big part of today's mass philanthropy. The community foundation has kept its local focus. Community foundations have generated funds from local, medium-sized estates for community projects, not from the poor as Goff had, perhaps wishfully, hoped. Nonetheless, the two projects sprang from a common idea of pooling resources in an enlarged community. Both promoted an original synthesis between charity and philanthropy, between volunteers and professionals, between lodge and town, between rich and average Americans, based on a vision of a metropolitan society.

Fundraising in World War I: A Giant Leap

As part of the dramatic mobilization required by the First World War, the Federal government drew on philanthropy's expertise in mass fundraising and further established charitable giving as a permanent feature of twentieth-century life. The intensity of the effort reinforced the perception that giving was part of being an American. The way the fundraising was conducted added to a dramatic increase in the scope and outreach of philanthropic organizations, as well as their level of interaction with one another.

The government oversaw the work of the Red Cross, the one humanitarian organization with a federal charter; it entrusted other mass fundraising drives to other organizations. The community chest movement dramatically expanded. A host of institutions, large and small, joined the matrix of giving. At the same time, many Americans of modest means "learned for the first time the joy and dignity of giving."[45] While 5,000 in a city of 300,000 people had given to various causes before the war, that number now jumped to 55,000 individuals.[46]

Broad humanitarian efforts began as soon as hostilities broke out in Europe, before direct American involvement. Some especially able figures, mining engineer Herbert Hoover among them, rose to prominence through their World War I humanitarian work. Hoover set the tone in 1914 when he gave up his ambition to become president of Stanford University and, from London, launched the Commission for Relief in Belgium (with the unofficial sanction of the U.S. government), a temporary committee to secure basic foodstuffs in Belgium and the occupied areas of northern France for civilian populations on the verge of starvation.[47] Hoover paid expenses for some of the staff out of his own pocket; volunteers joined. As a result, the commission kept its overhead administrative cost at less than half of 1 percent, while soon dominating the American effort to bring humanitarian relief to war-devastated regions. The CRB distributed a total of $894,797,000, including contributions from the English and French governments, and American government loans. For food and other basic needs, the CRB raised from

governments and individuals the very large sum of $259,600,000 be-
tween 1914 and 1920. Of this amount (equivalent to the annual income
of over 250,000 Americans, or 75 percent of the Federal taxes collected
in 1913) Hoover raised 20 percent from charitable contributions worldwide, 14 percent if only American private contributions are calculated.[48]

Other efforts sprang up at the intersection of governmental and
private action. The American Relief Clearing House in France and the
War Relief Clearing House in the United States, the latter under the able
leadership of General Electric's Charles Coffin, coordinated the donations in kind and cash from over 6,000 American relief organizations,
ranging from the Daughters of the American Revolution to the Jewish
Joint Distribution Committee.[49]

Significant as these efforts were, Americans intensified their fundraising dramatically when they entered the armed conflict in 1917. This
led to the definitive breakthrough in mass philanthropy. The federal
government lent its full force to mass fundraising by officially sponsor-
ing massive appeals by the Red Cross and the United War Work Campaign. A host of other institutions joined in the effort to raise money.

President Wilson appointed Henry Davison (of J. P. Morgan & Co.)
in 1917 to head a New Council of the Red Cross. Davison immediately
launched the war campaign with a public request for funds. This was
a real new beginning for the still-small organization with a checkered
history and an ill-defined sense of mission. Its motto—"Everything is
needed; everything is welcome"—was a tacit admission that there was
no consensus on goals in disaster relief operations. In 1889, the *New
York World* had denounced the Red Cross for giving help out too easily,
hence "introducing pauperism" among Johnstown flood victims. Local
charities had not cooperated well with the Red Cross in the aftermath of
the San Francisco earthquake (1906).[50] More targeted rescue operations
after the Triangle Shirtwaist Factory fire in New York City (1911), or the
sinking of the Titanic (1912) had gone better, but the leadership worried
that chapters mobilizing only for "the raising of money and supplies
in response to relief appeals gradually lose interest." The tuberculosis
campaign helped the Red Cross's national visibility, but the organization itself did not conduct national fundraising before America's entry

into the war. In the wealthy Massachusetts town of Manchester-by-the-Sea (population of 2,700), churches and other groups raised money for the Red Cross disaster relief fund by selling lemonade, ice cream, and candy. Bag sales could only go so far, however.[51] Red Cross leader Mabel Boardman complained that the Japanese Red Cross was significantly better organized and funded than the American.[52]

National priorities and the federal government's new directive to the Red Cross changed this in short order. With 2.8 million American draftees departing for the front, Davison set a goal of $100,000,000 to be raised in mass collections in one week from June 18 to 25, 1917. He exceeded that goal by $15,000,000. A second campaign a year later raised $181,000,000—the "most stupendous fund-raising effort by a voluntary relief society that the country had ever known," remarked an observer.[53] In short order, the Red Cross became America's biggest mass charity, funded with the small contributions that the average American made in response to appeals at gatherings in churches, schools, theaters, and social clubs. The number of Red Cross chapters in the nation leaped from 107 chapters to 3,864, with membership growing from 16,708 members to more than 20 million between 1914 and 1918. More than 8 million adults served as volunteer collectors. Another 11.5 million youth claimed membership.[54]

The United War Work Campaign to aid prisoners of war, American troops abroad, and suffering civilians in 1918 was another instance of successful mass philanthropy inspired by the war. Here too the federal government played a role in its launching. Raymond Fosdick, a young lawyer who had worked for the Rockefeller Bureau of Social Hygiene before the war and was now chairing the Commission on Training Camp Activities, initiated the mass appeal at the request of President Wilson and Secretary of War Newton D. Baker. John R. Mott, a leader of the YMCA and the growing international ecumenical and Christian student volunteer mission movements, directed the campaign seeking $170,500,000. The Armistice was signed on November 11, 1918, which was the day scheduled for the drive to open. Mott immediately responded by redirecting the purpose of the campaign to peace readjustment. In a famous telegram, he instructed all operation participants to work to prevent the "period of demobilization" from becoming a period of "physical and mental demoralization." Not even the deadly influenza epidemic stopped the volunteers' door-to-door solicitations. Because of the flu, 40 percent of collectors in one state had to opt out of the collection, but the others combed the countryside in their Fords wearing gauze masks as they rang doorbells.[55] Only a few days later, the campaign had gone over the $200,000,000 mark, significantly exceeding its initial goal.

The United War Work Campaign efforts depended on new developments in the community chest movement, which made it possible for its drives to reach all the way down to virtually every American at the county and city levels. New war chests emerged across America as combinations of local charities and churches, as well as local branches of national charities (e.g., Knights of Columbus, Elks, YMCA and YWCA, Salvation Army). They became the locus for billions of dollars of American donations and for the purchase of Liberty and Victory bonds in 1917 and 1918.

By the summer of 1918, there were war chests in over 300 cities, where the prewar experiment in federated fundraising was transformed into a national phenomenon. They penetrated deeply into the population. The forty-three principal war chests, drawing on an aggregate population of 7,068,750 reached 2,273,216 donors or 32 percent of their population—more than one per family.[56] Appeals were dedicated to the war cause and parts of the collected funds returned to the various agencies involved in the local collections. "Sixty funds in one" said one chest; "Humanity calls you" another.[57] Almost all of these war chests were participating members of the larger United War Work whirlwind.

The Red Cross was not a part of these joint community efforts, because it preferred to keep direct control over its local branches. But local Red Cross headquarters were often used to organize war chests, and volunteers overlapped across organizations. In addition to war work, war chests in Cleveland, Detroit, Toledo, Indianapolis, and Rochester included in their appeals the provision of funds for local welfare, thus adding to the momentum for community chests after the war.

The federal government had ordered this massive fundraising for humanitarian purposes while leading its own campaign to convince the American population to invest in government bonds. This was necessary because the new income tax aimed at the wealthy was designed to cover only about a third of what was sufficient to finance the war; the remaining two thirds had to come from borrowing. Secretary of the Treasury William McAdoo therefore oversaw the sale of Liberty and Victory loans, which were government bonds issued to the public for coupon rates of between 3.5 to 4.5 percent. The newly created Federal Reserve kept interest low to help buyers in the securities market absorb the Treasury issues, while the Capital Issues Committee attempted (but not successfully) to prevent corporations and municipalities from issuing competing securities.

The bond campaign followed a strategy closely intertwined with the mass philanthropic movement, that is, of deep penetration into the recesses of local communities. People were constantly exposed to exhortations to give. Liberty and Victory loan drives, designed around local "precinct captains," drew heavily on the volunteers of mass philanthropy, such as the Boy Scouts, to go door-to-door to solicit funds for the war effort. They also included provisions for payroll deductions to ensure that workers' contributions were collected before they attended to other costs of living. Raising money in the mass was integral to the federal government's propaganda effort entrusted to George Creel's Committee on Public Information. Banks across the country helped their customers invest in the war; volunteers canvassed neighborhoods; preachers called on their parishioners; four-minute men spoke at intermissions in theaters. As a result, the four Liberty Loan campaigns (two in 1917, two in 1918) and the Victory loan campaign of early 1919 elicited a massive response from Americans in all walks of life. Frank Vanderlip, the president of National City Bank in New York City, surveyed the sale of war bonds in January 1918, noting "an almost religious fervor that has been manifested in the sale of these bonds."[58] This fervor played a role in enshrining philanthropy as part of American culture.

Liberty and Victory bond loan drives engaged more than 66 million Americans as subscribers for a rough total of an astonishing $25 billion to assist with funding the war.[59] The government bond market led also to much speculation. Small investor-patriots bought liberty bonds at face value and then sold them off when they needed the money but their value was falling, at which point more speculative investors swooped in to take up the government bonds at a discount. In other cases, bond buyers were chasing higher returns and traded their bonds for stocks from often-shady promoters.[60]

With money changing hands so rapidly, many small institutions were now organizationally linked in the matrix of giving. Everywhere groups of citizens who joined for one cause or another—Armenian relief, Syrian relief, the Jewish fund, soldiers' comfort, and prisoners' camps—were part of a common movement.[61] Some worked with the Red Cross, while others remained independent. Most collaborated, regardless of their philanthropic roots.

Large elite philanthropic institutions cooperated closely with the mass philanthropic movement and exchanged leaders, who as a result thought of philanthropy in more inclusive terms. The Rockefeller Foundation appointed Wycliffe Rose, the head of its International Health Division, as director of its own War Relief Commission. Ernest Bicknell, who had distinguished himself in the Red Cross rescue effort after the San Francisco earthquake and who had become its first full-time administrator in 1908, represented the Red Cross at that Rockefeller war commission.[62] As the Red Cross was the largest coordinating body, the foundation deferred to it, maintaining a leadership role only in the fight against tuberculosis in France. Livingstone Farrand, former secretary of the American Tuberculosis Society and first director of the Rockefeller Tuberculosis Commission in France in early 1917, became chairman of the Red Cross after the war.[63]

In many cases, wealthy donors and grassroots fundraising projects targeted the same causes. Anna Harkness (whose deceased husband Stephen had been one of the original Standard Oil investors) established the Commonwealth Fund in 1918, promoting child welfare, health, and education. The fund contributed to relief and rehabilitation in Central Europe, but so did modest Americans who had roots in the region, recent immigrants, and even refugees who engaged in wartime Diaspora philanthropy.[64]

While some fundraising persistently remained particular to one group (some Jewish fundraising, for example, over Julius Rosenwald's objection), and despite intense improvisation, the war effort led many organizations to share resources for a common purpose. At home, the YMCA cooperated with the National Catholic War Council and the Jewish Welfare Board.[65] At the front, the YMCA opened "foyers" in collaboration with the French army for French troops.

Wartime fund raising relied on mass advertising to penetrate deeply into the population. The federal government, the Red Cross, and the United War Work all hired major publicists, who advertised giving for the war just as they advertised consumer goods for other clients. For the United War Work, Bruce Barton, one of America's greatest publicists (he later masterminded GM's marketing in the 1920s), took care of the publicity.[66] The Red Cross War Council got help from Ivy Lee, public relations counselor for the Rockefeller interests during the deadly labor violence of 1913. Red Cross chair Davison called in fundraiser Charles Ward, who in turn enlisted Lyman Pierce. These two public relations men with experience managing YMCAs had promoted the idea of the "blitz" fundraising campaign in which an organization concentrates large resources on canvassing all possible respondents quickly and mobilizing them for a cause. Focusing everybody's attention on specific programmatic goals for a brief period of time brought in significantly more money than a more diffuse campaign. This was the first instance of what Arnaud Marts, one of the first professional fundraisers (who trained with Pierce) termed the "modern 'whirlwind' campaign."[67] In New York City in 1913, Ward and Pierce had led the YMCA and YWCA in a campaign to raise four million dollars in "one week."[68] Now they helped the Red Cross divide the nation's cities and towns into units, establish local committees, set fundraising quotas, and put all to work, from Hollywood stars to the Boy Scouts.

All this fundraising naturally led to greater sophistication in targeting different social classes. In Springfield, Ohio, leaders of the war chest decided that 40 percent of the total should come from wage earners, 30 percent from people with larger incomes, and 30 percent from corporations. The poor should give the equivalent of about one hour of income per month, while more privileged workers should go to one day a month or 4 percent of income.[69] In Elmira, New York, the tables the war chest provided suggested that those with salaries between $500 and $1,000 give $1 per month, those with $4,000 to $5,000 salaries, $20 per month. All should realize, the war chest insisted, no doubt wishfully, that "one hundred cents out of every dollar that he contributes will go directly for war needs."[70] Moreover, war chests aggressively campaigned among local businesses, making corporate giving an important new partner in mass philanthropy.

The principal fundraisers took on the rich, who responded. J. P. Morgan gave $1,000,000 and Henry Ford, his peace ship a thing of the past and his factory operating for the government "without one cent of profit," gave ambulances valued at $500,000 to the Red Cross.[71] For the United War Work, Mott himself focused on the "big givers" like John D. Rockefeller, Jr., (who was campaign chair for New York State) and U.S. Steel's George W. Perkins, and also approached Americans living abroad via his international YMCA contacts and branches.[72] Campaign managers reported impressive results among other social classes. Pierce at the YMCA reported "middle class giving on a hitherto undreamed-of scale." Postville, Iowa, Mott's tiny hometown, contributed $2,800 to the United War Work.[73] A female volunteer for a war chest encouraged other women to postpone buying new hats and give for the war instead. Her solution was simple: "Ladies, do touch up your old hats by moving around your birds of paradise."[74] In Switzerland County, Indiana, sixteen-year-old Robert Gross gave all that he had saved for a new suit to the local war chest when the solicitor came to his family home. Some school children and girls working in offices, stores, and factories repeatedly gave so much as to be left hungry.[75]

In marketing giving among the working classes, the federal government-philanthropic partnership dwelled specifically on the moral connection between "saving" and "giving" that earlier social workers had pointed out. In her *Development of Thrift*, Mary Wilcox Brown had observed the personally beneficial effects of giving. Persons engaged in philanthropy almost "inevitably become more simple and frugal in their own way of living."[76]

As if to make the point that investing in victory was another form of savings, the Treasury Department designed a program to sell "thrift stamps." Not large or particularly ornate, thrift stamps were roughly the size of a standard postage stamp and cost 25 cents each. With the first purchase of a thrift stamp, the purchaser was "given a card containing spaces for 16 thrift stamps, with the expectation that when the card was filled, this having a value of $4.00, it would be exchanged for a war savings stamp, or as it was sometimes called, a war savings certificate."[77] At maturity, on January 1, 1923, the Federal Reserve Banks would pay to the purchaser at any post office a total of $5 per certificate issued as of January 2, 1918. The ability to redeem at any post office (e.g., as opposed to a national, state, or federal bank) made this outreach national and gave the stamps an appeal to rural and urban Americans alike.

To help subsume the thrift movement into the war drive, the YMCA launched a "Thrift Movement" and "Thrift Week" observance in 1916. "Thrift Week," symbolically opened on Benjamin Franklin's birthday (January 17), aimed to encourage funding the war. English teachers were recruited for the effort. A 1918 editorial in the *English Journal* directed teachers to explain grammatical and stylistic "conventions" "as the accessory of clearness and force in persuading one's hearers to buy Liberty Bonds or save for Thrift Stamps."[78] The students could take the message home. With public officials and civic leaders together articulating the view that funding the war was a form of *public* thrift, giving in this instance took on the aura of thrift.

Contributing to the war effort was also marketed as national duty and a means to victory. It made individual giving part of American culture for generations to come. But not all of this giving was really voluntary; it was sometimes the result of what might be called compulsory voluntarism. Giving to appeals became a public measure of every American's patriotism. Gone were the early days of the European war when groups of German Americans could object to the fundraising effort on behalf of the Entente and offset it with their own, which had led to violent encounters in Midwestern communities. Or when the government felt it was necessary to launch a special campaign in New York among Russian Jews, who had escaped pogroms, to support Russia against Germany. Giving was often enforced, being voluntary in name only. Employers not infrequently told workers how much to give and sometimes took that amount out of pay envelopes without workers' full consent. Eugene Crippen, like every worker at the Willys-Morrow motorcar plant in Elmira, New York, had no option but to give one week's wages through payroll deduction so that the company would meet its targeted $100,000 in war contributions.[79] With the war, responding to fundraising appeals became not only an act of generosity but also a test of nationalism and obedience. Before America's entry into the armed conflict in April 1917, fundraising had been much less demanding. But in 1917 and 1918, it was turned into a mechanism for enforcing loyalty, and giving became a tangible proof of it. The Red Cross abandoned any pretense of relying only on voluntary contributions. In Josephine County, Pennsylvania, whenever a parent or guardian refused to approve the signing of a loyalty pledge by a child, the Junior Red Cross reported the person to the local board of the National Council of Defense. War chests did much the same with those they perceived to be "slackers," as the chest in Switzerland County, Indiana, called the better off people who refused to give.

Coercion prompted suspicion. In Cleveland, Ohio, the very place where the federated movement had initially taken off (in the years when now Secretary of War Newton Baker had been mayor), citizens concerned about the bona fides of the charities and about the infringement of their freedom launched a National Investigation Bureau of War Charities in 1918 to evaluate war relief organizations before endorsing them.[80] Intransigence at home towards civilians who did not give money or not enough of it mirrored that on the front where dissent could not be tolerated. But at the same time, humanitarian work gave many a conscientious objector a viable alternative to direct military engagement. American Quakers launched the philanthropic American Friends Service Committee in April 1917 for this very purpose.[81]

The scale and scope of World War I fundraising obviously rested on the collaboration of many of the institutions of civil society (from organizations like the Red Cross to churches, libraries, and elementary schools that served as the natural sites for collection), while the federal government put its full power behind the bond drives. The war emergency helped make fundraising a permanent fixture of the country's routine. "Giving" became a symbol of American nationalism and a measure of citizenship. Europeans understood the movement as a special additional contribution by the American people to the cause of democracy.[82] It is in this context of massive government and civil-society investment in the techniques of fundraising that Americans created a mass philanthropy of unprecedented magnitude that continued to operate long after the mobilization effort, when giving was once again strictly voluntary.

Widening the Circle of Giving

The great expansion of mass giving led to the professionalization of philanthropy. Before and during World War I, volunteers raised most of the money. But after the war, full-time professionals organized specialized fundraising firms and sold their services to colleges, churches, hospitals, and cultural institutions. While injecting a new level of expertise into the process, fundraising firms were primarily mobilizers and consultants. They still relied in large part on their clients and the volunteers they recruited among university alumni or church parishioners to do the actual fundraising. Thus professionals and volunteers came to coexist in mass philanthropy. They oversaw its postwar consolidation and its success in the 1920s.

Fundraising firms took off rapidly after 1919. Charles Ward ended a thirty-five-year career as YMCA secretary to establish in 1919 the firm of Ward & Hill Associated, which soon became Ward, Hill, Pierce & Wells. Many others followed his lead, including Marts & Lundy, Ketchum, and Tamblyn & Brown. There were twenty well-known fundraising consulting firms in New York City by the end of the 1920s. The growth of professionalism raised the level of giving. The fundraising firm of John Price Jones reported that by 1929 the average philanthropic contributions of all persons filing income-tax returns had almost reached the record wartime level achieved in 1917.[83]

Institutions of higher education, as they had been the first beneficiaries of big-money philanthropy, became professional fundraisers' biggest clients. Already in 1914, Ward had assisted the University of Pittsburgh with an alumni drive relying on what had come to be known as the "every-member canvass" method.[84] John Price Jones left the deepest imprint in academia. Graduated from Harvard in 1902, Jones was loaned in 1917 by the advertising firm where he was employed, to work on the Liberty loan drives in New York City.[85] After the armistice, Jones directed the Harvard Endowment Fund campaign. Taking the college well beyond State Street, as Boston financial circles are called, he raised an unheard of $14.2 million from alumni in less than one year. In November 1919, the month the campaign was completed, Jones incorporated his own John Price Jones Company. Dismissive of earlier efforts by YMCA "Christers," "High Price Jones," as he was nicknamed, directed fourteen fundraising campaigns for universities between 1919 and 1925.[86] At a cost of 2.34 percent, he raised a total of $68 million for academic endowment and plant.[87] He also advised schools where collectors worked on salary, not on a percentage of total funds raised. Other fundraising firms orchestrated the work of church parishioners. Tamblyn & Brown guided Episcopal Bishop William T. Manning in 1925 in building the Cathedral of St. John the Divine on Morningside Heights in New York City.[88]

Health associations, which had initiated the mass philanthropy movement and had accelerated the professionalization of social work, called on fundraising firms to assist them. Tamblyn & Brown led a campaign for the Missouri chapter of the American Society for the Control of Cancer that aimed at putting to rest the idea that cancer was a disease brought on by personal indulgence. The firm orchestrated speeches, distributed literature and newspaper articles, prepared slides in movie theaters, designed bus posters, and insured the showing of films distributed by the YMCA. The society canvassed, on its own, various populations in New York State in census-like fashion. Its Rochester chapter designed a three-year campaign by estimating potential returns on the basis of the population in surrounding counties.[89]

Civic institutions came to rely on fundraising firms. Founded in 1913 by the publishers of *American City* magazine, the American City Bureau assisted only three local chambers of commerce with their fundraising campaigns in 1914. But in the six months following the signing of the Armistice, it helped carry out thirty fundraising campaigns to prepare cities for the "new era of peace." The American City Bureau expanded rapidly throughout the 1920s as civic groups sought its advice about how to gain greater membership and money from philanthropic appeals. It also ran exhibitions of local and foreign city planning and annual Summer Schools of Community Leadership.[90] Progressive boards of trustees and staff in large museums, libraries, and symphonies increasingly sought professional advice to gather cultural capital and broaden their appeal to middle-class visitors and donors.[91]

To become a professional fundraiser was, according to some, rather easy. "Almost anyone of good appearance with a flair for selling, organizing, and publicizing could conduct successful campaigns to raise moderate sums for popular causes," said Cornelius Smith, a former reporter for the *Baltimore Sun* and a cofounder in 1919 of the fundraising firm of Will, Folsom, and Smith.[92] But there was a need for agreed-upon qualifications as well as rules of engagement. In 1935, nine major fundraising firms created the American Association of Fundraising Counsel, which established a fair practice standard. For Arnaud Marts, a two-time president of the AAFRC, this event signaled the professionalization of fundraising, though it would take another twenty years before social critic Vance Packard would actually popularize the term "fundraiser" in *The Hidden Persuaders* (1957).[93]

The broadening of the circle of giving, a consequence of professional fundraising, was a significant social transformation. Membership organizations benefited from it. Although the NAACP, founded after the Springfield riot of 1908, had always been open to all individuals regardless of color as well as to members of all churches or lodges, more than half its income in 1914 still came from only fourteen big donors like Julius Rosenwald. By 1919, after an extensive membership campaign, some 62,300 members tripled the NAACP's income with their dues and contributions.[94] The following year the membership increased by 46 percent to 91,203, and the number of branches leaped by 70 percent to a total of 310. From then on, most of the funding for the NAACP's work came from black Americans through modest dues, contributions, and the proceeds of local events.

Not every organization relied on the advice of a high-profile fundraiser, but all sought to build on the war momentum and keep giving high. Community foundations continued to foster "the mental, moral, and physical improvement" of residents.[95] Young Raymond Moley, who would later join the early New Deal, headed the Cleveland Foundation after the war. He conducted numerous surveys and strengthened the city's civic institutions. By 1930, twenty-one American cities had community foundations with assets in excess of $100,000.[96]

The community chest movement spread from about forty cities in 1919 to about 350 by 1929. As one participant put it, the more people participated, the more understood that giving was one of "the real responsibilities of citizenship."[97] But gone was the wartime coercion. In 1920, community chests raised $19 million; by 1930, the figure had increased almost three-fold to $75 million. With chambers of commerce promoting the chests, many contributions now came from corporations (29 percent in Milwaukee; 26.5 in Cincinnati; 35.5 in Memphis; 48.8 in Seattle in 1929).[98] The proportion of individuals in the general population who contributed to a charitable organization grew with alacrity as well. By 1928, one in five citizens in Toledo contributed to a community fund; in Dayton, slightly more than one in four, in Cleveland, two in five; in Cincinnati, just under one in five; in Columbus, just over one in ten.[99] In 1930, Boston, Chicago, and New York were the only major cities without community chests. Part of the reason was the mutual avoidance among Catholic, Jewish, and Protestant charities in these cities that persisted well into the Great Depression.

Despite these achievements, in the self-serving judgment of some New Dealers, the community chests of the 1920s promoted social and political conservatism. Abraham Epstein (known for his work in the Social Security Administration) criticized them for concerning themselves not with large social reforms that would address the root causes of poverty, but with promoting case-by-case individual "adjustment" to existing social conditions and norms, in the manner of old-style charities. They did not support the federal program for mothers' pensions out of a fear of potential political favors being played out in their distribution. They gave only lip service to the child-labor amendment crusade. "The only spirited enthusiasm they evidenced," Epstein complained, "was during the annual 'zip-zip' community chest drives for funds."[100] But in fact, the federation movement was a critical phase not only in the professionalization of social work but also in the extension of the welfare state. The movement drew the attention of communities across the country to local welfare issues and eventually helped dramatically expand the pool of public funds. Several members of the New Deal "Brains Trust" had their first encounters with welfare in working with the community chests.

Although the New Deal eventually denied private agencies access to federal funds (see chapter 4), President Roosevelt himself and some of his advisers were critical players in the expansion of mass philanthropy. A great boost to mass fundraising came from the national campaign against poliomyelitis. Just as Harry Hopkins, the architect of the New Deal's recovery programs, had once led the tuberculosis campaign, his boss spearheaded the fight against polio, the disease that afflicted him.

Franklin D. Roosevelt first went to Warm Springs, Georgia, in 1924, seeking the therapeutic effects of the town's waters. In 1926, he purchased the property from George Foster Peabody, the philanthropist who had funded the Southern Education Board earlier in the century (see chapter 1). FDR established the nonprofit Warm Springs Foundation with the help of his former law partner, Basil O'Connor. O'Connor believed that a successful election in 1932 would be the key to raising money for polio, and events proved him right. In 1933, he initiated a mass fundraising campaign in Georgia instead of limiting his appeals to wealthy Georgians. As a result, the people of Georgia contributed over 60,000 gifts "ranging from a dime to $5,000," and "from farm produce to hand-made articles," for the construction of a new hospital building for infantile paralysis, to be named Georgia Hall.[101] From then on, the circle of donors grew. Beginning in 1935, postmasters in many communities nationwide, and not only Democrats, organized "President's Birthday Balls." O'Connor thought they could raise $100,000. But with

FDR as the public face of the campaign, they collected $1 million the first year.[102]

In January 1938, Roosevelt established the National Foundation for Infantile Paralysis. Former vaudeville star comedian and Democratic fundraiser Eddie Cantor coined the phrase "March of Dimes," a play on the name of the popular newsreel feature "The March of Time," and he appealed to radio listeners all over the country to send their dimes directly to the White House. The campaign proved hugely successful. In 1939 the national office initiated a "Mile O'Dimes" campaign, with towns competing to produce the "longest line" of coins. In 1940, O'Connor organized the viewing of short polio movies at theatres around the country where a "March of Dimes mother" would pass through the audience collecting donations. The most famous of these short clips was "The Crippler."[103] Soon after began the so-called "porchlight campaigns."[104] People turned on their lights to announce that they would welcome a campaign volunteer to their door. Thus the March of Dimes reinvigorated the techniques of neighborhood canvassing initiated in the fight against tuberculosis before World War I and used extensively thereafter by the Red Cross, the United War Work, and the war chests. With the March of Dimes, grassroots campaigning again connected all (willing) citizens in a great philanthropic chain that linked the White House to modest houses in remote communities and indeed to just about every dwelling and workplace in America.

In 1928 the *American Mercury,* edited by H. L. Mencken, focused attention on the changing locus and operation of organized giving by highlighting the rise of new professional fundraising techniques and new forms of philanthropic management. Referring to a "Big Wind" sweeping across American philanthropy, the magazine observed: "Where money-getters on the prowl once devoted themselves almost solely to the Big Money Boys, they now seek to be democrats, giving everybody, high or low, a fair chance to do his bit for the Worthy Cause." Fundraisers claimed that their newfound profession status enabled them to reach deeper into society, and, as the magazine rightly observed, profit much themselves in the process. "Instead of chasing after fat checks of six figures, they snatch up whatever is offered—dimes and nickels, and even pennies. And what was once a simple art, practiced exclusively by amateurs, is now in the hand of Science and Organization. It has become, indeed, a Great Profession, with trained specialists who, for a fee and expenses, stand ready day or night to raise funds for any Great Cause."[105]

Philanthropy as Part of the Standard of Living

With each successive drive, participating in mass philanthropy became more firmly established as an American value and even as a part of the American standard of living in the sense that a greater number of families would routinely budget small contributions.

The mass philanthropic movement could not have kept its wartime momentum in the 1920s without a rising standard of living. There was a steady increase in disposable income. Counting in 1914 dollars, average annual pay went from $696 in 1914 to $898 in 1929, a 29 percent jump. Therefore more Americans had the means to give some money away periodically to philanthropic causes.[106]

Earlier appeals for humanitarian causes at home or abroad had called on Americans' Christian sense of charitable duty, while appeals for national emergencies invoked patriotism. Increasingly campaigners added to their pitch the donors' contribution to their own well-being. In appealing to ordinary Americans, fundraisers expanded on the earlier notion of a public thrift. They emphasized that it was in the givers' self interest to contribute to the common cause, because they would ultimately benefit from the expected results. To the extent that the money raised would help eradicate diseases, create a healthier environment, lengthen life, and other such collective enterprises in which all Americans stood to gain, a personal contribution was an investment in a safety net for all that was well worth the momentary sacrifice. Giving for all competed with saving for oneself and one's immediate family. But with greater disposable income and clear collective goals, the two behaviors became increasingly intertwined and nonexclusionary.

This self-taxing for the common good is what Tocqueville labeled "self interest properly understood" when he observed and codified Americans' involvement in voluntary associations in Jacksonian America.[107] This same principle that once motivated participation in community institutions was now also driving contributions to larger national organizations through mass philanthropy.

In *How Much Shall I Give?* (1921), social worker Lilian Brandt assessed these changes with the war over and the community chests again on the rise. Brandt argued that the federation of philanthropy and the new techniques of mass fundraising implemented during the war had democratized giving in important ways. Although skeptical at times, she concluded: "In the last year or two, with the shifting of what might be called the center of comfort from the professional class and those whose income is derived from conservative investments to the wage-earning group, individual societies have been trying to get more support from the industrial classes." Brandt noted that in "cities where joint appeals have been made, it has been demonstrated beyond any possibility of doubt that much larger sums and the substantial interest of a much larger proportion of the population can be assured, and that the support of social work can be made a genuine community responsibility instead of being left to a handful of the relatively well-to-do."[108] "What was once the task of the privileged few has become the job of the common man," a community chest worker remarked in 1924.[109]

A small group of economists who in the 1920s conducted family budget studies focused on giving, showed that families planned their contributions to mass philanthropy alongside other regular expenses. In the budgets the economists worked out, they estimated what the American worker could "afford to give." While debating the degree to which philanthropy had been democratized, these economists took for granted that every citizen should give some money routinely. Writing in 1920, Harvard political economist T. N. Carver saw greater thrift and a higher wage-based standard of living as opening possibilities for targeted philanthropic engagement.[110] In "What Can a Man Afford?," published in 1921, Carl Joslyn, an economist more prone to moralizing than his colleagues, argued that individual Americans would be able to give more to charity if they would only spend less of their discretionary income on drinking and going to the movies. From a large number of family budgets, he estimated that a single American making $10,000 a year could give as much 5.35 percent of his income. He suggested only

0.28 percent for a family of six with an income of $1,800. Joslyn saw this giving as something most Americans with a "heart" and a "dollar" should do as one of the "elemental joys of life" in order to contribute to "the happiness of that great multitude of fellow-beings called 'society.'"[111] Giving money that might otherwise be used for consumption was, like thrift, an expression of virtue and also of regard for the well-being of society, and forethought. It was not only more altruistic than thrift but also more useful, including to the giver.

Surveying the standard of living for farmers and their annual budgets in 1929, Ellis Kirkpatrick, an expert agricultural economist in the Division of Farm Population and Rural Life at the Department of Agriculture, found that "closely allied with the church contributions is the expenditure of $1.10 per family for Red Cross and other welfare, by the 2,886 farm families" [in a survey of eleven states across the nation].[112] This was a part of purchasing "advancement goods"—a category that comprised "schooling, reading matter, organization dues, church, the Red Cross and other welfare"—and would prove of personal benefit as well as being a public or civic duty.[113]

We see similar patterns emerge in the results of a later study of those living on moderate incomes. For clerks as well as streetcar men and their families in the San Francisco Bay region in 1933, Emily Huntington and Mary Luck found that fully 93 percent reported donating on average 1.5 percent of their annual earnings to church, charity, or other organizations during the hard Depression year 1933. Eighty-eight percent of these families donated to organized charity, while 61 percent gave to the church. Remarkably, many family budgets included a line item dedicated exclusively to the Red Cross.[114]

The San Francisco study captured the most important trend. Individual giving remained at the same level but there were many more givers. Even though Joslyn's hope for greater family giving was not realized, the numbers of givers and total philanthropic giving went up markedly in the 1920s. On average, 3 percent of the population of a city gave to philanthropic causes in 1900, but by the 1920s, the percentage jumped to 35. By 1928, more than 100 million Americans were giving more than $2.5 billion dollars per year for philanthropic causes. These numbers increased from $1.75 billion in 1921 to $2 billion in 1924, and they continued upward.[115] Many Americans had adopted an ethic of giving.

Given the relatively constant proportion of religious and secular giving, the economist Willford King confirmed the democratization of giving in a study of New Haven in the 1920s. He underscored that the number of givers increased, and with it the dollar amount going to philanthropic organizations. "In this city, at any rate," King wrote in 1928, "it is not true that all that has occurred has been a substitution of a few large organizations for many small organizations."[116] Community chests and the Red Cross demonstrated these changes. During the early years of the Depression the chests built on the notion of American philanthropy as public thrift and were able to meet a significant amount of the nation's need. In some instances they even raised larger sums than they had in previous years. "In every city," reported the Association of Community Chests and Councils in November 1930, "a large part of the increase has come directly from job-holders—persons who may at any time have to turn to the chest for aid."[117] The association saw giving as a form of social insurance. Reciprocity was the key. President Herbert Hoover, himself a former administrator of World War I philanthropic efforts at home and abroad, hoped to rely on these organizations to stave off national calamity (see chapter 5).

"Giving is regulated by habit and tradition," noted President Hoover's Research Committee on Social Trends in 1933. In responding to mass appeals, the many had become participants in philanthropy. The committee reported that Americans' private giving "for purposes of public interest" was predictable and "irrespective of income, tax rate, or any external circumstance."[118] John Price Jones underscored, in the first issue of *Public Opinion Quarterly* in 1937, that mass giving had withstood the worst of the depression.[119] It had become a routine part of American life. While public opinion determined the success of any mass campaign, it affected the choice of a philanthropy but not the underlying philanthropic impulse.

CHAPTER 3

The Regulatory Compromise

As American foundations pursued a new open-ended philanthropy, one that broke away from centuries of targeted giving, and mass philanthropic institutions systematized fundraising to the broad American public, the nonprofit sector quite naturally began to weigh in on public issues. The growth and rising influence of this privately-funded sector posed anew the old question (at the origin of the British 1601 Statute of Charitable Uses) of what constitutes an eleemosynary (or charitable) gift and what its role should be in public discourse and policy. At the dawn of the twentieth century, many Americans found themselves using philanthropic resources to which they had access, including some very large ones, to wage political campaigns and push for new legislation. Inevitably the intersection of philanthropy and politics would become explosive.

The federal government welcomed the wealth of new resources that could be applied to the common good. Congress and the Treasury Department adopted the long-standing tax-exemption policy already benefitting philanthropic institutions in the individual states. Even more importantly, as the opportunity arose with the dramatic growth of both taxation and philanthropy during World War I, they extended the exemption policy not only to philanthropic institutions but also to the men and women who underwrote them.

Before tax exemption became a major issue in regulating gifts, the probate courts were the main arena for controversy. Probate judges were of two minds when they ruled on a challenge to a will intended to support political activity or to otherwise confront the law. Even though American states had abolished British laws during the Revolution, the early seventeenth-century statute continued to carry much weight in many American courts. It listed acceptable categories of gifts—for relief of the indigent, medical care, learning, religion, and other objects of public utility. Some judges relied on these precedents to invalidate a will and return the money to heirs in cases where the charitable gift was intended to support a politically controversial activity, or propaganda, as it was called time and again. Other judges interpreted these precedents loosely or ignored them, and in doing so they not infrequently broadened the scope of philanthropy.

As time went on, however, the question arose as to whether philanthropic institutions and the donors who supported them deserved tax exemptions. The issue of political activity began to be a factor in administrative rulings and tax courts under pressure from politicians who did not welcome challenges to their constitutional privilege of lawmaking. In essence, the state proposed to sponsor an apolitical philanthropy that would not limit its ability to legislate.

It is remarkable how much effort lawmakers, regulators, and philanthropists alike have invested throughout the twentieth century in the nearly impossible task of maintaining a solid distinction between philanthropy and politics. Promoting the common good often leads to political advocacy. All the same, the prevailing view was that philanthropy could educate but it could not advocate, a distinction that depended on an artificial boundary between communication and lobbying. In this dichotomy, policymaking is eligible for a tax exemption but political strategizing is not. Such rules were just as impossible to precisely define as it would be to construct a biracial society where blacks and whites were "separate but equal," another dramatic invention of the same period.

How the Courts Let Politics and Charity Mix
in the Nineteenth Century

American probate courts, traditionally the main regulators of charity, took a permissive approach towards advocacy in the nineteenth century. Judges left a great deal of leeway in the interpretation of what was

permissible in philanthropic funding, including in the area of engagement with politics.

The Second Great Awakening of the 1840s prompted the appearance
of all kinds of charitable associations on the American scene. These associations did much more than help indigents. They promoted contentious ideas, such as temperance, and the reform programs to implement
them. Frustrated heirs, objecting in the courts to bequests for these controversial projects, gave an opportunity to judges to affirm, if only cir-
cuitously, a broad mission for charitable institutions. Judges considered
the legal charitable rationale behind the gifts and their consistency with
previous interpretations of the eleemosynary statutes. Their landmark
decisions are very instructive of the arcane ways judges, when free from
issues of taxation, in effect recognized the indissoluble combination of
giving and advocacy.

Judges always asked first whether a contested gift could be used for
challenging existing laws. They declared time and again that citizens
could not attempt to alter the law through a bequest of their private
wealth. Lawmaking had no place in philanthropy. A gift must be "applied consistently within existing laws," wrote Massachusetts Chief Justice Horace Gray in *Jackson v. Phillips*, a famous civil rights case of the
Reconstruction years. Gray cited previous authorities who insisted, "the
bounty must be 'according to the law, not against the law' and 'not given
to do some act against the law.'"[1]

The seeming simplicity of Judge Gray's dictum hid subtleties that he
himself was about to resort to in mixing giving and politics. Centuries
of precedent had defined the proper spheres of charitable giving, but
Gray now had the authority to interpret the precedents and to broaden
charity. Although it may seem obvious that the first rule to follow for a
donor is to make a lawful gift to a lawful cause, in an imperfect world it
is often necessary to challenge bad laws in order to better society.

Judge Gray's moment came when heirs to Boston merchant Francis Jackson protested the latter's 1861 bequest to a prominent group
of abolitionists and feminists. Jackson had written his will in the days
when the two movements were still closely allied, that is, when advocates of civil rights for blacks and women argued together that race and

sex were merely "two 'accidents of the body' unworthy of constitutional recognition."[2] In 1867, one year before the case was first heard, Susan B. Anthony, one of the bequest's beneficiaries, founded with Frederick Douglass the American Equal Rights Association for a joint fight for gaining the vote.

In the bequest, the clauses pertaining to African-Americans and women were differently worded, and this proved to be critical. The money was to be used on behalf of African-Americans "for the preparation and circulation of books, newspapers, the delivery of speeches, lectures and such other means as in their judgments will create a public sentiment that will put an end to Negro slavery in this country." There were also some funds "for the benefit of fugitive slaves who may escape from the slaveholding states of this infamous Union from time to time."

The testator's heirs claimed that the trust had failed simply because the Thirteenth Amendment abolishing slavery had made a gift to slaves and fugitives obsolete. The court, however, held that the doctrine of *cy-près* (or respecting the donor's original intent under new circumstances—see chapter 1) was applicable, for "neither the immediate purpose of the testator—the moral education of the people; nor his ultimate object—to better the condition of the African race in this country; has been fully accomplished by the abolition of slavery." "Slavery may be abolished," the court recognized, "but to strengthen and confirm the sentiment which opposed it will continue to be useful and desirable so long as selfishness, cruelty, the lust of dominion, and indifference to the rights of the weak, the poor and the ignorant, have a place in the heart of men." Moreover, and perhaps more importantly, what made the court so sure that it could uphold the bequest turned on the question of political activity. According to the ruling, "the manner stated of putting an end to slavery is not by legislation or political action but by creating a public sentiment . . . or another name for public opinion or a harmony of thought."[3] For the court, creating public opinion was nonpolitical.

For women, the gift was intended not simply to shape public opinion but to intervene directly in the political process. It was meant to help "secure passage of laws granting women, whether married or unmarried, the right to vote; to hold office; to hold, manage, and devise property; and all other civil rights enjoyed by men; and for the preparation and circulation of books, the delivery of lectures, and such other means as they may judge best." The court denied the validity of the gift for women's rights precisely because it was aimed "directly and exclusively to change the laws; and its object cannot be accomplished without changing the Constitution also." The cause might be just, the judge admitted, but "in a free republic, it is the right of every citizen to strive in a peaceable manner by vote, speech or writing, to cause the laws, or even the constitution, under which he lives, to be reformed or altered by the legislature of the people." Judges should administer the laws "as they exist." Therefore "trusts whose expressed purpose is to bring about changes in the laws of the political institutions of the country are not charitable." Not on the list of charitable uses sanctioned by precedent, they are not "entitled to peculiar favor, protection, and perpetuation from the ministers of those laws which they are designed to modify or subvert."[4]

The civil rights case *Jackson v. Phillips* was only an initial installment in a long series of court battles involving philanthropy and advocacy. Barely two years after Judge Gray rendered the court's decision, the alliance African-American leaders and feminists had forged dramatically collapsed, and it would take the civil rights movement of the 1960s to rebuild it. Women, excluded from the Fifteenth Amendment (ratified in 1870) that guaranteed the right to vote irrespective of race but not gender, angrily broke their civil rights alliance with blacks. The Amendment forced them to forge ahead and stage their own independent battle for enfranchisement.

Judge Gray had been keenly aware that women did not have the right to vote. This had a major bearing on his resolution of the case. In his reasoning, the judge articulated an evolving theory of separation between thinking politically and acting politically. It was possible to construe the first as educational, but not the second. The court sustained the gift to advance the cause of justice for blacks because of its didactic means; those for women, the court rejected as narrowly political. In deciding the case, the court laid out not a firewall between philanthropy and politics, as some later regulators would insist, but a more subtle rule to separate permissible educational action from non-permissible political lobbying, which was increasingly described as "propaganda."

Thus American lawyers, judges, politicians, and other interested parties worked together to differentiate between different realms of philanthropic intervention. Financing for a political campaign, even when the ultimate goal was to change the law, was permissible, but *only* if the funds were allocated for the education of the public and not for direct lobbying of those in a position to act. Giving could serve advocacy at a remove, so long as it did not technically encroach upon the territory of formal politics.

The distinctions were influential even if ambiguous. As a result of this decision and others, giving for advocacy was increasingly directed at educating the public rather than influencing lawmakers. A close reading of the cases clearly shows that the important distinction was not between the political and the apolitical; it was between the broadly political and the technically political. Donors could serve political ends if they could find nonpolitical means for doing so. It became critical to word their intentions carefully so as not to arouse suspicion and challenge.

A few other late nineteenth-century court cases help us see that under the rubric of education, judges affirmed charitable trusts whose underlying purpose was in the final analysis political advocacy. This is an important point to establish because the Treasury Department would at times be far less flexible than the probate courts when regulating tax exemption for charities. The goal of the probate judges, one should keep in mind, was to add as much charitable money to special causes as possible. Treasury officials wanted instead to set limits on exemptions so as to add to their revenues.

To keep plaintiffs at bay, probate judges adhered to a very narrow technical definition of politics. So long as the challenged charity did not directly intervene in the government, they could legitimize its purpose, and they did. When Henry George's great campaigns in New York City against "unearned" "speculative profits" led to a landmark race for the mayoralty in 1886— George's third party received significantly more votes than Republican Theodore Roosevelt and kept the Democratic Party on high alert—many gifts went to the single-taxer. One of George's supporters left him his fortune in 1887 "for the express purpose of 'spreading the light' on social and political liberty and justice" by means of the "gratuitous, wise, efficient and economically conducted distribution all over the land of said George's publications," including his *Progress and Poverty* and his *Problems of the Times*. When the supporter's heirs attempted to recover the money for themselves, they failed. Changing public opinion, the court told them in 1889, was legitimate so long as it was not designed to promote a specific political action.

Thus, while distributing the works of Henry George obviously served a political agenda, it was understood as "public education." In other words, the dispersal and explanation of George's works and ideas represented a worthy charitable cause at law, provided the works contained "nothing hostile to morality, religion or law." In *Henry George et al., appellants v. William S. Braddock* at the New Jersey Court of Errors and Appeals, Judge Beasley seized on the African-American portion of the *Jackson* case to affirm his position. He further asserted that unless this bequest was upheld, it would become "altogether impracticable to disseminate, by means of a charitable use, the works of any of the leading political economists, either of the present or past age, for it is believed that none can be found that do not, in material particulars, make war, more or less aggressive, upon some parts of every legal system as it now subsists. Certain it is that neither the *Political Economy* of Mr. Mill, nor the 'Social Statics' of Mr. Herbert Spencer, could be so circulated."[5]

Conceptually, the judge added additional maneuvering room for those tax-exempt organizations later facing tax examiners whose ultimate goal was political advocacy. He legitimized a powerful new way for philanthropy to engage politics. All trustees had to do to fulfill their duties was simply to proceed within the framework of existing laws and they would not have to worry about their charitable status. The judge was very clear on this: "A proposition to alter the law according to the law" had a legitimate charitable purpose.[6]

How does one, then, alter the law in accordance with the law outside the formal realm of democratic politics? Again, the key lay in resorting to educational means of persuasion rather than the technically political ones of changing the law. Consider the case of a bequest to further racial integration that the plaintiff firmly believed to be invalid, but that the Supreme Court of Pennsylvania adjudged valid in 1893. In *Lewis's Estate*, the court upheld a gift to prevent "discrimination by the well-known persons and places, viz: Labor organizations, common carriers, hotels, business houses, schools, all places of moral amusement, cemeteries, and in defense of all other rights to which any respectable citizen is entitled by moral right." The donor's intention was to "protect citizens of the United States of African descent in the enjoyment of their civil rights, as provided by the first section of the Fourteenth Amendment to the Constitution of the United States and the Civil Rights Act of Congress based thereupon, and so also of the Fifteenth Amendment thereof."

The plaintiff thought he could not be on firmer grounds. As he correctly argued, the Supreme Court had overturned the Civil Rights Act of 1875 precisely because the Fourteenth Amendment forbade segregation of African Americans only in publicly-owned places. Not only was the will "inconsistent with existing laws," "it is hardly conceivable," the petition read, "that a trust could be valid which had for its object to overthrow a decision of the Supreme Court."

The judge simply retorted that the will was perfectly legal because it did not recommend any direct means of action, political or not, to help the beneficiaries. This made it a valid trust. "It does not offend against any rule of public policy and the main object sought to be promoted is not only lawful, but commendable."[7]

When in doubt, the judges usually sided with the charitable cause. In the new age of open-ended philanthropy, judges actually welcomed a level of vagueness in the bequests they reviewed. Donors responded by being fuzzy. To put philanthropy to the service of advocacy, it was best to leave the means untold and give every appearance of staying within existing laws. Thus giving became another instance of American pragmatism, where ambiguity was elevated to a philosophical principle. When the political encompasses the "educational," as has happened time and again, form matters more than substance, and equivocation becomes a way out of political and legal dilemmas.

An 1897 Illinois case concerning women's rights, *Garrison v. Little*, is telling in this regard. The trust did not tell the grantees what to do with the money for the attainment of woman suffrage. Rather, they were merely to use "their best judgment." Because the means to the political end remained pragmatically unspecified, the judge argued that the court was "bound to carry the gift into effect, if it can see a general charitable intention." A possible illegal application was no deterrent. Rather, "the word charity in its widest sense denotes all the good affections men ought to bear toward each other. A charitable use, where neither law nor public policy forbids, may be applied to almost anything that tends to promote the well doing and well being of social man." Charity is "whatever is given for the love of God or the love of your neighbor, in the catholic and universal sense—given from these motives and to these ends—free from the stain or taint of every consideration that is personal, private or selfish."[8]

This judicial interpretation of charities' purposes continued well into the 1920s in probate cases, even though federal tax policy simultaneously initiated a far more restrictive track. Thus the Pennsylvania Supreme Court decided in 1922 in favor of "improvements in the structure and the methods of government." The decision clearly authorized the trust to fund political action. Its ambitious agenda was to reform "the initiative, referendum, and recall; proportional representation; preferential voting." The sponsor did not want the funded work to be theoretical (limited to an academic political science that was hardly established) but to make a difference in "ballot reform; the simplification of municipal, state and national government; and the revision or remaking of city charters, state constitutions and our national constitution." The broader idea was "to promote efficiency and popular control of government." And the means were expansive, including an effort "to employ and pay lecturers and writers," "to print, publish and distribute pamphlets, magazines and newspapers," and in fact "to use any and all lawful means to increase the knowledge of the citizens of the United States of America upon these governmental and political questions." Trust monies might be used to draft "bills and acts, laws and other legislation and use all lawful means to have them introduced and passed to the end that popular democratic and efficient government may be promoted in the United States of America."

Was the gift to be understood as political science or political advocacy? In validating the trust, the court struggled with the boundary between the two but decided that even though success for the new institution "might involve changes in the Constitution and existing laws," this was no reason to rule against it. Instead the judge in the case argued forcefully that Americans had to engage in a continuous study of the laws of politics, lest they would "discourage improvement in legislation" and be compelled "to continue indefinitely to live under laws designed for an entirely different state of society."

Another estate case that came before the California Supreme Court at the end of the decade confirmed the important distinction increasingly made between policy expertise and political advocacy but protected the latter. At issue this time was the creation of a foundation to promote a broad miscellany of causes: improvements in the structure and methods of government in the United States; in living and working conditions for the working people; the economic conditions of the country; cooperation between employer and employee; education; the practicable application of the "science" of eugenics; prohibitive legislation affecting intoxicants and narcotics; justice for American Indians; and the right of free speech and assembly. After reviewing all the available case law since the *Jackson* case, the court recognized that the opportunities for slipping into pure politics were plentiful but affirmed the trust on educational grounds. At issue was "the creation of a more enlightened public opinion." The "consequent change in laws," should it happen, was merely a consequence of "human relations" and "rights in a republic."[9]

How the United States Treasury Kept Advocacy and Education Apart

With the growing importance of the income tax over the tariff in financing the federal government and the enormous increase in the sums devoted to philanthropy, tax-exemption policy eventually became much more salient than probate rulings in determining the purpose and limits of philanthropy. Twentieth-century federal regulators and lawmakers took a more restrictive view of the adjective "educational."

The Federal government at first took its cue from state governments in defining its own tax-exemption policy. State governments granted not only charters of incorporation but also exemption to organizations devoted to religious and eleemosynary purposes. In the late nineteenth century, about a third of the states revisited their constitutions to take into account changes in the scale of philanthropy. The new provisions fused rationales from common law and equity, some of which had prevailed since colonial days, in defining exemption policy. They reaffirmed the exemption of institutions dispensing social benefits through their religious activities and/or discharging state burdens through charity.[10] Colleges (whose main function prior to disestablishment was to train ministers for the national church) continued to benefit from exemption during the great expansion of higher education, when reformers called on new fortunes to build the American academic system.

All states periodically reviewed their provisions. New York legislators, worried about the negative market effects of land held in perpetuity, had capped the amount of property an exempt institution could hold. But in due course they realized the needs of large universities like Cornell (see chapter 1) and raised the property limit they had initially set on educational institutions.

Harvard president Charles W. Eliot defended the Massachusetts tax-exemption provisions for eleemosynary institutions in 1874 as "not a form of State aid" but "an inducement or encouragement held out by the State to private persons or private corporations, to establish or maintain institutions which are of benefit to the State." As Eliot explained it, the income churches, academies, colleges, hospitals, asylums, and similar institutions of learning and charity were earning was already committed "forever" to public use; therefore it could not be "diverted by the State to other public uses."[11]

There was no reason for state tax policy to affect the broad definition of philanthropy or to curtail the permissiveness toward advocacy that the courts had been inclined to allow. But that changed dramatically when the federal government adopted its own tax policy towards charity. Federal tax policy, which had played no role in the initial surge of American philanthropy, became the major instrument by which the government could define how much to subsidize giving, under what circumstances, and for what reason. With the rise of direct taxation on individual income and inheritance, exemption became a mechanism to encourage individual taxpayers to make gifts to existing charitable institutions or to create new ones.

While nineteenth-century probate judges had asserted that "an appeal to political institutions to improve the lot of mankind" was "entirely consistent with a broad and dynamic conception of charity," treasury officials instead saw an apolitical philanthropy as a necessary justification for the exemption.[12]

Federal tax policy towards charity began with the doomed federal income tax introduced as part of the Wilson-Gorman Tariff Act of 1894, which lowered protective duties on manufactured goods. The income tax, designed to make up for the loss of tariff revenue, included exemptions for "corporations, companies, or associations organized and conducted solely for charitable, religious, or educational purposes," but the Supreme Court struck down the proposed tax because it violated the constitutional provision of uniformity. Only with the Sixteenth Amendment did Congress gain the power to collect income taxes without "regard to any census or enumeration."

What is known of the legislative history of the exemption provision does not suggest a rationale for it other than the long history of state precedents.[13] In 1909, a federal corporate excise tax exempted institutions "organized or operated exclusively for religious, charitable or educational" programs. The Revenue Act of 1913 added "scientific" organizations to the exempt list. The Act of 1916 expanded it to include those "for the prevention of cruelty to children or animals." Literary groups were added in 1921, as were community chests, funds, or foundations, the latter under the impulse of the U.S. Chamber of Commerce, which pressed for an exemption for the civic and social welfare organizations that had benefitted from the dramatic expansion of mass philanthropy.

The states had also pioneered in providing exemptions to individual taxpayers for donations to charitable, religious, and educational institutions, as had North Carolina in 1901 for gifts above $2,000.[14] But it was only in 1917, with the war, that the federal government extended the exemption to individual taxpayers contributing to charitable causes. Senator Henry French Hollis from New Hampshire introduced an amendment to the War Revenue Act of 1917 that allowed 15 percent of personal income to be deducted.[15] Many senators considered the deduction a temporary wartime measure. This new charitable deduction arguably contributed significantly to the success of the United War Work Campaign.[16]

What was supposed to be temporary became permanent. The 1918 Revenue Act not only kept the personal income tax deduction but also widened it to allow estates and trusts to take the deduction for charitable contributions. The Revenue Act of 1924 permitted a small group of taxpayers who had contributed over 90 percent of their income to charity in each of the preceding ten years to deduct all charitable giving, not just 15 percent of personal income.[17] Personal deductions encouraged a great many more Americans to participate in philanthropy and so became an important factor in the success of mass philanthropy. Enshrining the deduction in statute also reinforced the notion that contributions were part of an American's civic obligation.

Thus the principle of encouraging individual Americans to give to exempt institutions, prompted by the national emergency of World War I, was written into federal tax policy almost at its birth. It did not matter much at first, for only 2 percent of the work force had to fill out the first income tax form 1040, produced in 1914. The federal income tax contributed only 9.7 percent of the government's revenue, almost all of which still derived from customs and excise receipts. But modern direct federal taxation had come to pass. Two years later, the Revenue Act of 1916 doubled the income tax rates. Soon after America's entry into the war, Congress dramatically expanded them again. By the 1920s the combination of corporate and personal income tax accounted for 55 to 60 percent of federal tax revenue. By then, exempting individual gifts to charity was becoming a major regulatory tool to make the cost of giving more affordable for many Americans. But the corresponding revenue loss was also a liability for the federal government. Treasury officials were therefore keen to limit it. As donors came to use the increasingly complex tax code creatively to push their political agenda onto the public scene, the Treasury Department responded by drawing a line in the sand. In 1919, the principle of no political advocacy for charities appeared for the first time in Treasury regulations declaring that "associations formed to disseminate controversial or partisan propaganda are not educational within the meaning of the statute."[18] The choice of the adjective "educational" was certainly consistent with past court rulings on bequests, but its application was now much narrower and therefore a significant departure from the legal precedents.

Regulators wanted to make sure beneficiaries of the tax exemption did not engage in politics under the cover of educational activity. During the 1920s, the Treasury Board of Tax Appeals, which reviewed disputed cases before they went to the federal courts, increasingly tightened the definition of "education" that had guided judges in their decisions on challenges to bequests. The Board rejected not only political lobbying but also anything they could construe as propaganda, as they called it, being disseminated as education. The compromise rulings of the probate courts, premised on broad definitions of charity and judicial discretion, were no longer acceptable models. The mere intention of being charitable was not enough. Instead, there was a hardening of the line against charitable corporations and associations that, in the words of the 1919 tax law, disseminated "controversial or partisan propaganda." By using exemption as a tool to regulate charity, Treasury officials sharpened the distinction between knowledge and advocacy, which judges had left vague.

Some cases of 1926 and 1927 settled by the Tax Appeals Court are particularly telling because the charities' objectives seem hardly controversial, and yet the donors were denied a tax exemption. Treasury lawyers advanced a very narrow conception of education. They argued against exemptions for activities that would have easily passed for education or "raising a public sentiment" among most observers. The first case included a 1919 donation to the League to Enforce Peace, as well as a gift to the Mining and Mechanical Institute of the Anthracite Coal Region in Pennsylvania, which had been incorporated in 1894 for the purpose of affording educational and scientific advancement for the men and boys in those fields. The court upheld the gift to the institute because with its narrowly defined educational purposes, it could be considered a charitable organization. The gift to the League was disallowed because the court deemed the "win-the-war" program it had adopted upon America's entry into the war, political. Even though the donor had given his money to a patriotic cause, he was denied the tax privilege.[19]

The Tax Appeals Court issued another ruling that confirmed the anti-propaganda principle in a case otherwise as suggestive of consensus as they come. The court denied a tax exemption for a gift to the North American Civic League for Immigrants, "a group of philanthropists, social workers, writers, and industrialists" who promoted nothing else than Americanization, a campaign of persuasion broadly endorsed by industrialists around the country during the World War to assimilate immigrants into the American melting pot.[20] Again, the probate courts would have easily passed such a program as educational. The tax board also turned down donations to the Scientific Temperance Federation, the Massachusetts Anti-Saloon League, and the Massachusetts Anti-Cigarette League, arguing that they were all formed to disseminate "controversial or partisan propaganda" and therefore "not educational within the meaning of the statute."[21] A gift to the International Reform Bureau (later called the International Reform Federation), a missionary and prohibitionist organization, met the same fate because it "supported candidates for public office who stood for the principles advocated."[22] By the late 1920s, then, the Treasury Department was set on making the tax exemption available only to those donors committed to helping noncontroversial educational causes that could not be construed as remotely political or even merely ideological.

The enormous difficulties in sustaining the distinction between education and advocacy were thrown into high relief when the matter affected all Americans, as did the battles for the legalization of birth control in the 1920s and 30s. American women's right to make their own reproductive decisions was morally controversial and yet central to all aspects of marriage and education. No issue came closer to embodying all the difficulties inherent in attempts to define the proper nature of philanthropic causes and the limits on philanthropic action and its interaction with democratic politics. Proponents of distributing birth control information battled on two fronts: that of legalizing distribution, and that of securing a tax exemption for their funders. While birth control advocates eventually won on the first front, they lost on the second; that is, they were unable to change Treasury's position that the state could not subsidize challenges to existing law, regardless of the flaws of that law.

Victorian laws considered birth control pamphlets pornography (thus illegal). Educated women knew better, read them, and practiced birth control. Those who wanted to change the obsolete laws often broke them. And those who provided them with the funds to break the law were guilty as well. If the latter claimed a tax exemption for giving support to a cause they believed in, they were directly challenging the state.

Margaret Sanger's successful fight on behalf of birth control did not prevent the simultaneous strengthening of the judicial firewall between philanthropy and politics. Sanger won her case, but the court battles waged on behalf of her Birth Control League did not make it easier for donors to support birth control or other controversial causes. When birth control was finally legalized in 1936, donors could claim a tax exemption when supporting the clinics, but by that time the restriction on political activity had been inscribed into the 1934 Revenue Act, thus making it the law of the land, not just an administrative regulation.[23]

Federal obscenity laws had targeted birth control ever since young dry goods clerk Anthony Comstock launched a social purity crusade from New York City's YMCA in the 1870s.[24] As a result, using the mail to distribute information on contraception was a serious offense. Medical journals refused to publish papers on birth control for fear of losing their mailing permit. For the same reason, standard medical textbooks often ignored the matter. Poor women most in need of reliable information could not get it by any practical means, even though everybody knew the hypocrisy involved in withholding the facts of birth control when it was widely practiced by the Protestant American middle class.

Margaret Sanger, a nurse practicing in New York's Lower East Side slums early in the century, was among the many social workers who witnessed time and again the devastating consequences of the lack of birth control for poor women, unsafe and often fatal cases of abortion being the most poignant. Both federal and state statutes stood in the way of Sanger's efforts to distribute birth control information. She and her estranged husband William were constantly harassed by the authorities. Comstock himself, still leading the New York Society for the Suppression of Vice he had started as a young man, arrest warrant in hand, detained William Sanger for illegally distributing his wife's pamphlets in 1915. Margaret Sanger went to jail in 1917, engineering her own imprisonment in part by refusing to acknowledge wrongdoing.

Sanger fairly rapidly realized that if she was to be successful in convincing judges and the public alike of the righteousness of her crusade to legalize birth control and in raising money for her campaign and clinics, it was important for her to move out of the feminist and radical camp and into the center of American politics and culture. Only then could she make her cause palatable enough to gain political traction and acceptance. She transformed herself, therefore, from a controversial Wobbly organizer, which she had been during the Lawrence textile strike of 1912, into the respectable leader of a movement that the middle class could embrace. The less controversial the campaign, the less likely it was to be treated as political propaganda.

Sanger won her first major victory in January 1918 when a New York judge construed the state's obscenity law as allowing physicians to prescribe contraception "for the cure or prevention of disease." This gave the campaign credibility, and some physicians joined Sanger's birth control clinics once they could distribute birth control information for medical reasons.

From then on, Sanger continued to target the center of American politics. She became especially eager to embrace eugenics, which had gained influence in scientific and policymaking circles. The term "eugenics" was coined in 1883 by Francis Galton, Darwin's cousin, to describe scientifically informed efforts to encourage persons with high intelligence to have children and to discourage reproduction among persons thought inferior. Charles Davenport, America's principal investigator in the field, and his associates collected data from prisons, almshouses, institutions for the mentally deficient, the deaf, the blind and the insane to measure the transmission of character traits. The result was a huge "inventory of the blood in the community," *Scientific American* noted.[25] Having learned eugenics from her British friend Havelock Ellis, Sanger campaigned for controlling the birthrate of the "unfit." She found natural allies among social workers, public health workers, charity volunteers, and medical personnel, who worked daily with tragic cases of people afflicted with hereditary diseases. Sanger also adopted Malthusianism—which insisted that population growth pauperized—for much the same reasons that she had embraced the precepts of eugenics: to justify the one movement she cared about and raise the necessary funds for it.

Davenport (who himself stayed aloof from Sanger) had attracted large donations from wealthy philanthropists, irrespective of a federal tax exemption that did not yet exist. His funding was never challenged under the new tax rules as eugenics was widely considered a mainstream science. In the summer of 1905, Davenport approached the mother of Mary Harriman, a Barnard undergraduate, settlement-house worker, and student in his Cold Spring Harbor Biological Lab, and stimulated her interest in the cause. Mrs. E. H. Harriman, who had recently taken over the management of her late husband's immense railroad fortune, rapidly agreed to fund Davenport's research on a grand scale. She established the Eugenics Record Office and turned the entire establishment over to the Carnegie Institution of Washington, which incorporated it in 1918 as its Department of Genetics. Mrs. Harriman's gift to the Carnegie Institution amounted to $300,000. John D. Rockefeller, Jr., also supported Davenport with fellowships for the summer training of field workers. College women with some background in biology were the most common recipients.

The American eugenics movement received its most official sanction when Congress passed the Immigration Restriction Act in 1924 to keep, its sponsors believed, undesirables out. Then, in 1927, the Supreme Court upheld the 1924 Virginia sterilization act, and Justice Holmes declared that "three generations of imbeciles are enough."[26] The irony in the Court's decision was not lost on Sanger. The state could legally sterilize people deemed mentally deficient and yet simultaneously prevent the distribution of birth control information, products, and services designed to help all individuals to make their own reproductive decisions.[27]

Moving to the center of political and scientific discourse paid off. Integrating eugenics into a larger rationale for birth control got Sanger closer to real money. She began to attract the attention of the major philanthropists who were funding eugenics. While Comstock had proudly reported to John D. Rockefeller, Sr.'s staff, in 1899, on his good work with "86 arrests, 78 convictions and more than two tons of obscene matters seized," Sanger received help from the younger Rockefeller.[28] Ever since his college years John D. Rockefeller, Jr., had been thinking through the lessons of Brown University professor Elisha Benjamin Andrews, a disciple of Thomas Malthus, on overpopulation.[29] After his grueling experience on the White Slave Grand Jury on prostitution in New York City in 1910, Rockefeller decided to fund a Bureau of Social Hygiene. He hired Katherine B. Davis, former New York City Commissioner of Corrections, and others who had investigated human sexual behavior, endocrinology, and the hormonal regulatory system, to run the Bureau. Davis reported in 1924 that 75 percent of college-educated women practiced birth control.[30]

Raymond Fosdick, who served briefly as the general counsel for Sanger's Birth Control League and also as a consultant for the Bureau of Social Hygiene, steered Rockefeller, Jr., toward Sanger. Sounding the Malthusian threat, Fosdick wrote the philanthropist, "I believe that the problem of population constitutes one of the great perils of the future, and if something is not done along the lines that these people are suggesting, we shall hand down to our children a world in which the scramble for food and the means of subsistence will be far more bitter than anything we have at present. Scientists are pointing hopefully to such methods as Mrs. Sanger and her associates are advocating."[31] As a result, Rockefeller personally authorized grants to Margaret Sanger's Birth Control Clinical Research Bureau and Dr. Robert L. Dickinson's newly formed National Committee on Maternal Health. Well aware of the contentious nature of the gift and not intending to challenge the IRS, he made these grants anonymously. Other potential donors such as the Milbank Memorial Fund also came through.[32]

The federal government rarely prosecuted cases of mail fraud for literature on contraception or contraceptive material. Still, the state was likely to deny a tax exemption to any contribution openly made to alter these laws. The exemption issue came to a head when Noah Slee challenged the IRS. Sanger had agreed to marry the wealthy and conservative manufacturer on the condition that they maintain separate quarters and he finance her birth control clinics. The older suitor, who never gave up pursuing a wife who preferred her life without him, went through extraordinary efforts to keep the clinics running. He gave large amounts of money and also smuggled birth control material from Canada into the United States.

Although Sanger's Birth Control League was officially chartered as a charitable and educational association under New York law (a status it lost and regained several times), the IRS rejected Slee's return on the grounds that he supported an organization devoted to political lobbying on behalf of a controversial issue. Slee challenged the ruling in 1926 but lost in 1930 after four years of legal wrangling in federal court.

The Court of Appeals for the Second Circuit affirmed the decision of the Board of Tax Appeals, holding that gifts made by a taxpayer to the American Birth Control League could not be deducted from income. In his decision, Judge Learned Hand, otherwise a noted free speech advocate with libertarian inclinations, made it clear that tax exemption could not be used for "political agitation." Judge Hand was not afraid of innovating in legal matters. But in this case, he had no legislative statute to elaborate on. He stuck to Treasury Department rules.

Judge Hand questioned the tax-exempt status of the League itself, but he admitted that "a free clinic, or one where only those who can pay, is a part of nearly every hospital, a recognized form of charitable venture." He appreciated "the good faith of the enterprise." But he found that the League had gone beyond its initial stated goal of disseminating "lawful information regarding the political, social, and economic facts of uncontrolled procreation" to enlist legislators for "the lawful repeal" of statutes regarding the "prevention of conception" and to publish a magazine. Hand confirmed the Board of Tax Appeals' view that an exempt civic league must not be operated for "effecting the removal of state and federal statutes," even though these very statutes encouraged "dysgenic breeding."[33] It is the almost exclusive dedication to "political agitation," Hand made clear, that "must be conducted without public subvention."

Hand took issue with labeling political "agitation" "propaganda." He even admitted that "there are many charitable, literary and scientific ventures that as an incident to their success require changes in the law." He went on to explain: "A state university is constantly trying to get appropriations from the legislature; for all that, it seems to us still, an exclusively educational institution. No less so if, for instance, in Tennessee it tries to get leave to teach evolutionary biology." But in these other cases, "the agitation is ancillary to the end." Concerning the efforts to control the procreation of children, Hand saw the political agitation as the primary purpose. He could not describe it as educational, the adjective he rightly chose from the statute that defined charitable activity.[34]

It was common enough for reformers and advocates of various causes, Hand recognized, "to say that the public must be 'educated' to their views" while they are in fact engaged in a political campaign. Hand thought "it would be perversion to stretch the meaning of the statute to such cases; they are indistinguishable from societies to promote or defeat prohibition, to adhere to the League of Nations, to increase the Navy, or any of the many causes in which ardent persons engage."

Slee lost the exemption in 1930. After a $40,000 settlement with the IRS, he was effectively bereft of disposable funds and was therefore unable to help the League any longer. The case was closely watched by philanthropists of all stripes, as other foundations and donors feared running the same risk if they contributed to charitable organizations engaged in political activities.

The court proceedings did not deter Sanger herself, who, without waiting for the outcome, further broadened her fundraising campaign. The question for her was never one of choosing between legislation and education; new legislation was required in order to proceed with education, and vice versa.[35] Quite cognizant of the modernization of fundraising, Sanger selected an expert in mass campaigns to achieve her goals. She turned to professional fundraiser John Price Jones for advice on mass solicitation (see chapter 2). Jones was unsure whether Sanger could control the required networks of volunteers and organizers necessary to implement a mass fundraising campaign. He feared that the anticipated solicitation might be handicapped by the continued dissension within the movement over the proper type of legislative amendment.

But if Jones doubted Sanger's ability to recruit enough volunteers to raise money broadly, he underestimated her. She launched a ninemonth campaign in January 1930 to raise $100,000 nationally "to promote legislation which would allow physicians to give contraceptive advice and to aid the further dissemination of birth control information."[36]

In 1931, Sanger located the National Committee's headquarters in Washington, D.C., as a lobbying office. From 1932 to 1936, she and her chief financial assistant raised more than $150,000, much of it in the form of small contributions. A direct-mail campaign produced hundreds of $25 gifts. Wealthier women in the New York area gave money in increments of $1,000. Although the Bureau of Social Hygiene in New York turned down an initial request on grounds that it did not support lobbying, the Rockefeller family contributed to the campaign and the Milbank Memorial Fund agreed to finance an effort to have poor women seeking contraceptive advice write to their congressmen.[37]

Whether Sanger's contributors could deduct their gifts was no longer an issue after the legal battle was won. In 1936, the now rarely enforced Comstock laws were finally rendered moot by the courts. The United States Court of Appeals for the Second Circuit legalized contraception in *United States v. One Package of Japanese Pessaries.* Judge Augustus Hand wrote the majority opinion. His cousin, Learned Hand, who had ruled against Slee, was also a judge in the case. He wrote a concurrence to express his reservations that the liberalization should have come from a legislative act rather than a judicial decision. But all agreed on the ruling. It took only a few more years for federal programs to be actively involved in promoting birth control, now repackaged more obliquely as "planned parenthood," in an organization one step removed from the fiercely contentious leadership of a victorious but aging Mrs. Sanger.

But whereas Margaret Sanger had won her long battle, J. Noah Slee had lost his. Slee's loss did not appear to be very critical at the time, but in effect it was. The principle of the separation of advocacy from giving endured. Philanthropy could not underwrite lobbying or any other means of influencing legislation. The case set the precedent for impending disputes over the definition and regulation of philanthropy. Conceptually, the Slee loss coupled with the Sanger victory revealed a schism between social support for reformist philanthropy and the legal strictures placed on the lobbying activities of charities. The principle of giving for education but not for advocacy would only be reinforced in the coming decades, and it would leave a deep and lasting impression on modern philanthropy.

Affirming the Separation of Education and Advocacy in the Tax Code

The inscription in the Revenue Act of 1934 of the formal separation between education and advocacy was a major turning point in the regulation of philanthropy. The first such act formally to single out political advocacy as a reason for not granting a tax exemption, it was a direct outcome first of the Slee case and then of a battle in Congress over veterans' benefits.

Learned Hand's motivation for keeping advocacy out of philanthropy went beyond the blind application of some Treasury Department rule. It was also an expression of his belief in expertise as the source of policy. For a generation, professionals of all stripes had grounded their authority on "scientific" knowledge, which had to be free from political influences. They saw objectivity and advocacy as separate endeavors, and objectivity as the reliable source of authority. At the Laura Spelman Rockefeller Memorial Foundation, Beardsley Ruml put the full weight of Rockefeller money behind the emergence of a distinct "policy science." Charles Merriam championed it at the Social Science Research

Council, while the historian Charles Beard, a progressive fighter for just causes, often learned the hard way that funding was going in the other direction, toward scientific inquiry.[38] Critics charged that funding an objective social science was an easy way out of contentious issues, and yet it became the project of a new generation. Hand saw Slee entrenched in the political rather than the educational camp.

Hand wanted to do the right thing in the Slee case. Most politicians, however, were more grounded. They saw the removal of tax exemption as a tool to silence their opponents. Such strategic attempts, often the outcome of bitter disputes between exempt groups, frustrated those regulators who hoped to manage the state subsidy to philanthropy to serve widely shared purposes sanctioned by law and practice. But competing interests turned the exemption into a political weapon.

As the Great Depression set in, a group of taxpayers advocating for good government, who wanted to help alleviate the government deficit, created the tax-exempt National Economy League. The association, a "non-partisan citizen's organization for public service," was organized in May 1932 under the chairmanship of Antarctica explorer Rear Admiral Richard Byrd. Archibald B. Roosevelt (FDR's distant cousin) served as secretary. The association recruited a distinguished roster on its national advisory council—including Calvin Coolidge, Al Smith, Newton Baker, Elihu Root, and General Pershing. Their general purpose was to secure "the elimination of wasteful or unjustifiable governmental expenditure."[39]

This was of course a worthy goal in those years of economic collapse, but it was at the same time a politically contentious one, especially as the National Economy League targeted for budget reduction "benefits to veterans of the Spanish and World Wars who suffered no disability in fact through war service" or who were no longer handicapped. Veterans were the one group in America granted preferential tax treatment regardless of the Treasury Department's 1919 rules on political lobbying. In the Revenue Act of 1921, Congress had specifically listed contributions to organizations of war veterans and their auxiliary units as deductible from taxable income. Although Congress did not identify the American Legion by name among the exempt organizations, it was widely recognized that the Legion was more than a fraternal order, a recreational club, and a service organization; it regularly lobbied for legislation of interest to veterans.

The National Economy League (whose membership included distinguished veterans) developed a strong case against the veterans as the Depression deepened. In late December 1932, William Marshall Bullitt, onetime Solicitor General of the United States, appeared as the league's volunteer lobbyist before a joint Congressional committee investigating veterans' legislation with the mission to "lop some $450,000,000 from the $1,000,000,000-per-year appropriations for veterans." This was only five months after President Hoover had ordered the troops to remove the "bonus army" of unemployed World War One veterans who were haunting the Capitol grounds asking for advance payments on their benefits. "Pitted against the League" was the American Legion and its "super-lobby." Bullitt was "severely heckled" by some senators. "Chief heckler" was Indiana's Republican senator and World War I veteran Arthur Robinson, who denounced the league for supporting wealthy taxpayers "trying to shirk their share of war costs." Robinson extracted from a reluctant Henry H. Curran, director of the National Economy League, the promise that the organization would release names of all its contributors of $25 or more. Curran in turn argued that the American Legion should also be required to make public a list of the sources of their financial supporters.[40]

Once more the debate centered on the appropriateness of tax-exempt organizations engaging in law-making. "Your purpose is to influence legislation," Robinson rightly observed in a jab at the National Economy League's tax-exempt status. The League vehemently denied that they were engaged in a political rather than an educational mission. "Our purpose is to get the facts before the people—and I believe they will influence legislation," Curran disingenuously replied.[41]

The National Economy League won the first round. One of its directors, lawyer Glenville Clark, a former classmate of Franklin Roosevelt at Harvard, drafted the Economy Act of 1933 in the New Deal's first hundred days. The measure cut drastically the veterans' pension and disability budget.

The league pursued its educational-political campaign by sending to every member of Congress evidence that disabilities not infrequently due to causes other than war service accounted for an increasingly large share of the cost of veteran relief. Already 8 percent of the veterans' budget in 1925, the cost of disability had jumped to 40 percent by 1933.

Having suffered a defeat at the hands of the league, the veterans responded by developing a different strategy. They pulled strings in the Senate to have the National Economy League's tax-exempt status revoked. They charged that, despite its official claim of being educational, the Economy League was nothing but a political advocacy group. In 1934, in the second round of their battle, the veterans, confident that their own (well-known) preferential status was safe, backed a rewriting of the tax code to restrict the political activities of tax-exempt organizations. This was an important move that inserted restrictions heretofore existing only in Treasury regulations into the code itself. Meanwhile, Congress restored some of the veterans' benefits over FDR's veto.

To proceed with the change in the tax code, Senator Byron Patton Harrison, Democrat from Mississippi and chairman of the Committee on Finance, proposed an amendment on the Senate floor. Although there was little discussion, its origins in the political infighting over the veterans' budget were clear. Senator David Reed of Pennsylvania revealed as much by declaring on the floor, "There is no reason in the world why a contribution made to the National Economy League should be deductible as if it were a charitable contribution if it is a selfish one made to advance the interests of the giver of the money."[42]

As if to keep their options open, legislators remained hesitant to define exempt categories as they wrote the revenue act. The House struck as too vague a clause forbidding "participating in politics." In the Senate, Robert La Follette, Jr., supported broad language because it would facilitate enforcement by the IRS.[43] In the end, a seemingly innocent adjective provided the compromise language needed to pass the legislation. The tax code would now include as a prerequisite for tax exemption that "no *substantial* part of the activities" of "corporations, community chest, fund or foundation" operated "for religious, charitable, scientific, literary, or educational purposes, or for the prevention of cruelty to children or animals" "be carrying on propaganda, or otherwise attempting, to influence legislation." Contention would hence revolve around the meaning of the adjective "substantial." By inserting the modifier, Congress made some room for the proposition that it was acceptable to "alter the law according to the law" or to allow efforts to change sentiment "by lawful means."[44] There would be countless interpretations of what constitutes a substantial attempt to influence legislation, as well as of what constitutes controversial and partisan action.[45]

Senator Reed had hoped to bar tax exemption for "any organization that is receiving contributions, the proceeds of which are to be used for propaganda purposes or to try to influence legislation."[46] But Congress chose instead to favor some tax-exempt organizations over others. When Congress amended the law in 1934, it did so in both the sections on exempt organizations and on individual deductions. Both sections included the propaganda clause. Veterans, quite conscious that their voting power protected them, fully expected preferential treatment, and they were not disappointed. They were technically permitted to lobby, as Congress did not insert the firewall language in the special section concerning them.[47] Fraternal societies operating under the lodge system were similarly spared. So were labor organizations. With the addition of the adjective "substantial" to the tax code of 1934, Congress formalized restrictions on the political activities of all other charities and educational institutions. Thus Congress made for the first time a distinction that has become increasingly important between different kinds of exempt groups, a distinction that reflected political muscle more than logical categorization (a feature of the law to which I shall return in examining the civil rights era 1969 tax code—see chapter 7).

The new legislation was as much the fruit of recent political infighting as of any sustained reasoning on membership composition or the meaning of advocacy. But it was nonetheless critically important in the sense that Congress posed anew the large question of how to support philanthropy's contribution to the common good.

Could the act of giving be meaningful in a democracy and yet not encroach on politics? "It must be hard sometimes to draw the line between education and propaganda," answered the *New York Times* in

1928, commenting on a tax audit of the Anti-Saloon League.[48] That the 1934 legislation was, in part, the outcome of a rivalry between two lobbying groups proved sufficient indication that it would indeed be complicated to distinguish between the two purposes. The 1934 legislation became to American philanthropy what the 1601 statute had been to philanthropy in the British kingdom. But the language of the act clarified matters much less than its sponsors intended. Lawmakers would find that maintaining a firewall between education and advocacy would require them to compartmentalize thinking and acting in American life, a task that was rarely, if ever, possible.

CHAPTER 4

The Private Funding of Affairs of State

Herbert Hoover, who had been one of the great spokesmen of voluntarism during the First World War, sought to make institutions of philanthropy full participants in the "compound republic," as James Madison characterized the nation and its different levels of government. In formulating policy as secretary of commerce from 1921 to 1928, Hoover sought technical support from foundations and think tanks; in directing disaster relief, he orchestrated the work of the Red Cross, community chests, and other institutions of mass philanthropy. Hoover expanded his experiment in federally directed philanthropy when president of the United States in an effort to confront the large-scale unemployment and poverty facing the nation at the onset of the Great Depression. There his attempt to integrate philanthropy into the federal mix proved inadequate. It collapsed under the sheer scale of what was needed and under the pressure of conflicting visions of social justice.

In the process, though, Hoover set in motion an enduring debate on the role that philanthropy should play in affairs of state. Should philanthropic institutions take part in governmental decision-making or governmental actions or both? Conversely, to what extent should the federal government enlist philanthropy in pursuing its ends? Could private partners maintain their autonomy from government when emergencies arose and yet follow Washington's guiding hand? Hoover's experiment is extremely important because he was able to turn institutions of civil society, from philanthropic foundations to community organizations, into instruments of the executive branch while calling on them for voluntary action. Hoover wanted at once to control and also to stimulate philanthropic institutions' initiatives. His was an idiosyncratic synthesis of authoritarianism—in its will to subordinate citizens' organizations to executive authority—and voluntarism—in claiming merely to channel the flow of voluntary energies to the collective good. In partnering with philanthropy, Hoover fostered a mixed political economy that enlarged the federal government's reach without formally reorganizing it.

Previously only state and local governments had supported philanthropic institutions. In the New England towns of early America, government and eleemosynary institutions were organically coupled. In eighteenth-century Philadelphia, Benjamin Franklin counted the matching (or joint) grant among his inventions. With his persuasion, the General Assembly of Pennsylvania passed legislation to house his private Library Company of Philadelphia in the State House, as well as to give land to the Academy he had founded. In nineteenth-century New York, Tammany politicians diverted the public treasury to charities, hospitals, and orphanages, expecting the immigrant vote in return.

But the federal government had previously stayed at a safe distance from such arrangements. The Smithsonian Institution stood as a notable exception, and here Congress had hesitated for a long time before accepting Smithson's bequest. In the 1830s and 1840s, John Calhoun was among the politicians who argued on constitutional grounds that the federal government should not broaden its mandate by taking on the added responsibility of running an institution of knowledge or, by extension, any charitable institution. The debate lasted for two decades. The federal government did not want to go into welfare either. In 1854, President Franklin Pierce vetoed a bill that Dorothea Dix had advocated and Congress had passed that authorized the federal government to fund institutions for the deaf and insane. The bill would have put the federal government on the slippery slope to supporting private charitable institutions.

What President Hoover did in fostering a partnership between philanthropy and the federal government was therefore new, but it turned out to be short lived. Hoover's hopes that charitable organizations might provide enough relief to get the country through the growing Depression proved illusory. To provide Americans with a lasting safety net, President Roosevelt changed course. Roosevelt established a clear sepa-

ration between publicly and privately funded action. By increasing federal authority over state and local governments, he went so far as to
sever their traditional connection with philanthropy. But the partnership between government and philanthropy to address the large issues
of job security, welfare, and even racial integration had its supporters
and did not so easily disappear. It returned, albeit in a different form, in
the Great Society of the mid-1960s—forty years after Hoover had first
attempted it.

Hoover's No-Cost Federal Governance

Hoover was called a "food czar" for his work during World War I. Success in persuading so many Americans to give money and volunteer
time to assist the victims of war gave him an unswerving confidence
that civil society, with strong governmental guidance, could to a significant degree alleviate national and international disasters. Hoover was
optimistic that the successful spirit of mobilization that he had tapped
during World War I could be replicated during peacetime and, moreover, that it could then be applied not only to humanitarian emergencies but also to peacetime issues, to promote economic progress and
improve standards of living.

Before President Harding named Hoover as commerce secretary,
the cabinet post had been only a part-time position.[1] Hoover made it a
much bigger job from which he launched his experiment in the large-
scale partnering of the government with the philanthropic as well as the
business communities. He extended to the new philanthropic institutions the "cooperative committee and conference system" (through the
federal encouragement of trade associations), which he was simultaneously developing with business, and which historian Ellis Hawley has
aptly labeled the "associative" state.[2] Hoover declared in 1920 that while
he was not "a believer in extending the bureaucratic functions of the
Government," he was "a strong believer in the Government intervening
to induce active cooperation in the community itself." That same year
in a commencement address at Swarthmore, he told students that he

wanted to draw upon the "vast sense of national service and willingness to sacrifice" he had encountered during the war.[3]

Hoover was genuinely committed to the traditions of localism and private initiative. To him, concerned citizens earned their democratic freedom by governing themselves at the local level. In a phrase he could have borrowed from Alexis de Tocqueville, Hoover argued, "Where people divest themselves of local government responsibilities, they at once lay the foundation for the destruction of their liberties."[4] At the same time, Hoover believed that only the federal government could orchestrate on a national scale a creative synthesis of the many overlapping philanthropic programs. In his short book on *American Individualism* published in 1922, Hoover argued his case for developing "a large field of cooperative possibilities."[5] *Cooperation* was always Hoover's preferred word—and he stretched the meaning of it considerably over the course of his career in public service. Hoover's plan required that his private sector partners pay the bills and do the work but follow his orders. In addressing the St. Louis Advertising Club in 1920, he defined his strategy of no-cost federal governance as "a new basis of community action."[6] Essentially, philanthropies would become an expression of the executive branch, which would coordinate all matters of policymaking.

Hoover had entered public service at a time when foundations and think tanks, although in their infancy, were already influential. They had joined the federal government in a number of projects. President Theodore Roosevelt had asked the Russell Sage Foundation, the original general-purpose foundation, to fund his Country Life Commission, which had as its goal collecting first-hand information on farming conditions. William Taft had chosen Frederick Cleveland, who led the Rockefeller-funded New York Bureau of Municipal Research (one of the first think tanks devoted to governmental research), to head his commission to reform the national budget, which he had funded with a congressional appropriation. When President Wilson, fearing defections among Democrats, abandoned the project of reforming the national budget, Jerome Greene, then secretary of the Rockefeller Foundation, founded in 1916 the Institute for Governmental Research to keep the reform plan going.[7] Hoover joined the board in 1918. The Institute was eventually renamed the Brookings Institution in 1927 to recognize its biggest funder.

Other influential think tanks were created in these years to address social, political, and economic problems and inform policymaking. Department store owner (and leader of the credit union movement) Edward Filene launched the Twentieth Century Fund in 1919 to investigate the needs of a mass consumption society. In 1920 AT&T statistician Malcolm Rorty and economist Nahum Stone created, with Commonwealth Fund support, the National Bureau of Economic Research, where Wesley Mitchell pursued his studies of the business cycles that proved so important to Hoover's Commerce Department. In the arena of international affairs, Carnegie had set up the Carnegie Endowment for International Peace in 1910; a group of Versailles Peace Conference participants founded the Council on Foreign Relations in 1921. Hoover contributed to this institutional development by forming the Hoover Institution on War, Revolution, and Peace, a specialized collection of documents on the causes and consequences of World War I, in 1919 at Stanford, his alma mater.

From his cabinet post, Hoover turned to these think tanks for ideas and policy proposals. In one of his first acts as commerce secretary, he called on them to help American companies acquire new tools of economic analysis, effectively breathing life into the small field of labor statistics. Hoover convened twenty-five business, labor, agriculture, and nonprofit leaders to serve on the President's Conference on Unemployment.[8] This initial meeting of the working group was a formative moment in Hoover's personal effort to work out an association with the nonprofit sector. Presumably, unemployment should have been an interest of the labor secretary, James J. Davis, but he had no such intention. A director general of the Loyal Order of Moose, Davis preferred to attend his lodge meeting rather than the ambitious conference launch of September 1921. The National Bureau of Economic Research and the American Statistical Association reported on figures and measurement techniques. Mary Van Kleeck of the Russell Sage Foundation and Bascom Little, head of Cleveland Community Chest, were the two prominent representatives from philanthropy.

There was plenty to do to expand the knowledge base of federal policymaking.[9] After a nationwide strike of coalminers in 1922, Hoover asked the Russell Sage Foundation to develop a study of employment patterns of workers in European coalmines, especially in Germany, to generate comparative statistics. Hoover was curious also about another Russell Sage regional planning project that had brought together hundreds of experts to devise plans for orderly metropolitan growth. The Regional Survey and Plan for New York under the guidance of planner and life insurance executive Charles Dyer Norton was emblematic of Hoover's associative outlook.[10]

Hoover also embraced big philanthropy's agenda of supporting universities. As commerce secretary, he attempted to steer academic research efforts towards applied projects. Following the advice of National Research Council leaders Nathan Hale and Robert Millikan, he raised money from industry for research at universities to foster technological innovation.[11] These efforts to improve the scientific performance of the nation dovetailed with those of Rockefeller Foundation president George Vincent, who had emerged from the war years with a similar belief in applied science and in the benefit of cooperation among diverse segments of society.[12] The Commerce Department commissioned some studies, while others emerged independently from the new foundations. For example, the Guggenheim Foundation invested heavily in aviation safety, and Lindbergh's endorsement gave these studies visibility. Hoover's vision of cooperative possibilities was becoming reality.

At times, the partnership between the Commerce Department and nonprofit organizations became so critical that Hoover would not hesitate to absorb an organization into the department if he saw the need to do so. He requested and received congressional approval in 1921 to create a Division of Building and Housing, a field he considered "critically important to the health of the entire economic system," as well as to individual families.[13] The division relied much on the nonprofit organization Better Homes, Inc., which Mary Maloney of the magazine *Delineator* had created, for developing housing codes and launching educational campaigns. With Maloney limiting her activities in 1923 and Hoover fearing her departure, he integrated the nonprofit organization into the new division to maintain access to Better Homes' volunteers, who distributed Department of Commerce materials in their communities.[14]

Hoover's embrace of think tanks was necessarily politically tainted, as it was impossible to draw a clear line between a policy science designed to improve governing, which was what foundations and think tanks were supposed to develop, and the partisan debates in which they engaged. Hoover's cooperative formula was, therefore, plagued by a continuous ambiguity between politics and policy, just as similar conflicts played out in tax courts and IRS review boards (see chapter 3). Hoover seemed oblivious to this conflict because he expected to have it his way, but there were tense moments. While he was serving as a trustee of the Brookings Institution, its Institute of Economics embarked on a series of reform proposals that called for lower tariffs. In response, Hoover denounced Brookings's first president Harold Glenn Moulton as a liability to the United States whose policy recommendations, if listened to, were likely to cost the nation tens of millions of dollars. Hoover resigned from the Brookings board in protest of this "politicizing" of social science research. In turn, Moulton joined the ranks of many economists who favored freer trade agreements and later protested the passage of the Hawley-Smoot tariff in 1930.[15] But even though politics sometimes derailed the effort, and policymaking proved elusive, Hoover's pragmatic partnership between the federal government, foundations, and think tanks was a significant innovation.

The opportunity for Hoover to place not only foundation philanthropy and think tanks but also mass philanthropy firmly under the aegis of the federal government and to apply his new framework for philanthropy and American governance came unexpectedly in the administration's response to the great Mississippi flood of 1927. The flood, which began on April 16, broke the Mississippi levee system in 145 places. The waters covered 27,000 square miles, caused over $400 million in damages, and killed 246 people in seven states. Arkansas was hardest hit, with roughly 13 percent of its area flooded. By May, the Mississippi River below Memphis, Tennessee, formed a vast watery ellipse up to sixty miles wide, across which farmers could row a boat without touching the ground. The Delta, also flooded, was the heart of a great plantation system where white landowners employed thousands of black sharecroppers. Until the water finally subsided in August, 700,000 people were displaced, including 330,000 African-Americans who were moved to 154 relief camps.

President Coolidge appointed his commerce secretary to serve as head of a Special Mississippi Flood Committee. Hoover's performance in that role not only enhanced his reputation as a very able administrator, but also gave him a chance to return to the limelight again as a great humanitarian. That the Republican nomination might possibly be within his reach was not lost on him or anybody else.

The relief operation was Hoover's best opportunity for calling American voluntarism to governmental service. As relief czar for a second time he implemented his vision of a federal chain of expertise and action, linking all levels of government to business interests, foundations, and social welfare and humanitarian agencies. Whether the federal government could serve simultaneously as both a participant in and an umpire of this arrangement, as Hoover wanted, was questionable. But the emergency was the occasion to try. If significantly successful, the relief effort might seal a new top-down federal formula where the top echelons of federal administration directed the entire chain of participants all the way down to communities.

As was the case during the war, Hoover induced institutions of mass philanthropy (most notably the Red Cross) and private social services to cooperate with local, state and federal agencies and also with business to provide immediate disaster relief. Hoover mobilized resources from the Departments of the Navy and War, the Treasury Department (especially its subsidiary, the Coast Guard), the Agriculture Department, and his own Commerce Department. To supplement federal action, Hoover called out and federalized National Guard units normally under the command of individual state governors. He then asked for help from state militias and state and local departments of health, as well as already operating special relief committees. From civil society, Hoover relied most heavily on the American Legion, local and national Red Cross chapters, and local citizens' committees to bring relief to the displaced populations. Finally, he also involved large philanthropic foundations. The Rockefeller Foundation financed one hundred county health units, eighty-five of which its International Health Division had helped create in cooperation with the U.S. Public Health service during the early 1920s.[16]

Hoover was the great conductor. He established a clear chain of command to oversee housing the displaced populations. From Washington came the design of various programs such as credit corporations and plans for shantytowns. From nonfederal sources—local governments, business, and philanthropy—came money and execution.[17] Banks and other commercial interests in the states provided as much as 50 percent of the various credit corporations' capital. Under Hoover's direction, local grassroots organizations secured sites for rebuilding, obtained the materials, and built the shantytowns.

Most importantly, Hoover put the Red Cross at the very center of this no-cost-to-the-federal-government relief effort. With its federal charter that gave the president power to appoint half of its central committee, complemented by grassroots financial support and a network of volunteers, the Red Cross became the best emblem of Hooverism. The previous year it had been designated the official relief agency in the aftermath of the 1926 Florida hurricane but had failed to meet its goals. Judge John Barton Payne (Wilson's last secretary of the Interior), president of the Red Cross, had blamed Florida politicians for the failure. He accused them of downplaying the severity of the disaster in order to protect the state's tourism and real estate, and held them responsible for the shortage of funds. With Hoover now in charge of the flood-relief operations, all this changed. Volunteers arrived in large numbers. Of 33,849 Red Cross workers, only 2,438 were paid by the Red Cross.[18] Local communities organized benefits and special fundraising events at every opportunity.

The Mississippi flood-relief effort was the proof that a new associative federalism could work well enough in facing a major emergency. On the eve of the presidential campaign, one photographer caught the future candidate in Opelousas, Louisiana, beaming over newborn triplets named Highwater, Flood, and Inundation.[19] It was good for the

political ambitions of a compassionate engineer, whose successes in orchestrating relief during World War I and now in the great flood led him
to the Republican nomination in 1928.

Hoover's efforts in Mississippi, impressive in coordinating a powerful response to a natural disaster, also revealed the dramatic limitations
of no-cost federal governance. There were naturally no provisions within
disaster relief to alter the status quo of the Southern race hierarchy. Not
considered were the harder questions of social justice. Municipalities
counted on African-Americans to rebuild the levees. Southern planters
expected them to be ready to return to their plantations as sharecroppers once the water receded. Hoover pushed the federal government
to direct local and philanthropic efforts towards recovery, but he was
unprepared to break the thick layers of racial prejudice encountered in
the process. Neither was the Red Cross.[20]

Hoover was troubled enough to order a report on the condition of
African-Americans in the camps. But for his large scheme of ordered
cooperation to bear fruit, there needed to be significant agreement on
the moral and economic goals of the recovery. Accordingly, Hoover ac-
quiesced to Southern planters' pressure on the Red Cross and the National Guard to keep sharecroppers from leaving for the North. Relief
workers recruited locally actually prevented displaced sharecroppers
from stepping on the train to Chicago. They enlisted them at gunpoint
to work along the river to repair the levees. In the camps, they gave
them only meager food and leftover medical supplies. Hoover seemed
willfully blind to these issues. He dismissed much of the criticism of
black treatment in the camps contained in reports that he himself had
ordered from Robert Moton, the head of Tuskegee, and he absolved the
Red Cross while chastising Moton for not being grateful enough.[21]

Even though Hoover had not defied the Southern planters and confronted the Red Cross on the race issue, he did have a tentative scheme
of his own to improve race relations. Not surprisingly, he would involve
philanthropy in a big way. In alleviating the abject conditions induced
by the flood, Hoover had seen an opportunity for an experiment in reducing sharecropping in the United States by redistributing some of the
land to the rural poor. The floods had bankrupted many of the valley's

planters, putting a glut of affordable land on the market. If it could be purchased, at least some African-American sharecroppers might be turned into landowners. For an advocate of social engineering, the flood was, perhaps, a long-awaited opportunity—Hoover's chance to try out Jeffersonian democracy. "Over-riding all of this are the infinite values to good citizenship, stronger stability to the economic structure and the state that comes with a population who have a stake in the land," he wrote.[22] The plan was to work as follows: a private corporation would begin with capital of between $1 and $2 million to purchase plantations, subdivide them, provide tenants with equipment and working capital. Annual income on interest and repayments of mortgages would allow the program to expand to include more families. Hoover figured the corporation would begin with a thousand families, and new income from their mortgages would allow the program to add 180 families per year.

Hoover spelled out his plan in a July 1927 memorandum that he shared with only a "few acquaintances," including Harvey C. Couch and L. O. Crosby, both Southern industrialists who acted as flood-relief administrators in Arkansas and Mississippi. Others in whom Hoover confided his ideas were Judge John Barton Payne of the Red Cross and Dr. Robert Moton of Tuskegee.[23] Although it is unclear what role the Red Cross would have taken in such a plan beyond the logistics of settling people and equipment on newly created parcels of land, Barton steadfastly refused to even consider the idea. Hoover's efforts did, however, raise in Moton's mind the idea that significant improvements for black farmers were in the offing and motivated him to enlist black support for Hoover during the presidential campaign, even though Republicans were still taking the black vote for granted.

Who would underwrite such an experiment? In March 1928, Hoover approached Edwin Embree, who headed the Julius Rosenwald Fund.[24] Turning to Rosenwald made perfect sense from Hoover's standpoint. "Herbert Hoover is by training and experience a leader," Rosenwald would say during the presidential campaign, during which he supported Hoover. "I regard him as fitted beyond any man of this generation for the presidency of the United States. I know of no man at present in public life who has displayed such extraordinary vision in dealing with many stupendous and wholly novel problems, crucially affecting human welfare."[25]

Hoover and Rosenwald had collaborated for some time. After the Russian famine of 1921, Hoover, with President Harding's official endorsement, had worked with many American relief organizations to feed starving Russians. The Joint Distribution Committee, which had worked efficiently during the First World War, operated in areas where Jews were numerous, and Felix Warburg, chairman of the Committee, began raising money for permanent settlements for Russian Jews in the rural Ukraine and along the Crimean Sea in support of a Russian government plan to move Jews to the countryside. Rosenwald, who believed relocation would help persecuted Jews, joined in this effort to turn Russian Jews into farmers. By 1928, after a series of initial gifts, Rosenwald had pledged over eight million dollars. John D. Rockefeller Jr., contributed $500,000 "out of respect for Rosenwald's and Felix Warburg's interest in the work."[26]

Upon the announcement of Rosenwald's offer, Herbert Hoover had characterized the gift as "a great experiment in human engineering," which will make it "possible for people who have been striving as petty tradesmen, to return to their ancient calling and become producers of the necessities of life from the soil."[27] It seemed to Hoover now that Rosenwald, who had spent his fortune funding schools in poor southern black communities (see chapter 1) and supported the Russian resettlement, would be a likely person to fund the land transfer in the Delta that Hoover envisioned for African-Americans.

Rosenwald demurred, however. Even a philanthropist of his stature had reservations about how far Hoover could go in persuading philanthropy to take on problems that Rosenwald believed belonged to the federal government. In this case, his objections were compounded by the absolute need to overcome local segregationist forces. Rosenwald did not give an immediate answer to Hoover, but he eventually made it clear to him that his associative formula could go only so far and that

American philanthropy could not commit to a level of social engineering of this magnitude without real legal and financial backing from the federal government.

Rosenwald told Hoover in 1929 that there were inherent limitations to the formula of no-cost federal governance. It was up to the federal government not only to recognize large social issues of equity, he declared, but also to foot the bill for the required human engineering. Rosenwald urged the President to help directly with federal funds for breaking down race hierarchy, if only because "12 million colored people constitute one of the great potential markets for American industry. The measures to be adopted are many," Rosenwald continued, "but three stand out conspicuously. First, educational programs should be accelerated, with particular reference to the elimination of illiteracy. Second, health activities should be restudied to make sure that this group of people, whose conditions of life are in many ways different from those of whites, are receiving the aid in the elimination of disease that is desirable for their health and for the protection of the rest of the population. Third, the improvement of opportunities for employment should be made the serious concern of the government and such agencies as chambers of commerce and farm boards. No case can be made for employing an inefficient black man in preference to a more efficient white, but when employment can be given to the colored man on a sound basis, the national welfare and prosperity are promoted since on the whole the opportunities for employment for the Negro are much more restricted than for the white."[28] Rosenwald did not believe in no-cost federal governance when it came to fighting racism, and he believed it had to be based on a comprehensive plan, not just an experiment in land redistribution.

That role the federal government was not yet willing to play, even at a modest level. At the White House, after what most believed a successful recovery from the flood and a huge electoral success, it was easy to forget the missed humanitarian opportunity. In his 1929 inaugural address as president, Hoover insisted on Americans' "capacity for cooperation among themselves to effect high purposes in public welfare." Hoover was sure he had the authority to set the terms of teamwork.

Hence he laid out the "field of cooperation by the Federal Government with the multitude of agencies, state, municipal and private, in the systematic development of those processes which directly affect public health, recreation, education, and the home."[29]

When the stock market crashed, it was only natural for Hoover to stay the course and extend the federal reach through various associations. He set all his Cabinet secretaries searching for funding for programs of old-age pensions, unemployment insurance, and healthcare, insisting that the money would come from private resources.[30]

In November 1930, as the economy kept worsening, Hoover appointed Colonel Arthur Woods (who had coordinated the successful 1921 Unemployment Conference) director of a new President's Emergency Committee for Employment. Again, Washington's blueprint called for encouraging the various levels of government to cooperate with industry and charitable organizations to increase employment opportunities and alleviate suffering. In response, most cities around the country organized citizens' committees or mayors' committees, semipublic agencies that conducted large fundraising drives. These emergency committees deployed the methods of mass philanthropy, in particular the whirlwind campaign, to draw upon the purse strings of all able to give.[31] Not funded by tax money, they usually covered the expense of direct relief but were unwilling to fund work programs that state legislatures would not consider supporting.

As the Depression set in, Hoover's formula seemed to hold promise only in a few privileged communities where local institutions had the funds to respond to the economic decline. Hooverism worked where there were deep-pocketed philanthropists willing to support local efforts and behave in ways consistent with the President's directives. This was certainly the case in Delaware—the last stand of Hooverism. There, the population was concentrated around Wilmington, in New Castle County, where the influence of the du Pont family was strongly felt, ever more so as the Depression worsened. Delaware has in fact been called a "company state," so deeply did the giant Dupont chemical company infiltrate all levels of politics as well as civil society.[32] The du Ponts were in a unique position to do what Hoover expected them to do, that is, support the coordination of local governments, local business, and local charity into a powerful response to the downturn. The du Ponts did not channel their philanthropy through a large foundation like the Rockefellers, but nonetheless they rose to the occasion by giving on a large scale.

There was no doubt about the need for strong intervention on the part of the rich. The caseload at the Associated Charities of Wilmington jumped 43 percent in July 1930 over the previous year, and relief expenditures doubled.[33] Never before "have we been called upon to meet so many demands for food, fuel, clothing, and shelter," Lammot du Pont, chairman of the Associated Charities' Finance Committee testified. "Unemployment and illness are bringing to us men and women who are appealing for the first time in their lives."[34] His cousin Pierre S. du Pont, who headed the giant chemical concern, personally underwrote all of the administrative costs of the Mayor's Emergency Relief Committee in Wilmington in the first two years of its existence, so that all of the funds it raised could go directly to relief. Pierre loaned his personal secretary Frank McHugh and continued to pay his salary while he served the city as the committee's chairman. The du Ponts used their leverage to pressure other local companies to help as well. The local telephone company extended to the mayor's committee the use of its former headquarters. Many other companies and their employees participated in the effort.

Local governments and nonprofits devised relief strategies together, dividing the responsibility. By May 1931, the state legislature and city hall recognized the Associated Charities, renamed the Family Society, as the official agency to administer relief to families and single women. The Salvation Army administered help to single men without dependents. The Travelers' Aid Society assisted transients. The Visiting Nurses' Association secured medicine for special cases and assessed the medical needs of the families. The Wilmington Board of Public Education provided milk and lunches for undernourished school children.[35]

In December 1930, Wilmington mayor W. K. Forrest launched a fundraising campaign together with Lammot du Pont and Francis du Pont that aimed to raise $100,000 for the immediate winter-to-spring relief of unemployment. Pierre du Pont subscribed the first $10,000 dollars before the formal campaign began.[36] Although fundraising was more difficult than expected, by May 1, 1931, a total of 3,000 families had contributed.[37] In the special report Wilmington sent to the U.S. Bureau of Census for the first quarter of 1931, total relief expenditures were estimated at $198,618. Of that, $188,618 came from private contributions, the rest from local government. This represented a 1,349 percent increase over relief expenditures for the same quarter in 1929.[38]

Pleased with the outcome, and eager to have the federal government place its stamp of approval on this effort, Hoover sent his labor secretary, William Nuckles Doak, the man *Time Magazine* dubbed the "handsomest Secretary of Labor in American history," to address the newly renamed Mayor Employment and Relief Committee in 1931 and congratulate them on their perfect example of Hooverism at work.[39] A new mayor, Frank Sparks, welcomed the secretary. By then, Dupont had adopted an automatic 1 percent payroll deduction for those of its employees willing to sign up and contribute to the committee. Other companies did the same.

Doak singled out the men of Delaware as embodiments of the president's approach to moving the country out of the Depression. "We realize," he said, that "you are conducting a program which is one of the most outstanding in the United States. It is a centralized program, with decentralized operation. You have financed your program by arousing your own community and your state to the amount of money necessary to care for your own."[40] Hoover followed through with a congratulatory note of his own in early 1932, addressed to William du Pont, not in his corporate guise but as chair of the finance committee. At least in Delaware, as well as in a limited number of other similar places, this "decentralized" Hooverian-style "centralized" organization, with encouragement from the federal government, operated seemingly efficiently, with an association of private philanthropies and public agencies under Washington's benevolent guidance. The Wilmington response showed that Hoover's approach could be sustained; but by April 1932, the limits of the approach were evident. The Mayor's Emergency Relief Committee was forced to shut down because its funds were exhausted.[41] And of course the circumstances that had made it possible for Delaware briefly to rally around Hoover's program were not replicated in many parts of the country. Philanthropies found themselves having to provide not for emergencies but for long-term welfare, a task altogether outside of their means and know-how.

When in 1930 a drought hit a much larger region of the Mississippi Valley than the flood had earlier devastated, Hoover quite naturally tried his rescue system first, but it quickly collapsed under the sheer scale of the required effort in a climate of economic crisis, financial losses, and uncertainty about the proper responsibilities of philanthropic institutions. The Red Cross, the organizational embodiment of Hoover's federalist system, buckled under the sheer weight of the project, even though its leaders tried to focus on drought assistance, not on unemployment and welfare, fields wholly outside the organization's mandate. It was a very tough situation: the disaster was huge, the Red Cross mandate impossibly broad, and the underlying economic crisis made it hard to raise money.[42]

The flood involved 170 counties, the drought at least 1,000. Twenty-three states were affected. To "lay the foundation" for disaster relief, Hoover called the governors of the afflicted states to meet with him in Washington, where, on August 14, 1930, he outlined his plan for creating once again an elaborate hierarchical organization with the Red Cross as the major nonprofit group collecting contributions from the mass of Americans and delivering the aid.[43] At the top there would be a National Drought Relief Committee, chaired by Secretary of Agriculture Arthur Hyde and made up of representatives from the Federal Farm Board, the Federal Farm Loan Board, the Red Cross, the Federal Reserve Board, the Treasury Department, the American Railway Association (important in moving goods at a discount), and the banking establishment (decisive in providing credit). This system was duplicated at the state and county levels. Each governor was to appoint a state drought-relief committee comprised also of a state agricultural official, a leading banker, a Red Cross representative, a railway representative, and a leading farmer. Once the state committees had determined which counties needed organized relief, they would then appoint county committees, each again comprised of a similar mix of prominent citizens and officials.[44]

The goals of the organization, as Hoover outlined them, were in line with previous relief operations he had conducted: to assist needy families over the winter, prevent unnecessary sacrifices of livestock, and protect the public health. As in the Mississippi Flood program, the provision of credit was considered critical. Local relief committees estimated the level of aid lending institutions, businesses, local governmental agencies, and Red Cross chapters would provide.[45] The latter mobilized volunteers. The federal government was not funding direct aid to families, the infamous governmental dole, or paying for meals for the starving poor, only subsidizing animal feed to the farmers. The Red Cross, for its part, was willing to help with groceries but reluctant to provide full meals. In line with its anti-welfare stand, the Red Cross's food distribution was generally limited to an order of staples in the local country store, garden seed, a canning program, and the distribution of yeast. Even with such limitations, conservative planters, sticking to the attitude they had displayed during the flood, refused to participate in the Red Cross garden seed distribution for fear that croppers, who had already had their wages cut by 50 percent, might perceive any mark of compassion as an encouragement to leave the plantations.[46]

As the emergency showed signs of becoming permanent, the debate on federal funding—the proper use of public funds, the mandate of respective partners, the place of local autonomy, the enforcement of welfare policy—came to a head. Several senators had aired the idea of providing the Red Cross with public funds for direct relief, when Arkansas Senator Joseph Robinson introduced in Congress in January 1931 a resolution that the government grant $25 million to the Red Cross for use in food and unemployment relief.[47] The Red Cross, in the midst of its own fundraising, made it known that it would turn down the offer on principle. Judge Payne explained to the Senate Appropriations Committee that his organization would not accept a government grant because it did not want to become an unemployment relief organization, which is what the grant would have intended. Hoover stood by the Red Cross, as did the press and a number of prominent Americans who believed the federal government had no business turning a mass philanthropy dedicated to disaster relief into a welfare agency. Thomas Edison went so far as to put his eighty-fourth birthday cake up for auction for the Red Cross. It is "a good cake," Edison said, well worth buying for the "greatest organization in the world."[48]

Hoover was as anxious as Payne to avoid direct government support of relief. He feared it would dry up private charity. So did House Majority Leader John Q. Tilson, Republican from Connecticut, who remarked that, "Once the Red Cross is destroyed, as it must inevitably be by a Federal dole, and our local charities paralyzed, as they will be when the Federal Government takes over responsibility for charitable relief, the appropriations that must follow as a consequence of such a policy would now stagger belief. We are now at the cross-roads so far as our charities are concerned."[49] Indeed we were. Between 1929 and 1932, as the Depression deepened, one-third of the private charitable agencies in the United States disappeared for lack of funds.[50]

Both houses passed a compromise $20 million aid package on February 14 for "agricultural rehabilitation," a term sufficiently ambiguous to allow farmers to buy food for themselves, not just their animals. This allowance put an end to the no-cost federal welfare on which Hoover had heretofore insisted. Responsibility and lines of command began shifting. Because Payne, who adhered to the letter of the Red Cross federal charter, declined the money, even as a loan to his organization, the Treasury Department distributed it directly to emergency relief committees at state and local levels.[51] When Payne also refused to help coal miners in drought areas because their problem did not originate in the drought, Hoover finally reconsidered his unconditional support of the Red Cross position and turned to another charity close to his heart. He asked his fellow Quakers of the American Friends Service Committee to carry out a program financed by the American relief administration and also the Rockefeller Foundation for feeding children in these regions.[52]

Wilmington's relative self-sufficiency until 1932 was the exception. Most other cities felt the pressure much earlier and were in dire straits. In many the situation was urgent. Municipal budgets and private philanthropic efforts had difficulty in New York, Chicago, and Detroit, their safety nets strained to the breaking point. Foundations, community chests, and family relief societies could not come to the rescue. The

Rockefeller Foundation Division of Social Sciences, under Edmund Day's leadership, responded that the division should keep its focus on university research but do a better job of focusing that research on national needs.[53] The Russell Sage Foundation, which had helped Hoover so much in the Commerce Department in the 1920s, keenly felt the limits of its capacity as conditions worsened. In late 1931, New York City alone was already spending roughly $18 million a month on relief. At that rate the annual expenditure of the Russell Sage Foundation would have been depleted in less than two days; hardly an effective use of its funds, or so it seemed to its trustees.[54] In 1932, the Foundation put its larger policymaking ambition on hold and instead published manuals on *Emergency Work Relief* and *Cash Relief* for use by social workers.[55]

At the same time, mass philanthropy appeals fell short of their goals. No fund appeal since the great drives of the World War I period had been so ambitious or received so much professional planning as the community chest whirlwind campaign of October through November 1931. The appeal was made at movie theaters, in amusement parks, and in places of employment across the nation, with free advertising billboards provided by major advertising agencies. The president's Unemployment Relief Organization, led by AT&T's Walter Gifford, orchestrated the campaign and sought to raise $175 million. Advertising for the drive boldly proclaimed, "In one month . . . every city and town in the land will raise the funds that will be necessary to banish from its borders the fear of hunger and cold."[56] However, despite Hoover's personal attention and his enlistment of one hundred leaders from industry, business, and philanthropy, the fund raised just short of $100 million, a real achievement considering the economy, but far short of the goal. Twenty-five percent of all community chests failed to meet their goals by 10 percent or more, and the money raised would cover only 30 percent of the expected need in chest cities, leaving fully 70 percent of this need to be addressed by tax-supported institutions.[57]

Charitable organizations like the Red Cross lacked the flexibility and the experience to rise to the occasion. The Red Cross had staunchly refused to be involved in cities, for fear of being transformed further from a disaster relief agency to an unemployment agency. As a result,

urban politicians had resented proposals to fund the Red Cross so long
as it was ignoring the cities. Senator Robert Wagner and Representative Fiorello LaGuardia wanted instead to nationalize the issue of relief,
that is, "treat all needy American citizens" alike.[58] Under pressure from
big-city mayors, especially Detroit's Frank Murphy, Hoover proposed
to Congress a Reconstruction Finance Corporation in December 1931.
The RFC was passed in January 1932, its purpose to provide businesses,
banks, railroads and other institutions with loans to spur investment. Its
lending authority was augmented as part of Senator Wagner's July 1932
Federal Emergency Relief and Construction Act, which authorized the
RFC to provide loans to states (that no one apparently expected to be
repaid) to fund welfare and public works. With federal dollars came
supervision. RFC leaders were not shy in denying loans when they believed the state could do more for its citizens.[59] From then on, the federal
government was directly involved in relief in all parts of the country,
and it would be only a short time before it would redefine its relationship with philanthropic institutions because it held the purse strings.
The Red Cross had marginalized itself, and no-cost federal governance
was no more.

When Hoover became president, he had asked the Rockefeller
Foundation to support a Committee on Social Trends in 1929, where
academics and government bureaucrats met to diagnose the nation's
problems. After four years of research conducted at the Rockefeller-
funded Social Science Research Council, the committee published its
report, *Recent Social Trends*, in 1933.[60] But in the elapsed time, the original goal and purpose of data collecting had been lost. In drafting the
report John Dewey, William Ogburn, and Wesley Mitchell endlessly debated the distinction between facts, problems, and programs and what
they were supposed to report on in the midst of a Great Depression.
Overwhelmed by the problem, they ended up recommending old-age
pensions, a six-hour day, and unemployment compensation.[61] Others
in the group were not so accommodating in presenting everything in
neutral sounding language. Disillusioned with having to navigate between politics and policy and losing faith in the ability of social science

to provide the practical knowledge Hoover sought, the Council's Robert Lynd simply asked, "Knowledge for What?" but provided no answer.[62]

Rosenwald had criticized the kind of philanthropic-federal government alliance that Hoover advocated because it lacked both the commitment and the means (which only the federal government possessed) to reform society. Rosenwald's argument would rapidly come to the fore in the early 1930s, as the full scope of the Depression was understood. Government intervention proved increasingly necessary; the great Rosenwald Fund itself suffered economic setbacks to the point where Rosenwald asked the Rockefeller and Carnegie foundations to meet some of its obligations.

The New Deal Formalizes the Separation between Private and Public Efforts

Such was the state of affairs when Franklin Delano Roosevelt moved into the White House. Roosevelt echoed Rosenwald in singling out the federal government as responsible for a larger share of relief and reform. From Albany, New York, in August 1931, Roosevelt had issued a warning about the extent to which the nation could fall back on civil society to meet the pressing needs of the day. Predicting that private charity would be unable to provide adequate relief to the unemployed during the coming winter, Roosevelt argued that government aid needed to be extended "not as a matter of charity but as a matter of social duty."[63]

As the country experienced long-term unemployment, it became increasingly difficult for government and private philanthropies to embark on joint welfare ventures and a carefully coordinated unified strategy without an explicitly shared vision of the common good. Charities sought to improve their immediate environment, and this had seemed right to Hoover. To the new administration, however, it seemed critical to put resources where they were most needed, and that would necessarily conflict with local priorities. The need to govern the nation as a whole in a time of crisis was the reason why President Roosevelt rejected his predecessor's model of associative governance and instead favored a clear distinction between tax-supported and privately funded intervention in the economy and society. Roosevelt wanted a freer hand to govern and sought to prevent richer states from tapping private resources in order to claim matching funds from government. He dramatically increased the power of the federal government and revived the idea of a compound republic in which all branches at all levels had a clearly defined role to play.

Hoover had shown that it was possible in the proper circumstances to create an unprecedented chain of association between all levels of government and civil society for disaster relief and social reform. But his insistence that the government should write the rules—except when they interfered with racial segregation—while charging civil society with their cost and implementation could not survive a broad-scale systemic crisis. Roosevelt faced up to long-term unemployment nationwide by clearly separating government from charity and accepting the need for government to foot the bill.

In March 1933, Roosevelt summoned Harry Hopkins to Washington to head his new Federal Emergency Relief Administration. Hopkins had come of age as a social worker in New York City and embodied the professional ethos of the social-welfare progressives of the 1910s and 1920s. As a social worker in 1913 with the Association for Improving the Condition of the Poor under John Kingsbury (later head of New York State's Department of Public Charities), he had set up its unemployment agency and convinced New York to let men whom the charity supported work on state projects.[64] In 1915, Hopkins had lobbied for and received an appointment as executive secretary of the newly formed New York Board of Child Welfare.[65] He moved on to become divisional director of the Red Cross in Louisiana during World War I and then, back in New York, became executive director of the New York Tuberculosis Association in the 1920s. He helped draft the charter of the American Association of Social Workers. When Hopkins became the head of the Temporary Employment Relief Administration that FDR created as governor of New York, he was fully cognizant of the methods of mass philanthropy and its interaction with local and state governments.

By the late 1920s much of the burden of the relief effort had already been transferred to various governments. In 1928, 71.6 percent of all relief in the nation's fifteen largest cities came from public funds, according to the Federal Bureau of Social Statistics, which concluded that private citizens' efforts "dwarfed by comparison."[66] C. M. Bookman, director of social agencies and of the community chest in Cincinnati still emphasized the good of private charities when he addressed the 1930 National Conference of Social Work, but the following year he pointed instead to the limits of voluntary action and called for larger government support for the poor and unemployed.[67] Social worker Josephine Brown reported that, based on a U.S. Census study of public relief in 116 cities, private charities could still be counted on for covering about a quarter of the needs in 1929. A mere six years later, in 1935, she found that after massive federal intervention, private money accounted for only 1.3 per cent of total relief funds.[68]

As "the world's greatest spender," Hopkins was the person responsible for the shift. Most important was the way in which he oversaw the distribution of federal dollars, directing the states to put an end to their traditional mixed political economy of giving if they were to receive their share. It was of absolute necessity to find a redistribution formula that prevented rich states from claiming a disproportionate amount of federal funds compared with poor states. On June 23, 1933, Harry Hopkins issued his first and most significant rule governing how Federal Emergency Relief funds would be disbursed. Hopkins' directive prohibited the turning over of federal funds to a private agency. "The unemployed must apply to a public agency for relief, and this relief must be furnished directly to an applicant by a public agent."[69] Not only were public and private accounting to be kept apart, but the states could not entrust private institutions to administer federal funds. Although both government and philanthropy worked for the common good, the source of their funds—tax money and private donations—took on a new significance. They could not be combined any longer.

Hopkins' rule barring private agencies from administering public funds had a profound impact on philanthropy. As Frank Bane, previously the director of the American Public Welfare Association, a professional association, and one the leaders of the FERA, explained it to Aubrey Williams, a new recruit to the organization from a private agency in Milwaukee, the agency's motto was "public funds should be administered by public agencies."[70] The change was "epoch-making," said Josephine Brown. It cleared out the "confused" thinking that had prevailed when public and private funds were combined.[71] The ruling also revealed two sharply contrasting visions of the federal government's relationship to philanthropy. Hoover had wanted to make eleemosynary institutions full partners in a federal design. While granting power to these institutions by not challenging their ideological assumptions and racial attitudes, he also made them subservient to Washington's rules and required private philanthropists to pay for federal programs. Roosevelt and Hopkins provided a clear alternative. The federal government would pay, but it would also be fully in charge.

Hopkins knew private philanthropies well. He had worked with them for years. Now he was relegating them to a secondary role. He justified this move by developing a critique of the way in which they operated, noting that they made the poor feel guilty for accepting their help. Hopkins believed that the rise in the number of people involuntarily out of work called for a new rationale, different from the rationale of charitable work. As in his support of widows' pensions, he fought the stigma associated with receiving charitable gifts, the notion that it implied some kind of character flaw, when in fact the systemic problems of industrial society were responsible for the crisis. Hopkins's biographer (and also granddaughter) argues that he had convinced himself that only government could "rescue the needy from the indignity of private charity."[72] In other words, relief was their right as citizens, not a gift. He also saw a national commitment enforced by federal standards as essential for helping migrants, who were usually ineligible for receiving aid from local private charities, but who should be assisted as much as "settled" people.[73]

Hopkins's good intentions aside, the history of welfare before, during, and since the Great Depression clearly suggests that this justification was beside the point. His purpose was to find a coherent and systematic way to confront the crisis on a national basis, and that was something that only the federal government could do. In describing a speech he was about to give in June 1933, Hopkins announced that he was "going to say that the federal government has a responsibility for the distribution of funds which are appropriated by Congress for the relief of the unemployed which it cannot delegate, in good conscience, to any other agency, but must itself assume the responsibility for their disbursement."[74] The bill establishing FERA went so far as to give the federal administrator the right to appoint a state administrator if this was the only way to carry out the intentions of the act. Another amendment gave the federal administrator the right to assume full control of unemployment relief in any state if, after an examination of relief management in the state, he was unsatisfied with the current leadership. The motivation was not just to sever public from private funds, but also in part to keep the states under close supervision.

While arguing that their work was only transitory, the New Dealers transformed the nation for the long haul. Their rhetoric was often at odds with their actions. Josephine Brown, who was both witness and party to this policy shift, pointed out that Hopkins considered federal relief policy to be only temporary, but felt all the same that private philanthropies would resist retrenchment. Based on his New York experience, Hopkins feared that private charity interests, if allowed to administer funds from federal programs, would feel invested in those programs and make it difficult politically ever to terminate them. The idea, as Hopkins put it, was "to see that the unemployed get relief, not to develop a great social work organization throughout the United States."[75] Hopkins was also interested in returning charity to philanthropy. He did not want the federal government to take on permanent responsibility of caring for "unemployables," whom he defined as "old people, widows, persons who were breadwinners but now are in TB institutions, insane asylums, the crippled and handicapped."[76] Rather he would leave these to the responsibility of private charities, knowing very well that philanthropists had worked for decades to abandon almsgiving and to move their organizations towards finding solutions for root causes (see Chapter 1).

The often impossible effort to distinguish between the two populations ended up plaguing government programs and leading to the "two-tiered" welfare system—generous toward the employed but tightfisted toward the unemployed—that historians usually blame on the Social Security Act.[77] President Roosevelt and Senator Wagner extended to a large population of older Americans a version of retirement benefits that large corporations had privately implemented for their management (and Carnegie for teachers) a full half-century earlier, but they were much more timid about a safety net for the poor.

Hopkins' injunction shook up dozens of city, county, and state agencies across the country that had been using voluntary agencies and private philanthropies as a major arm of their operations. Hopkins gave states and cities only five weeks to create public welfare structures to receive and disburse FERA funds. The impact on philanthropy was massive. And not surprisingly, the turn over was less than smooth.

In at least one highly symbolic instance, the New Deal began by breaking its own rule because it made sense politically to do so. It allowed the Archdiocese of Chicago to administer federal funds. Roosevelt needed the support of Midwestern Catholics, and Chicago's Cardinal Mundelein worried about how federal welfare spending might undermine the loyalties of Catholic workers to the church. Mundelein, who enjoyed close ties with Mayor Kelly and also with the president (especially significant at a time when other Catholics like Al Smith and Father Coughlin were turning their back on the New Deal), had the Central Charities Bureau and the Society of St. Vincent de Paul named units of the Illinois Emergency Relief Commission in August 1933. This would make it possible for them to distribute FERA funds. Professional social workers protested the move as a violation of professional standards and of the separation of church and state. But the exception stood. FERA required only that the church agencies put "visible evidence" of their connection to the agency in all of their offices, and on the checks they sent.[78] Meanwhile, Hopkins denied similar exemptions to the Salvation Army and Jewish charities.

By the end of 1933, Delaware, such a bright spot in the Hoover design, had adopted a significantly altered operating model, one which disaggregated the previously well-oiled machinery that had married the Family Society and the Salvation Army to local government employment and emergency relief committee organizations under the approving eye of the federal government. Civil Works Administration reports for the beginning of 1933 already revealed a marked absence of budget line items devoted to private philanthropies, such as the Family Society and the Salvation Army, which had appeared on the state and municipal budget rolls mere months before. By late 1934 the emergency relief reports produced by the state of Delaware and its various cities and counties no longer contained any budget line items for private philanthropic organizations.

But despite instructions to the contrary, Delaware Governor C. Douglass Buck, who had married a cousin of Pierre du Pont, blurred the lines separating public and private aid administration by creating the Relief Commission, Inc. In part to circumvent the state legislature's strict application of the federal rule, Buck helped form the relief commission to take over operation of unemployed assistance in New Castle County in June 1934. He achieved this by resurrecting a charter granted by the legislature to the Associated Charities in 1885. Under this charter, the association was incorporated with "perpetual existence" to "obtain from the proper charities and charitable individuals funds and supplies for the relief of the deserving classes." The charter also empowered the county court, known as the Levy Court, which still operated in the traditional manner as a small elected body charged with assessing and collecting taxes, to appropriate money to the Associated Charities "in the pursuance of its charitable purposes."[79] This maneuver made it clear that, at least at the county level, there were still means of creatively channeling limited city, county, and even state funds to local philanthropies.

More common were various strategies to maintain, at least for a while, the existing blend of public and private funds by turning social workers into public servants with the approval of the FERA. In Pennsylvania one study found a "large transfer of workers from private to public agencies" across the state in the eighteen months following the FERA order, transforming some nonprofits, at least in part, into branches of government. Another survey in 1935 revealed that family agencies in many middle-sized cities such as Bridgeport, Connecticut, Grand Rapids, Michigan, and Tuckahoe, New York, had witnessed similar shifts of workers; while for some larger cities such as Wilmington, Delaware, Norfolk, Virginia, and Springfield, Illinois, board members and executives of nonprofits helped to plan and operate the newly created public agencies.[80]

Private agencies often had their trained and experienced staff appointed as public officials. In Wilmington, the Temporary Emergency Relief Commission (TERC) absorbed the operations and staff of the Mayor's Employment and Relief Committee, previously underwritten by Pierre S. du Pont. As of the middle of 1933, the Family Society continued to administer relief to families in need with emergency funds, though it had shifted roughly half of its cases to work relief projects run by the TERC. Ethelda Mullen, the peripatetic executive secretary of the Family Society, was made the executive secretary of the TERC. She thus became an eligible "agent" to administer relief funds, and while she could not channel them directly to the Family Society, she could put those on their unemployed rolls onto the TERC rolls and then administer aid.[81]

Mullen was also able to bring in other personnel from private voluntary agencies and have them appointed. Such efforts helped keep skilled individuals in the loop. Facilities were often shared, further blurring the lines of public and private. The TERC continued to operate in an office donated by the Dupont-owned Delaware Trust Company. In November 1933, Hopkins, acting as Federal FERA administrator, designated the Delaware Temporary Emergency Relief Commission as the Civil Works Administration for the state. He accepted the appointment of all the existing members of the Relief Commission as part of the CWA.[82] But these interlocking personnel networks only delayed the inevitable. They did not reverse the trend separating the public and private spheres and walling off federal unemployment relief funds from private philanthropies.

The New Deal held firm to the notion that the federal government was responsible for redistributing resources across regions as needed, and this created additional conflicts with local philanthropies. The principle affected philanthropy directly, because states could count only their own tax funds for matching purposes with the federal government. The issue of the federal government preventing states from including private funds in matching allocations once more came to a head in Delaware with the first federal grant-in-aid issued to the state as the FERA's matching fund. By June 1933, the sum had reached $481,815, but it would have been higher had private contributions from the county committees been taken into account. This led the influential Jasper Crane, a vice president and director of the Dupont Company, a director of the local YMCA and Red Cross, and then chairman of the State Temporary Emergency Relief Committee to write to Harry Hopkins on June 19, 1933, to ask for federal matching funds for these contributions.

Crane argued the case by pointing to the old organic association between the state government and private donations by ordinary residents in the various Delaware counties, which attested to vibrant communities responsible for their own. Crane pointed to Delaware's rule that "none of the money appropriated by the state may be used for direct relief in any county unless that county contributes . . . 20 percent of the whole cost of direct relief in the county." He concluded, logically, that "private contributions are thus the keystone of the arch of our relief work in Delaware." Crane saw limiting matching funds "as working hardship on our State and discouraging private citizens from making private contributions to our relief funds."[83] That did not move Hopkins who felt national issues trumped local ones.

Under the new Washington policy, local public agencies could no longer raise donations from residents, which previously had been quite generous, with the expectation of receiving equal support from the federal coffers. Although dire predictions of the imminent "exhaustion" of "all resources" proved inaccurate, there was a growing understanding that philanthropy would no longer be a main source of public funding for poverty relief.[84] As a result New Castle and other counties discontinued fundraising "except as a last resort." It was best to ask citizens to send their donations (which they had previously directed to the Mayor's Committee in Wilmington) directly to private philanthropies such as the Family Society, which supported women and unemployed families.[85] Public agencies should not compete for charitable funds in the population at large.

The Delaware state legislature, controlled by Republicans, resisted this separation of the public and private spheres. In 1934, Delaware was one of only four states to put a Republican in the Senate, John G. Townsend, Jr. Delawareans also elected a new Republican representative, J. George Stewart, from Wilmington, who had been a member of the Temporary Emergency Relief Commission. The two men attacked the New Deal on the basis of unfairness. They argued that in the first half of 1934 Delawareans had paid an average of $5.20 in taxes to the federal government for every dollar they received back in relief funds. Pierre du Pont, who had emerged as one of the leaders and funders of the anti New Deal Liberty League, sounded the same note in October 1937 when he computed that total federal assistance to the state had amounted to $28,400,000, just 17.7 percent of the $160,266,000 in taxes flowing out of the state to the federal government.[86] According to du Pont, this data indicated that the state could have taken care of its own relief needs had those funds remained within state borders and continued to be applied in the voluntary mode in which early relief had operated, with the distinction between voluntary contributions and compulsory taxes conveniently blurred. But residents had stopped giving money generously to local causes in alliance with local governments because the federal government was going to redistribute their wealth nationwide.

The Works Progress Administration became the key federal relief agency after 1935. The local Family Society, still running with the benefit of some tax appropriations from local coffers via the Levy Court, gave welfare relief only to families who were deemed unemployable according to state and federal standards. Broadly speaking, the federal government had severed much of the traditional organic relationship between the state and private philanthropies and co-opted the state in a more coercive if limited version of federalism.

These drastic changes were national. New-style federal agencies, not the Red Cross, took charge of addressing such crises as the 1930s "Dust Bowl" calamity. Intensive farming combined with poor agricultural practices had destroyed the protective cover of vegetation across much of the northern and southern plains. In 1934, the convergence of high winds and the worst drought in American history affected more than 75 percent of the country, impacting twenty-seven states. The outcome was a giant dust bowl covering an area of more than 50 million acres in Texas, New Mexico, Colorado, Kansas, and Oklahoma. The Red Cross was not completely absent from the ensuing rescue effort. It made the drought a part of disaster relief for Red Cross Month in March 1934 and called for dust masks, especially for children. Junior Red Cross members were enlisted. But the role that the Red Cross played in alleviating dust bowl conditions in 1934 and 1935 was minor compared to its part in drought-relief efforts in the Mississippi Valley in 1930–31 or in the 1927 flood. Federally-funded New Deal relief and policy-planning had become the preferred method for confronting disasters.

Federal assistance became the primary relief for citizens in need in the states affected by the Dust Bowl. Congress took action, deployed experts and aid agencies, and no longer expected civil society to pay the bills. In the summer of 1934, President Roosevelt secured $525 million for drought relief from Congress. Around the same time the Department of Agriculture began purchasing cattle from distressed farmers at above-market prices—helping ranchers hold onto their land and distributing the beef to the needy—and by 1935 the federal government was the world's largest cattle owner.[87] Perhaps the most devastating moment of the Dust Bowl came on April 14, when immense dust storms struck the Great Plains— the day came to be known as "Black Sunday" (and the term "Dust Bowl" itself was coined in the storm's wake).[88] Congress followed up by declaring soil erosion "a menace to the national welfare" and established the Soil Conservation Service in the Department of Agriculture, which developed conservation programs to protect topsoil.[89]

The federal government disrupted the long-standing partnership between philanthropy and local and state governments twice, and in contrasting ways. Hoover's no-cost federal governance put philanthropic forces at the center of the governing process. Roosevelt ended Hoover's experiment and designed policies that forced Americans to draw stricter boundaries between public and private funds. Neither Hoover nor Roosevelt implemented his vision fully. The New Deal formula lasted for thirty years, but the federal government engaged private philanthropic forces again in the Great Society's funding of privately run social services (chapter 7). In response to widespread grassroots pressure from the civil rights movement, the government designed entirely new rules of engagement. All along, a war of ideas, with powerful political consequences, unfolded over the place of philanthropy in American governance and the wisdom of collaboration between the state and the institutions of civil society.

CHAPTER 5

From Humanitarianism to Cold War

The clear division of labor between government and civil society that the New Deal had insisted upon to lift the country out of the Great Depression became irrelevant during and after World War II. American philanthropic organizations now turned their attention overseas to rescue war victims and assist in reconstruction. Although there was no grand design, the ways in which Americans combined government and philanthropic resources made humanitarianism an important part of the Pax Americana. Humanitarian aid emerged as, in Secretary of State John Foster Dulles's words, "a force of enduring strength that can bind together the peoples of the world."[1] Big foundations provided the organizational framework and personnel to help the U.S. government achieve its policy goals. Mass philanthropies collected millions of individual remittances from ordinary Americans who wanted to participate in alleviating suffering and restoring "normal" life in liberated countries.

For the American administration, philanthropy became at once a resource and a force to reckon with. At home, the courts, Congress, and the Treasury Department insisted that philanthropy not interfere with the political process, but on the soil of freed nations, government policy mixed humanitarian action with politics.

As the Cold War came to dominate international relations, philanthropic programs more than once became entangled in the ideological battles that pitted Washington against the Kremlin. Several foundations—most prominently the Ford Foundation—played a major role in rebuilding local civil societies in Western Europe capable of shouldering the American "psychological war" against communism. In the Third World, philanthropic institutions pioneered American methods of agricultural development and technical aid before Washington embraced these same programs selectively as Cold War strategy.

Focus on Humanitarian Aid

By the time Germany invaded Poland in 1939, little was left of the League of Nations' fragile institutional network that had linked peoples of different countries together. Economic protectionism and nationalist movements had gained ground over cultural exchanges, industrial standardization, and a common science. In the United States, isolationist feelings that Americans had overcome in the 1920s had resurfaced in the 1930s. While maintaining official neutrality early in the war, the American government was suspicious of its philanthropies sending money abroad; its immediate concern was to prevent American aid from falling into the hands of belligerent governments. Thus the Roosevelt administration required all voluntary agencies engaged in soliciting and collecting donations for countries in the war to register with the Department of State under Section 8(b) of the Neutrality Act of 1939.[2] The initial registration measure applied only to organizations providing aid to belligerents and left organizations helping other countries outside of State Department supervision.[3] However, in March 1941, with the lend-lease act signed, and "neutrality" finally redefined to favor Allied forces, Secretary of State Cordell Hull wanted greater control over the maze of ongoing private fundraising and relief activities. President Roosevelt appointed his former Ambassador to the Soviet Union, Joseph E. Davies, to head a President's Committee on War Relief Agencies.[4] Charles P. Taft (son of President William H. Taft and former president of the International YMCA) and Frederick P. Keppel (president of the Carnegie Corporation) also sat on the committee.[5] The committee's contribution was initially modest, as it established only a voluntary reporting procedure for these agencies not registered with the State Department under the Neutrality Act.[6] This changed when the U.S. became involved in the hostilities.

Entering the war paradoxically gave Americans an opportunity to start anew a humanitarian movement through which they could eventually reconnect a fragmented world. President Roosevelt enlarged and recast the Davies Committee as a proactive President's War Relief Control Board.[7] The board launched large, nation-wide campaigns to raise funds for the aid of troops and victims (as had been done in World War I—chapter 2). At the board's behest, Winthrop W. Aldrich, chairman of Chase National Bank, coordinated a national campaign to provide humanitarian relief on the front in the fall of 1943. Two more would follow in 1944 and 1945. In his fundraising, Aldrich joined forces with local community chests, which were in the process of launching a national drive of their own, and together the war board and the community chests created the National War Fund, a private philanthropic federation.[8]

President Roosevelt understood the potential benefit of this philanthropy for Americans' image in the world. He saw the National War Fund as evidence that "Our men and our allies know they have made no covenant with our Government alone. They know that they have the backing of all the resources and spirit of the American people themselves. In that conviction alone lies the winning morale which no slave of a dictator can ever know."[9] The war board timed its appeals to avoid competition with Red Cross drives or the sale of U.S. bonds.[10] The war board also intervened in the administration of philanthropy, consolidating agencies licensed to operate abroad whose missions overlapped (their number dropped from 300 in 1941 to 67 in 1943) and thus drastically reducing overhead.[11] It insisted that charities, regardless of the sectarian nature of their appeal, adopt a single image of America that they would project abroad. It applied special pressure on refugee organizations that dedicated all the money they raised in America to their homeland to rename themselves. The French Relief Fund became American Relief for France, the Queen Wilhelmina Fund became American Relief for Holland, and Russian War Relief became the American Society for Russian Relief.[12]

Religious charities with their established networks of donors created their own wartime federations. In 1943, the Roman Catholic Bishops of the United States and the National Catholic Welfare Conference began War Relief Services (which later changed its name to Catholic Relief Services) under the leadership of Monsignor Patrick O'Boyle. The Protestant churches also collaborated, forming the Church Committee for Overseas Relief and Reconstruction, which gave way in 1946 to the Church World Service.[13] The war board endorsed the United Jewish Appeal to run a combined campaign on behalf of the American Jewish Joint Distribution Committee, the United Palestine Appeal, and the National Refugee Service.[14]

This large humanitarian mobilization on the part of the American population, important in itself, took on an entirely new dimension when put to the service of the first international organization in charge of feeding the liberated populations—the United Nations Relief and Rehabilitation Administration (UNRRA), which the Allies created in 1943. As early as 1940, Britain had floated the idea of creating a novel transnational agency for the future peace, whose mission would be to make such basic commodities as food and medicine available and to provide technical aid in health, education, and industrial rehabilitation. In the U.S., Assistant Secretary of State Dean Acheson was independently drafting a plan for a United Nations Relief Administration. In 1942, the Soviets also submitted proposals to the U.S. and the U.K. Meanwhile, the U.S., Great Britain, Australia, Canada, and Argentina were setting aside wheat reserves in anticipation of famine following the end of hostilities.

The U.S. government took the first concrete step towards creating an international relief organization by setting up the (short-lived) Office of Foreign Relief and Rehabilitation Operations (OFRRO) in September 1942.[15] Roosevelt asked his friend, New York governor Herbert H. Lehman, to resign his position and become its head. Putting an American Jew in that position was important symbolically. OFRRO then administered relief work in North Africa in the wake of military advances there in early 1943.

In the fall of 1943, the federal government closed the national OFRRO to join other nations in the newly formed United Nations Relief and Rehabilitation Administration, which it dominated by virtue of being its main funder. Forty-four nations joined in the consortium. Roosevelt again appointed Lehman to head the new organization, and Lehman, in turn, brought in the private charities as partners. He needed them to carry out his humanitarian mission free from constraints imposed by the various constituent governments. That Lehman could count on the active collaboration of a large charitable network in his own country made an enormous difference in shaping the humanitarian movement, and conversely the new organization gave American charities access to means never before at their disposal and dramatically broadened the scope of their relief missions. From this beginning, American humanitarian agencies would not only participate in the creation of the postwar network of international organizations but would provide it with direction.

American philanthropy kept UNRRA's humanitarian mission on track and helped the new international agency keep some political independence. While private voluntary organizations had paid for the bulk of American charitable work in World War I, this time the voluntary sector raised the equivalent of only from 7 to 10 percent of U.S. government appropriations.[16] But UNRRA's effectiveness nonetheless depended in large part on its ability to cooperate with private philanthropy, as Congress put severe restrictions on the funds it appropriated.[17] In a move designed to mollify those American congressmen who resented long-term American commitments around the world, UNRRA was not to give away commodities but to sell them at subsidized prices in local currency (collected by local governments from the sale of UNRRA-delivered supplies). Hence the need Lehman felt to supplement revenue from these sales to liberated countries with food and medical supplies offered free of charge, and for this he needed private American organizations. In addition, voluntary organizations lent experts to UNRRA. Thus, Wilbur Sawyer, director of the International Health Division at the Rockefeller Foundation, became director of UNRRA's Health Division.[18]

As American troops made progress first in North Africa and then Europe, the American army was initially reluctant to permit American voluntary organizations to work in occupied territories. In principle, the army was to retain full control of operations in all occupied zones, while UNRRA would begin its work in countries only after governments had been re-established. But the situation on the ground was unstable. It became critical to provide humanitarian aid to war victims to forestall food riots and to prevent the black market from dominating food distribution. The army soon let UNRRA distribute relief in not-fully-pacified areas, and UNRRA, in turn, brought in the private agencies.[19]

Lehman struggled to get the army to free up some of its own supplies for relief operations and to provide cargo space for their transport. As the war drew to a close, in December 1944, Roosevelt responded to Lehman's many pleas by instructing the War Shipping Administration to provide shipping space for UNRRA. Roosevelt also pressured the army to allocate some of its supplies to civilian relief. Better able now to achieve its goals, UNRRA became the chief organization supporting refugees, administering camps, and supervising the work of the voluntary agencies that staffed the camps.[20] Within them, groups like the Red Cross, the YMCA, Friends' Relief (rewarded after the war with a Nobel Peace Prize), and the Jewish ORT provided educational and training programs.[21]

In a separate effort, American voluntary organizations had for some time been working on the problem of distributing relief in war zones. Solving it required some institutional creativity. Already in November of 1942, Joseph P. Chamberlain, a professor of public law at Columbia, had brought together seventeen private voluntary organizations, including the YMCA, the American Friends Service Committee, the Joint Distribution Committee, the Near East Foundation, and Catholic Agencies. Together they approached the War Relief Control Board to outline their intended course of action in the territories under army control. These seventeen organizations formed the nucleus in 1943 of what would become in 1944 the American Council of Voluntary Agencies for Foreign Service, the organization that would prove most effective in working with the American army in distributing supplies in the occupied territories. At Charles Taft's suggestion, the new body represented all voluntary agencies in dealing with army relief operations in liberated Europe, with the War Relief Control Board acting as liaison.[22] The

American Council of Voluntary Agencies for Foreign Service became the coordinator for mass philanthropies dedicated to humanitarian aid. It created specialized committees, such as one on the Balkans and one on displaced persons. Among them was the Council of Relief Agencies Licensed to Operate in Germany, formed in 1946, which in the next two years would distribute several hundred million pounds of clothing, food, and medicine, especially much needed penicillin and insulin.[23]

In April 1946, eleven participating relief organizations, including all the members of the American Council of Voluntary Agencies for Foreign Service, as well as many of the agencies that had formed the Council of Relief Agencies Licensed to Operate in Germany formed Licensed Agencies for Relief in Asia. This was the only voluntary organization authorized by the Supreme Command for Allied Powers to ship supplies into Japan. General MacArthur was so impressed by the member agencies' ability to provide food in time to avoid riots that he asked them to continue and expand operations in 1948.[24]

To foster the new charitable internationalism, two important figures devised a plan that would encourage all Americans to send packages abroad. Arthur Ringland of the War Relief Control Board, who had acquired key experience with food relief during World War I with Hoover's American Relief Administration, and Lincoln Clark, a professor at the University of Maryland, also an official in UNRRA, in 1943 convinced members of Catholic Relief Services and the American Friends Service Committee to join in their project. By 1946, with pledges from twenty-two member organizations, they created the Cooperative for American Remittances in Europe or CARE (the name was later changed to "Relief Everywhere").[25]

CARE built on the vast distribution systems that the army had created during the war, but made it possible for every donor to make his personal mark by identifying package recipients. By personalizing contributions to such a large-scale organization, CARE became associated in everybody's mind with enlarging the meaning, as historian Merle Curti explained, of the "old American custom of neighbor helping neighbor."[26] At the end of its first five years, CARE packages had reached one out of every five families in Germany and one out of every five persons in Austria. Many recent immigrants or American-born children of immigrants working at blue-collar jobs and making inroads into the middle class were also sending goods to family members in Eastern Europe and thus taking a small role in the beginning of the Pax Americana.

While running UNRRA, Lehman gave CARE a boost. By 1946, UNRRA controlled 7.7 million Ten-in-One packages initially meant for the army (each designed to feed one soldier for ten days or ten soldiers for one day). With the army releasing supplies, Lehman sold 2.8 million of these packages to CARE once he was satisfied that the organization had its financing in place as well as adequate storing and shipping facilities.[27] Davies of the War Relief Control Board also assured availability of supplies before he licensed CARE. Once this was done, the U.S. Army assisted with logistical support, as did the War Relief Control Board and the State Department. This translated into distributing agreements with the governments of Norway, Finland, the Netherlands, Belgium, France, Italy, Greece, Yugoslavia, Czechoslovakia, and Poland, and with the military authorities in Austria and Germany.[28]

The value of CARE overseas relief peaked in early 1948 but fell after that, in no small part due to Stalin's decision in October 1947, after refusing Marshall Plan aid, to cut off the Soviet satellites from all aid—first governmental, and soon thereafter private—from the United States. The "people-to-people" connection, which kept many recent Americans rooted in their countries of origin, stopped at the Iron Curtain. The Detroit auto worker, symbol of American postwar prosperity and emblem of the victorious American century, could no longer send some of his excess income to help family members in Poland or elsewhere in the Soviet bloc, any more than American government and philanthropic organizations could. And yet, the knowledge of such aid was critical in promoting a benevolent vision of America throughout the world.

Unfortunately, UNRRA's ability to manage budgetary constraints and political pressures, and its relationship with the army, proved fragile. The Office of Strategic Services precipitated the early end of UNRRA when its head, William "Wild Bill" Donovan, suggested assigning men to UNRRA offices in the Balkans who would relay information back to him. Lehman, who refused, resigned in March 1946, citing health reasons.[29] Fiorello LaGuardia, who replaced Lehman, remained an indefatigable advocate of UNRRA's humanitarian mission, even to communist-dominated countries. But the danger of American aid landing in the communist camp, as well as OSS pressures, kept undermining the organization. When Tito attacked U.S. forces even while he was receiving UNRRA supplies, the U.S. withdrew from the organization.[30] Shortly thereafter UNRRA, which was primarily funded by the U.S. government, ceased operations—in Europe in 1947 and in China in 1948.

The international humanitarian cause did not die with the demise of UNRRA, however, nor did the activities of the voluntary agencies that played such an important role in it. Rather, as initially envisioned, UNRRA's multiple functions were absorbed by the new international institutions of the postwar world, most prominent among them the United Nations. Technical services to promote industry, agriculture, and health became the purview of the new array of private agencies affiliated with the U.N., which were designated as nongovernmental organizations (also called PVOs for private voluntary organizations, a broad term that included philanthropic foundations). Americans took the lead in carving a place of choice for NGOs during the United Nations' formation, a natural consequence of the role they had played in the humanitarian effort after the North African and Italian invasions. Practically all NGOs representatives who attended the August 1944 Dumbarton Oaks planning conference for the establishment of the United Nations were Americans. Forty-two primarily American NGOs served as advisers to the first American delegation and signed the U.N. charter as "consultants."[31] They earned for all NGOs a place in Article 71 of the charter, which provided for further "consultation with nongovernmental organizations" by the economic and social council. In the years following, the U.N. created sixteen specialized agencies dedicated to particular global issues. These included the United Nations High Commission on Refugees, the World Health Organization, the Food and Agriculture Organization, and the United Nations Educational, Scientific, and Cultural Organization (UNESCO). Private groups assisted in fundraising for U.N. programs, and oftentimes the U.N. channeled its funds for the

administration of these programs to them. UNRRA's closing thus signaled the advent of a more integrated and wide-ranging international
structure of world relief and development, one that American philanthropy had done much to launch.

As if to symbolize American philanthropy's lead in this international
humanitarian movement, the Rockefeller family helped attract the new
United Nations' headquarters to New York by donating the land.[32]
After considering the gift of one of the family's country estates, Nelson
Rockefeller scrambled to purchase a seventeen-acre tract in Manhattan that was slated to become a new office complex. His father, John D.
Rockefeller, Jr., agreed to put up the money, and the U.N accepted the
large donation. Congress even passed a special bill to make the gift tax
deductible.

Focus on "Psychological Warfare"

American ideals of postwar philanthropy as embodied in the early history of the United Nations were quickly challenged. Hopes to export
capitalism for the world's greater good turned into ideological confrontation. When President Truman declared the Cold War in 1947,
American philanthropy came to shoulder the national encounter with
communism. Commitments to promoting peace, freedom, and democracy abroad became interwoven with programs to alter public opinion and undermine communist ideology and Soviet power. America's
largest foundations provided funds and collaborated in organizational
strategies with the U.S. government. They invested heavily in European
cultural and educational institutions in an effort to put culture to the
service of what became known as "psychological warfare" against communist ideology. Grassroots organizations were involved as well.

In devising Cold War strategies, the alliance between American diplomats, intelligence agents, and a small group of foundation officials was
held together not only by common institutional goals, but also by a tight
professional and social network linking them. The early history of the
Ford Foundation—then a newcomer to the big philanthropic scene—

(the creation of which I examine in some detail in chapter 6) suggests the closeness of these ties.

Henry Ford II and the foundation's trustees appointed Paul Hoffman its president in 1950. Who could possibly be better qualified for the job of running the world's newest giant of private philanthropy than the former Studebaker salesman who had risen first to the presidency of his automobile company and then become the successful administrator of the Marshall Plan in Europe?

Hoffman brought several of his former Marshall Plan staffers to the foundation, including Harvard law professor Milton Katz and also Richard M. Bissell, who had worked for the Office of Strategic Services and pushed for a firm but open-minded approach to the Soviet Union.[33] Hoffman consulted with George Kennan, one of the chief architects of America's "containment" policy. Kennan presided over the Free Russia Fund, a nonprofit corporation Ford established to help resettle Soviet exiles in the U.S. One objective of the fund was to learn from exiles about life behind the Iron Curtain. When John J. McCloy, U.S. High Commissioner to Germany (who had administered Marshall Plan aid), returned home in 1952 to head up the Chase Manhattan Bank, he joined the Ford Foundation's board of trustees.[34]

McCloy also chaired the Council on Foreign Relations, a New York-based think tank founded in 1921 that counted among its members virtually the entire foreign-policy elite (including Kennan and the Dulles brothers), and was funded by the Carnegie Corporation and the Rockefeller Foundation. The Ford Foundation joined in funding it during the postwar years. It was in the council's journal *Foreign Affairs* that Kennan published in 1947, under the pen name Mr. X, "The Sources of Soviet Conduct," which would serve as a guiding text for the policy of containment. Other important figures of the foundation world emerged from the foreign-policy elite. Dean Rusk, Rockefeller Foundation president during the 1950s, came from the State Department (later returning as President Kennedy's and then President Johnson's secretary of state).

Hoffman made the Ford Foundation a full partner in foreign policy during his short tenure. As the Cold War intensified, Hoffman launched the foundation's international program, openly acknowledging that is was a means to export American values against communism. He hired McCloy's public affairs officer Shepard Stone to direct the foundation's division of international affairs.[35] There is "no doubt that every effort must be made to unite the free world," Hoffman reported to the Board of Trustees, and to achieve this, the free world must "do more than arm itself; it must develop its strengths."[36] To that end, Ford officials conferred directly with officials from the State Department and the Central Intelligence Agency in plotting out a European program directed in some fashion at fighting communism and promoting Western culture and democracy—as well as defusing European antipathy toward America and American culture.

Education and cultural activities were an important part of this psychological warfare. In West Berlin, the Ford Foundation directed huge resources towards the new Free University. Organized in 1948, the university could count an enrollment of 5,500 students by 1951 with about 40 percent coming from the Soviet Sector. McCloy, in particular, praised this program as advancing education and morale in Germany in a way that even more substantial government funding could not.[37] Maintaining a center of intellectual accomplishment and democratic education, the foundation knew, was "playing a significant role in the ideological conflict between the Soviet Union and the West."[38]

In 1951 the Ford Foundation gave $500,000 to aid Reinhold Niebuhr's campaign to relocate professionals from European refugee camps to America.[39] Churches and civic groups the foundation supported were involved in the related work of teaching democracy. The Unitarian Service Committee, a Massachusetts nonprofit corporation, developed in the Western zones of Germany a cooperative German-American project to improve human relations and to inculcate the German people with democratic practices and principles. The organization developed workshops to disseminate knowledge and practical techniques related to mental health and childcare so as to free the youth from their parents' predisposition towards authoritarianism in family and institutional life. As the Ford Foundation described it in the behavioral language of the 1950s, "A primary task of psychological warfare is to analyze the beliefs and attitudes of the people of each area and to develop techniques for manipulating these factors to evoke desired behavior responses." Milton Katz assigned as the project's final goal destroying the "enemy's will or capacity to fight or otherwise impair U.S. interests."[40]

Mutual understanding among nations was indispensable for fighting the battles of the Cold War. Senator J. William Fulbright conceived in 1946 of a bilateral international cultural exchange that would be funded by Congress through the sale of surplus military equipment.[41] By the late 1940s the program was sending hundreds of U.S. graduate students abroad, both to Europe and other regions, and it had gathered much needed support from private voluntary agencies that assisted with government-run visits.[42]

American families participated in the cultural cold war by receiving foreign students and sending their own sons and daughters abroad. At the high-school level, a broad array of voluntary associations supported exchange programs, including the International Christian Youth Exchange, the Conference on Christians and Jews, the International Farm Youth Exchange, the Grange and 4-H, Kiwanis, Rotary, Catholic Welfare Conference, and others. U.S. colleges and universities, too, began sending off increasing number of students, aided by improved language training at American schools, cheaper trans-Atlantic travel, and free tuition abroad. Many of these same institutions also attempted to offer financial incentives to bring foreign students to the U.S.[43]

These exchanges, conducted with close collaboration between state and civil society institutions, often had the intended outcome. Akira Iriye, a historian who grew up in Japan, remembers his discovery of the United States as a Grew Foundation scholar (Joseph Grew was a former ambassador to Japan) at Haverford College, from 1953 to 1957, as years of "virtually total" intellectual freedom. Although the Cold War dominated international relations, the young undergraduate encountered American ways in its civil society of "churches, farms, private homes, and colleges," from which he eventually emerged as a distinguished scholar of international relations.[44]

Efforts at mutual understanding were not limited to stays at small liberal arts colleges. American foundations were eager to promote "area studies" in large universities. In 1947 the Carnegie Corporation funded the creation of a new Russian Research Center at Harvard. Though not the first such institution devoted to the investigation of strategically important regions, it did represent the beginning of a postwar boom in the social science study of the problematical parts of the world. When Ford supported "area studies" in several schools, Hoffman reported to the Board of Trustees in 1951 that "no university has a center dedicated to discovering the common elements in the eastern and western traditions and to arranging for intellectual exchange between the east and west."[45] Harvard would soon boast programs devoted to East Asia and the Middle East, while Carnegie would support additional ones focused on Latin America, Japan, and East Asia.[46] The new centers moved away from traditional emphases on history and literature in favor of the newer behavioral approaches of the social sciences that were transforming psychology, sociology, and political science. The study of international law also expanded in these postwar years. Aimed at measuring human action, the behavioral approach—when applied to Russia and elsewhere—thus meshed conceptually with the methods of psychological warfare. It was a matter of giving young Americans the tools for understanding different cultures in enough depth to effect changes in them.

Such psychological warfare entailed some division of labor between government and philanthropy, at least theoretically. When Hoffman directed the Marshall Plan, he believed that the government was totally justified in using at least 15 percent of its propaganda budget for covert operations. Keeping the source of funding a secret was often necessary. Propaganda, Hoffman felt, was not a job for those always moving "within a goldfish bowl."[47] But as head of the Ford Foundation, he refused to cross the line from overt to covert operation. In 1951, CIA director Allen Dulles approached Hoffman about using the foundation as a secret conduit for agency funds. After some soul searching, Ford officials declined to channel CIA money, satisfied that they were already helping the agency with anti-communist propaganda in Eastern Europe, the re-education of communist defectors in the U.S., and other CIA-supported causes.[48] This refusal stemmed in part from concerns that the foundation's goal of promoting peace not be conflated with the actual "prosecution of the cold war."[49] But Ford officials also believed that refraining from such direct collaboration would actually allow the foundation to promote American aims more effectively, taking action in areas where government involvement was impossible or ill-advised.

The CIA, however, feeling that the Soviet government's own covert cultural activities of funding newspapers and symposia were enough of a justification, found other foundations willing to transmit its funds and created some philanthropic organizations of its own for this express purpose, most notably the Farfield Foundation.[50] CIA-funded foundations supported newspapers, magazines, and other cultural events in Europe, including the Congress for Cultural Freedom (CCF). At its first meeting in June 1950 in Berlin, the CCF attracted much of the liberal intellectual elite from both Western Europe and the United States—many of them former communists now intent on discrediting their earlier creed. Designed to counter similar congresses run from Moscow—including one such event at New York's Waldorf-Astoria Hotel in 1949—the CCF's major target was European intellectuals on the non-communist left, men and women prone to denouncing the dehumanizing traits of American mass culture as well as McCarthyism, but who had not become communists and might yet help tip the scales in favor of the West. Most CCF members were unaware of the CIA's support for the organization until CIA funding was finally exposed during the mid-1960s in the context of a congressional investigation of foundations' tax loopholes (see chapter 7).[51]

Focus on Development

While the psychological war was being pursued in Europe and Japan, in the developing world the state-philanthropy partnership focused on agriculture. Washington paid special attention to newly independent nations as a way of containing communism. Keeping the free world free would mean returning to the old philanthropic formula of development, that is, to attacking the roots of developing nations' economic distress, rather than simply securing their alliance in order to access their raw materials.

In launching its postwar foreign aid program, the U.S. government benefited from a few philanthropic experiments in public health and agricultural extension, going back to investments in the depleted American South during Reconstruction (see chapter 1). Philanthropies were as much precursors of rural developmental programs abroad as they were partners with government. In 1930, Near East Relief, an organization founded fifteen years earlier in a valiant American effort to provide humanitarian assistance to the victims of the Armenian genocide, transformed itself into the Near East Foundation for agricultural improvement and village life assistance. In the late 1920s, Harold B. Allen, a faculty member in vocational agriculture at Rutgers University, launched at Near East Foundation an experimental rural development program in forty-eight Macedonian villages on land donated by the Greek government.[52] Other agricultural demonstration projects, as well as home sanitation projects (mosquito control, sanitary latrines) followed in Syria, Albania, Bulgaria, and Iran. The Near East Foundation insisted "that native personnel, government agriculturalists, nurses, and ministries share in the work from the beginning," until such time as the project becomes "a completely native product."[53] The Rockefeller Foundation (which had contributed to Near East Relief from the beginning) provided continuous support to the Near East Foundation, which, lacking an endowment, had to raise its own money.[54]

The Rockefeller Foundation had been for some time the leading organization in the field of rural development both at home and abroad. The foundation achieved extraordinary new momentum in the 1940s with the "green revolution" that it initiated in Mexico after Henry A. Wallace, Vice-President of the United States, had casually suggested it.[55] J. George Harrar, the plant pathologist from Washington State University who directed the program, would later serve as foundation president. Mexico provided land, local labor, and covered construction costs, while the foundation paid for the operating costs and sent the professional personnel. Plant scientist Norman Borlaug endlessly crossed varieties of wheat under very difficult conditions until he achieved dramatically improved yields. Borlaug was eventually recognized with a Nobel Prize.[56] After him, hunger became a political problem of access to food and no longer an issue of productive capacity.

Rockefeller spent more than $12.5 million on its agricultural development program in Mexico between 1940 and 1949, and followed this up with similar programs in Colombia and Chile in the 1950s. Working with Mexican government officials, researchers, and agricultural colleges, the foundation developed a corps of Mexican agricultural experts trained at the college and graduate levels, sometimes in the U.S., in market-oriented farming techniques. The foundation's biggest failure was in its inability to reach out to the nation's small-scale subsistence farmers, a problem that would persist in exporting the "green revolution" to Asia.[57]

One of the Rockefeller brothers, Nelson, pushed hard for a philanthropy-government partnership for rural development in Latin American countries, where his family had large oil interests. He and New Dealer Beardsley Ruml, a former Rockefeller Foundation official and a major promoter of the modern social sciences, approached Harry Hopkins in 1940 about creating an office of Coordinator of Inter-American Affairs (CIAA) within the State Department. Hopkins, who had by then become FDR's closest confident of the war years, agreed, and the president established the agency by executive order with Nelson Rockefeller as its head.[58]

Rockefeller feared that a government program might be short-lived, so he founded with family money the Institute of Inter-American Affairs (IIAA, to which the U.S. Congress gave a charter of incorporation of the sort it had once denied the Rockefeller Foundation—see chapter 1). IIAA pioneered an administrative structure for government-NGO cooperation (including representatives of both U.S. and Latin American governments, as well as U.S. and indigenous experts) called a *servicio,* to conduct public health and agricultural productivity studies. The *servicio,* staffed initially with American experts, would gradually come under indigenous control.[59]

As in the case of other large philanthropic programs, rich Americans were not the only sponsors of rural projects. Now that the war was over, American missionaries resumed providing technical assistance in community development around the world. By 1950, U.S. Protestant groups (united under Church World Service during the war) engaged in overseas technical assistance spent $150 million. In comparison, in 1952 the U.N.'s Expanded Program spent just short of $23 million, while the U.S. government in 1954 spent $122 million.[60]

Despite the potential of the green revolution, feeding the world remained a major concern in the 1950s as demographers predicted a vast increase in the world population that revived fears of declining resources. Between 1900 and 1960, the world's population doubled, and after World War II a growing cadre of social scientists expressed grave concern that the planet might not withstand another such doubling in a mere thirty years.[61] Postwar America therefore experienced a resurgent wave of Malthusian thinking and was slow to recognize the mitigating effects of productivity.

John D. Rockefeller III, Nelson's older brother, played a historic role here. While the family foundation was a leader in agricultural development, Rockefeller pursued a long-standing interest in birth control, dating back to his father's financing of Margaret Sanger's efforts (chapter 3). He lent his considerable support also to the rejuvenated field of demography, which still retained the taint of its eugenic past, and to population research. Rockefeller's travels during the war had convinced him that population restriction was a worthy goal. Having developed an intense interest in the culture of the Far East, he worried especially about overpopulation there.

In supporting population research, Rockefeller followed in the footsteps of newspaper entrepreneur (and friend of Japan) Edward Scripps, who had created the Scripps Foundation for Population Research in 1922. Another precursor, the Milbank Memorial Fund, sponsored academic research and held a conference in 1931 that led to the formation of the Population Association of America. In 1936, Milbank supplied funds for the creation of the Princeton Office for Population Research, the base for many leading demographers to this day.[62] Rockefeller took over the leading role during the war. In 1943 he made a large personal gift to the Scripps Foundation. Nine years later, in 1952, Rockefeller convened a population conference in Colonial Williamsburg, Virginia (which his family had begun restoring in 1926), under the auspices of the National Academy of Sciences, and a few months later founded the Population Council, which was to take on the mission of bringing the overpopulation issue to the attention of governments and the public. His efforts brought in other large funders who supported a worldwide movement for population control. The same year, the Ford Foundation began investing in population control. Few then worried about such abuses as the involuntary sterilization programs in India and other places that have since been exposed.[63]

President Truman naturally turned to philanthropic programs and to the expertise of the people who had been instrumental in promoting them when he launched an official American plan of economic development and long-term technical assistance. Philanthropy would give the Cold War its humanitarian face. In the "fourth point" of his 1949 inaugural address, the president prompted Americans to "embark on a bold new program" for "the improvement and growth of underdeveloped areas." The International Development Act of 1950 established the Technical Cooperation Administration to carry out the program that became known as "Point Four." The idea was to blend humanitarian goals with those of economic development and American national interest and security.

Nelson Rockefeller's impact on Point Four was critical. In his more optimistic moments, Rockefeller believed that an effective blend of public and private action, as well as for-profit and not-for-profit enterprise, would render traditional philanthropy obsolete.[64] Benjamin Hardy, the speechwriter for the State Department's Office of Public Affairs, and the person who first floated the Point Four idea to Truman, had been a press officer in Rockefeller's office of Coordinator of Inter-American Affairs.[65] Hardy had begun to conceive of technical assistance as a major arm of U.S. postwar policy as early as 1948. Though confronted with resistance from his superiors in the State Department, Hardy managed to send his idea up the chain to members of the White House staff working on the president's 1949 inaugural address, where it was finally presented to Truman by advisor Clark Clifford. Truman wanted to use his address to make a major foreign policy statement and was enthusiastic about incorporating the idea, despite its lack of detail. Rockefeller later provided more substance on private enterprise's ability to undertake public work and deliver social services in his 1951 International Development Advisory Board report *Partners in Progress*, which Truman read closely.[66]

In his inaugural address, Truman advanced humanitarian and developmental goals for the Cold War. He sought support by appealing to democratic impulses. His agenda was to contain communism by teaching poor countries how to raise their own standard of living. As Samuel P. Hayes, Jr., special assistant secretary of state for economic affairs explained to the League of Women Voters of Massachusetts in January 1950, "We cannot . . . entrust our security even to a possible preponderance of power." Instead Hayes believed in the classic philanthropic formula, temporarily suspended during the war, of attacking the root causes of social problems. As he put it, "we cannot confine ourselves to dealing with symptoms. We must go much deeper and try to root out the germ causes of mankind's chronic ailments. We must help build a world society in which every man has a real personal stake in peace. Then, if tyrants and governments try to disturb the peace, they will stall against the abrasive antagonism of the great mass of peoples."[67]

The tight interweaving of philanthropic and government projects in rural development abroad was nowhere clearer than in India. The first head of Truman's Technical Cooperation Administration, Henry G. Bennett, and Douglas Ensminger, the long-term Ford Foundation representative in India, were almost mirror images of one another. A former president of Oklahoma A&M, U.S. delegate to the Food and Agricultural Organization in Quebec in 1945, and a member of an agricultural survey mission for the U.S. Army in Germany, Bennett was an evangelical Christian who believed in the export of "Christian democracy" as a concomitant of technical assistance.[68] He saw Point Four as a self-help program that would operate not through large infusions of monetary aid but through the "people to people" dispensation of knowledge and training. His models included the agricultural extension service that employed county agents to bring new agricultural technologies to American farmers. Bennett saw the need to recruit similar agents for work overseas. Under his watch, educational institutions in the U.S. and abroad came to absorb the largest share of the Point Four budget.

Ford's programs in India preceded Point Four. In New Delhi, Ensminger immediately developed a privileged relationship with Prime Minister Nehru, who otherwise protested America's intrusion into Indian affairs.[69] As a result, American ambassador to India Chester Bowles made sure Ford was closely associated with Point Four programs. The legislation contemplated from the start the utilization of private agencies "to the greatest extent practicable." To congressmen who wondered why a governmental agency was necessary if private businesses and agencies were to be so relied upon, Secretary of State Dean Acheson responded that "many of the projects were not financially attractive to private enterprise" and that the resources of "the great foundations" were "limited."[70]

Ensminger was impressed with the direction Bennett gave to Point Four. The two men understood one another. Ensminger had degrees in agriculture and rural sociology and had worked with the USDA from 1939 to 1951. While at USDA, he had taken a deep interest in the *servicio* program of Nelson Rockefeller's Institute for Inter-American Affairs and was in fact about to join the Rockefeller program in Latin America in 1951 when he decided to join Ford.[71] Ford's programs in India (and also Pakistan) mirrored Rockefeller green revolution activities in Latin America. Ford and Rockefeller eventually created together the International Rice Research Institute in the Philippines in 1960. With their cooperation, the green revolution would put an end to the huge deficit in wheat, corn, and rice production in the region.

Bennett for his part was an effective defender of the developmental-educational-humanitarian ideal of Point Four, which undergirded its connection to philanthropy. There were those in the State Department who believed that massive infusions of aid oriented for short-term political and economic ends would be more effective than a long term program, but we will never know how much longer Bennett might have resisted their influence. On December 22, 1951, the developmental-educational-humanitarian option suffered a tragic setback when all of its most important advocates died together in a plane crash over Iran.

Bennett along with Point Four originator Benjamin Hardy and fourteen other administrators of the program were surveying the Middle East in search of new projects. As Douglas Ensminger noted after this tragic accident, "the Point Four program lost its direction and never regained it."[72] The other side quickly won in the State Department. In 1952, with a new Mutual Security Act, the State Department succeeded in turning Point Four increasingly into a way to pump short-term economic aid into developing countries in the name of fighting communism, a strategy more in line with the military directives of NSC 68 than Bennett had been willing to follow.

The state-philanthropy partnership, based on a blend of humanitarian aid, technical assistance, and democratic proselytizing, proved fragile. Its progressive elements were no more effective at escaping the strategic Cold War framework than other parts of American society. Challenges came from aid recipients as often as from Washington. Dictators understood how they could use American foreign aid to achieve their ambitions. Ethiopia was among the more important sites of early Point Four programs, as the administration had an erroneous image of Emperor Haile Selassie as a progressive leader and of the country as a breadbasket of Africa, an image based on local reports of its alleged fertility. Bennett himself had given one of the first Point Four contracts to his own Oklahoma A&M College for establishing a new A&M college in Ethiopia.[73] Its goal was increasing food production and improving storage and distribution facilities. Selassie had little interest, however, in adopting the kind of land-tenure reforms needed to raise the country's productivity. He accepted the program's assistance in hopes of parlaying it into military aid as well as U.S. support before the U.N. for annexing Somaliland. When he did not get the military aid he wanted, Selassie accepted development aid from the Soviet Union in 1959 as a way of leveraging more support from the U.S.[74]

In other places, the alliance remained productive. Some voluntary agencies were successful in aligning government efforts at technical assistance with their own "experience and altruistic purposes."[75] International Voluntary Services was one of these. Charted in 1953, it was a Christian organization with a board comprised of representatives from

fifteen denominations. It received funds from the Technical Cooperation Administration as well as from the Ford Foundation, the Rockefeller Brothers Fund, the Arabian American Oil Company, and World
Neighbors. By 1960, young volunteers recruited by the organization had
completed agricultural and village projects in Egypt, Jordan, Iraq, and
Nepal. But many NGOs and university extensions operating abroad
feared partnership with the government, preferring not to be perceived
as government agents. The American Friends Service Committee established a program in India in 1951 under the TCA. After five years,
the AFSC bowed out of the relationship when the TCA required that its
personnel undergo security checks.[76] The fewer agreed-upon U.S. requirements, the more fragile the alliance. Philanthropists had wanted to
see their work as enlarging American foreign policy. Paul Hoffman of
the Ford Foundation thought as much. It was a vision that turned out to
be more utopian than real.

Cracks in the Government-Philanthropy Partnership: American Jews and U.S. Policy Towards Israel

The mid-century philanthropy-government partnership experienced its
most significant test with the creation of Israel. The birth of the new
state provoked a deep crisis between a vastly expanded American Jewish philanthropy, which stood behind Israel, and an American government preoccupied with befriending the oil-rich Arab states so critical
for supplying Europe. The government had at first allowed philanthropy
to play a political role, but then found that it could not always control
the outcome. Objecting to the political obstacles the Eisenhower administration was posing to Israel, philanthropies supported by American Jews took matters into their own hands. With huge donations to
Israel they countered the official U.S. stand of support to Arab countries
so effectively that American policymakers several times threatened to
prevent them from doing so. But in the long run the tide ran in the opposite direction and a dramatically enlarged, Zionist-inspired Jewish-
American mass philanthropy helped push a reluctant Eisenhower ad-

ministration to take a more conciliatory stance towards the Jewish state and clearly affirmed philanthropy's ability to influence foreign policy.

The American Jewish community's support for the new Jewish state after World War II represented a dramatic but understandable change of heart for a community that had been historically apathetic toward Zionism. Of the several forms of Zionism that had competed in the early days, the dominant view did not advocate that American Jews should settle in Palestine. For American Jews, America was already Zion. Justice Brandeis thought Palestine should be the homeland of refugees and the destitute, not of established American Jews.

The likelihood that Palestine could someday become an independent Jewish state seemed very remote to Jewish-American philanthropists. Five times as many Arabs as Jews lived in Palestine in the interwar years, and consequently American donors supported other settlement projects instead—especially in Russia, but also in Argentina. Julius Rosenwald, a major figure in American philanthropy and definitely not a Zionist, gave money to Palestine only for some agricultural experiments in which botanists at the University of Chicago had expressed an interest.[77] Most American Jewish philanthropy was oriented towards local community needs in the United States.

Germany's increasingly virulent anti-Semitism led to an increase in Jewish-American philanthropy abroad before World War II, but still little of it went to Palestine. Although American Jews had practiced federated fundraising early on (see chapter 2), American Zionists, feeling cheated in the distribution of funds, were reluctant to work with the United Jewish Appeal after its creation in 1929. They agreed to help raise funds for non-Zionist activities only after the burning of Germany's synagogues in November 1938. Thus in 1939 the separate campaigns of the Joint Distribution Committee, the United Palestine Appeal, and the National Coordinating Committee Fund (refugee assistance) were all conducted by the United Jewish Appeal. But final totals for Palestine still disappointed the Zionists in the early 1940s. In the 1930s American Jews sent only about $1 million a year to Palestine. By 1948 that figure had risen to $98 million.[78]

After World War II, when American efforts to help holocaust victims finally began in earnest, the Zionist project became a great experiment in social engineering. American Jews, the only Jewish community in the world that still commanded large wealth, were the sole source of continuous financial support for the resettlement of Jews in Palestine and, after 1948, for the new state of Israel. Guided by their own convictions and under pressure from Israeli leaders, American Jews sent hundreds of millions of dollars to the new Jewish nation during the late 1940s and 1950s. Their financial contributions to Israel amounted to twice the amount of money provided by the United States government.[79]

This philanthropy had major repercussions for Israelis and American Jews alike. Israel's economy was small enough that American philanthropic money really made a difference for economic development and refugee settlement, and also enabled the purchase of the arms and military equipment that Washington refused to provide. Fundraising for these goals became the overriding preoccupation of the American Jewish community, but this put the community at odds with official American policy.

At the White House, President Truman personally supported the 1947 U.N. resolution partitioning Palestine into separate Jewish and Arab states.[80] He did not depart from the established policy of friendship with the Arab states, but he helped Israel in several important ways. Among other gestures, he made sure the United States was the first country (before the Soviet Union) to recognize de facto the newly proclaimed state in May of 1948, over the objections of both the State Department and the Pentagon.[81] When the State Department proposed to withhold the unallocated portion of a recently approved $100 million loan from the Export-Import Bank over the issue of Palestinian refugees, Truman did not permit it. And when the State Department again moved to take away the tax-exempt status of the United Jewish Appeal, Truman killed the idea.[82]

President Eisenhower was less inclined to support Israel. With Adlai Stevenson winning 75 percent of the Jewish vote in the 1952 election, Eisenhower felt he could disregard American Jewish entreaties. This led to a major rift between American Jews committed to Israel and the administration, which maintained a policy of so-called "friendly impartiality" in the Middle East.

Although the UJA directed the bulk of its funding to Palestine during the late 1940s, American Jews were eager to display their loyalty to the United States and its foreign policies, and UJA leaders stressed the essential Americanness of their mission. In a speech delivered in Tel Aviv in October 1948, Henry Morgenthau, Jr., former treasury secretary in the New Deal and a key leader of the UJA, asserted that the new nation's struggle was a replay of George Washington's fight against the British during America's "early critical days." As a defender of Holocaust survivors, Morgenthau was doing for his fellow Jews what his father, Henry Morgenthau, Sr., had attempted to do for the Armenians when serving as Woodrow Wilson's ambassador to the Porte.[83] Upon his return to the United States, Morgenthau recast his remarks in Cold War terms, claiming that Israel would become a "hard core of resistance" against communism in the Mediterranean.[84] Leading Americans, including Eleanor Roosevelt, Supreme Court Justice William O. Douglas, Democratic Senator Paul Douglas, and New York Governor Thomas Dewey also endorsed the UJA objectives.[85]

That American Jews backed American Cold War policy objectives by supporting Israel was the key idea behind the UJA campaign. UJA advertisements published during the 1950s emphasized again and again the ideological and historical affinity between Israel and the United States. Displaying the faces of resolute-looking Israeli men and women, one 1954 UJA ad published in the New York Times insisted that Israelis were inspired by "a dream like our own American dream." Significantly, at a time when the U.S. government was trying to bring Arab states into its orbit, the UJA argued that these same nations opposed American goals in the Cold War. "Beyond the border is an enemy with contempt in his heart for everything your country represents; opportunity for all, aid to newcomers, democracy." "In his hands are late model communist arms—swift jet bombers, sleek fighters and heavy tanks—weapons designed for attack. On his lips is a threat—to sweep all Israel" and "Western-style progress into the sea."[86]

In 1950, Herbert Lehman, who had served as the influential director of UNRRA and was now a senator from New York, insisted that
the UJA helped advance democracy both at home and abroad. Morgenthau likewise noted Israel's value as a bastion of democracy. In contrast
to the Arab regimes that the American government supported, it was,
he argued, the one place in the Near East "where democracy is a vital
and compelling part of people and government alike" and would "given
time . . . serve to transform that whole region from its present feudal
state to that of a vigorous democratic society, fashioned in the image of
our own." "A democracy in Israel is a source of strength for America. A
focus of freedom in the Near East is a focus of freedom for the entire
world," he said.[87]

The UJA's fundraising ability matched its sophistication in public relations. By the end of the war, it was collecting money in 3,371 U.S. communities, many of which doubled their giving to the UJA each year from
1943 to 1948. The number of givers also increased rapidly, doubling
between 1945 and 1946, and then rising another 70 percent between
1946 and 1948.[88] The number of contributing Jewish organizations also
grew. In 1948, UJA collections added up to four times the total national
fundraising of the American Red Cross, and thirteen times that of the
American Cancer Society.[89]

National Jewish organizations increasingly booked their annual conventions in Miami Beach, where the peak winter season drew legions of
wealthy Jews from across the country. This time, it was the Zionists who
attracted the most money to the United Jewish Appeal and turned it
into a big show. The UJA therefore concentrated its efforts on refugee
resettlement in Palestine. Miami gave 58 percent of the proceeds from
its 1951 UJA drive to Israel. Other communities did the same. After
hovering around 60 percent at first, the national percentage went up
rather rapidly, reaching 80 percent in 1952–53.[90]

In Miami, the fundraisers resorted to all sorts of stratagems to locate
vacationing Jews. They acquired guest lists from hotel clerks and waited
for the guests at the hotel's beach club. The UJA threw star-studded galas
to kick off its annual drives.[91] UJA fundraisers in Miami Beach also
brought in Israeli leaders to help stimulate giving. At one such event in

February 1948, Golda Meir made it plain that the American Jews' role in the ongoing war for independence in Palestine was to give money: "This is your war, too. But we do not ask you to guard the convoy. If there is any blood to be spilled, let it be ours. Remember, though, that how long this blood will be shed depends upon you."[92]

Other Israeli leaders, who felt that more Americans *should* "guard the convoy," repeatedly called on American Jews to immigrate to Israel during the late 1940s. But while American Jews gave generously, fewer than 100,000 chose to settle in the Jewish state—and most of those ultimately returned home, leading to the charge that American Zionism was merely checkbook Judaism. It was a sensitive issue. In the late 1940s, the American Jewish Committee, a traditionally assimilationist (and formerly anti-Zionist) organization, even threatened to cut off aid to Israel if the state did not cease its efforts to recruit American Jewish settlers. Following a confrontation with AJC president Jacob Blaustein in August 1950, Israeli Prime Minister David Ben-Gurion finally relented and agreed to state publicly that "the Jews of the United States, as a community and as individuals, have only one political attachment and that is to the United States of America."[93]

After Blaustein and Ben-Gurion put the immigration issue behind them, the campaign for Israel Bonds in September of 1950 gave the Jewish state a new, direct, and powerful financial tie with their coreligionists in the U.S. American Jews could now invest directly in Israel's economic future and acquire a stake in a surrogate home. By offering the bonds for sale at numerous rallies, dinners, meetings, and receptions, Israeli officials created opportunities to approach American officials and lobby for their cause. As it turned out, U.S. Treasury regulations worked in favor of the bond campaign. Many who bought the Israel bonds, which came without a tax deduction, donated them to the United Jewish Appeal, a charitable organization, thus gaining for themselves the full deduction allowed by the IRS for charitable contributions, while at the same time supporting a controversial political objective in opposition to their government's foreign policy.

Jewish rhetoric notwithstanding, the Eisenhower administration did not see Israel as a bastion of democracy, nor did it discount the importance of Arab states and oil. In this context, two major crises during the Eisenhower administration brought the conflict between UJA fundraising and U.S. foreign policy into the open. Israel's Jordan River project of 1953 and the Suez Crisis of 1956–57 revealed the extent to which both Israel and the United States perceived Jewish-American giving as a major bargaining chip. In both instances, the Israeli government conceived of the Jewish-American community's gift as big enough to substitute for lost aid from the American government, and the American government implicitly agreed with this assessment by threatening to stop the flow of private money to Israel.

In the fall of 1953 Israel began constructing a hydroelectric power plant near the Syrian border at the B'not Yaakov Bridge, located in the demilitarized zone between the two countries. Syria objected, claiming it would rob Arab farmers of water from the Jordan River and give Israel a military advantage. Moreover, Israel had launched the project despite the fact that the dam threatened a soon-to-be completed U.N. plan for joint use of the Jordan River. The U.N. quickly demanded that Israel stop work on the project, and the U.S. supported the U.N. decision, cutting off public aid to the Jewish state.

In reacting to the sanctions, Ben-Gurion and the Israeli cabinet concluded that the hydroelectric project was important enough to defy the U.N. and risk the loss of U.S. aid. The Israeli cabinet debated whether American Jews would be able to increase their level of giving sufficiently to compensate for the loss of foreign aid from the U.S. Ben-Gurion believed that they would. Foreign Minister Moshe Sharett was the major voice of dissent. He did not object to Ben-Gurion's conclusion but was justifiably concerned that Eisenhower might move to block American Jewish money.

In the midst of the crisis, Israel decided to retaliate against Arab raiders from Jordan. In October of 1953, Ariel Sharon led a night assault on the Jordanian village of Kibya, an action condemned by the international community. The American government temporarily suspended aid to Israel, and Jewish philanthropic organizations responded with intensified fundraising efforts of their own. In early 1954, the UJA floated a five-year $75-million loan—in addition to the regular fundraising for the year—to help Israel meet its short-term obligations. By summer, the UJA had sent 80 percent of that sum to Israel.[94]

The American Jewish community again mobilized to raise emergency funds after Great Britain and France joined Israel in launching a military campaign against Nasser in the fall of 1956 in an unexpected retaliation for his restricting access to the Suez Canal. The attack, coming only a week before the American presidential election, took American Jews as much by surprise as the Eisenhower administration. Eisenhower strongly condemned the three countries, demanding their withdrawal, and, at least initially, the Presidents' Conference (of major American Jewish organizations) and other Jewish lobbying groups pursued a line that offered only limited support for Israel while carefully avoiding outright criticism of Eisenhower.[95]

But the crisis stimulated a massive new round of gifts to Israel. In November, the UJA launched an Emergency Rescue Fund seeking $100 million over and above the normal campaign goal to help 80,000 Jews depart from Egypt. At the kickoff meeting in New York City, Nasser was attacked as the "spiritual heir of Nazism."[96] In February 1957, the Israel Bond Organization made a record $15,450,000 at the organization's three-day conference in Miami—covering 20 percent of that year's goal of $75,000,000. In addition to a birthday celebration for celebrity entertainer Eddie Cantor, the event was highlighted by a keynote speech from Harry Truman railing against Eisenhower's Middle East policy. On March 3, 1957, two days after Israeli Foreign Minister Golda Meir announced to the U.N. General Assembly Israel's decision to withdraw from the Gaza strip and the Gulf of Aqaba, she again told UJA delegates that their fundraising work was an integral part of the "struggle for Israel's security, for Israel's welfare, for Israel's economic rights."[97]

Eisenhower saw the matter differently. In early 1957, after Treasury Secretary George Humphrey reported that Israel received about $40 million a year in private, tax-deductible gifts, and that about $60 million worth of Israel bonds were sold each year in the United States, Eisenhower pushed for proposing a U.N. resolution to suspend not only governmental assistance to Israel but also private assistance. In a last-ditch attempt to get some support from within the Jewish community, Eisenhower advised Humphrey to "get in touch with one or two leading Jewish personalities who might be sympathetic to our position and help to organize some Jewish sentiment."[98] But in effect, there was little Eisenhower could do, and he knew it. Given the state of Jewish-American public opinion, the notion that the Jewish leadership might support restricting aid was wishful thinking. This did not, however, prevent Eisenhower from cabling Ben-Gurion that the U.S. might vote for sanctions in the United Nations, and that those measures might include restrictions on private contributions.[99]

The administration, however, did not clarify its plans and seemed to be doing nothing more than sending a warning. As the *New York Times* reported in February 1957, "There appeared to be divided councils in the State Department on the question of private contributions." The issue remained cloudy: "It is uncertain whether the proposed resolution would apply only to United States Governmental assistance to Israel, or would also forbid private contributions through the United Jewish Appeal. The State and Treasury Departments would also have to decide whether private contributions could be stopped by executive action or would require new legislation," the newspaper reported in a later article.[100]

Mass giving on the part of American Jews combined with effective lobbying by the American Zionist Council, the American Israel Public Affairs Committee (founded in 1953), the Presidents' Conference, and others helped to secure bipartisan congressional opposition to Eisenhower's stance on unconditional withdrawal from Sinai and Gaza, as well as support for guaranteeing Israel's security.[101] Jewish-American lobbyists were able to muster the backing of the Democratic Senate majority under the leadership of Lyndon Johnson. To get Johnson to speak out against sanctions, Texas Jews—encouraged by both secular leaders and rabbis in Saturday sermons—inundated the Senate Majority Leader, as well as Speaker Sam Rayburn, with more than 5,000 telegrams in the course of a single weekend. In response, Johnson sent a letter to Dulles objecting to possible sanctions and then took the Senate floor to urge a settlement—and to assert that the administration policy would remain stalled in the Senate for as long as needed.[102]

The Israeli state-building project was the great unifier of American Jewish philanthropy. That Israel and American Jews ultimately prevailed on the United States government to establish a closer relationship with Israel undoubtedly had much to do with the Soviet's new commitment to the Arab states and Nasser's ingratitude towards the United States in the aftermath of the Suez Crisis.[103] But the Jewish community's fund-raising also played a major role in the policy shift. In order to sustain the historic movement unfolding in Palestine, American Jews had been moved to take action on an unprecedented scale, and in so doing they had challenged the Pax Americana. They had ventured beyond the humanitarian and economic initiatives that had up-to-now bounded the partnership between philanthropy and government.

CHAPTER 6

Philanthropy at Midcentury: "Timid Billions"?

By the middle of the twentieth century, Americans had created a large philanthropic enterprise that was part of the fabric of their daily lives. It included an impressively diverse set of institutions, ranging from local community chests to national health organizations, from small family foundations to wealthy general-purpose foundations. By 1938, there were still only 188 foundations in the United States, but for the first time a significant number of them were located outside of the Northeast. During the war years, the number of charitable foundations more than doubled, to 505, and this figure would nearly triple by 1955, when the number was estimated at 1,488.[1] Characterized by a mix of secular and religious purposes, the nonprofit sector as a whole provided a medium through which Americans channeled their excess income to help the poor, to enhance children's education, to promote cultural activities, to fund science, and to initiate agricultural reform in poor countries.

Concurrently, huge federal outlays in welfare as a response to the Great Depression, in big science for the country at war, and in education for veterans boosted fields heretofore in the province of philanthropy. In reporting these new government outlays (at all levels of government), some postwar economists at the National Bureau of Economic Research invented a new expenditure category they called "public" philanthropy, which accounted for 9 percent of a $482-billion GNP in 1959. Philanthropy, by contrast, claimed the equivalent of a little over 3 percent of GNP (and that included money raised by churches). Adding an estimated value for volunteer work would have raised philanthropy's percentage of GNP to 5 percent.[2]

The inherent variety of philanthropic endeavor, as well as competition with the state in science, welfare, and education placed it at the crux of key arguments over the makeup of the American political economy at midcentury. Philanthropists adopted different strategies of giving, depending upon where they stood politically within these debates. Liberal donors, who assented to big government, underwrote a large secular educational and scientific establishment that was both empirical and pragmatic in essence. Their conservative counterparts championed a smaller government, saw secularism as a threat that degraded American life, and resented America's entanglement in foreign affairs. The two groups of philanthropists openly opposed one another, and their feud, exacerbated by Senator McCarthy's anti-communist campaign, became a battle for the future of the country.

Philanthropy at Midcentury

During the New Deal, Roosevelt and Morgenthau had launched investigations into the finances of a few "economic royalists," as the president called them, carefully chosen from among his political opponents, who had seemingly used the charitable exemption as a means of tax evasion or taken advantage of other loopholes in income and estate taxes. It is easy to dismiss these prosecutions as politically motivated, because indeed they were. But in conducting his war against "the forces of selfishness," Roosevelt had not so much departed from traditional tolerance of inequality as insisted that the rich should return part of their wealth to the society that made it possible for them to acquire it in the first place.[3] His selective enforcement of tax laws gave the country the National Gallery of Art and a few other philanthropic institutions that came to life in the postwar years.

The president and his treasury secretary most famously targeted Pittsburgh banker Andrew Mellon (Morgenthau's predecessor in the previous administration). Mellon had masterminded vast investments in steel and chemicals in the Allegheny region and had created the monopolistic Aluminum Company of America. Throughout his public career as Harding's, Coolidge's, and Hoover's treasury secretary, Mellon continued to manage his private affairs, and suspicions had arisen that he was using his position for the advantage of his companies. In 1924, Senator James Couzens from Michigan denounced Mellon on the Senate floor for conflict of interest and launched an investigation into the workings of the Internal Revenue Service.[4]

Influenced by another Pittsburgh businessman, Carnegie's associate Henry Frick, Mellon had begun acquiring European masters in the 1910s. His buying reached a climax in 1930 after Josef Stalin authorized the secret sale of some of the Hermitage treasures to help finance the Soviet five-year plan. With the assistance of a clever London art dealer, one of America's greatest capitalists in the course of a single year purchased twenty masterpieces from the world's greatest communist, including works by Frans Hals, Rembrandt, Van Dyck, Velazquez, Botticelli, and Raphael. As these were secret purchases, the treasury secretary stored the paintings in the basement of the Corcoran Gallery in Washington, D.C., and also in an apartment below his residence, where only he and a few close associates had access.

Mellon transferred some of his paintings to the Andrew W. Mellon Charitable and Educational Trust he had created in 1930 for the "furtherance of the public welfare" and "to promote the well-doing or well-being of mankind." As Mellon gave the paintings to the trust, he took the tax deduction that the law afforded for such gifts, but in effect he kept the paintings in his private possession. He intended, he claimed later, to have the trust transfer the collection to the U.S. government to form the nucleus of a national gallery of art in Washington, D.C.

That this was in fact his intent is certainly plausible. As treasury secretary, Mellon had the task of overseeing the long-delayed beautification of the Washington Mall. The 1902 McMillan report commissioned by Congress—a classic document of the City Beautiful Movement—had recommended transforming the Mall from a jumble of commercial stands and railroad lines into a monumental space. Mellon oversaw the construction of the Federal Triangle and of John Russell Pope's National Archives.

Roosevelt and Morgenthau started the offensive in 1934. Whether Mellon had resolved early on to build a national gallery of art, and if so how firm his commitment was, we will never know for sure. Only after Mellon was charged with misusing the charitable deduction did he recruit Pope to be the architect for the gallery, and only at the end of 1936 did he begin negotiating infrastructure and design. Mellon died in 1937 at age 82. The Board of Tax Appeal exonerated him posthumously due to a lack of sufficient evidence, but Roosevelt clearly savored a victory on inaugurating the National Gallery in 1941. Having forced Mellon's hand, he now praised him as "a giver who has stipulated that the gallery shall be known not by his name but by the nation's."[5]

There had been no fiscal incentive for setting up philanthropic foundations in the early twentieth century (chapter 1), but that changed dramatically after the creation of the income tax in 1913. The New Deal administration broadened its probe by exposing the rich who evaded taxes, and the results were tangible for philanthropy. At congressional hearings in 1937, Treasury leaked the names of sixty-seven wealthy Americans who had lowered their income tax by transferring large personal revenues to holding companies after Congress reduced taxes on such enterprises. In addition to Mellon, the likes of banker Thomas Lamont, industrialist Pierre du Pont and his close associate John Raskob, newspaper owner William Randolph Hearst, and General Motors president Alfred P. Sloan (all personal foes of Roosevelt), had used this perfectly legal if objectionable device to lessen their obligations to the state.[6]

Sloan had invested in a yacht and incorporated it as a holding company (an "incorporated pocketbook," Morgenthau called it). When publicly exposed, Sloan argued he had not meant to evade taxes, only the liability associated with operating the sailboat. The bad publicity generated by this incident tarnished Sloan's public image, and he attempted to restore his reputation by accelerating giving to a philanthropic foundation he and his wife had created three years before, albeit one initially dedicated to promoting an alternative to the New Deal programs for the country.[7] The foundation would later play an important role in worldwide research on cancer.

The New Deal inheritance tax was directly responsible as well for the creation and vast expansion of the biggest American philanthropic institution of the postwar era—the Ford Foundation. In December 1934, Morgenthau proposed to the White House a graduated inheritance tax (on heirs' individual shares) in addition to the existing estate tax (upon the entire estate).[8] Creating the new tax turned out to be too complicated, but Congress instead raised the estate tax dramatically to a maximum of 70 percent for fortunes above 50 million.[9] Opponents denounced the measure as the "soak the rich" tax act.

The Ford case and its impact on American industry was heavily debated on the Senate floor. What would happen to the family-owned company if the Fords were forced to sell their shares to pay the increased estate tax (estimated at half the stock value—itself a matter of speculation since the company was not held publicly)? In going to Ford's rescue, Senator Arthur Vanderberg of Michigan prophesized the end of the great industrial empire: Under "this proposed tax confiscation . . . it will be driven into the hands of Wall Street, or its equivalent; and the money-changers, who have striven vainly in years past to achieve this end and whom the administration says it proposes to drive from the temple, will have been handed the dominion which in no other manner could be obtained."[10]

Vanderberg's protests were to no avail. The act went into effect on January 1, 1936. The same month, Henry and his wife Clara, and their son Edsel incorporated the Ford Foundation as a benevolent corporation under the laws of Michigan, in part to consolidate administration of the family's good works in and around Detroit.[11] More importantly, the foundation gave the Fords the means simultaneously to avoid the huge inheritance tax and to pass on the company to the next generation without losing control of it. Their decision to resort to a perfectly legal mechanism ultimately proved to be a turning point in the history of the nonprofit sector. In February 1936, Henry Ford willed most of his stock not to his son but to the foundation; Edsel did the same.[12]

Edsel died first, of cancer in 1943, three years before his father. With the two men's estates being settled at about the same time in 1947, the foundation received about 90 percent of the non-voting stock in the

company. By this means the Ford family avoided much of the tax burden and Henry II, Edsel's son, kept full control over the ailing automobile company his grandfather was leaving behind. If it had not been
for the foundation, Henry II and his two brothers would have paid an
estimated federal estate tax of $321,000,000 and lost control of the com-
pany.[13] This was also how the Fords not-so-consciously created the largest foundation in the United States in a single stroke. Hence the commonly heard charge that the leading American foundation of the 1950s
began as a tax-dodge.

Although foundation dollars never accounted for more than 10 percent of overall giving, the large foundation became better established in
these years. In 1930, Frederick Keppel, head of the Carnegie Corporation, had reflected on the foundation as a "factor in American progress."[14] At midcentury, a handful of big foundations constituted a sub-
sector of their own, one of great wealth and consequent influence over
the worlds of knowledge and policy. Four foundations (Ford, Rockefeller, Carnegie, and Duke) had assets of over $100 million in the 1950s;
fifty or sixty more had assets exceeding $10 million. By the end of the
1950s, the Ford Foundation's estimated resources were at least twice the
size of Harvard's, the wealthiest university in the country. In fact, Ford's
$3.6 billion endowment was the equivalent of 67 percent of the esti-
mated total endowment for all American colleges and universities.[15]

It was also during the New Deal that corporate foundations began to
appear. These were yet another variant of the foundation idea, in which
the funding came from current corporate revenue rather than from a
separate endowment income.[16] Badly in need of money during the Depression, community chests lobbied Congress for a corporate tax exemption, so that they could more easily entice local corporate contributions.
Despite opposition from both President Roosevelt and Treasury Secretary Morgenthau, the Revenue Act of 1935 exempted charitable contributions for corporations of up to 5 percent of net corporate income.[17]
This should have provided corporations the required incentive to give,
but enlarging philanthropy at the expense of stockholders' returns involved considerable legal wrangling. Following the accepted wisdom
that only stockholders owned corporate profits and that management

was not free to distribute even a small percentage to charity, most state corporate charters had no clause authorizing such disbursements.

During the 1930s and 1940s, several states responded positively to pressures from community chests and enacted legislation allowing corporate contributions. By 1956 three quarters of the states had such laws on the books.[18] The corporation's right to give away stockholders' profits was tested in the New Jersey Supreme Court in *A. P. Smith Manufacturing Company v. Barlow* in 1953, after stockholders in this company manufacturing equipment for gas and water industries had successfully blocked a small donation to Princeton University. Frank Abrams, of the Standard Oil Company of New Jersey, who wanted to develop corporate philanthropy, joined by the Ford Foundation in its own effort to expand the boundaries of the nonprofit sector, funded a successful appeal where the court upheld the contribution to the university, clearing the way for a broad-based corporate philanthropy.[19]

Even though the 5 percent maximum donation authorized was rarely met, the Korean War tax on excess profits spurred corporate donations. College administrators naturally sought out their many alumni in positions of responsibility across corporate America. Prominent among them, AT&T public relations executive Arthur W. Page devoted considerable skills to attracting corporate gifts to Harvard.[20]

Another reason that the philanthropic sector grew was the successive revisions of the tax code, which made it increasingly cheaper for Americans in the middle and higher tax brackets to give money away by reporting charitable contributions along with the other allowed deductions itemized on the long-form tax return. In 1949, depending on the giver's income, a $1,000 gift translated into a tax savings of between $228 and $765.[21] Both community foundations and community chests benefited. Community foundations had fallen on hard times in the early years of the Depression, but they grew again as donors wanted to lower their inheritance tax but insisted their gifts be used locally. From total capital assets of just about $54 million in 1941, the estimated resources of community trusts climbed to just over $100 million in 1949.[22]

Taxpayers became ever more familiar with the mechanisms by which they might secure tax credits by engaging in philanthropy. Local lawyers and numerous manuals instructed potential donors on how to create their own foundations to trade charitable contributions for considerable tax advantages.[23] In 1952, Treasury raised the allowable charitable deduction from 15 to 20 percent of income.[24] Among wealthy taxpayers, an increasing number turned to the family foundation as a more effective way to shelter dollars than contributing to an existing charity. Instead of giving to local community chests, museums, libraries, colleges, or other fundraisers, they gave to their own foundation, and this allowed them maximum flexibility. They could accumulate money for several years before making gifts while sheltering the donated income from taxes, or they could give only in good years. As these small funds greatly augmented philanthropic dollars, chambers of commerce and local charities endorsed them. The majority of foundations created at midcentury were small family foundations—over 5,000 existed by the mid 1950s—and had no big plans and no staff to carry them out.[25] They were products of American capitalism and the tax code. A good many were scrutinized by the IRS for various forms of self-dealing and delayed disbursements.

The mass philanthropy that had come of age during the previous half century dramatically expanded in the 1950s, engaging in a dizzying array of overlapping charitable campaigns, involving both fundraising and volunteer work. America now entered the golden age of mass fundraising. To enlarge the pool of donors, mass philanthropies perfected fundraising techniques they had pioneered during the war. National health organizations and community chests canvassed American neighborhoods in annual drives. In addition to door-to-door collections, bake sales, and even barn dances helped raise money.

Modest contributions from ordinary Americans provided the backbone of this form of giving. In 1950 one analyst for the Russell Sage Foundation estimated that Americans with incomes below $3,000 accounted for 60.4 percent of all charitable contributions; the figure jumped to 80 percent when incomes under $5,000 a year were considered. Beginning in 1944, all taxpayers filing a short form could claim a standard deduction on their tax returns, whether they made donations or not. Some in the nonprofit sector feared such a deduction for all would hurt charitable donations, but it became clear that Americans' charitable giving was not motivated solely by tax incentives.[26] In fact, donors in the lowest tax brackets remained among the most generous of Americans.[27] By 1950, 1,318 chests (up from a mere thirty-nine chests in 1920) received contributions from 57 percent of the U.S. population.[28] In Indianapolis, community chest leaders, who prided themselves in promoting the "goodness of people," recommended that wage earners give four or six, or even up to eight hour's pay per annum to the chest.[29]

Community chests continued to coordinate local efforts through federated fundraising drives, and they apportioned the money raised. A signal event was Detroit's United Foundation-Torch Drive in 1949, which collected over $9 million, a year after local businessman Walter C. Laidlaw merged the community chest and other Detroit charities into the United Foundation. Henry Ford II, as well as UAW's Walter Reuther, helped organize the campaign. That same year, federated charities in Boston recruited 35,000 volunteers, a "veritable army of solicitors," many of them among lower-middle-class housewives.[30] A great many United Funds across the country eventually came under the aegis of a national governing body known since 1970 as the United Way. Such national offices of charities often called on experienced professional fundraisers in these years to oversee their campaigns and to ensure that local agencies adhered to the best fundraising practices.[31]

Mass philanthropy penetrated not only American neighborhoods but also factories and offices, where payroll deductions helped expand collections. New Deal tax withholding had generalized the method. The charitable payroll deductions enabled corporations to manage solicitations more effectively, siphoning donations to federated charities and away from individual charities. In addition, after the passage of the Taft-Hartley Act, management saw the payroll check-off as a way to prevent union personnel from engaging in ancillary union activities on the shop floor.[32] For its part, labor used its promotion of philanthropy to strengthen its community-leadership position. In 1941, Ford became the first major automaker to agree to a check-off of UAW union dues. Dues were deducted automatically from paychecks, and a charitable contribution could be added to this deduction. About 40 percent of all labor agreements provided for such charitable withholdings by 1946.[33] In 1949 in Detroit, the federated campaign suggested that hourly employees make an annual donation equivalent to five hours of pay and that executives give from 0.5 to 2 percent of their annual salary.[34]

Americans naturally continued to give vast sums to religious institutions, but the portion of those gifts that went to philanthropy is difficult to evaluate, as churches have no reporting requirements. The bulk of the money collected from parishioners went to church maintenance. One of the few reliable estimates available comes from a 1957 survey conducted by the National Council of Churches of fifty-two Protestant and Eastern Orthodox churches in the United States. These churches spent 81.1 per cent of the money they collected for local congregational expenses and a significant 18.9 percent on benevolences, including foreign missions and relief abroad.[35]

Despite the American population's intense level of commitment to philanthropy at midcentury, some insiders expressed worries that regardless of their wealth, philanthropic organizations were not responding to the new circumstances of state competition with ambitious enough goals. They felt the challenge of "public philanthropy." Edwin Embree, a veteran of both the Rockefeller Foundation and the Rosenwald Fund, feared that, with the first generation of institution builders gone, the big foundations were spending only "timid billions." The largest foundations had become bureaucratic organizations in their own right, with well-connected boards of trustees and a professional staff to distribute the money. "In spite of the increasing number of funds and the desperate needs of the world," Embree wrote in a 1949 *Harper's* article, "there is an ominous absence of that social pioneering that is the essential business of foundations." Embree denounced the lack of "creative attacks on basic problems." He recalled Frederick Gates's warning against a "scatteration" of philanthropic resources, "the sprinkling of little grants over a multiplicity of causes and institutions," and projects too "narrowly defined." Quoting a study critical of philanthropic practice by sociologist Eduard C. Lindeman, Embree expressed fears that there were too many conservative bankers and lawyers "and friends of the founder" among trustees, and that they all wanted to play it safe. He urged the new generation of leaders to "turn these great social forces" to "fresh attacks" "on social frontiers."[36]

Identifying such problems in the face of the huge investments of public philanthropy posed a challenge. The military's large-scale venture into science had brought the state into research fields that foundations had funded in the 1920s and 1930s. The Rockefeller Foundation had been at the forefront of advances in physics worldwide, for example. Now John D. Rockefeller III struggled to "make the peaks higher" at the family foundation.[37] With defense R&D in World War II and the Cold War, scientists had come to depend on a level of funding that only the state could provide. The same was true of advances in biology and medicine. In 1938, the Federal government spent only $42,430,000 funding natural science and technology research; in 1940 the figure was $770,120,000.[38] One foundation official complained in 1949: "We raised three million dollars for cancer research and then read that the government proposes to appropriate thirty million to the same cause; it's very discouraging."[39] Moreover, by sending veterans to school and paying their tuition, the GI Bill of 1944 put more resources at the disposal of American universities than all foundations combined. In 1950, the creation of the National Science Foundation—the brainchild of Vannevar Bush's wartime National Defense Research Council and the Office of Scientific Research and Development—led many to believe that science might no longer need philanthropic funding. A decade later a quarter of the annual income of Harvard University (fully 57 percent in the medical school) came from one or another federal agency.[40]

Mass philanthropy faced a similar dilemma when it came to social welfare services. In a typical year during the 1950s, state and federal governments covered about 73 percent of such services, ranging from school lunches to veterans' programs, and up to 95 percent of the cost of assistance to the elderly. This forced a great many charities to rethink their mission. Some found niches in such social services as family counseling and juvenile delinquency.[41] In Indianapolis the Family Welfare Association became the Family Service Association and its program "changed from one of serving only the economically disadvantaged to one of providing casework service, no longer just to the poor but to any person in the community who might request it, regardless of economic and social status."[42] All residents seeking services became eligible irrespective of their personal resources. In Wilmington, Delaware, the Family Society shed its welfare past to focus on therapy, including marriage counseling.[43]

Philanthropic leaders found themselves operating in a world where every program they put forth competed with a federal program. Anxious about a big government takeover, they argued before congressional panels and in public debates that philanthropic dollars ought to be spent as "venture capital," a term they used repeatedly to mean that they would engage in experimental projects too risky for tax dollars (most often without explaining what exactly they had in mind).[44] At the Russell Sage Foundation, the leading philanthropy in social work, trustees invested their resources in the new behavioral and social sciences.[45] Officers of the Kellogg Foundation, which had focused its energy on fostering community around rural Battle Creek, Michigan, began thinking of problems affecting metropolitan and industrialized areas.[46] But it was at the Ford Foundation that a few executives came together to write the postwar textbook for a liberal internationalist program for philanthropy.

Liberal Philanthropy at Midcentury

Henry Ford II brought considerable managerial ability to the foundation. He had been still in his twenties when he revitalized the automobile company by hiring able managers away from GM, as well as Harvard-trained "whiz kids," Robert McNamara among them. Together they retooled the production line and returned the company to profitability. Henry II turned next to the foundation. He was well aware that all potential beneficiaries (including the IRS), who could claim a share of the bounty, would closely watch this new giant of philanthropy. Cultural critic Dwight Macdonald later derided the Ford Foundation in the *New Yorker* as "a large body of money completely surrounded by people who want some."[47]

Henry sought advice from one of the foundation's trustees, physicist and MIT president Karl Compton, on how to get "the best thought available in the United States" so that he could "most effectively and intelligently" put the foundation's enlarged resources to work for "human welfare."[48] Compton recommended enlisting the services of a young lawyer by the name of H. Rowan Gaither, Jr., who had distinguished himself as assistant director of MIT's Radiation Laboratory during the war and had since gained visibility by overseeing the RAND Corporation's conversion from Air Force-sponsored to civilian think tank.[49] He was chairman of its board when Henry Ford II contacted him in 1948 about the foundation.

Gaither was swayed by Ford's commitment to an organization that was independent of family control and that possessed vast resources. Both conditions were equally important to develop a program capable of energizing the foundation. While there was still some uncertainty about what the foundation's assets might be worth on the market, Ford was essentially asking Gaither to dream up ways in which he could use a large endowment for the betterment of humanity, and fast. He estimated that the Ford Foundation would have $10–15 million to spend in 1949, and perhaps as much as $40 million by 1952. John Gardner from the Carnegie Corporation expressed the hope that 98 percent of the foundation's funds could be allocated to the solution of critical problems. Others believed that was much too ambitious considering overhead expenses. A 50 percent efficiency after five years was perhaps more realistic.[50]

In 1948, then, Gaither brought together eleven men with experience in public policy and academia. Although none rose to lasting prominence, they were among the brightest of the generation that reached major positions of responsibility in the war. Together they brought to the task of reinventing the foundation much knowledge of their own, as well as an extensive scientific and academic network on which they could rely. Some were Gaither's friends from his University of California days; others, he had met through war work. Like Gaither, they had been involved in national defense but were now committed to world peace, greater American participation in world affairs, and the United Nations as the privileged medium through which to negotiate international tensions.[51] Although the Cold War would eventually force them to reconsider this hopeful vision, together they defined a liberal internationalist program for the foundation. This was the most influential philanthropic program of the postwar years, emblematic of how liberal and educated members of the generation perceived their future.

Donald G. Marquis, department chair in psychology at the University of Michigan and president of the American Psychological Association, represented the social sciences. Marquis had served on the Research and Development Board of the National Military Establishment—the immediate successor to the War Department and forerunner to the Department of Defense—and it was there that Gaither had first heard of him. Gaither also called on Peter H. Odegard, who had written on interest-group politics and become chair of Berkeley's political science department, and on Thomas H. Carroll II, a friend from undergraduate days at Berkeley, now dean of the University of North Carolina's business school. William C. DeVane, a dean at Yale recognized for curricular innovations integrating science, the arts, and international affairs, represented the humanities. For education, Gaither brought in Francis T. Spaulding, a former dean of the Harvard Graduate School of Education and a trustee of the Rockefeller's General Education Board, now serving as the New York State Commissioner of Education.

For the sciences, Gaither relied on Danish-born Charles C. Lauritsen, a pioneer in nuclear physics and a contributor to Vannevar Bush's National Defense Research Committee. Lauritsen, who had spent much of the war developing rockets and proximity fuses, was a staunch opponent of the development of the H-bomb. The hope for lasting peace shaped his participation in the study committee. Finally from medicine came Thomas Duckett Jones, a graduate of the University of Virginia's medical school who had become research director at Boston's Good Samaritan Hospital.

Gaither recruited four more men to staff the planning team. William McPeak had worked for the Association for the Aid of Crippled Children and the American Heart Association, where he had acquired experience in mass philanthropy. Don K. Price, Jr., like McPeak a Southerner, had helped draft the legislation establishing the National Science Foundation; he was especially interested in mediation between politicians and scientists over research policy, the topic of his 1954 book, *Government and Science.* The other two staffers were again friends from California days, Dyke Brown, a partner in Gaither's San Francisco law firm, and Paul Bixler, a cofounder of the *Antioch Review.*[52]

While early-twentieth-century philanthropists who established foundations had left few detailed blueprints, this group deliberately defined one generation's main philanthropic agenda. They answered Embree's call for big ideas. Their proposal was to recognize the "interdependence" of human actors, and then turn all manner of social interaction into productive events and sources of happiness.

That the Gaither committee intended to speak in the name of a much larger group of philanthropic leaders, civil servants, professionals, and academics is clear from the way they went about preparing their blueprint for reform. The team consulted experts nationwide and supplemented expert testimony with opinion polls revealing what had caused Americans distress and what, in the years ahead, might add most to their enjoyment of life. In all, they traveled an estimated 250,000 miles, interviewed over 1,000 specialists, and wrote twenty-two interim reports before completing their final document, which was published in 1949.[53]

Imbued with the optimistic postwar spirit and steeped in the grand philanthropic tradition of working for the good of mankind, the Gaither team targeted nothing less than providing "each human being optimum spiritual and political freedom, opportunity, sense of responsibility, and happiness."[54] Throughout the Gaither report, a call for respect for human dignity—rather than specific plans—dominated discussions of the political process, labor-management relations, racial inequality, and international relations.

Inspired by America's new place in the world, the committee insisted on the vital connections between international and domestic situations. It was not enough to insure peace; what was needed was a peace that would "assure the ever-increasing realization of democratic ideals." Only we Americans could lead the world in this direction, they concluded, and only if the country maintained "internal strength, stability, and vitality in our political, social, and economic institutions, and in our people themselves."[55]

With its emphasis on a new behavioral science of social interaction, the committee grouped its proposal under five program areas. It did not feel constrained by the federal government's competition but instead stressed overlapping goals in each area. A program for "the establishment of peace" was grounded in the realization that the United States was then "the only country able to provide even a part of the urgently needed assistance"; "the strengthening of democracy" was meant to insure that "a fair share of our national talent is attracted to those enterprises which serve the common good";[56] "strengthening the economy" was designed to help realize a combination of high output and full employment; a program for "education in a democratic society" promoted equal opportunity in a fluid society; and, finally, a program in "individual behavior and human relations" proposed understanding "interdependence" as the "realization of common interests, common efforts, common humanity, and common fate."[57] The proposed areas of support theoretically encompassed the entire breadth of the social and behavioral sciences. The hope was to provide "a rational basis for planning and responsible decision making" through "an understanding of human behavior" that was necessary to "maintain the democratic nature of such planning and control."[58]

Although the Gaither report was not intended to provide specific disbursement guidelines, the expanded foundation committed resources to the social sciences on a level never envisioned before. In the 1920s, under Beardsley Ruml, the Laura Spelman Rockefeller Memorial (later the social science division of the Rockefeller Foundation) had paved the way with significant funding for the social sciences.[59] More recently the Carnegie Corporation had taken the lead in exposing segregation, commissioning Gunnar Myrdal's *American Dilemma*, the landmark study that revealed the distance between the American creed of equality and the American conduct of segregation. Carnegie had also commissioned a comprehensive survey of *The American Soldier*.[60] But these were only the beginnings of a new initiative into which Ford was now infusing major resources.

The field of social science application, Ford suggested, was immense, encompassing the homes, schools, factories and offices where Americans lived and worked. Research at educational institutions had an enormous role to play, and Ford gave it top priority in outlining the program. This was of course in line with traditional philanthropic support of higher education. But in behavioral and social research, teamwork would now replace the lone scholar. And teamwork required funding strategies and programmatic skills that the lone scholar of the past did not have. As Harvard president Nathan Pusey remarked in 1953, research that had been a kind of "professorial avocation," turned now into a major enterprise.[61]

The proposed study of human behavior was the most innovative of the Gaither proposals (although it would have only limited application in the early years of the foundation) and stands out as a major new insight into improving human relations, one with broad policy implications. The Gaither team argued that the problem could no longer be evaded. Too many Americans were having trouble adjusting to modern life. The world's biggest philanthropy should therefore help them understand that they needed to adapt their habits and lifestyles to one another if they were to live at peace with themselves and find happiness. The shift from rural to urban living, from an agricultural to an industrial economy, from a local to a mass society, combined with racial and religious conflicts, tended to create a society of maladjusted individuals.[62] Too little was known about the motivations and processes that explained individual behavior and human relations, and to the members of the committee, this knowledge seemed especially crucial if democracy was to be strengthened. Adjustment to modern life was the new frontier, for "men live together whether they want to or not; all are thrust, from birth, into an immense network of political, economic and social relationships. This interdependence can be the most abrasive of conditions in societies where men are enslaved as tools of other men or of a state machine; it can be the source of greatest satisfaction if it means the enrichment of personal life by the sharing of the best by the most."[63]

In working on this report, the Gaither team attempted to clarify key concepts so as to render them operational at a practical level. Critic Dwight Macdonald later mocked the document for lapsing into a jargon he called "foundationese," and this was certainly true.[64] Nonetheless, the Gaither team clearly focused on where the foundation had a chance to innovate, and it is for this reason that Dyke Brown insisted on distinguishing foundation programs from "conventional fields of interest."[65]

The foundation declined to commit funds to fields that were already adequately covered by public and private philanthropy. Thus it would not engage in traditional welfare activities. It could not be a private WPA or a super community chest.[66] Funds were dedicated instead to one form or another of adjustment to modern life. That Ford wanted to make an original contribution is also clear from the decision not to go into the natural sciences.[67] The team consulted broadly before leaving the health sciences out as well. Thomas Jones's committee of doctors recommended that the foundation refrain from assigning top priority to the medical field because of the considerable resources (including those of mass philanthropies such as the American Cancer Society and the March of Dimes) that were already available. Ford had no desire to become a new General Education Board (which had poured $82 million into medical education between 1910 and 1925) or to compete with the expanded National Institute of Health, any more than with the National Science Foundation.[68]

The Gaither blueprint was a textbook for postwar liberal venture philanthropy, but applying its lessons turned out to be a different matter altogether. With the report complete, Henry Ford II asked Marshall Plan administrator Paul Hoffman to become foundation president. Hoffman seemed the ideal choice—a very good mind and proven leader (see chapter 5). When he was struggling to bring Studebaker back during the Depression, he had willingly engaged in collective bargaining, opened the books for union leaders, and avoided strikes. A supporter of conservative unionism, he had tried to moderate Taft-Hartley in 1946. He saw the Marshall Plan, which he ran successfully, not only as a check against communism but as a way to secure American prosperity. He defended American free enterprise while supporting Keynesianism as a means to raise the standard of living for average Americans. The trustees were so eager to have him when they appointed him in November 1950, that they let him run the foundation from Pasadena, California, where his wife preferred to live. Hoffman brought in Robert Hutchins as second-in-command. Hutchins was a thirty-year-old law professor when he was selected president of the University of Chicago in 1929. He remained in that post until 1945, thereafter serving as chancellor until 1951, when Hoffman (a University of Chicago trustee) brought him to Ford.

All of Hoffman and Hutchins's talents did not, however, suffice for turning Gaither's ideas into actual programs. Egos caused delays while accumulated funds needed to be spent to meet IRS requirement. Personality clashes and conflicting policies undermined Gaither's lofty goal of promoting adjustment to modern life. Hoffman pushed the international program hard (chapter 5). Hutchins prompted the trustees to create two separate funds. The Fund for the Advancement of Education supported professional development for high school and college teachers. Conservative in his views on curriculum—Hutchins loved great books and hated vocational education—he got a cold reception from most teachers, who took instead their cues from John Dewey and believed in learning by doing. Hutchins established a Fund for Adult Education, which supported pioneering work in public television as the means to break down social and religious barriers and help Americans understand one another.[69] The Fund took the lead in pushing for educational channels—a move supported by a broad constituency from Protestant churches to organized labor.[70]

Henry Ford and Paul Hoffman realized they did not see eye to eye almost as soon as they got down to working together. The conflict between the two came to a head when Hoffman, who feared Robert Taft's isolationism, requested time off to run Ike's campaign in April 1952. The trustees, already irritated by his independence and the lack of results, reluctantly granted him a three-month leave of absence. At the end of the year, Hoffman convinced the trustees to create the Fund for the Republic, which would have as its mission defending civil liberties. With Senator McCarthy quite active, and an investigation of foundations led by Senator Eugene Cox under way, the separate institution was to take the measure of the international communist menace while combating restrictions upon academic freedom; defending due process and equal protection of the laws; protecting minority rights; stopping censorship, boycotting and blacklisting activities; and fighting the principle of guilt by association.[71]

The Fund for the Republic was incorporated in December 1952, with former Republican Congressman Clifford Case of New Jersey (an Eisenhower Republican endorsed by both the AFL-CIO and Americans for Democratic Action) as its first president. It attempted without much success to appease Southern segregationists by fostering a biracial dialogue. The more immediate result is that Henry Ford II heard much grumbling from Ford dealers throughout the South about the Fund's liberal stands. The complaints did not help Hoffman's case with the trustees, and the creation of this Fund turned out to be Hoffman's severance pay. The "young ignoramus," as Hoffman not so kindly referred to Henry Ford II (although Hoffman had not graduated from college either), delivered the bad news at Ike's inauguration.[72] Hoffman, let go, resumed his presidency of Studebaker.

Gaither returned as foundation president from 1953 to 1956, but, impaired by ill health and not much of an administrator, he was unable to jumpstart the program he had not, after all, clearly defined. To disburse the necessary foundation funds, Gaither made a huge grant to hundreds of private colleges in 1955 to raise their faculty salaries in response to state governments investing much of their postwar tax revenues in building their own state systems.[73] The foundation also established the Center for Advanced Study in the Behavioral Sciences at Stanford, but the larger behavioral program lagged behind. Understanding interdependency was left to the future.

So were civil rights. The Gaither team had proposed a universal program with "no distinction of race, religion, class or nationality." But in the section of the report on education, Dean Spaulding still advocated local autonomy for schools, which assured segregation.[74] Gaither as foundation president did not challenge established patterns of race hierarchy. Following Gaither in that position was Henry Heald, president of New York University. Heald disliked reform. He ended the foundation program in behavioral sciences as well as mental health. He considered black spokesmen Roy Wilkins and Martin Luther King, Jr., "propagandist politicians," and he turned down a request for funds from Whitney Young of the Urban League.[75] The Ford Foundation did not come out in favor of racial integration until the 1960s. For the time being, the promise of scientific inquiry served only to mask a timid policy.

The Conservative Reaction

Despite the issues that kept it from realizing its ambitious goals, the big foundations' hopeful visions for a different kind of future succeeded in stimulating opposition. A conservative alliance challenged the liberal establishment. Opposition came from those Americans the report had neglected to take into account. Some noted that the Gaither team had traveled thousands of miles to put together their report without interviewing a single clergyman. By and large, the Study Committee saw religion more as a source of social conflict than of spiritual fulfillment. Instead, the committee had placed its hopes for the advancement of human welfare in economic prosperity (and socioeconomic mobility), civic engagement, lifelong education, political and civil rights, peace, and the notion of "adjustment," advocated from within the behavioral sciences. They showed no concern for the spiritual life and values that many Americans held dear.

To ensure the place of spirituality at the center of American life, conservatives countered the liberal philanthropic program with philanthropic means of their own, including the tools of mass philanthropy. Their alternative philanthropy promoted religious values and a political economy that would be truly free because unencumbered by state regulation and social programs. One of the leaders of this effort to extract piety from individualism and free market values was an oilman from Pennsylvania, J. Howard Pew, one of the ten wealthiest Americans and a devout Presbyterian. Pew's ire was initially drawn by the collectivism of the church. He spoke for many conservatives in denouncing the Social Gospel as a way to take the religious out of religion. In addition, he felt that the Social Gospel threatened individualism, and that it was a form of communism. Not surprisingly, Pew brought a distinctly evangelical tone to philanthropy. In his hands, philanthropy was neither about good works nor science. It was nothing less than the arena in which the battle for eternal salvation was fought.

Born in 1882, Howard Pew was the son of Joseph N. Pew, Sr., founder of the Philadelphia-based Sun Oil Company. After attending the small religious evangelical Grove City College in Pennsylvania that his father supported and doing some graduate work at MIT, Howard joined the company in 1901. He became president in 1912 at age thirty after his father's death. Under the second generation of Pews (with his twenty-six-year-old brother Joseph as vice president), Sun Oil flourished. In addition to its oil and gas interests, the company invested in shipbuilding during World War I, and by 1941 it had become the largest manufacturer of oil tankers in the U.S. The company integrated vertically even further by developing an extensive retail business. It opened its first automobile filling station in Ardmore, Pennsylvania, in 1920.

The Pews' experience with the federal government during the New Deal provides a taste of the way Howard Pew pursued the merger of politics and religion through philanthropic means. They initially cooperated with the National Recovery Administration to explore guidelines for prices and wages in the oil industry as the legislation required, but they quickly parted ways with the administration when it came to fixing prices. The Pews joined the Du Ponts in the Liberty League in vehement opposition to the New Deal. Such opposition often took a religious cast. In 1936 Pew worked closely with the League and Irénée du Pont to help an enterprising minister produce and distribute a film defending private property against New Deal collectivizing. The minister had the idea of depicting the U.S. Constitution as a work based on the Ten Commandments, especially "thou shall not steal."[76]

These efforts to use philanthropic resources to challenge the welfare state were not isolated. In the 1940s a number of conservative interest groups—including the National Economic Council, American Action, and the Committee for Constitutional Government—carried on extensive lobbying and propaganda campaigns modeled after the Liberty League. Funded by the Du Ponts and their allies, these groups railed against "collectivist" ideologies.[77]

In attacking the pernicious effect of collectivism on the American political economy, Pew drew inspiration from economist F. A. Hayek's 1944 work, *The Road to Serfdom*, which argued that the growth of the state in the U.S. and other Western countries augured the rise of totalitarian regimes akin to Nazi Germany or the Soviet Union. Pew regularly attended the meetings of the Mont Pelerin Society (named after the village in Switzerland where Hayek assembled a conclave of conservative economists).[78] This association gave a degree of philosophical rigor to Pew's fight against "Socialism, Welfare-state-ism, Marxism, Fascism and any other like forms of government intervention . . . antithetical to the teachings of Jesus, to our American way of life and to the dignity of the individual."[79]

Pew's main challenge was to communicate his message to a large number of Americans. While the liberal foundations were spreading their version of the common good by funding the new social sciences in the elite universities of the nation, dispensing millions on schools, launching public TV stations with educational programs, and so on, Pew's lone effort at communication, namely the funding of conservative seminaries, did not reach very far. He was in fact preaching to the converted. The money he invested in theology programs across the country to counter social Christianity failed to have the multiplier effect he was hoping for. In order to realign the American political economy with God's design, Pew soon realized, he first needed a vehicle to advertise his views.

This Pew tried to do quite early by supporting Reverend Norman Vincent Peale's publication *Guideposts* in 1945. As the pastor of the Fifth Avenue Marble Collegiate Church wrote to Pew, "All we need to do is to state our case" and "keep driving it home. It will win its own way, I am sure, because it is the truth."[80] Peale eventually published a toned-down version of the ideas he shared with Pew in his 1952 best seller *The Power of Positive Thinking*, in which he hit upon the right mix of pietism and mass psychology to sell millions of copies. Pew also supported the Los Angeles "Spiritual Mobilization," a spiritual movement against "stateism" that numbered Peale and physicist Robert Millikan among its directors.[81]

In closer geographic proximity to Pew was his close personal friend Jasper Crane, a Dupont executive and the main organizer of the federated philanthropic movement in the Mid-Atlantic States. Crane and Pew shared the same goal. As Crane wrote to John Foster Dulles, freedom explicitly entailed "self-reliance" and the rejection of all forms of dependency. "The mollusk is secure as he clings to his rock, but he isn't free. Self-reliance is a tough doctrine but it is the only way for the spread of the Kingdom of God."[82] Crane rejected the program of the liberal foundations. In 1947, eleven years after helping found the Wilmington Community Chest and Council as well as the Wilmington Community Foundation, Crane attracted twenty welfare and "character building" institutions to participate in a United Community Fund of Northern Delaware.[83] He saw locally centered drives as "really a test of the American way of voluntary cooperation. If some of these institutions are not supported by this cooperative effort of individuals," he wrote Eugene du Pont, "the government will take over some of the functions of some of them. Then their activities become extended beyond reason, costs go up, and more taxes ensue."[84] Crane was also wary of dangerous influences on the federation movement. He was kept informed of all of the details when the Wilmington YWCA welcomed W.E.B. Du Bois, whom he considered a dangerous communist, to deliver an address in 1947.[85]

In 1948, the Pews created the Pew Memorial Trust in honor of their father. In contrast to the liberal foundations seeking social change, it supported traditional causes. The first grant went to the Pennsylvania chapter of the Red Cross, and it was made anonymously, again as a conscious rejection of the ostentatious secular giving of the day. As Pew recorded then, quoting Matthew, 6:3, "when thou doest alms, let not thy left hand know what thy right hand doeth."[86]

As a way to mobilize people to a cause, anonymity is not very effective. Soon, however, the occasion for conservatives to go public against liberal and secular foundations presented itself in a big way. The country was following Senator McCarthy in his relentless denunciation of communism as the fifth column destroying America. Pew, who did not want the government to intervene in his affairs, did not object at all when the same government harassed those he believed to be enemies of the

"American way." Congressional hearings into foundations were a real opportunity for conservatives to go after their liberal enemies and nail them down. Pew seized the opportunity to advocate that the IRS selectively remove some tax exemptions so that the government would cease subsidizing subversive organizations.

Eugene Cox, a U.S. senator from Georgia, launched in 1952 an investigation of "educational and philanthropic foundations and other comparable organizations" for possible "un-American" or "subversive" activities of a "socialistic nature." Cox felt that foundations, which were "all creations of capitalism," "had in many instances operated to bring the system into disrepute." The Cox hearings—a public encounter between liberal and conservative philanthropies—were a disappointment, however. The communists were more accurate in their denunciations of liberal foundations for funding CIA spies (see chapter 5) than the McCarthyites were in their claims that tax-exempt institutions harbored and funded communists.[87]

Cox was keen on investigating the Carnegie Endowment for International Peace's support of the United Nations. By the time he launched his committee, the endowment's former president Alger Hiss had already been in jail for two years. Cox nonetheless called the two former chairs of the endowment who were responsible for Hiss's appointment. John W. Davis (the Democratic nominee for the presidency in 1924, but best remembered as the lawyer who defended segregation in *Brown v. Board of Education*) was his irenic self in standing by his choice of a suspected Soviet spy.[88] Future Secretary of State John Foster Dulles declined to appear, referring the committee to his lengthy testimony before Senator McCarran's Committee on internal security.

Cox had other big foundations in his sights as well. He pointed his finger at the Rockefeller Foundation for its support of Owen Lattimore, a distinguished China specialist whom McCarthy had accused of being a Soviet spy at the Institute of Pacific Relations. As a southerner, Cox was displeased by the Carnegie Corporation's funding of Gunnar Myrdal's *An American Dilemma*. As an isolationist, he objected to Carnegie's funding for area studies programs—an endeavor in which Ford had joined. When the two foundations were asked to defend their support for Russian studies centers at Harvard and Columbia, they pointed to the obvious distinction, which Eisenhower himself had made at Columbia, between training communists and teaching about communism.[89]

On the stand, Robert Hutchins of Ford was as usual unrepentant, brilliant, and polarizing. Hutchins was genuinely liberal in his politics and had zero tolerance for any challenge to academic freedom. In 1944, he had stated his position rather concisely: "No faculty member can ever be fired except for rape or murder committed in broad daylight before three witnesses."[90] To the committee, he reasserted his position in defense of academic freedom with the proposition that "there is no necessary correlation between political sagacity and scientific eminence."[91] Despite rubbing the committee the wrong way, the investigated withstood the investigation well. In the end, the Cox committee (after the untimely death of its chair) cleared the foundations of wrongdoing, except in a few minor instances.

This disappointing outcome did not frustrate opponents of the liberal foundations for long. Tennessee Congressman B. Carroll Reece—a former chairman of the Republican National Committee and a supporter of isolationist Robert Taft—engineered a second round of investigations, which Congress authorized in July 1953.[92] As Reece put it on the floor of the House: "Some of these institutions support efforts to overthrow our government and to undermine our American way of life. These activities urgently require investigation. Here lies the story of how communism and socialism are financed in the United States, where they get their money. It is the story of who pays the bill."[93]

Behind Reece stood a number of influential conservatives, among them Howard Pew. Pew saw in the congressional investigation an opportunity not only to support the right wing of the Republican Party (Joseph Pew, Howard's younger brother, was a staunch supporter of then junior senator Goldwater), but also to launch a counteroffensive of his own and to push his program of saving the country from the Social Gospel. In a letter to Reece in spring 1953, Pew equated the social commitments of the large foundations with communism. He wrote that "there are certain subversive activities which have been developed with foundation money which should be studied by such a committee

with great care," His target was the Rockefeller Foundation-backed report "Basic Christian Principles and Assumptions for Economic Life,"
an expression of the Social Gospel.[94] While Reece rehashed old charges
about grants provided by Rockefeller and Carnegie to the communist-
infiltrated Institute of Pacific Relations, Pew instead attacked Rockefeller for the National Council of Churches' newly released book *Goals
of Economic Life* (1953). The authors (Reinhold Niebuhr among them)
clearly stated their commitment not to take "ethics into the stratosphere
and separate it from practical economic concerns."[95] Pew, who felt religion was only about faith, not at all about social issues, called it "a
subversive book." Six other "subversive" volumes were in the works and
already announced.

Pew's real nemesis was Niebuhr, not Khrushchev. But it seemed to
him that the two battles ought to be joined. Putting a stop to the Social
Gospel at home would be the first step. "Ways and means must be provided to stop just that kind of thing," an enraged Pew wrote to the leader
of Spiritual Mobilization in Los Angeles, denouncing the Rockefeller
Foundation's funding of Niebuhr and informing him of Reece's plans.[96]

Reece's timing was poor. McCarthyism was losing its momentum,
and in the end Reece only succeeded in discrediting himself by articulating an imagined liberal conspiracy of fantastic proportions. He alleged that the foundations and established scholarly organizations (the
American Historical Association, the American Council of Learned
Societies, and the Social Science Research Council among them) had
worked in tandem since the early 1900s to indoctrinate the American
public to accept internationalism and collectivism (as exemplified by
the New Deal). Hutchins was again a major target of the congressional
ire, but this time for his new role as president of the Fund for the Republic, where Hoffman had appointed him as a parting shot at the Ford
Foundation. Hutchins had broadened the Fund's investigation into the
federal loyalty program and blacklisting in the entertainment industry.[97]

The Cox and Reece congressional investigations failed to convict
the liberal foundations, but they put them on alert. In response to the
Reece investigation, the Carnegie Corporation joined with other foundations to create the Foundation Library Center, which collected data

on budgets and procedures and brought a degree of transparency to the field. The (renamed) Foundation Center was the first sector-wide institution.[98] Others would emerge in the next two decades. Although few were still listening in 1954, the Reece Committee recommended that the tax statute be further broadened to provide for "the complete exclusion of political activity" by tax-exempt organizations. Ironically, Congressman Reece and his Republican colleagues, and Pew and his allies, got what they wanted by a strange accident of history. Liberal Senator Lyndon Johnson, unexpectedly and without any prodding, orchestrated the change. What motivated him?

Only recently the Texas senator had worked on behalf of American Jews to save their tax-exempt donations to Israel from any interference by the Eisenhower administration (see chapter 5). But now, Texan politics caused Johnson to switch positions. In 1954, a young, wealthy oilman and state senator named Dudley Dougherty challenged Johnson in the Democratic primary—which at the time effectively served as the general election in an all-Democratic South. Dallas millionaire H. L. Hunt's Facts Forum, as well as newspaper magnate Frank Gannett's Committee for Constitutional Government backed Dougherty. Dougherty, who had a track record as a McCarthyite, denounced Johnson for being too liberal.

Johnson easily won the primary but remained incensed that two tax-exempt foundations had contributed to his rough treatment. In retaliation, he single-handedly managed, without debate, to write an amendment into the internal revenue code in July of 1954, strengthening rules prohibiting tax-exempt foundations from influencing legislation (as it had since 1934, with some rephrasing in 1950). His amendment denied them permission to "participate in, or intervene in (including the publishing or distributing of statements), any political campaign on behalf of any candidate for public office."[99] Johnson's move pushed political activism off limits, but it did not serve as an absolute deterrent.

For his part, Howard Pew had made it clear that losing the tax exemption would not prevent him from funding his favored conservative causes. A year after his family consolidated their three hundred trusts, pension funds and investment accounts into the Glenmede Trust Company (named after their estate in Bryn Mawr), Pew created, in 1957, the J. Howard Pew Freedom Trust (by transferring 5,000 shares of Sun Oil Co to the Glenmede Trust) for reaching the "hearts and minds" of Americans by promoting "the true concepts of individual liberty and freedom."[100]

The trust promoted a "limited form of government," "the values of a free market," and "the philosophy that we must first have faith in God before we can enjoy the blessings of liberty."[101] Pew had definite opinions about social programs. As he put it, setting aside in one sentence the entire program of social justice advocated by the likes of Gaither at the Ford Foundation, "Communism, crime and delinquency are not caused by poverty, unequal distribution of wealth, bad laws, poor housing, or any other economic, social and political condition. They are caused by sin."[102] The connections Pew had established with Peale as well as Crane gave him confidence that he could dramatically broaden his message if only he could find the right man to deliver it. It was not long before he found the perfect messenger.

A well-known radio preacher of the 1940s, the Reverend Billy Graham was also able to attract large crowds at personal appearances. In 1944, 30,000 people came to hear him speak at Soldier's Field in Chicago. Graham gained an even broader national audience when the Hearst newspapers chose to "puff" Graham's Youths for Christ, and he received similarly favorable coverage in publications like *Time*, *Life*, and *Newsweek*.[103] He represented a convergence of political and religious convictions that Pew found congenial. He saw the Cold War as an evangelical crusade, and like Pew, he applied the communist label very broadly to secularists, unbelievers, and Marxist-Leninists alike. "There are communists everywhere. Here too for that matter," Graham said in a speech in North Carolina in 1947. During a sermon in Los Angeles in 1948, he added, "Communism is not only an economic interpretation of life—Communism is a religion that is inspired, directed, and motivated by the Devil himself who has declared war against Almighty God."

Graham campaigned for Eisenhower in the final stages of the 1952 presidential campaign, because he had sensed in Eisenhower "a dependence upon God" and had the conviction that "the Christian people of

America" should "not sit idly by." Closer to the center and in search of a national consensus, Eisenhower promoted a religious nation rather than a Protestant nation, but Graham was determined that Protestants were "going to vote as a bloc for the man with the strongest moral and spiritual platform." A moderate on race, Graham invited Martin Luther King, Jr., to say a common prayer at his New York crusade. He also insisted that his Southern revivals not be segregated by race. Furthermore, despite a 1948 sermon entitled "The Sin of Tolerance," he did not engage in anti-Catholicism or anti-Semitism.

Pew first contacted Graham in 1954.[104] Although some of Graham's pro-Israel remarks had actually irritated him, Pew saw in Graham an opportunity to put in front of a broad public his vision of a scripturally sound political economy.[105] Graham was the best hope he had and certainly the one person who was already taking an important part of the message to larger crowds. Pew began funding Graham that year—at first concealing his gifts from the public eye through anonymous donations—providing support to Graham's evangelical association as well its key publications like *Christianity Today,* which was enjoying a growing circulation.[106]

By aiding Graham, Pew masterminded a highly successful partnership with the larger evangelical movement and also, it turned out, with mass philanthropy. Since Graham had already established himself as a successful mass evangelist, he provided the Freedom Trust with a ready-made medium through which to connect with a great many Americans and return the practice of American democracy to what Pew saw as its Christian underpinnings. The genius of working with Graham lay in Pew's ability now to advocate a political agenda as part of God's design for America. That Graham had already moved away from his early more extremist positions also helped in reaching a mass audience, and this was something Pew understood. Broadening the message would entail, eventually, a softening of his own political position.

The high point of Pew's relationship with Graham came during Graham's 1957 summer interdenominational crusade in New York, in which 2 million people participated (and 1,500 churches). The crusade staff kept Pew informed of how the gatherings proceeded and the numbers of conversions or, as Graham called them, "decisions for Christ." Graham's secretary wrote Pew, "On Wednesday night, the [Madison Square] Garden was filled and there were 704 decisions for Christ. On Thursday night there were 13,000 persons in attendance, with 550 decisions. The impact of the Crusade is already tremendous."[107] The crusade, which started on May 15, was extended into July (100,000 people gathered at Yankee Stadium on July 20), then to September 1. On that last day, Graham claimed up to 200,000 supporters on Broadway. The Protestant liberals carefully avoided Graham. Reinhold Niebuhr turned down Graham's request for a meeting and ridiculed his crusade as "an obscurantist version of the Christian faith" sold to the public with "all the high pressure techniques of modern salesmanship."[108]

Pew's seed money to fund Graham's Crusades for Christ acted as a kind of providential multiplier. Conservative philanthropy countered liberal philanthropy by engineering a connection with mass philanthropy. It would not be long before a flock of converts would in turn contribute their own dollars to the evangelical cause. The postwar effort to build a more Christian America thus rested on the convergence of big money and mass giving.

If Graham's crusade did not convey quite the full message of the Freedom Trust, Pew's friend Robert Welch took care of the rest in launching the John Birch Society in 1958. Pew, who denied having been a member, was listed on the editorial Advisory Board of the society's publication, *American Opinion,* and as a stockholder of Robert Welch, Inc., the society's publishing arm.[109] But the association with Graham, who had moved away from initially extreme positions to the evangelical "center," was an incredible success for Pew. For Graham provided a genuine alternative to the liberals' program expressly addressed to ordinary Americans.

To help Graham reach beyond the crowds gathered at revival meetings, Pew, after some hesitation, (anonymously) funded Graham's first television appearances—four one-hour live broadcasts direct from Madison Square Garden.[110] Graham saw the potential of the new media as a tool for education and civic engagement. He promised Pew "some of the largest television audiences in the history of television," followed by a "great spiritual outpouring, such as this generation has not yet experienced."[111] The program was successful, and viewers sent in small contributions. With his canny blending of elite and grassroots philanthropy, the evangelist had raised almost $3 million by the end of the New York crusade and ended up with a cash reserve.[112] The crusade had acquired a broad legitimacy from its depth of support within American society. TV was on board, and so were Eisenhower supporters, evenhanded John D. Rockefeller III as well as "hard drinking, poker playing" Texas's oil millionaire Sid Richardson.[113] This mass-based evangelical campaign had made its way closer than ever before to the political center. Meanwhile, tax-exempt philanthropy, forbidden by law to carry on propaganda or attempt to influence legislation, had turned a blind eye on these restrictions and engaged the full spectrum of political activity. Philanthropy was "timid" no more.

CHAPTER 7

Investing in Civil Rights

As the civil rights movement gained momentum in the early 1960s, a small group of philanthropic foundations threw themselves wholeheartedly into the national campaign to end racial segregation. The Taconic Foundation, the Field Foundation, and the Stern Family Fund among the small foundations and the Ford Foundation and Carnegie Corporation among the larger ones provided civil rights leaders with seed funds to register black voters in both North and South, boost minority entrepreneurship, and shore up education. They remained committed to supporting civil rights even as the movement radicalized. The overall mandate was "equality of opportunity," said national security adviser McGeorge Bundy on taking the presidency of the Ford Foundation in 1966.[1]

This chapter tells the little-known story, very important for understanding the politics of philanthropy, of the hostile encounter between this small group of foundations and an uncomfortable alliance of segregationists in Congress and tax lawyers in Treasury. The politicians opposed foundations' investment in civil rights, and the civil servants suspected foundations of tax fraud. At stake was how much a foundation with its tax-exempt but privately managed budget could influence social change in America. The concurrent political and fiscal attack on foundations culminated in 1969 when influential politicians in Congress sought (but failed) to set a term on the life of foundations or to otherwise drastically restrict their influence on public policy.

Singling out Foundations for Fiscal Regulation

The McCarthy-inspired loyalty investigations of the 1950s had left foundations reasonably unscathed. But segregationists in Congress resented the advantage the tax code afforded the wealthy to shape public life through their foundations. These resentments found voice first in 1961, when a Southern populist politician set in motion a broad campaign to restrict foundation activities.

A Democratic congressman from a small town in East Texas, Wright Patman had been reelected time and again since 1929. Patman hated the arrogant wealthy, and their philanthropic efforts did nothing to lessen his disdain. Toward the end of the Hoover administration, he had joined Senator James Couzens in proposing to impeach Treasury Secretary Andrew Mellon, and he had felt vindicated when President Roosevelt pursued the former secretary for tax evasion (chapter 6).[2] During the New Deal, Patman successfully sponsored the Robinson-Patman Act of 1936, which protected country stores from encroaching chain stores such as A&P and Kress. That chain store owner Samuel Kress eventually donated some of his Renaissance paintings to Mellon's National Gallery only reinforced Patman's negative feelings towards him.[3]

In 1961, when he first launched an investigation into 500 nonprofit foundations, Patman again went after chain stores owners, as he had in 1936. He singled out the Hartford Foundation, which A&P founder John A. Hartford had created. Devoted to medical research, the foundation controlled more than a third of A&P stock, giving it an estimated annual income of $7.5 million in 1960.[4] To Patman's mind, this sum was simply too large to be controlled by a private entity without government oversight. As an inveterate New Dealer, Patman saw little use for civil society's intervention in public affairs. The only part of big government Patman took exception to was the Federal Reserve, because, in his estimation, it catered to the needs of large corporations.

Patman pursued his investigation of foundations throughout the 1960s. He argued that the proliferation of philanthropic foundations was evidence not of increased American generosity but rather of growing fiscal abuse, which removed "over $11.5 billion" from taxation.[5] He was determined to expose philanthropy as yet another pretext the wealthy used to avoid inheritance taxes, keep control of companies from one generation to the next, and receive handsome tax deductions when dumping unwanted assets. He also believed philanthropy was a means to avoid antitrust legislation, hide dubious financial transactions from scrutiny, and influence the public through the funding of media. Despite egregious errors in his reports, which he stubbornly refused to correct, Patman uncovered real evidence of malfeasance. He argued that wealthy philanthropists abused the generous charters the state had granted them and put tax-exempt money to work for personal goals unrelated to charity. At heart he was deeply suspicious of the wealthy as a class, and for that reason he reserved special contempt for the academic and cultural programs American foundations supported.

Although Patman wielded some influence as chair of the House Small Business Committee, the investigation was his own. Some congressmen, most notably Missouri Republican Thomas B. Curtis, denounced it early on as an individual crusade that would only yield findings that corresponded with Patman's own long-held conclusions.[6] Soon, however, Patman drew support from Ways and Means chair Wilbur Mills, who was concerned about abuses of the charitable deduction, as well as from Senator Albert Gore, Sr., who denounced the deductions because they made it possible for "the vested wealth of this country to be tied up in perpetuity for the descendants of a few people who have waxed rich, sometimes by chance or inheritance."[7]

Patman was prone to hyperbole, but some of his facts were remarkably accurate. He was the first person to reveal that the CIA had been using private foundations as fronts to channel money to anticommunist activities in Europe (chapter 5).[8] This was only additional evidence of how easily foundations could be distracted from their initial charitable purpose. The leak did much damage to the standing of those pro-American European intellectuals who were now exposed and condemned in their own countries as CIA agents. Embarrassed, the White House quickly pressured the congressman to abandon that part of his investigation.

As a longtime isolationist, Patman wanted to abolish all fiscal exemption for Americans' gifts abroad. If foundations wanted to spend money abroad, he said, they would do better to support the troops; he would have later confiscated all foundation income to pay for the Vietnam War. Moreover, Patman proposed early in his investigation a moratorium on creating new foundations, and then later a twenty-five-year maximum on a foundation's life.[9] The time limit was not a new idea. Adam Smith had long ago advised against perpetuities for fear of the "dead hand." During Patman's years in Congress, Sears's Julius Rosenwald had set a term on his own Rosenwald fund, because he felt that new philanthropists would emerge in due course to engage the problems of their day.

Patman focused on economic issues, not racial matters. But he also resented foundations' forays into civil rights. As a Southerner in Congress, who had once sponsored an (unsuccessful) bill in the Texas legislature to prohibit interracial intercourse, and who had signed Strom Thurmond's 1956 Southern Manifesto challenging the Brown decision, Patman stood firm for segregation.[10] He wanted local communities to set their own standards as a constitutional means of preserving the status quo in race relations.

Patman's crusade coincided with a reconsideration by the Treasury Department of the regulations governing foundations. Unlike Patman, tax lawyers at the Treasury did not see foundations as the embodiment of East Coast wealth eluding legislative oversight and corrupting American core values, but like him, they saw in many foundations classic instances of tax abuse.

Treasury lawyers began an investigation of 1,300 foundations in 1964.[11] Aware of Patman's investigations but anxious to protect professional integrity, the tax community at Treasury kept the noisy congressman at a safe distance. They had little use for his populist rhetoric, advocating instead firmly worded laws that would make it possible for IRS agents to prevent donors from mixing foundation and private affairs. Even though the tax code forbade donors from using the funds they donated on themselves, through so-called "arm's length" provisions, the language in the tax code was cluttered with such adjectives as "reasonable" or "substantial" that shielded abusers from prosecution.

In targeting foundations as a special part of the nonprofit sector, Treasury lawyers formalized a distinction they had begun to make in the 1940s between public charities (like community chests) and private foundations. The former were the collective expression of multiple donors, whose checks on one another provided natural fiscal oversight. The latter were instead idiosyncratic creations of private wealth, not infrequently inclined towards secrecy and tax evasion.

Ultimately, Treasury discovered that the cheaters were not the holders of great wealth that Patman (and FDR and Morgenthau before him) attacked, but rather small foundations and independent businessmen of the kind Patman defended. It was the more modest donors who took advantage of the loopholes in the tax code, with principal donors at small family foundations often resorting to their philanthropic funds for private purposes—a practice regulators denounced as self-dealing. They made loans to themselves, to officers, or to trustees without adequate security or without charging a reasonable amount of interest. Treasury wanted foundations to disburse money every year, but many foundations delayed making grants for years while engaging in the unprosecuted accumulation of capital. As part of their investment portfolios, foundations frequently operated corporations unrelated to their charitable purpose, a practice Treasury wanted to limit to 20 percent of the total voting power or value of these corporations' equity.[12] To hold back excessive involvement in business, Treasury also sought to prevent foundations from borrowing money for purposes other than charity.

The most important of the abuses, because it encompassed several of the others, was the practice of establishing foundations not (or at least not primarily) to do good, but as vehicles for maintaining control of a private business within a family while substantially diminishing the burden of income, gift, and estate taxes for that family. It was well known that this was how the big Ford Foundation had started, before transforming itself into the world's largest philanthropic organization. Many smaller businessmen followed this perfectly legal practice as well, but they did so without putting their foundation to work for any substantial charitable purposes, perhaps because they functioned below the regulatory radar. *Business Week* noted in 1960 that "the real motive behind most private foundations is keeping control of wealth."[13] According to Treasury, the proportion of abusers was closer to 10 percent, but that is still a very significant number.[14]

In the end Treasury lawyers concluded that there was no evidence that the growth of foundations had eroded the tax base or that the foundations "represented a dangerous concentration of uncontrolled economic and social power." They therefore saw no reason to limit their existence. But they did recommend no self-dealing, annual payouts, and restrictions on business holdings in a 1965 report Congressman Patman and Senator Al Gore, Sr., quickly denounced as too lenient.

Treasury lawyers had made the decision not to address the political activities of tax-exempt foundations in their 1965 report because, as they announced publicly, the IRS already had good controls in place. In actuality, they were uncertain about how to distinguish the political activities of foundations from those of public charities. They of course knew that the courts had protected the political speech of public charities against some IRS decisions. In *Seasongood v. Commissioner,* not even one year after Senator Lyndon Johnson had single-handedly inserted an amendment to the 1954 tax code that made it illegal for tax-exempt organizations to help office seekers in an election (see chapter 6), the Sixth Circuit had confirmed the tax-exempt status of the Hamilton County Government League, which the IRS had disallowed. The court deemed that the Ohio charity's general public campaign for better government constituted permissible educational activity; only direct appeals to legislative and executive authorities and the support of candidates constituted "tainted political activity."[15]

In the 1960s, nonprofits began taking advantage of this trend—ultimately provoking a backlash. A number of tax-exempt organizations became openly defiant of tax rules on propaganda. Thus Sierra Club head David Brower fought Congress's proposal to build two dams on the Colorado River. The dams, designed to deliver water from the Northwest to the Southwest, would have flooded part of the Grand Canyon. The day before the House subcommittee was to vote on the bill, the club took out full-page ads in the *New York Times, Washington Post,* and other papers, chiding Congress. However upsetting it may have been to some, the club could legally claim the ads as part of an educational campaign. The ads included, however, a form to be clipped and mailed to Colorado Democratic congressman Wayne Aspinall, to pressure him to oppose the proposed legislation. The incensed congressman called on the IRS for quick retribution. The IRS suspended the club's tax exemption while it conducted an investigation, an IRS first. It ultimately revoked the club's 501 (c) (3) status, though the dams were never built and the publicity actually enhanced the Club's public image.[16] Writer Tom Wolfe noted accurately that "the Sierra Club's preeminence in the conservation movement began at precisely the moment when the federal government declared it a political organization."[17]

It was debatable whether the IRS should have viewed this campaign as "substantial" lobbying, for in monetary terms the publicity cost only $10,000 of the club's $1.5 million budget for the year. IRS supporters pointed out, however, that the Sierra Club intended to continue its political lobbying. Whether or not disregarding the tax consequences of political uses of philanthropic funds would become "radical chic," as Wolfe predicted, liberal nonprofit groups were already facing a new alliance between IRS law enforcement and a number of politicians in Congress.

An incident involving lobbying, however well-publicized, would hardly have led to a major reassessment of tax exemption laws, especially since the Patman and IRS investigations uncovered only repairable wrongdoing, had it not coincided with the continuing mobilization of a few foundations for the funding of the civil rights movement and for the better economic and educational integration of the black community in America.

Early Philanthropic Investment in Civil Rights

At the start of the 1960s, the halting pace of the federal government's response to the civil rights movement created an opening for liberal foundations. With the Brown decision unenforced, segregation remained the most intractable of issues. Little progress on civil rights legislation had been made during the Eisenhower years. President Kennedy was at first more concerned with preserving his friendship with influential Southern senators than with listening to African-American civil rights leaders. As the latter deepened their resolve, however, Kennedy together with his brother Robert, whom he had appointed attorney general, responded by implementing a level of reform at the executive level, with the stroke of a pen, as it came to be said, thus bypassing congressional oversight. The president appointed minority officials and issued an executive order to create an Equal Opportunity Employment Committee.[18] But lacking a congressional appropriation, the Kennedys needed philanthropic funds to put their plan into action on the ground.

The Supreme Court had outlawed segregation in trains and buses and public facilities used in interstate transportation in December 1960, but to no avail in the South.[19] As Freedom Riders were subjected to extreme violence, Robert Kennedy and a few Justice Department lawyers—Assistant Attorney General for Civil Rights Burke Marshall first among them—offered civil rights leaders a strategy: they should help register black voters in the South and send them to the polls.[20] Voter registration became the first educational project that brought together the administration and philanthropy.

In the 1950s there had been challenges to Southern white registrars' denial of voting rights to African-Americans, but with limited results.[21] Civil rights leaders were skeptical of the Kennedy plan, which they took as a diversion and ultimately a submission to the status quo. Bayard Rustin, a founder of the Congress of Racial Equality (CORE) and a close associate of Martin Luther King, Jr., alleged of the president: "He calls the Negro leaders together and says in effect, 'I want to help you get money so Negroes can vote.' That's when he is bowing towards us. Then he turns and bows to the Dixiecrats and gives them Southern racist judges who make certain that the money the Negro gets will not achieve its purpose."[22] Nonetheless, the strategy provided an opening for foundations to enter the civil rights struggle by funding educational pursuits, such as registration campaigns. Philanthropists were not supposed to go into politics, but they could legally promote voter "education" aimed at teaching citizens how to pass the literacy tests segregationists had set up to prevent them from casting their votes.

A handful of philanthropists already involved in civil rights causes were eager to fund these voter registration drives and participate in their organization. Prominent among the few wealthy Americans committed to the cause of racial justice was Stephen Currier, a young Harvard graduate, who was close to Burke Marshall and married to Audrey Bruce, Andrew Mellon's granddaughter. The couple had eloped in 1956 when students at Harvard and Radcliffe, and their investment in civil rights made their family relations even tenser. Audrey never got her mother's approval for devoting Mellon's money to the cause.[23]

The Curriers' Taconic Foundation took the lead. As National Council of Negro Women president Dorothy Height remembers him, Stephen Currier was deeply troubled by philanthropy's long submission to the strictures of "separate but equal."[24] He brought together in 1960 the leaders of CORE, SNCC, SCLC, NAACP, the NAACP Legal Defense Fund, the Urban League, and the National Council of Negro Women and formed the United Civil Rights Leadership Council. In 1961, he worked closely with the Justice Department to devise a funding plan for the voter registration drives. He secured participation by the Field Foundation, which Marshall Field III's widow Ruth was ably running.[25] Harris Wofford, special assistant to Kennedy on Civil Rights, further enlarged the circle of philanthropy by persuading the Edgar Stern Family Fund from New Orleans also to underwrite the effort. It was a small circle. Edith Stern, Edgar's wife, was none other than Julius Rosenwald's daughter. She had already been active in voter registration work in New Orleans.[26] The Rockefeller Brothers, the New World Foundation, and the Norman Foundation (which Patman had exposed for having channeled CIA money to Europe) also helped fund voter registration.[27]

To put money in the hands of civil rights groups, philanthropists used the Southern Regional Council (SRC) as a special conduit for foundation dollars. A progressive institution committed to ending segregation through grassroots educational campaigns, the SRC, headquartered in Atlanta, had been supported throughout the 1950s by Hutchins's Fund for the Republic and the Fund for the Advancement of Education, two offshoots of the Ford Foundation.[28] Although the Fund for the Republic was no longer under the control of the foundation trustees and operated totally independently, the organization remained associated in the public mind with the name Ford, and its efforts to mend race relations in the South continued to be the subject of complaints from Ford customers to their dealers.

As a registered tax-exempt charitable organization, SRC could receive and administer foundation grants, whereas civil rights organizations had no such privileges. Attorney General Robert Kennedy solved the problem by arranging with IRS commissioner Mortimer Caplin (his former University of Virginia law professor) a special dispensation that allowed the SRC to distribute the tax-exempt funds it received from foundations to non-tax-exempt civil rights advocacy organizations.[29] Hence the key role SRC played in allocating the money. SRC executive director Leslie Dunbar and his young assistant Vernon Jordan negotiated strategies and also settled rivalries as they channeled philanthropic funds to the NAACP, SCLC, SNCC, CORE, and the National Urban League (which Jordan would head in the 1970s), as well as to the local African-American organizations and churches that would lead the registration drives.[30] The Field Foundation in Chicago funded the United Church of Christ Citizenship education program, beginning in 1961, something it was able to do directly because the funding was going to a church. Andrew Young, a minister in the church, directed it while also working for King in Atlanta.[31]

Many volunteers, men and women from all over the South, joined in the effort to tutor prospective voters in how to take a literacy test and then "how to go back where they came from to teach other people how to take the literacy test" recalls SRC's Dunbar.[32] On the ground, it was a matter not simply of teaching black voters how to take a test but also of how to avoid risking one's life in doing so, for the police protection promised by the administration was not always forthcoming.[33] The Curriers redoubled their funding and fundraising efforts following Mississippi NAACP field secretary Medgar Evers's assassination in June 1963. Not long after, in January of 1967, the generous couple tragically disappeared in a plane crash over the Caribbean.[34] In their short lives they had shown how philanthropists could change the American political landscape.

The disenfranchised were for the most part identical with the poor. The foundations that supported voter registration therefore also came to play a major role in launching an array of social services in poor communities and programs of community action that made the nonprofit sector a partner with several levels of government. These efforts served as models for Great Society programs. In the late 1950s, the Curriers' Taconic Foundation launched a program in Harlem that was the precursor to Head Start.[35] After Ford Foundation Vice President Dyke Brown (a member of the original team Gaither had assembled) hired Paul Ylvisaker away from the Philadelphia mayor's office to head Ford's Public Affairs Program in 1956, the Ford Foundation became a pioneer in the War on Poverty. Daniel P. Moynihan later credited it with inventing "a new level of American government" by bringing together federal, state, and local governments as well as private nonprofit organizations. The outcome was the inner-city community action agency, where poor residents set their own priorities and pursued their own programs with a mix of private and public funds at their disposal. Moynihan told the story of a foundation advancing "creative federalism"; that is, government officials and philanthropists joining to connect separate public agencies and combine public and private funds while running programs jointly.[36]

Ylvisaker, the son of a Lutheran minister and quite religious himself, taught on the economics faculty at Swarthmore and had been serving as executive secretary to Philadelphia mayor Joe Clark when he joined the Ford Foundation in 1956 at age 34. Ylvisaker found his new workplace "paralyzed," its grant-making unimaginative and risk-averse, dedicated largely to academic research and hospitals.[37] The cautious president of the foundation, Henry Heald, was anxious to avoid the kinds of conflicts with Congress that had prevailed in the days of the Reece committee. Heald did spend a lot of money on Public TV, but he kept Whitney Young of the Urban League and other African-American leaders at a safe distance. Civil rights was not on his agenda. In his first eighteen months, Ylvisaker resigned three times out of impatience, and then at last he made his mark in New York City's Lower East Side.

Traditionally Jewish, the Lower East Side had become home to increasing numbers of blacks and Puerto Ricans. Gang warfare and interracial youth violence were commonplace. At the famed Henry Street Settlement House (founded by progressive reformer Lillian Wald), director Helen Hall worked with city youth board officials, as well as neighborhood associations, churches, synagogues, social agencies, parent-teacher associations, local businesses and labor unions, on organizing a large-scale crusade against juvenile delinquency. Overcoming resistance from several local organizations that feared her dominance, Hall coordinated the work through a joint program called Mobilization for Youth and raised money from the J. M. Kaplan Fund (Patman would soon expose this foundation, too, as having channeled CIA money abroad), as well as from widow and socialite Brooke Astor's Vincent Astor Foundation.[38]

Ylvisaker helped turn Hall's local effort at combating juvenile delinquency into a nationally visible experiment that combined government and philanthropic resources. From his position at Ford, he funded Richard Cloward and Lloyd Ohlin of the Columbia University School of Social Work to develop what they called an "opportunity theory" of juvenile delinquency by tying delinquent behavior to low income, neighborhood decline, diminished social and economic opportunities, and the severe constrictions that all these factors place on normal aspirations to upward mobility. The National Institute of Mental Health agreed to fund Mobilization for Youth in 1961 after Cloward and Ohlin gave it greater theoretical weight and became involved in its planning.[39]

The Ford Foundation contributed money to establish the program as a demonstration project (thus sharing funding with the National Institute for Mental Health and New York City), and Ylvisaker was instrumental in bringing in additional funds from the newly formed President's Committee on Juvenile Delinquency. All of the pieces of Moynihan's "creative federalism" came together as Mobilization for Youth promised a combination of neighborhood-based job training, education, community organizing, and family services.[40]

Kennedy's economic planners liked the demonstration project. It was focused and experimental, involved only a modest commitment of federal dollars, and bypassed federal bureaucracies as well as Congress. By 1961, then, the Ford Foundation, New York City's government, and the federal government (under the guise of the National Institute of Mental Health, the President's Committee on Juvenile Delinquency and Youth Crime and the Labor Department) had fused different levels of government and civil society into a common effort to tackle social problems in a meaningful way. Mobilization for Youth was limited in scope, covering a mere thirteen census tracts in New York City, but one had to begin somewhere. In May of 1962 at a White House ceremony, President Kennedy recognized the three-year project for community action as the pilot for a coming wave of jointly run government-civil society projects. Attorney General Robert Kennedy and New York City mayor Robert Wagner, Jr., were in attendance.[41]

Ylvisaker channeled other Ford Foundation resources towards helping poor people participate in community institutions and planning. He launched the "Gray Areas" program in 1961, borrowing a phrase from Raymond Vernon's Ford Foundation-supported Regional Plan Association studies of the New York area. Gray areas were transition zones. Vernon used the term to describe those areas that lay between healthy urban areas that did not need help and slums that were past the point of intervention. The idea was to select these gray areas carefully so as to maximize resources "at points of leverage."[42]

The goal was not to gentrify the city, but to help the urban poor. The core of the program was resident participation in educational reform, job training, housing, health, and other social services. By 1965, the Ford Foundation had opened Gray Area agencies in Boston, Oakland, New Haven, Philadelphia, and Washington, D.C. Dyke Brown and David Hunter from Ford convinced Presidential Committee on Juvenile Delinquency director David Hackett to co-fund four of the five projects.[43]

In late October 1963, only a month before his assassination, President Kennedy gave Hackett the go-ahead to implement a national program of community action. In time, President Johnson and Sargent Shriver made community action "the basic concept" of the legislative program they pushed to the center of American politics.[44] Mobilization for Youth's insistence on poor people's participation in their community affairs eventually translated into the legislative language of "maximum feasible participation" in the Equal Opportunity Act of 1964.

A New Mixed Political Economy of Social Services

President Johnson turned pilot programs of "creative federalism" into large congressional appropriations, dramatically altering both the amount of funding available and the relationship between the government and the nonprofit sector. Small alternative structures like the ones a few foundations had pioneered were becoming the focus of national action, and the federal government the largest funder of social services delivered by private agencies. This was the real beginning of a new mixed political economy of social services. Instead of the no-cost federalism of the Hoover years or the separation of public and private funds Roosevelt and Hopkins had insisted on, an expanded federal bureaucracy would now develop criteria and funding formulae for channeling money to the nonprofit sector, either directly or using state agencies as intermediaries.

The 1964 Economic Opportunity Act created the Community Action Program, which distributed federal funds to local community action agencies, staffed by city and/or county leaders, representatives of private voluntary agencies, and also representatives of the poor. By the end of 1966, the federal government had made more than 900 grants for Community Action Programs in some 1,000 counties.[45] The move to utilize non-governmental organizations had by 1967 become a central pillar of Great Society liberalism. The outcome was a nonprofit sector tied to all levels of government and challenging traditional political channels for control of welfare.

But as is well known this was not a peaceful process. Chaos prevailed in many Community Action Programs. Social workers promoted conflicting theories of action while leading rent strikes and resistance against city governments. The poor participated only minimally. Not surprisingly, Moynihan entitled his retrospective book *Maximum Feasible Misunderstanding,* as he wanted to highlight the fundamental defects of the War on Poverty. All the same, "creative federalism" did engage philanthropists, bureaucrats, and citizens alike in an experiment in defining and fostering community.

With government a big funder of nonprofit agencies, the tide had turned for the nonprofit sector. The larger welfare reforms of the 1960s—the successive amendments to the Social Security Act, first in 1962, and then in 1967—led to an immense expansion of government funding for private social services and with it a complete overhaul of the nonprofit sector.

The small group of foundations that played a role in civil rights was also influential in welfare reform. Wilbur Cohen, who headed President Kennedy's task force on health and social security, enlisted the services of the Field Foundation as the main think tank to review the Aid to Families with Dependent Children program. The Field Foundation called on a wide group of consultants from the American Public Welfare Association, the National Social Welfare Assembly, the Child Welfare League of America, and the National Urban League, as well as academics in schools of social work, and it charged them with making recommendations for welfare reform.[46] It was on the basis of this study, made possible by one of the most progressive foundations in the nation, that Cohen prepared the "amendments" to the Social Security Act that required the states to establish childcare facilities, apprenticeship programs, and counseling centers in poor communities across America. The federal government, never having paid for more than 50 percent of the social services available nationwide, committed itself to pay up to 75 percent of the cost of "anything that would help troubled, handicapped or dependent people."[47] The policy, as Health, Education, and Welfare Secretary Abraham Ribicoff shrewdly put it, was to "wage war on dependency," and the way to win that war was to mix private and public programs. The result was a large expansion of the private nonprofit sector.

The 1962 amendments gave state agencies the authority to manage federal grants. But, in contrast to the New Deal, which had prevented states from subcontracting federally-funded programs with civil-society organizations (see chapter 4), the federal government now clearly sanctioned such previously-forbidden arrangements. Further opening up the law's scope, the federal government authorized funds to be spent not only on welfare recipients but on anyone "likely to become" a welfare recipient, thus broadening further the range of services the government could purchase from nonprofits.

Federal funds flew to nonprofits at an even greater rate in 1967, after another round of Social Security amendments. John Gardner was then at the helm at Health, Education and Welfare. After working for the Office of Strategic Services during the war, Gardner had joined the Carnegie Corporation in 1946 and was among those Carnegie officials who read anew the famous report on *The American Dilemma* that Gunnar Myrdal had written for the foundation in 1941. As president of the Carnegie Corporation and of the Carnegie Foundation for the Advancement of Teaching since 1955, Gardner had committed more funds to social justice and civil rights.[48] When the President appointed him to the cabinet post, he was able to successfully expand a partnership between the federal government and the nonprofit sector.

Gardner worked with Wilbur Cohen, now undersecretary, on the 1967 Social Security amendments. To lower the number of women on welfare, Title IVA of the Social Security Act obligated the states to provide day care and other forms of family aid to all parents in apprenticeship programs. Again, the states were encouraged to contract with nonprofits and again the term "social service" was used very freely. Probably as the result of an oversight, and contrary to the 1962 law, the department of Health, Education, and Welfare did not even retain supervision of these contracts after they were funded.[49]

The new law also allowed for states to use privately donated funds as the 25 percent match needed to get federal reimbursement, thereby abolishing yet another New Deal rule that forbade matching funds from private sources.[50] The provision strengthened the new alliance between states and private agencies. Nonprofit agencies increasingly generated their own programs and offered their services to the states, which then counted those agencies' privately funded budgets in the formulae for federal matching grants.

The federal contribution was modest at first. A survey of nonprofit health and welfare agencies in thirteen cities in 1965 found that public funding accounted for only 6 percent of their budgets. The Family Service Association of America reported the same year that public funds accounted for 8 percent of affiliated agencies' income.[51] But federal spending for social services exploded after 1967, regardless of executive efforts to rein in the budget. By 1968, 51 percent of surveyed agencies had some sort of government funding, with 21 percent receiving funds from a local Community Action Agency, either as a "delegate agency" administering a program or through a purchase-of-service contract. For agencies receiving Community Action Agency funds, the average grant accounted for 34.1 percent of the budget.[52] Federal spending for social services jumped from $281 million in 1967 to $740 million in 1971 to $1.69 billion in 1972.[53]

Philanthropic institutions were willing to take financial risks in the War on Poverty, and the federal government was firmly committed to funding nonprofit groups in helping the poor. This was when McGeorge Bundy, who could no longer justify to himself the Vietnam policies he had helped design as national security advisor, left the administration and joined the Ford Foundation as its president in 1966. There he oversaw the expansion of civil rights and poverty programs. Ylvisaker claimed with some justice that the Great Society commitment to community action originated with his investment in Mobilization for Youth and the Gray Area project. But Ylvisaker's own days at the foundation were numbered. Bundy and Ylvisaker had irreconcilable personalities, and the latter resigned. Paul had more "sail" than "keel," Bundy would later say, a remark that more accurately describes their different styles than Ylvisaker's weaknesses.[54] In effect, Bundy stayed the course.

Urban renewal initiatives created the conditions for Bundy to support a new program of loans (rather than grants) to stimulate business ventures in the ghetto, and hopefully to integrate minority entrepreneurs into the capitalist economy. Foundation deputy-vice-president Louis Winnick had the idea of supporting at-risk local entrepreneurs with low-interest loans. Unlike the bankers, he believed that the poor could be trusted. Bundy advised him to team up with John Simon, a professor of law at Yale, who had become president of the Taconic Foundation after the Curriers' death in January 1967 (he was also their children's legal guardian) and was working on a similar scheme.

There were precedents for philanthropic investments in poor neighborhoods, as the protagonists themselves pointed out. In the nineteenth century George Peabody, an American-born banker prominent in the reconstruction of the American South (see chapter 1), created the concept of a limited dividend corporation to develop and manage low-income housing in England. Early in the twentieth century, the Russell Sage Foundation had developed the Forest Hills garden community in Queens; and John D. Rockefeller, Jr., had built the Paul Laurence Dunbar apartments in Harlem, where several notables of the Harlem Renaissance lived. But what Bundy, Winnick, and Simon discussed was quite different from those projects. They were looking for a way to help local minority entrepreneurs revitalize their own neighborhoods and increase their participation in American business. Winnick began promoting the idea that loans could substitute for grants after reviewing a proposal to help minority youth rehabilitate a tenement building. At the same time, Simon probed the legal implications of foundations' laying aside the stricture of maximum return on investments in order to endow risky projects with social potential. Simon and Winnick developed the concept of "program-related investments," chancy capital ventures consistent with their larger institutional goals. This was an important legal innovation and one that was in sync with the times.[55]

In late 1967, Simon created the Cooperative Assistance Fund (incorporated under Delaware Law in 1968) to invest in minority business. The nine foundations that participated in the fund (Field, Ford, New York, New World, Norman, Ellis L. Phillips, Taconic, Rockefeller Brothers, Sachem Funds) were veterans of the civil rights movement. Simon devised the fund as a section 501 (c) (3) organization "whose purpose is combating poverty, prejudice and community deterioration through assisting members of minority and poverty groups to improve themselves economically and to have access to improved and integrated housing."[56] Its first president was Edward Sylvester, among the first African-American professionals to step into positions of national leadership. He had been the first director of the Labor Department's Office of Federal Contract Compliance in 1965 and then an assistant HEW secretary.[57] The idea caught on. Soon, the Carnegie Corporation revised its charter to permit its participation in the fund. The Unitarian-Universalist Association, important in voter registration in the South, made a commitment, as did the Danforth Foundation in the St Louis area.[58]

Program-related investments were to be used to help charitable and educational organizations reduce their dependence on gifts by launching income-generating activities. They could also be used to identify and encourage individuals with talent for building economic institutions, and to help minority communities achieve self-sufficiency. In September 1968 the Ford Foundation initiated such investments. The loaned funds would return a modest interest and would eventually be repaid and reinvested in other social enterprises. In 1968, not a year after a deadly riot destroyed downtown Detroit, Ford loaned $500,000 to Detroit's Inner City Business Improvement Forum. Local business interests matched the program-related investment, and the combined funds were then used to generate an additional $5 million of conventional financing. The Ford program benefited causes other than minority entrepreneurship. Ford in 1968 opened a $6 million line of credit to the Nature Conservancy to help the Washington, D.C. environmental nonprofit acquire ninety-seven parcels valued at $12.6 million. By 1972, the Conservancy was sufficiently established that it could secure all of its credit needs from traditional lenders. The foundation also enabled state agencies to acquire strategic land.[59]

The Ford Foundation invested most heavily (with a $3.4 million loan guarantee) in the Bedford-Stuyvesant Restoration Corporation to finance construction of a commercial center. That program-related investment was the most publicized because Senator Robert Kennedy had targeted this very area for ghetto rebuilding in 1966. Kennedy spearheaded an amendment to the Economic Opportunity Act of 1966 to make it possible for Congress to invest in Community Development Corporations to provide not only social services but also housing, offices, and shopping centers. To underwrite Bedford-Stuyvesant's development corporation, Kennedy called on a few friends and courted local politicians. He got immediate support from Ford and Taconic, and also from the Astor Foundation (among the first to fund Mobilization for Youth). For Ford, investing in minority entrepreneurs was a natural extension of the community programs the foundation had pushed much earlier. Young black lawyer Franklin Thomas headed the development corporation, a job that would eventually lead him to the presidency of the Ford Foundation.

In Bedford-Stuyvesant, the Ford loan supported construction of a 157,000 square-foot commercial center that served a community of 75,000 people with retail, commercial, and cultural facilities. The project was a major test of whether a community development organization with sufficient technical and financial assistance could reverse the deterioration and improve the quality of life in blighted areas.[60] Hopes for the project rested in large part on a core of middle-class families that still resided in the area. These families were expected to provide sufficient buying power to support a shopping center. In the past, commercial banks had declined to underwrite such a commercial center until a sufficient number of leases had been negotiated. It was this vicious circle that the program-related investments idea was designed to break.

Regulatory Action In Congress

Rebuilding the inner city was a worthy goal, but race riots threatened to destroy it faster than it could be rebuilt. The small group of foundations committed since the beginning of the decade to civil rights strongly felt that only by strengthening community life could they hope to temper the violence that periodically erupted in America's ghettos. It was therefore essential to keep supporting local communities, even if this meant crossing the political line and funding militant black power groups.

James Farmer had committed to nonviolence in founding the Congress of Racial Equality in 1942 at the University of Chicago, and he was still advocating reconciliation when he promoted Freedom Rides as well as the Mississippi Freedom Campaign. When Floyd McKissick, the first African-American to attend the University of North Carolina's School of Law, replaced Farmer as national director of CORE in 1966, the New York Times said of him that he had not yet "crossed the line that divides militancy from hate." But reformist McKissick soon stood behind his base, ending its commitment to nonviolence at the 1966 CORE convention.[61]

While McKissick stayed close to the membership, he was also pragmatic, looking for resources wherever they were to be found. It made good sense to approach the Ford Foundation for financial support. CORE was broke, and its leaders were often at odds with the local machine politicians who dominated Community Action Program boards. Bundy for his part was eager "to demonstrate to the black community that the establishment would not turn its back on black militant organizations." He and other Ford officials saw in McKissick an opportunity to temper violence, if only they could make "it possible for CORE to operate within the system" rather than becoming like the more radical SNCC.[62] But Bundy had to present to the foundation trustees a proposal with a reasonable goal and all the proper accounting safeguards, and this was not so easily done.

The foundation settled on Cleveland after studying fifteen cities, including Baltimore, where CORE was solidly implanted. Ford staffer James Cunningham who conducted the investigation reported in an internal memo in March 1967 that he had come "to have considerable respect for the brand of militant organizing advocated by CORE, and its ability to produce some young male leaders who can get away from the 'strong older woman' leadership dominance of the poverty organizations." At the same time, Cunningham cautiously underscored, "the Foundation should not expect too much from such a project. . . . It would not prevent riots in Cleveland this Summer. . . . It would not end Negro poverty, or elect a Negro Mayor. But it could help get the present Cleveland poverty program moving, and could help defeat the present hopeless mayor."

Helping CORE organize the Hough district on the east side of Cleveland was necessary, Cunningham added, "so Negroes can bargain from strength and dignity for a fair shake in the city."[63] Indeed, six days and nights of rioting from July 18 to July 23, 1966, had destroyed their community. The hapless mayor, Ralph Locher, had been unable to capitalize on four years of federally funded urban renewal programs. CORE brought new hope for social and political reform, and even some expectation of controlling racial violence.

In 1967, at the time McKissick was calling on Ford, the Field Foundation had created a new policy-oriented research institute, the Metropolitan Applied Research Center, and persuaded black psychologist

Kenneth Clark to serve as its first president. Clark's famous early-1950s doll tests showing that little black boys preferred dolls representing little white girls over dolls representing little black girls, had played an important role in persuading the court in *Brown v. Board* that segregation damaged children's psyches. In his new role, Clark cleverly guided McKissick through Ford's elaborate application process.[64]

The outcome made the headlines. The *New York Times* announced Ford's grant to CORE for registering voters on its front page on July 14, 1967. The newspaper reminded its readers that CORE had become "an increasingly vocal champion of the black power concept" and had struck the word "multiracial" from its constitution. It quoted Bundy as saying that the two organizations did not have "to agree on all public questions," but that he expected CORE to behave in a "businesslike" fashion. Also announced on the same day were Ford's grants to the Businessmen's Interracial Committee on Community Affairs of Cleveland and, also in Cleveland, to the National Catholic Conference for Racial Justice and the American Council for Nationalities Service for Project Bridge, a church-centered effort to improve "understanding between Negroes and white ethnic groups."

As CORE got funded, African-American local politician Carl Stokes announced that he would again challenge the Democratic mayor in the Democratic primary. Born in poverty, Stokes had attended college on the GI bill before going to law school and was now serving his third term in the Ohio House of Representatives. He began campaigning by highlighting the failings of federal urban renewal programs under Mayor Locher. At the same time, Stokes feared that too much black activism would scare white voters, and he tried to dissuade Martin Luther King. Jr., from marching through Cleveland in the summer of 1967.

It was a good thing for Stokes that King did not heed the advice. How influential CORE really was in inducing black voters first to register and then to vote in the Democratic primary is much harder to say. But Locher was quick to denounce the Ford grant as East Coast money and the source of his political problems. "New York City will never win an election as long as you support Ralph Locher," he declared. Addressing members of white ethnic groups, he pointed to "$175,000 from the

Ford Foundation for the aid of CORE and for the aid of having voters register." He added, "Not one nickel came to the Fourth ward. Not one nickel came to most wards. But many, many thousands of dollars went to certain wards on a restricted, limited basis in this city."[65] He was right. Stokes won the primary and later the election, beating his Republican opponent, Seth Taft, grandson of President William Howard Taft and nephew of Senator Robert Taft.[66]

What was new in the Ford grant was that the money had gone for the registration drive in one specific electoral contest. The targeting made this effort quite different from the Southern Voter Education project that preceded it, a fact Republicans and Southern Democrats were quick to note. The political power that a large private American foundation could exert spread alarm in political circles. All of a sudden, any candidate could be thus targeted, if only a well-funded outside organization decided to do so. That the organization was tax-exempt made it all the more unacceptable. Segregationists in Congress were on the alert. By the time of the tax hearings in 1969, a leading Brooklyn congressman, John Rooney, also accused his pro–civil rights opponent in the Democratic primary of using his private tax-exempt foundation to attempt to unseat him, albeit this time unsuccessfully.[67]

When Ford crossed the divide from education to advocacy, some within the philanthropic community feared regulatory reprisal, but not McGeorge Bundy, who knew the politicians and paid no attention to their feelings. Racial tensions were at their highest in the spring and summer of 1968, and Bundy seemed to delight in intervening in some of the crises.

Two months after Martin Luther King, Jr., was shot, Senator Robert Kennedy suffered the same fate on the very night of his victory in the California primary. Loyal to the Kennedys, Bundy decided to make a few Kennedy aides the beneficiaries of an existing Ford Foundation program for travel and independent study that would give them a chance to reorganize their lives in the aftermath of the assassination. A Ford Foundation grant to eight staffers of the late senator was perhaps a small item in the larger scheme of things. But many in Congress perceived this gesture to be part of a larger political blueprint already clear after

Stokes's election.[68] Texas representative Wright Patman asked whether the socially active Ford Foundation had "a grandiose design to bring vast political, economic, and social changes to the nation?"[69]

It was not enough for Bundy to alienate the segregationists. He managed also to find himself implicated in a controversy deeply dividing the left across America. In the Ocean Hill School District, a largely abandoned subsection of Bedford Stuyvesant where the Ford Foundation had a huge program-related investment, and in the adjacent Brownsville community, the foundation funded an experiment in school decentralization. Mayor Lindsay had asked Bundy to preside over a blue-ribbon commission on the future of New York City schools and the possibilities of decentralization. Opting for "maximum feasible participation" on the part of local communities, the commission recommended moving control away from the centralized Board of Education to the school districts. But when the local black principal charged thirteen teachers and six administrators, most of them Jewish, with neglecting local pupils and then fired them, the teacher's union under Albert Shanker organized resistance to the decentralization plan. New York City teachers went on strike three times that fall for a record five weeks. The confrontation turned ugly. Jewish teachers and local black residents traded widely publicized charges of anti-Semitism and racism.[70]

Ocean Hill-Brownsville was a small area. But the controversy fractured America's big liberal community. One faction clung to the meritocratic ideals of the educational system that had served the Jews but not African-Americans. African-Americans felt that the union was patronizing them and that they had a right to educate their own children. James Baldwin summed up the situation when he wrote, "It is cowardly and a betrayal of whatever it means to be a Jew, to act as a white man."[71] The days of blacks' and Jews' joint pursuit of integration had come to a very sad ending with their different versions of communitarian and universal ideals at odds. Bundy had once more demonstrated his polarizing skills.

Such were the events that preceded Wilbur Mills's hearings on the 1969 revenue bill, which promised a reexamination of the tax exemption for foundations. In the highly charged context of 1969, Treasury could no longer ignore the political implications of its recommendations as it had done only five years earlier. Treasury Secretary Joseph Barr set the tone of the congressional debate with a public denunciation of a number of wealthy Americans for paying no taxes, a tactic reminiscent of the charge Roosevelt and Morgenthau had leveled against economic "royalists."[72]

Although there was no obvious connection between civil rights activism and tax evasion, the segregationists in Congress fused them into a single issue—the misuse of tax-exempt money. Segregationists saw in this wide-ranging tax investigation their opportunity to attack a major source of financial support for the civil rights movement. A platoon of Southern Democratic politicians, including Oklahoma Representative Tom Steed, Louisiana Senator Russell Long, Arkansas Senator J. W. Fulbright, and Georgia Senator Herman Talmadge were exercised by philanthropy's increasing investment in civil rights. They drew attention to the illegal investment in politics that theoretically neutral organizations were making on behalf of minority rights. It was a convenient way of putting on the defensive an influential part of the nonprofit sector at a moment in American history when it was particularly vulnerable to these charges. Most philanthropists and foundation executives remained guarded in their communications with Congress, though they understood the underlying motivations for congressional scrutiny. Bundy did not. At the tax hearings he refused to concede any ground to those whose attempts to preserve segregation was garbed in fiscal probity. Like Robert Hutchins in the 1950s Cox and Reece loyalty investigations, Bundy openly expressed doubts that Congress could ever enforce a clear line between philanthropy and politics.[73]

In drafting the tax legislation in the Senate Finance Committee, Senator Gore introduced an unfriendly clause that limited the life of foundations to forty years, only slightly more generous than Patman's initial proposal of a twenty-five-year limit. A moderate on race, Gore had refused earlier in his career to sign Strom Thurmond's 1956 Southern Manifesto challenging the Brown decision, but he harbored a deep suspicion of wealth and was the senator who most closely supported Congressman Patman's investigations. "The record shows," Gore argued, "that in overwhelming proportions and instances foundations are created for the purpose of tax avoidance, to extend economic benefits to members of the creator's family and to continue family ownership and control of property. Let us take one of the good ones: Kellogg. It was created approximately forty years ago for charity. What has happened? The corpus has increased—and here is the report—from $41 million to $408 million. Not one dime of this increase has gone to charity; some of the income has. Here is a 168-page report. And what is the purpose? To advertise Kellogg, Kellogg, Kellogg. Can you see it? Kellogg, Kellogg, Kellogg."[74]

Gore's populism was no greater threat to foundations than Patman's, though both rallied much Southern support. As chair of the Senate Finance Committee, Russell Long argued for the limit on the Senate floor. He denounced foundation incomes as covered "with a cloak of tax immunity." Long had consistently voted against civil rights, including the 1965 Voting Rights Act and, like Patman, he gave only timid support to the Great Society. Most Senators who supported the "death sentence" for foundations, as foundation executives tagged it, resented the foundations' civil rights activities. Talmadge, from Georgia, argued during the debate that "a foundation is the only thing in the world that is permanent in scope. Individuals die, corporation charters expire and must be renewed, all life on earth and vegetation die. Has the Treasury given any thought to the fact that sometime the life of the foundation ought to expire?"[75] Talmadge was quite explicit as to the source of his anger. "Recently many foundations have gotten themselves involved in areas that are really quasi-political. Some of them are subsidizing research in school busing, birth control, and one foundation even went to the extent of subsidizing a former Senator's staff in a trip around the world. Why should the taxpayers of our country subsidize these questionable activities?"[76] Twelve of the nineteen senators who had voted for the Southern Manifesto were still in the Senate in 1969. Of these twelve, nine voted to keep the "death sentence."

There was also some support on the left for putting a legal limit on a foundation's life. Ruth Field (widow of Chicago businessman Marshall

Field III and head of the Field Foundation) made it known that she supported the limit.[77] But other liberal philanthropists were opposed because they believed in the ability of their institutions to recreate themselves to address the changing problems of the day. In early 1969, John D. Rockefeller III charged Peter Peterson, the president of Chicago manufacturing firm Bell & Howell, to form a "Commission on Foundations and Private Philanthropy" to help review the sector's options and find a common voice in responding to Congress.[78] The commission did not report on time, but Rockefeller and Peterson enlisted Senators Percy, Mondale, and Curtis to sponsor an amendment against the threat of mandatory termination after forty years. Perhaps it was never a serious threat, but the senators who came to the foundations' rescue argued effectively that Congress was in this instance acting against the public good. Contrary to Gore's theory of wealth hegemony, they showed that it was not the "dead hand" that ran American foundations but instead trustees who adjusted philanthropic deeds to the needs of the time. The senators reaffirmed one of the essential characteristics of modern American philanthropy, its open-endedness (see chapter 1).

Mondale was the most articulate on this point. He noted that in 1969, twenty-seven American foundations had been in existence for at least forty years. If the Rockefeller Foundation had been forced to liquidate in 1952, it would not have carried out the Green Revolution. If the Carnegie Corporation had been shut down in 1951, it would not have achieved its widely acclaimed Children's TV Workshop and its extended investment in preschool education. If the Commonwealth Fund had ceased its activity in 1958, it would not have had a major impact on medical education. If the Danforth Foundation had shut down at forty in 1967, it would not have had the capital to strengthen Negro colleges in the South.

Most importantly, of the 6,800 foundations that controlled 98.5 % of total foundation assets, 5,300 with 91% of the assets were operating under a broad charter, with the trustees deciding what to do, not the heirs of inherited wealth or the "dead hand" of the founder. Trustees had ample legal recourse for adapting donor intent to changing conditions, perceptions, and means of activity.[79] The foundations countered the charges against them effectively, and the amendment to defeat the death sentence passed the Senate 53–35.

The Southerners failed to get the death sentence into the law, but they did restrict political activism. Congress passed a 1969 comprehensive tax reform act that tightened regulations governing foundations and made them more accountable. The legislation was balanced even though Russell Long, who had fought so vigorously against the foundations, called the moderate bill the "Attorneys' and Accountants' Relief Act of 1969" because of its bewildering complexity.

There had been no connection between the tax evasion of family foundations that Treasury had denounced earlier in the decade and the civil rights activism Southerners in Congress were upset about. But one unsuspected connection burst in the middle of the tax debate and gave it the air of being surreal. President Johnson had already announced he would not run again when he nominated Supreme Court Associate Justice Abe Fortas, close friend and long-time personal lawyer, for the job of Chief Justice. A highly respected figure, once a protégé of Felix Frankfurter and a judicial activist, Fortas was the perfect nominee to replace Chief Justice Earl Warren, at least so it seemed until a journalist exposed an excessively lucrative teaching arrangement that Fortas's business associates had procured for him with American University, and the opposition seized on it to derail the nomination. Several other justices were known to supplement their salaries, but in the summer of 1968 all attention was on the nominee for the top job.[80] It did not help that Fortas and his wife Carol Agger were known for their expensive tastes and luxurious life style. Surprised and embarrassed, Lyndon Johnson had to withdraw the nomination.

The matter should have rested there, but the press kept the investigation alive. As the tax debate proceeded through 1969 a new scandal erupted, and it proved just what the segregationists needed to turn liberal philanthropists into crooks. Abe Fortas had been involved with one of them, reported *Life* on May 5, 1969. Fortas and his wife had been on the payroll of the Miami-based Wolfson Foundation for three years. Louis Wolfson, a Jewish businessman who had made a fortune in TV stations in Florida, actively supported local civil rights causes. But Wolfson had also been indicted for securities fraud (not tax fraud). "The Justice . . . and the Stock Manipulator" read the magazine article's title. A liberal businessman suspected of illegal financial practices was using his family foundation to provide a Supreme Court Justice with a retainer widely perceived as the purchase of immunity, all the while funding a political civil rights movement with tax-exempt money. In the climate of suspicion surrounding foundations, the notion that they were buying influence intensified and clouded the tax debate. Senator John Williams of Delaware successfully called for legislation to penalize any judge or public official accepting any money from a tax-exempt foundation.[81]

By nominating Fortas, Johnson had unwittingly created the perfect storm. He had brought to the public's attention a family foundation that was not only guilty of financial fraud, but had perpetrated that fraud while supporting the civil rights movement and keeping on its payroll the one Supreme Court justice whom the former president had nominated the year before for the top job at the Court.

Although a clean separation between philanthropy and politics was likely impossible, as Bundy was warning Congress, the final revenue act specifically required exactly this separation from foundations, though requirements were more flexible for public charities funded from multiple sources. The 1969 code reasserted that nonpartisanship was essential to secure a tax exemption, no matter how "unsubstantial" foundation budgets for such activity might be.

In response to the foundations' investment in civil rights, the act specifically stated that voter registration activities would be permitted only if a grant was made to an organization working in five or more states and supported by five or more nonprofit organizations, not one of which provided more than 25 percent of the total support. This certainly insured that the Ford grant to the Cleveland chapter of CORE could not be repeated.[82] In addition to preventing any investment in grassroots politics, the law stipulated penalties for activities generally referred to as lobbying expenditures.

In direct retaliation for the Ford Foundation's controversial grant to Bobby Kennedy's staff after his assassination and in response to the Fortas scandal, foundations were now forbidden to make payments directly to government officials of federal, state, or local governments. Government officials were to resign their jobs before accepting foundation assignments. Taking a leave of absence was not enough.

Acting on old Treasury recommendations, the act explicitly forbade self-dealing and other fiscal abuses that had been so carefully documented over the years. Foundations were also prevented from making investments that "jeopardize charitable purpose," but an explicit exception was granted for program-related investments, which played an important role in the implementation of Great Society programs. There was at least this one victory for the Ford and Taconic foundations.

Most importantly, the act required foundations to make annual disbursements starting in 1972: a minimum of 4.5 percent of assets the first year, 5 percent in 1973, 5.5 percent in 1974, and 6 percent in 1975 (later reduced to 5 percent). And the law required foundations to pay a 4 percent excise tax to provide Treasury with sufficient funds to perform its oversight responsibilities. There were as well several other provisions preventing grants to individuals and foreign organizations unless the foundation exercised "expenditure responsibility." Contrary to the fears of many within the sector, the law did more good than harm by setting disbursement rules on which all could agree and by which all could abide. In the end, the U.S. Senate had been reasonable enough and the philanthropists determined enough that the final legislation reflected compromises.

In reasserting a firewall between philanthropy and politics, Congress had singled out foundations without fully realizing that this was again an exercise in wishful thinking considering the drastic transformations of the nonprofit sector that had just taken place. In the preceding years, all levels of government had become partners with the nonprofit sector in programs that were here to stay. Given the need for frequent revisions of both programs and legislation, it would soon again be impossible to draw a clear divide between policymaking, a technical field eligible for tax exemption, and political action, an activity that could not be subsidized.

By 1969, the foundations targeted for retribution had achieved much beyond helping the civil rights movement. Their leaders had orchestrated some of the more significant institutional changes that were part of the War on Poverty and in the process had transformed the nonprofit sector as a whole by initiating key joint ventures with the state. They had also brought the larger field of philanthropy back into the federal system of governance (as in the Hoover years), this time not as a subordinate but as an ally in reform. In the Great Society, civil society partnered with all levels of government in providing services to the poor while (theoretically) enlisting the poor in the effort as well. The outcome was a mixed political economy of social services, in which it was possible for public and private money to work together for the common good.

CHAPTER 8

In Search of a Nonprofit Sector

The challenge was to find a common voice for a sector of American society that had long resisted aggregation. The task fell to a small group of philanthropists and politicians who were deeply concerned about the future of American private philanthropy. Prominent among them in the decades between the mid-60s and the1980s were John D. Rockefeller III, a third generation philanthropist; John Gardner, a former president of the Carnegie Corporation who, as President Johnson's Health, Education, and Welfare Secretary, had introduced Medicare; and Daniel P. Moynihan, a U.S. senator from New York steeped in political science. These men now saw the federal government's massive spending as a threat to private philanthropy. They believed that institutions ranging from foundations to mass charities would have to speak in one voice if they were to be heard.[1] They therefore sought to federate all nonprofit organizations as a discrete sector of American life. Rockefeller proposed to call it "the third sector"; others talked of a "voluntary sector" or an "independent sector," until most Americans acknowledged the existence of a "nonprofit" sector.

At stake was how Americans should volunteer time and give money away in the era of big government. On volunteering, Alexis de Tocqueville had long ago provided a body of important ideas in positing "the art of association" as the "fundamental science" everyone observed and applied.[2] By coming together, like-minded Americans exercised their freedom of action. They mustered means not available to any individual. In comparatively small groups, they better achieved their personal goals. Thanks to their associational habits, they avoided much of the homogenization of modern mass society.

But what would happen to volunteering and giving if government now funded an ever-greater share of American life? Would Americans remain resilient joiners?[3] Would they still spend enough of their money on civil institutions to support a nonprofit sector? In negotiating a continuing partnership with government, Rockefeller, Gardner, and even Moynihan, who had been openly critical of many Great Society programs, promoted a sector balancing public and private sources of support. They wanted it to be independent from government, but they also intended for the government to honor its commitment to fund social services.

At the same time, they faced opposition from a conservative coalition, which also included nonprofits and had access to its own philanthropic sources. This coalition was intent on stopping the flow of federal government money for social services in the name of defending capitalism and promoting the moral regeneration of the poor. Among conservatives intent on "defunding the left" were Richard Scaife (heir to the Mellon fortune), Associate Justice Lewis Powell, and Treasury Secretary William Simon, who refused to acknowledge the limited financial reach of the nonprofit sector. They considered the social welfare of Americans the proper sphere for voluntary contributions, state or local government assistance to charity a matter of local autonomy, and the federal government altogether out of place in charitable transactions. For thirty years liberals and conservatives fought to make their idea of the nonprofit sector the accepted view of civil society. The nonprofit sector as we know it today emerged slowly from this confrontation.

Envisioning a Third Sector

What prompted a few philanthropists to champion a federation of nonprofits was their fear that the third sector might otherwise be absorbed into government. One of the first to sound the alarm was Carnegie Corporation president Alan Pifer, who succeeded John Gardner. Pifer was instrumental in promoting the Great Society programs his foundation had helped shape, but he worried that the federal government would assert its dominance and authority in any partnership with philanthropy. Federal oversight, he thought, had already reduced many nonprofits to "little more than appendages of government."[4] With the federal government making civil society institutions accountable to it rather than to private citizens, federal dollars were rapidly eroding the independence that was a distinctive quality of private philanthropy.

The amount of federal funding funneled through nonprofits certainly supported his judgment. The mixed economy of giving begun under Johnson's Great Society continued to expand during the early 1970s. By 1974 government funding for the nonprofit sector nearly equaled that of private giving. In that year alone, nonprofits received $23.2 billion from government and $25.3 billion from philanthropy (another $32.1 billion came from their own endowment income and fees for services).[5]

Federal money came in the form of state contracts. In 1971, states still devoted no more than 25 percent of their social services budgets to contracts with nonprofits, but by 1976 they were spending nearly 50 percent on such contracts.[6] *Non Profits for Hire* was the title Steven Smith and Michael Lipsky chose for their study of the state of Massachusetts' funding of social services. The Massachusetts Department of Public Welfare, they discovered, had doubled the amount of purchase-of-service contracts, most of it with federal money, between 1977 and 1981.[7]

Smith and Lipsky reported that settlement houses and other private agencies, which had previously relied on private gifts, were at first cautious about accepting government contracts because they worried that their mission as "truly voluntary" associations would be compromised, but the contracts presented them with opportunities to grow and gradually pushed them into the fold. The Ecumenical Social Action Committee of Jamaica Plain in Boston was founded in the late 1960s by local clergy to help neighborhood youth, and its budget jumped from $92,000 in 1971 to over $1.1 million in 1980, with 70 percent coming from the government. The Friendly House of Worcester, a settlement house, was designated a community action agency under the Office of Economic Opportunity program in the mid-1960s and received federal funds for daycare services for abused and neglected children in the 1970s. By 1980, the government was providing 49 percent of the agency's total revenues of $677,000. When early supporters resigned over the issue of outside control, trustees more willing to serve as brokers of social services paid for by the government replaced them.[8]

Dependency on government was the price for the ability to fight the War on Poverty, but was it worth it? In asking the question, Pifer realized that these partnerships between government and local organizations (such as community action agencies) had begun with good intentions, but he argued that they were not "true" voluntary associations"; their roots had not "sunk into the social structure."[9] Poor residents were supposed to participate in all decisions but in effect had to abide by Washington's rules.

Worse, the federal government proved to be an unreliable partner, often turning its back on the poorest and channeling more of its money to the middle class, which voted. This was the consequence of giving states and local governments greater freedom to spend federal funds. Grants to rustbelt states continued to boost Great Society programs, but this did not happen in more conservative Sunbelt states where enforcement of civil rights laws remained lax.[10] This was possible because of block grants, the hallmark of President Nixon's New Federalism. Experts had proposed block grants as a reform to federal aid programs as early as the 1940s—and President Johnson had actually enacted two, in healthcare and law enforcement—but President Nixon saw them as a way of undermining liberal interest group lobbying and bypassing a federal bureaucracy dedicated to supporting these groups. The administration consolidated scores of existing (narrowly defined) categorical aid programs into block grants covering community development, job training, rural development, law enforcement, education, and transportation.[11]

The first two block grants that Congress passed carried the proviso that the states and localities must respect the rules of the old so-called categorical grants that were replaced, but accountability and reporting requirements were minimal. In the South, Nixon's Comprehensive Employment and Training Act in 1973 and Community Development

Block Grants in 1974 benefited an expanded Republican constituency among the middle classes. One Brookings monitoring study showed that most funds went to suburbs and small towns rather than distressed inner cities.[12] These funds were still entrusted to nonprofits, but they served a much broader constituency than in poorer communities.

In watching the government create a federative structure and yet direct fewer resources to the truly needy, Pifer despaired of a "philanthropy" entering an "age of transition" and a nonprofit sector speaking in "a babel which amounts to no voice at all."[13] Sharing Pifer's concern over the fragility of the overall philanthropic enterprise, John D. Rockefeller III appointed himself chief coordinator to jumpstart a federative effort that would increase philanthropy's influence on the nonprofit sector and recommit the philanthropic enterprise as a whole to the most pressing issues. For Rockefeller, who was at the time trying to conceptualize a book on American philanthropy, it was a deeply personal commitment and one that had long been in his thoughts.[14] He had proposed a "third sector" commission as early as 1964, and in 1969 he had convened the short-lived Peterson Commission (see chapter 7) largely to fend off Wright Patman's congressional attack on foundations. The Commission had issued a report, but it came out only after the Tax Reform Act and was largely ignored.[15]

Rockefeller tried again in 1972 to create a federative structure capable of holding together the diverse institutions of a third sector. Congress was preparing new hearings on tax revisions to address "various tax preferences," including issues of importance to rich donors, such as equity in estate and gift taxes, capital gains, and accelerated depreciation.[16] Rockefeller and a small group of advisors, characteristically naming themselves the "501(c)(3)" group because the tax code lumped most sector institutions in this one fiscal category, turned to Harvard economist Martin Feldstein in 1973 to review how federal fiscal policy affected gifts from all taxpayers, not just the rich. Feldstein correctly predicted that with Treasury increasing the standard deduction ordinary Americans could claim on their returns, fewer of them would have an incentive to make a gift that they could later itemize as a tax deduction.[17] Whether fewer Americans made gifts or not is unclear but, as

Feldstein anticipated, the percentage of itemizers declined from 57 to 38 percent of taxpayers between 1973 and 1978. In consequence charitable organizations became more dependent on the wealthy for support.

With the encouragement of Ways and Means Committee chair Wilbur Mills and Treasury officials within the Nixon administration (the president himself suggested a few appointees to the panel), Rockefeller moved to organize a Commission on Private Philanthropy and Public Needs in the summer of 1973. While tax legislation was the immediate impetus for the panel, Rockefeller wanted a review of the entire collection of issues facing the third sector—from taxation, to government support, to advocacy.[18]

Rockefeller tapped John Filer to chair the panel, and the commission informally took on his name. Filer, a lawyer, was chairman and CEO of Aetna Life and Casualty, the nation's largest publicly owned insurance corporation, and had a personal record of philanthropic activities, but he was not a person of national standing and did not rise to the occasion. In addition to Filer, the commission included twenty-six members representing foundations (Alan Pifer was a commissioner), higher education, churches, the United Way, the NAACP, Blue Cross, and other civic institutions. But the commission lacked women and minorities at a time when affirmative action was becoming national policy. This omission would weaken its credibility considerably, despite a research effort that called on a phalanx of more than a hundred consultants—including economist Feldstein as well as foundation veteran Paul Ylvisaker—and produced eighty-five studies taking the measure of American philanthropy.

The commission's 1975 report, *Giving in America*, largely accepted government's enlarged role as a fait accompli, especially in fields like health, education, and welfare, which had not only become too big for philanthropy to address on its own, but were also increasingly accepted as "broad social needs to be attended to as rights of citizenship rather than as benefits charitably and selectively bestowed."[19] The commission also asserted that there remained a need for a "vigorous public-minded and independent sector" to experiment in areas where government could not venture, foster citizenship through voluntarism, assist public agencies in delivering services, and in some cases, act as a counter-weight to centralized government power.[20]

Reversing Pifer's formulation, the commission argued that the prob-lem of tax-exempt organizations was not excessive government influ-ence limiting their autonomy but insufficient private contributions to balance government's role. They did not object to big government and did not foresee government retrenchment. Rather, they feared instead private retrenchment as the outcome of the severe recession and infla-tion that followed the 1973 oil embargo.

Identifying giving (not volunteering) as the "fundamental under-pinning of the voluntary sector," the report identified signs of an alarm-ing decline in private giving during the 1960s and early 1970s as the central threat to the nonprofit sector. Measured in purchasing power, giving fell roughly $8 billion between 1960 and 1974, an amount equiv-alent to just under one third of all private philanthropy in 1974.[21] One of the Filer Commission's studies also showed that giving fell as a per-centage of GNP (from 1.98 percent in 1969 to 1.8 percent in 1974) as well as personal income (from 1.97 percent in 1960 to 1.67 percent in 1972). What is more, the biggest drop in giving came from the low- and middle-income households who provided the "bulk of donations."[22]

The reduction in gifts affected a broad swath of charitable institu-tions. Mainline churches suffered the most, and indeed according to the commission accounted for "much of the overall decline in giving." The trend affected both Catholics and Protestants, and paralleled a long-term decline in both churchgoing and enrollments in parochial schools.[23] But the reductions in donations also hit secular organiza-tions like the United Way. To make matters worse, the fall off coincided with skyrocketing labor costs in social services, only marginally offset by resorting to volunteers.[24] Labor costs were especially problematic in education—where they had risen about 76 percent since the early 1960s—and healthcare, where they rose 1.5 times faster than consumer prices.[25] Foundations also accounted for the shrinking of the third sec-tor as nearly 3,000 of them closed their doors between 1968 and 1972.[26]

The commission noted that the 1973 recession had hit an already ail-ing philanthropic sector harder than the rest of the economy—bringing low even affluent institutions like Harvard and the Ford Foundation.

After the Ford Foundation's endowment lost $1 billion in the stock market—a third of its value—the foundation announced in early 1975 that it would cut both its staff and grants by half.[27] The recession only exacerbated the devastating combination of rising costs and falling gifts that had afflicted the sector since the more prosperous 1960s.

The proposed solutions in the Filer report centered on a series of modest revisions to the tax code aimed mainly at shoring up private giving and protecting capital. But the political landscape complicated efforts to enact the commission's fiscal proposals into law. Nixon— whose administration had early on encouraged the formation of the commission—had resigned in the wake of Watergate, and Wilbur Mills, who for years had been the major figure behind tax reform, had stepped down from his chairmanship of the powerful House Ways and Means Committee because of alcoholism and his dalliances with Argentine stripper Fanne Fox.

John D. Rockefeller III nonetheless played a role in convincing the Treasury Department to implement a few of the Filer recommendations in the 1976 tax code. By the time of the hearings on the new revenue bill, he had become more influential in Washington. Despite their tense relationship, he was helped by his brother Nelson, the newly confirmed vice president under President Ford. Nelson brought into the fold Treasury Secretary William Simon (who had supported the commission as undersecretary in the Nixon administration), before Simon joined conservative philanthropy's effort to defund the left.[28] As a result, the 1976 Tax Code adopted, in part, two Filer Commission recommendations. The commission wanted Congress to replace the 4 percent excise tax imposed under the 1969 tax act to pay for audits of tax-exempt organizations. The tax raised roughly three times the amount of money necessary to cover the costs of the actual audits. A fee that more closely matched the cost of the procedure was put in its place. As requested by Filer, Congress also lowered the required minimum payout rate for foundations from 6 percent of assets to 5 percent. This was an important safeguard against depleting principal in bad years. But the major elements of Filer's tax recommendations, including expanding the charitable deductions to stimulate more giving among low- and middle-income families, did not make it into the final bill.

One sign that the commission had accepted federal government rule and a mixed economy of giving as the norm was its recommendation to create a public umbrella organization for philanthropy, not unlike the regulatory body existing in Britain.[29] The Filer Commission proposed a permanent quasi-public "national commission on the nonprofit sector" that would serve as a clearinghouse, forum, and general advocate for philanthropy. In January 1977, the Treasury Department did create a Treasury Advisory Committee on Private Philanthropy and Public Needs composed of *ad hoc* follow-up groups to the Filer Commission, but it was a short-lived effort. Rockefeller's call for liberalizing lobbying rules for most nonprofits also fell on deaf ears. His personal intervention at the White House (he had voted for Carter against Ford) had no effect.[30] When he died in a car crash near the family's Pocantico estate in 1978, he had little tangible to show for his last few years of work.

Rockefeller himself had been aware that the Filer recommendations were too narrowly focused on fiscal issues to foster a broad new alliance among the wealthy, the larger giving public, and reformers in a rejuvenated third sector. A dissenting group of commissioners also felt the report was too narrow but for different reasons. As the commission was about to issue its report in 1975, they emerged from within the commission to represent the interests of those targeted by Great Society programs. They felt that the report was timid, and they feared the negative consequences of Nixon's New Federalism. Calling themselves the Donee Group, they came from Great Society organizations devoted to minority rights, housing in the inner city, the environment, public interest law, women's rights, community organizations, and other social advocacy goals.[31] They had failed to push the commission beyond technical tax issues to embrace larger questions: Who benefits from philanthropy? Can philanthropy really play the role of the "venture capital" of social change, capable of promoting innovations on the margins? What are its commitments to public purpose? How does it promote equity, justice, service, and leadership? Can philanthropy produce an antidote to capitalism's excesses? Both Rockefeller and the Filer Commission felt they should provide funds for this Donee Group to establish a permanent organization, the National Committee for Responsive Philanthropy.[32]

The members of the committee focused so intently on their role as the voice of nonprofits dedicated to social advocacy for minorities and the poor that they failed to see the larger threat of a conservative movement intent on putting an end to the Great Society. Instead, they pressured the philanthropic establishment to open itself up to minorities and to be more transparent in their distribution of funds. They meant to break the United Way's monopoly over workplace fundraising in order to make room for minority charities, which were not well represented and often involved in advocacy work. The National Committee spearheaded the creation of "alternative funds" and fought to gain access for them in workplace charitable drives, especially the Combined Federal Campaign, the annual charitable drive to raise money from federal employees.[33] As things stood, the United Way received about 70 percent of the money raised by the Combined Federal Campaign. National health agencies such as the Red Cross and the American Cancer Society, under an umbrella agency called National Health Agencies, got another 23 percent, and international organizations like CARE (under another umbrella organization called International Service Agencies) most of the rest. The campaign also collected money for a few other national organizations in the health and welfare fields. The Combined Federal Campaign raised $80 million in 1979 from 2.8 million federal employees.[34] With significant help from NCRP, the National Black United Fund, an umbrella organization of black charities brought suit in federal court over charities to be included in the CFC.[35] While the suit was in litigation, a congressional panel largely agreed with those critical of the campaign and called for Office of Personnel Management head Alan K. Campbell to change the criteria for inclusion, which he did.

A Pluralistic Sector

What was really needed was an umbrella organization with broad aims for the nonprofit sector as a whole. Institutional circumstances helped. In August 1978, two small organizations, the National Council on Philanthropy (NCOP) and the Coalition of Voluntary Sector Organizations

(CONVO), were in search of new CEOs. NCOP, an institution founded in Cleveland in 1954 as the Conference on Solicitations, changed its name in 1965 to signal its effort to provide "a national voice for the total field." Rockefeller had helped create CONVO in 1976 when it became clear that a public commission was not going to materialize. CONVO's mission was to assess emerging public needs and the extent to which the voluntary sector could meet them. The two organizations merged to form Independent Sector, which was chartered in March 1980.[36] Founding chairman Gardner chose Brian O'Connell, of the National Mental Health Association, as the first executive director.

After Rockefeller's death, Gardner had become the leading figure in the federative movement, and its most forceful proponent. As a long-time president of both the Carnegie Corporation and the Carnegie Foundation for the Advancement of Teaching, he knew the foundation world. He was a serious intellectual whose 1961 book *Excellence* helped shape the course of American education; in the subtitle, Gardner asked *Can We Be Equal and Excellent Too?* As President Johnson's Health, Education, and Welfare Secretary, he was responsible for many Great Society programs that required contracting with nonprofits. Head of the Urban Coalition in 1967, founder of Common Cause in 1970 (a grassroots organization pressing for peace in Vietnam, civil rights, voter participation, governmental accountability, and transparency), Gardner had no difficulty developing a broad vision for the sector. He felt that the nation would "suffer irreparable damage if it were to lose the tradition of private giving, lose the variety and vitality supplied by our wealth of voluntary associations."[37]

Striking a familiar note, Gardner wanted the federative institution to free the nonprofit sector from a "steadily increasing dependence on the federal government" and keep the government "rulebook" at a distance because, should the trend continue, "many of our voluntary institutions will be arms of government." Gardner insisted that the federation would not attempt "to bring order to a field whose tumultuous variety is its greatest source of creativity." He maintained that he did not want "to coordinate a sector that would break out in rebellion at the very thought of coordination." But at the same time, Gardner sought to bring together the different kinds of nonprofit organizations. He expressed his vision accurately when he said the sector was not to be an institution only for the traditional nonprofits but also "the natural home of non-majoritarian impulses, movements and values. It comfortably harbors innovators, maverick movements, groups which feel they must fight for their place in the sun, and critics of both liberal and conservative persuasion." Gardner saw the Independent Sector's vitality "rooted in good soil—civic pride, compassion, a philanthropic tradition, a strong problem-solving impulse, a sense of individual responsibility." Combining voluntarism and pluralism, it rested on "the habit of exercising private initiative for the public good" in an always expanding and diverse civil society.[38]

In the organizing drive for Independent Sector, Senator Daniel Patrick Moynihan, who followed its development closely, echoed the widely shared feeling that it was time for the independent sector to be independent again. Noting that in 1980 the government funded 50 percent of Catholic Charities' budget, Moynihan mused that "private institutions really aren't private anymore."[39] Moynihan and Gardner were quintessential "pluralists," to use the political language of the 1970s. Both had crossed party lines, Gardner as the only Republican in the Johnson cabinet; Moynihan, as a Democrat advising President Nixon and maintaining close ties to neoconservative circles. The two were committed to the goals (if not all of the methods) of the War on Poverty. In the 1970s, they drew their inspiration from the broad ideology of political pluralism rather than focusing on the tax code. Pluralism was a way to achieve unity through recognizing diversity, and the nonprofit sector was ideal terrain for turning that theory into action by bringing its disparate components together.

At the turn of the twentieth century, the Progressives resurrected James Madison's "Federalist 10" from oblivion to produce a theory of interest-group politics. Their work was widely read in the political science circles of the 1970s by scholars who formalized a new pluralist theory of American politics.[40] Moynihan, trained as a political scientist, applied their ideas to the nonprofit sector. Addressing Independent Sector, he underscored the fact that pluralists had "challenged both the absolute sovereignty of the individual and the absolute sovereignty of the corporate state. They argued that between the individual and the state were to be found a great array of social and economic entities, and that in the strength of these voluntary, private associations—church, family, club, trade union, commercial association—lay the chief strength of democratic society."[41]

One of the first and most consequential decisions of the new Independent Sector organization was to expand nonprofit sector boundaries by bringing church and secular charities under the same umbrella. A congregation was the model voluntary association, and religious toleration the best symbol of American pluralism. Churches were also quintessential tax-exempt organizations as, under the constitutional provision of separation of church and state, they did not have even a reporting requirement. Independent Sector, the older Council on Foundations (founded in the 1950s in the aftermath of the Cox investigation), and the Pew Charitable Trusts partnered in promoting mutual understanding between organized religion and institutionalized philanthropy. Considerable changes had taken place at Pew in the 1970s. In late 1972, the Pew Memorial Trust permitted Saint Luke's and Children's Medical Center to post a plaque acknowledging its gift, the first time the trust had dropped its policy of giving money only anonymously.[42] Now, in responding to the new federative effort, the trust completely lifted its veil of secrecy.

There were good reasons why the new philanthropic leaders attempted to bring the religious and the secular together. Churches had long been significant sources of social services for the poor, establishing missions to alleviate suffering in slums and poor communities across the country. Indeed, the Methodists had pioneered the Social Gospel early in the twentieth century, and the Social Gospel tradition remained very much alive in liberal churches that had embraced the Great Society, regardless of the commitment of the poor to religious conversion.

Independent Sector was correct in thinking that allying secular philanthropy with faith-based charities was an effective way of reinvigorating the field. With the Reagan administration wasting no time before cutting funding for social services, an alliance with churches was strategic for a nonprofit sector asserting itself. Even though donations to mainline denominations had been on the decline, churches still raised huge amounts of money, a part of which they redistributed in social services. Religious institutions were simultaneously recipients and donors of philanthropic money. Reviewing the work of 2,700 national and regional religious organizations that relied primarily on annual giving, the Council on Foundations found that nearly 50 percent were "donors." They acted "like foundations" by giving grants or loans "and doing much of it in ways that [were] blazing new trails for the philanthropic enterprise."[43]

Religious groups, in addition to making large outlays for feeding and sheltering the needy, were also "working for justice, human rights, and advocacy issues."[44] Even self-described conservative groups funded programs for social change. Other funding went to educational programs, health services, alcohol counseling, and housing. For example, the U.S. Catholic Conference had launched in 1969 a Campaign for Human Development to combat domestic poverty. A condition for funding that still applied in the 1980s was that members of the "poverty community" had to have the dominant voice in campaign-funded projects, which ran the gamut from reclamation of Indian land to education to basic infrastructure to loans to at-risk entrepreneurs. The same was true of the mainline Protestant denominations. The Coalition for Human Needs, a program of the national Episcopal Church, aimed at "outreach, social justice concerns, empowerment, and self determination" in communities across the country. The Self Development of People Fund of the United Presbyterian Church sought to effect "real changes" in "deprived and disadvantaged" communities." The United Church of Christ's Board of Homeland Ministries worked "on behalf of the overlooked persons of our society, our nation's rejects, those without advocates," such as homeless women or "bag ladies," the elderly, the handicapped, impoverished residents of Appalachia, Native Americans, and migrants. The Lutheran Church in America focused on minority economic projects and social justice issues. So did the United Methodist Church, committed as it was "to the needs of ethnic and language minorities, people in transitional relationships and those living under repressive systems."[45]

In turning to churches and their parishioners, Independent Sector wanted also to reinvigorate mass philanthropy, and this required strengthening volunteerism. O'Connell, the executive director, therefore commissioned a survey on volunteers in American society. He was pleased with the high level of participation the survey found. With volunteering broadly defined as "working in some way to help others for no monetary pay," 52 percent of all adults and 53 percent of all teenagers reported in 1981 having volunteered in the past year.[46] Five out of every six households in America contributed to one or more charitable organizations, 70 percent to a church or other religious organization, 28 percent to an educational group, 24 percent to a hospital, 67 percent to other health organizations, and 50 percent to other charities.[47]

The data on volunteering seemed to put to rest the dire predictions of the Filer Commission. But the level of giving remained a concern. As an estimated 85 percent of all charitable giving came from individuals earning less than $50,000, the organization attempted to reduce the price of giving for the mass of Americans with modest incomes.[48] Senators Moynihan and Robert Packwood (R-Oregon) had introduced legislation in Congress in 1978 to allow non-itemizers to claim charitable deductions on top of the standard deduction, again reiterating a Filer Commission recommendation. This so-called Charitable Contributions Legislation acquired renewed urgency when President Reagan lowered tax rates for the wealthy, thus reducing their incentive to give to charity. John Gardner, Brian O'Connell, Landrum Bolling (chairman of the Council on Foundations), and representatives of twenty-six 501(c)(3) organizations (the Red Cross, Marquette University, the Urban Coalition, the Nature Conservancy, the Council of Jewish Federations, and Goodwill Industries, among others) stressed deductibility as an incentive for small "entry-level donors."[49] Economist Martin Feldstein, who was soon to become Reagan's chief economic adviser, sided with them. Independent Sector lobbyists waited outside the Senate chamber on voting day. Colonel Ernie Miller of the Salvation Army and Mary Frances Peters of the Girl Scouts wore their uniforms so that there could be no doubts about the organizations they stood for.[50] Their bill became law in August 1981 and reality in 1982. The following year, the United Way experienced the greatest one-year giving increase in its history, 15 percent, and attributed much of it to the legislation. But the measure did sunset four years after passage.

Independent Sector had enough faith in its members and the worthiness of its cause that it stimulated the creation of a field of academic research on nonprofits. The idea was to create a body of knowledge about voluntary action and the nonprofit sector that philanthropy professionals, volunteers, the IRS, the Census Bureau, and the larger public could share. There were a number of precursors in this effort. The Association of Voluntary Action Scholars was founded in 1971 (renamed in 1989 the Association for Research on Nonprofit Organizations and Voluntary Action). Founded in 1971 as the Association of Voluntary Action Scholars, the Association for Research on Nonprofit Organizations and Voluntary Action (ARNOVA) is a neutral, open forum committed to strengthening the research community in the emerging field of nonprofit and philanthropic studies. The Yale Program on Non-Profit Organizations (PONPO) began work in 1978.[51]

Other universities followed Yale's lead by mobilizing experts from various disciplines and bringing them together. Columbia set up a University Seminar on philanthropy. Case Western University created a Center for Nonprofit Management, as did the Kennedy School, the City University of New York, and Duke. The Lilly Endowment was a major contributor to the Center on Philanthropy at Indiana University, founded in 1987. By creating the first fundraising school in the country, the center drew strength from the recent Supreme Court affirmation of charitable fundraising as an activity benefiting from First Amendment protection when advocating positions on matters of public concern.[52] Independent Sector made coordinating research efforts one of its major tasks and took over the management of the National Center for Charitable Statistics (NCCS), a program founded in 1980 by the National Charities Information Bureau and the United Way. These research efforts integrated studies of the nonprofit sector in economics, political science, sociology, and history.

An Alternative Nonprofit Federation

What the pluralists had not anticipated was that they were not alone in their desire to boost an independent sector and give new life to civil society. Conservatives wanted a voluntary society too, but on a radically different basis—uncompromised by government-funded programs. Many of them saw personal behavior as the cause of poverty and the welfare state as the source of dependency. As a group, conservatives felt they could develop their own network of nonprofit institutions to promote their program and perhaps seize the national agenda. The apparent leftward drift of the Nixon White House proved the catalyst for their action. While the likes of the Donee group feared that Nixon's New Federalism would undermine nonprofits, conservatives saw the administration's support of the welfare state as only more proof that policymakers were stuck in the grasp of the liberal nonprofits.[53] The solution was to separate real conservatives from pragmatic Republicans.

Lewis Powell, a Richmond, Virginia corporate lawyer soon to be President Nixon's nominee to the U.S. Supreme Court, was among the first personalities to promote an open confrontation with what Irving Kristol called the "new class" of liberal elites who controlled federal bureaucracies, nonprofit institutions, universities, the media, and the philanthropic dollars that supported many of them and their projects.[54] In a 1971 memo he drafted for the U.S. Chamber of Commerce, Powell argued that the American economic system was under "broad attack" by leftist extremists. Addressing businessmen, he predicted that corporate philanthropy would play a larger role in the future and pointed out to them that by giving to existing philanthropies they were all too often funding their "own destruction." Powell urged the business community to rally to its own defense by using the Chamber of Commerce as the focal point of long-term efforts to cultivate confidence in free-market institutions rather than the mixed political economy that the liberal foundations were pushing. In perhaps the most forceful espousal of philanthropy's role in the conservative movement, Wall Street financier and Nixon and Ford Treasury Secretary William E. Simon, in a change of face—he had earlier helped John D. Rockefeller III establish the Filer commission and push for tax reform to help philanthropy—called for alternative civil institutions that would support a new counter-intelligentsia comprised of all those opposed to the egalitarian ethic and collectivist ethos that fed the welfare state and undermined individualism and liberty. Powell, Kristol and Simon believed that a "massive and unprecedented mobilization" (Simon's words) was needed, intellectually and financially, to come to the aid of liberty.[55]

Their ideas resonated beyond conservative circles. At the Ford Foundation, the founding institution of Great Society federalism, Henry Ford II had until then persisted in his defense of liberal programs. But Ford resigned from the foundation board in 1977, declaring he had had enough of an institution that had lost respect for capitalism. As he departed, he declared, "The Foundation is a creature of capitalism, a statement that, I am sure, would be shocking to many professional staff people in the field of philanthropy. It is hard to discern recognition of this fact in anything the Foundation does. It is even more difficult to find an understanding of this in many of the institutions, particularly the universities that are the beneficiaries of the Foundation's grant programs."[56] In reacting to Ford's resignation statement, Kristol urged the readers of his column in the *Wall Street Journal* to consider their own interests and those of their shareholders when giving to various causes. "Corporate philanthropy," he wrote, "should not be, cannot be, disinterested."[57]

In the name of saving small government, the conservative coalition succeeded in turning their own charitable dollars into the engine of a powerful new political movement aimed at defunding the left and placing the newly formed "third sector" on notice. While the Donee Group was urging a more vocal role for nonprofit groups sparked by Great Society funding, the conservative coalition sought instead to cut state aid to nonprofit institutions invested in welfare, social advocacy, and minority rights. If the government's funding of extensive social services was the problem, then breaking up the mixed political economy that delivered those services was the solution.

The weapon the conservative coalition chose was the nonprofit think tank. Philanthropists regularly funded think tanks (independent tax-exempt nonprofit organizations that analyze public policy, conduct empirical studies, and formulate key policy positions). It was progressive reformers who had come up with the think tank concept early in the century as a way to champion governmental administrative and budgetary reforms at one step removed from partisan politics.[58] The Brookings Institution, founded in 1916, is a prominent example. Their aim was to end the corruption of political machines and put politicians who accepted bribes behind bars. Now conservatives were using their own think tanks in an effort to defund the left.[59] They successfully waged campaigns to reduce the budgets of welfare programs and restrict nonprofits' access to the remaining funds.

The number of conservative think tanks grew, and they became more powerful. Among the think tanks already dedicated to articulating a vision of free-market economics was the American Enterprise Association, founded in 1938 by a group of businessmen to promote free and competitive enterprise. During the 1950s, the American Enterprise Association expanded under the direction of William J. Baroody, Sr., a former economist for the U.S. Chamber of Commerce. Baroody cultivated relationships with corporate donors. He brought in economists Milton Friedman and Paul McCracken to help the organization fight the liberal "monopoly of ideas" in public policy.[60] But despite its roots, the American Enterprise Institute (renamed in 1961) had become politically cautious after the IRS investigated the organization for supporting Goldwater in 1964.[61]

Other pioneers of conservative philanthropy were the Smith Richardson Foundation, the John M. Olin foundation, and the Lynde and Harry Bradley Foundation. H. Smith Richardson (who inherited money from the chemical industry) started his foundation in 1935 and became an early supporter of the American Enterprise Institute. The foundation continued to fund conservative causes after Richardson's death in 1972. Munitions manufacturer John M. Olin created a foundation to support the conservative political agenda in 1953.[62] The Bradley Foundation originated as a local foundation in Milwaukee, Wisconsin in 1942, but grew immensely in 1985 when the Allen-Bradley Company was sold to Rockwell International, bringing the foundation's assets to nearly

$300 million. The deal helped make the foundation among the nation's twenty wealthiest and invigorated its mission to "de-utopianize political thinking."[63]

Among philanthropic newcomers, Richard Mellon Scaife, an heir to the Mellon fortune, became known as the "mystery angel" of the new right. Scaife redirected the Sarah Mellon Scaife Foundation away from his sister's focus on population issues and the arts and towards the new conservative agenda.[64] John D. MacArthur, head of Bankers Life and Casualty Co., died at the age of 80 in 1978 after donating his fortune to a foundation bearing his and his wife Catherine's name. Catherine expressed their wish that the foundation follow a different course from that of the internationalist, liberal-oriented philanthropy of Ford, Rockefeller, and Carnegie. They were not East-coast liberals but "a bunch of Midwestern businessmen devoted to free enterprise and opposed to more government controls," to quote Robert T. Ewing, one of the Bankers Life officials who directed the foundation.[65]

These foundations supported the think tanks that helped usher in the Republican ascendancy of 1980. They were remarkably successful at evading legal restrictions on funding political advocacy and made clever use of accounting tricks such as funding the basic administrative expenses of think tanks rather than programs the IRS could label politically controversial.[66] The most important of these new think tanks was the Heritage Foundation.[67] Its forebears were Edwin J. Feulner, who served on the staff of Illinois Republican Congressman Phillip R. Crane, and Paul Weyrich, press secretary for Senator Gordon Alcott of Colorado and the man who coined the phrase "new right." In 1971 they came up with the plan to form a new policy research center that would not be afraid to jump into policy debates when it mattered. They received a founding donation from Joseph Coors, who was "stirred" to action by the memorandum Powell had written for the Chamber of Commerce.[68] Richard Scaife helped transform the small research organization into the Heritage Foundation. In 1977, its budget was $2 million. It grew to $10 million in 1983 and $18 million in 1989, with corporate giving coming from GE, Kraft, Ford, Procter and Gamble, and GM.[69] The American Enterprise Institute also grew exponentially in the 1970s.[70]

Heritage and the new cadre of conservative nonprofits did not benefit just from the largesse of foundations. They relied also on donations from the many small, individual donors who funded the conservative movement, especially as it linked causes with high emotional content such as outlawing abortion, ending affirmative action, allowing prayer in public schools, with that of the free market. Richard Viguerie, executive secretary of Young Americans for Freedom and a fundraiser for George Wallace, helped secure funds from ordinary Americans by being among the first to use the computer effectively for mass mailing.[71] Donations of $25 to $50 to the Heritage Foundation accounted for as much as 40 percent of its annual budget.[72]

The conservative think tanks' strategies worked well. They focused on promoting a few key ideas and policy proposals for a retrenched government, social and legal conservatism, and the preservation of free market capitalism.[73] They objected, with some justice, to liberal and progressive nonprofits using government contract funds to lobby for ever greater government activity. At the Columbia University Seminar, whose members came primarily from the pluralist network, Michael Joyce of the Olin Foundation took on the left for pressuring unelected administrators in agencies with money to disburse, thus using "extra-political means" to achieve their political goals in an undemocratic way.[74]

At first the Treasury department objected to some conservatives' misuse of their tax-exempt status. The IRS tried in 1978 to strip independent Christian schools of their exemption because they were racially segregated. Conservative Christians saw the IRS action as evidence they had to organize for an offensive political battle. Weyrich and Howard Phillips, head of the Conservative Caucus, worked with Christian leaders Jerry Falwell and Robert Billings to found the Moral Majority (Weyrich also claimed credit for that phrase) and the National Christian Action Coalition. They campaigned for tax-exempt donations to spare poor white children from the "intolerable and repugnant 'other schools.'"[75]

By the early 1980s, conservative think tanks had entered a new era of influence, thanks to their receptive audience in the Reagan White House. It was the pluralists who were now on the defensive. Heritage delivered *Mandate for Leadership: Policy Management in a Conservative Administration*, which was a blueprint for conservative governing (tax cuts, missile defense, etc.) that influenced the new administration.[76] Michael Joyce of the Olin Foundation was on the president-elect's transition team. The Committee to Defund the Left and the Conservative Caucus complained that nonprofit groups that received funds were often against Reagan policies. Heritage explicitly recommended that "a conservative administration ought not to be funding organizations that might actively oppose its political agenda."[77] As part of the strategy to defund the left, the network of conservative philanthropy dedicated part of its resources to spreading its message on college campuses. It funded thirty conservative campus newspapers (called the Collegiate Network) to help campaign for conservative ideas and policies and recruit among young conservatives. Conservative foundations refused to join the liberal Council of Foundations, which they denounced for "politicizing philanthropy" (as if they were not), and formed their own Philanthropy Roundtable in 1987.[78] Funding came from fourteen conservative foundations including the familiar Lynde and Harry Bradley Foundation, the John M. Olin Foundation, the Scaife Family Foundation, and the Smith Richardson Foundation.

Conservatives were also successful in taking money away from the left. The Reagan White House halted a long-term trend of increased funding for social services. In 1986, nonprofit organizations received as much money as they had received in 1980, which in real terms meant a 25 to 30 percent decline in federal support, a shortfall that the states did not make up.[79] Tax cuts for the wealthy, which reduced the incentive for giving, caused further problems for nonprofits. The pluralist network panicked as soon as President Reagan started cutting the budget in 1981. Independent Sector estimated that giving would be $18.3 billion less over the next four years. A study it commissioned predicted that 15 percent of taxpayers with the highest incomes, who made 44 percent of all individual charitable contributions in 1978, would be responsible for the drop. As a result, educational, medical, and cultural institutions, which get a large portion of their support from the wealthy, would bear the brunt of these reductions. An Office of Management and Budget report projected that for nonprofits to maintain their existing revenues in 1982, offsetting both inflation and losses in public funding, they would need a 25.6 percent increase in support over that of 1981. Broken down by area, private giving for philanthropy needed to increase by 61.3 percent for social welfare groups, 17 percent for education, 12 percent for health, 11 percent for international programs, and 11 percent for the arts. All told, private giving would have to increase 144 percent between 1980 and 1984 (four times faster than it did between 1977 and 1980) to make up for inflation and lost revenues.[80]

But rather than fund social services through nonprofits, the Reagan administration moved towards giving tax breaks to the middle class for the purchase of social services. This accelerated a trend to help the middle class rather than the poor, a tactic already seen under Nixon's New Federalism. For daycare, federal spending dropped from $2.7 billion in 1980 to $2 billion in 1987. Meanwhile, the tax credit for child- and dependent-care expenses increased more than 400 percent after adjusting for inflation.[81] The same logic of extending government benefits beyond the poor applied to school vouchers. The only silver lining for liberals, though it was not immediately apparent, was that a concomitant downsizing of the federal workforce made nonprofit organizations more valuable in delivering essential services. Conservatives were less successful than appeared at first glance in their uncoupling of government and liberal philanthropy.

As a response to this coordinated attack, Independent Sector focused on keeping the federal government money flowing. The pluralist network, which had begun as an attempt to keep civil society independent from government, was now fighting to maintain government-paid services. It was counterproductive, O'Connell told anyone in Congress who cared to listen, to think that civil society could foot the government's bill. There was "a total lack of appreciation of the size of private giving." The more realistic assessment, he insisted, was that if "we overload voluntary organizations with the basic responsibility for services, undercut their income and limit their role for advocacy and criticism, they will fail us and we will be at another point of national breakdown when people will demand that government do it all."[82] Thus a way to achieve the conservative agenda was to fund nonprofit organizations dedicated to liberal social causes!

O'Connell continued this battle into the 1990s after George H. W. Bush issued his Points of Light initiative asking all Americans to contribute to the common good. "From now on in America, any successful definition of a successful life must include serving others," said Bush.[83] But "points of light" could not replace government funding when nonprofit institutions were receiving 60 percent of their income from the government in social services, 40 percent in community development and civic and organizational activities, and one third in health services.[84] To make his case, O'Connell invoked Reinhold Niebuhr's Depression-era pronouncement: "The effort to try to make voluntary charity solve the problem of major social crises . . . results only in monumental hypocrisies."[85] What was true in Hoover's days of Depression was now true in the midst of a stable economy. The nonprofit sector was never meant to be a substitute for the welfare state.

How the Pluralist and Conservative Networks Converged

It was hard to imagine the pluralist-liberal and conservative coalitions ever finding common ground, and yet their engagement with religious groups led to an unexpected convergence in which both could be seen as favoring government-sponsored faith-based organizations. Conservative groups came to compete for government support with their liberal adversaries.

Independent Sector had built on the Social Gospel and the civil rights tradition of the more liberal churches to extend the work of the Great Society. The conservative network, on the other hand, had initially relied on evangelical churches to dismantle the Great Society. For conservative Christians, there should be no confusion between the kingdom of God and the kingdom on earth. But now conservative politicians in the White House and Congress wanted to fund conservative churches to help fight the liberals, and some of these churches wanted their share of the federal pie. In the 1980s the Supreme Court helped dramatically in bringing the two nonprofit networks closer together. It was not of course a matter of welding a common ideology but rather of facilitating access to federal funding for faith-based organizations of both persuasions. The convergence was neither party's intent.

If conservative churches were to have an influence over the larger population, they too needed federal funds for family counseling, help for the homeless, and indeed the whole range of Great Society subsidized activities so as to cast them in their own religious mold, delivering these services in the interests of moral regeneration. After years of trying to limit federal funding to nonprofits, the conservatives changed tactics and looked for ways to increase federal funding to their own nonprofits. The best way for a conservative administration to serve this constituency was to fund conservative churches' outreach programs. Marvin Olasky argued in *The Tragedy of American Compassion*, a book he wrote during a fellowship at the Heritage Foundation in 1990, that offering material aid without attempting to reform the soul debased individuals and increased dependency. Olasky told the story of posing as a homeless man for two days and visiting various social service agencies where he was provided only material help. "There was one thing I did not get, even though I asked for it many times," Olasky reported, "a Bible."[86] The volunteers working at these institutions may have been nice, he reflected, but they were not compassionate. Olasky influenced Texas Governor and then President George W. Bush's agenda for funding faith-based charities, as well as Speaker Newt Gingrich's "Contract with America."

Was it constitutionally possible under the strictures of the separation of church and state to extend federal funding to evangelical programs? The wall that Jefferson had envisioned between the state and religion had in fact often been breached. Churches had long been recipients of both state and federal government money. But the courts, in interpreting the First Amendment, had traditionally made an important distinction between funding services that benefited the poor, the sick, and the young through church programs at home and abroad, and funding the churches themselves. At times, churches had to set up independent secular organizations to receive government money, but most of the time they did not. If the church served only as an intermediary to the recipient without imposing a religious condition, a government program was not seen as violating the First Amendment.

The battle over compassion in America revolved around federal intervention in church affairs. With the conservative coalition gaining strength in the 1980s, the Rehnquist Court pushed an increasingly permissive doctrine in state-church relations: to bar religious groups from receiving funds merely on the assumption that they might proselytize was a violation of equal rights; government could therefore support religious-based organizations so long as the funded activity appeared religiously neutral.

This was the start of the "charitable choice" idea. The debate took a definitive turn in a court case over the 1983 Adolescent Family Life Act, which authorized federal funds for teen pregnancy counseling and other educational programs, and which specifically allowed religious providers to participate. The ACLU, objecting to conservative churches using taxpayer money for teaching abstinence to adolescents as part of a larger religious education, filed a lawsuit on behalf of a group of liberal clergy, taxpayers, and the American Jewish Congress. When *Bowen v. Kendrick* reached the Supreme Court in 1988, the Court ruled that the law was "neutral on its face" towards religion and not unconstitutional. The religious groups were just one category of a long list of eligible providers. The court thus rejected the automatic presumption that financial aid to a religious institution would necessarily result in a constitutional violation.[87] The more permissible neutrality doctrine gained ground over the previous separation doctrine. Potential challengers had to show that aid was actually used to advance religion, not that it could be.

Bowen gave drafters of charitable choice legislation the precedent they needed to proceed with a broader government-religion partnership in social services. Conservative and liberals were divided no longer on the issue of whether social services could be funded through religious institutions, but only on the extent to which so-called "pervasively sectarian" institutions should exclude proselytizing when delivering state-funded services to the poor, and on ways in which to ensure fair treatment of recipients. The Welfare Reform Act of 1996 included a section commonly known as "charitable choice," championed by then-Senator John Ashcroft. The clause mandated that if states employed nonprofits to deliver federally funded social services, then they must treat religious organizations as "eligible contractees."[88] Furthermore, states could not require religious organizations *not* to use faith as a criterion for hiring decisions, nor would those organizations have to remove religious icons or symbols from their facilities. The provision did prohibit faith-based organizations from explicitly proselytizing or discriminating against recipients, and did mandate that clients be provided alternative secular services upon request.

The measure was in effect bipartisan. President Clinton signed it into law as part of welfare reform. Vice President Gore saw in it a "new era of civil society collaboration."[89] Both Gore and Bush supported versions of faith-based funding in the 2000 presidential campaign. Gore was more vocal about pluralism and the need for church-state safeguards. Bush instead promised to "look first" to faith-based groups to "rally the armies of compassion."[90]

In Bush's view, the alliance was absolutely necessary, for government can only spend money, "it cannot put hope in our hearts or a sense of purpose in our lives. That is done in churches and synagogues and mosques and charities that warm the cold of life."[91] Once in the White House, Bush created the Office of Faith-Based and Community Initiatives. He intended faith-based initiatives to appeal to the evangelical bloc, which was not traditionally inclined to provide social services, but he did not get as strong a response as he had hoped. To liberal churches, faith-based initiatives were merely an extension of their Social Gospel alliances with governments. But those evangelicals who insisted on converting the poor wanted no strings attached to government money. Echoing Olasky, they maintained that delivering services like job-training and drug rehab without actual conversion only attacks the symptoms of the problem and not the primary cause—that being sin. Despite these qualms, many conservative churches eventually jumped on the federal bandwagon, providing social services that the Great Society had initially extended to the nonprofit sector. The new welfare law erased much of the hard distinction between the religious and the secular that had heretofore prevailed, thus granting legitimacy to the idea of a vast contracting economy of social services involving all levels of government, and a nonprofit sector transcending the division between church and state.

The larger purpose of opening the nonprofit sector to political advocacy and lobbying was also achieved in the late twentieth century. In violation of the tax laws, conservative philanthropies went on funding the political agenda that was transforming America, and again the Supreme Court supported them. The court implemented a significant relaxing of the lobbying rules that both the Treasury Department and the Office of Management and Budget had previously maintained.[92] Conservatives were committed to two contradictory campaigns—one to extend the influence of their views by loosening restrictions on lobbying, and the other to limit the influence of liberals by making lobbying more restrictive. At the big liberal foundations that had been chastised in 1969, most still preferred to play it safe. Embree's "timid billions" had returned. Science provided them with a large and seemingly unending field of funding possibilities.

Inconsistent measures only reflected policymakers' confusion over the changing place of the nonprofit sector in the American political economy. The few liberal nonprofits involved in political advocacy remained under the close supervision of the executive branch. As a result of an investigation into Planned Parenthood and growing pressure from conservatives to check the political influence of government nonprofit contractors, counsel for the Office of Management and Budget proposed in 1983 new regulations to curb the use of federal funds in political advocacy. The Office of Management and Budget revised its Circular A-122, *Cost Principles for Nonprofit Organizations*, an accounting guideline the Carter Administration had created in 1980. The proposed rules not only barred any use of federal money for lobbying but defined lobbying so broadly as to include the routine exchange of technical information with legislators (even long before a legislator envisioned introducing a related bill) and endorsed an equally broad definition of grassroots lobbying. Zeal backfired as the proposed regulations went so far beyond the old 1934 IRS substantial rule as to endanger First-

Amendment rights. Opposition came from a diverse group of mainline charities. Whether involved in advocacy or not, they opposed having to comply with two sets of overlapping rules coming one from the Internal Revenue Service and the other from the Office of Management and Budget. With the White House registering intense protest across the board from the Red Cross, the U.S. Chamber of Commerce, the National Association of Manufacturers, and the American Civil Liberties Union, the Office of Management and Budget withdrew the proposed rules at the behest of Chief of Staff James Baker.[93]

Meanwhile Congress had already recognized in 1976 the arbitrariness of the old "substantial" test (see chapter 3) and substituted a percentage option: an exempt organization could elect legally to devote a portion of its budget to lobbying, provided it registered with the IRS first. In technical terms, a 501(c)(3) could become a 501(c)(3) H. The H election rules were very specific and set lobbying limits according to two sliding scales keyed to the size of an organization, one for lobbying legislators, the other for grassroots lobbying. But the IRS let ten years go by before implementing regulations for administering the law. Therefore few charities elected to use H rules during those years, mostly because of uncertainty over what it meant to "influence legislation" and what constituted grassroots lobbying. When the IRS finally issued rules, they were so stringent that they again generated an intense counterattack from Independent Sector. In 1988, the IRS heeded criticism from charities and their allies in Congress and offered a new proposal that defined grassroots lobbying in much more specific terms, which were adopted in 1990.[94] This time, the compromise measures prompted a Treasury official to complain that activities that had to be counted as lobbying expenditures were so few that "there was nothing left that's lobbying."[95] The door was open for nonprofits to assert their political voice. Still, in 2003, only 2.5 percent of nonprofits operated under the 501(c)(3) H rules, the remainder of the sector being still governed by the old "substantial" test.[96]

The main reason for not shifting to the H legislation was that the Supreme Court had meanwhile provided a much easier route to lobbying. Though most charities continued to operate under the original 1934 guidelines, new legal developments in the 1980s created much greater space for well-organized nonprofits to lobby. A most notable case was the 1983 U.S. Supreme Court decision in *Regan v. Taxation with Representation*. Taxation with Representation, founded in 1970, was a liberal group dedicated to fighting tax loopholes for corporations and the wealthy and backing tax legislation that would serve the "public interest" rather than "special interests." It was similar to Ralph Nader's Tax Reform Research Group.[97] In technical terms again, the organization received IRS recognition as a 501(c)(4) organization, that is a tax-exempt civic league but one not eligible to receive tax-exempt donations, a privilege that only a 501(c)(3) enjoyed. Taxation with Representation applied to be recognized as a 501(c)(3) but was denied by the IRS in 1974 because of its lobbying activities. After protracted negotiations and several organizational changes that failed to assuage the IRS, Taxation with Representation challenged it in 1977, claiming violation of free speech and equal rights. The case reached the Supreme Court.

While the Court upheld the lobbying restrictions on 501(c)(3)s, it also opened the door for charities to accomplish their same lobbying goals by recognizing 501(c)(4) organizations as legitimate additions to the 501(c)(3)s. The 501(c)(4)s could lobby and be tax exempt, serving essentially as alter egos of the 501(c)(3)s, except that they could not receive tax-exempt contributions or use any 501(c)(3) money for lobbying. Previously, the IRS had wanted to keep 501(c)(3)s and 501(c)(4)s much more separate, but the court essentially changed that. The IRS modified its guidelines in the 1980s to conform to the court decision. The IRS allowed full control of a 501(c)(4) organization by a 501(c)(3) organization and unlimited lobbying by the 501(c)(4) so long as it was related to its social welfare purpose.[98]

Consistent with the well-established distinction between private foundations (usually funded from a single source) and public charities (always funded from multiple sources), the law barring political activity remained unchanged for private foundations, but there too lines were blurred as conservative foundations had been involved for two decades in funding think tanks with openly political agendas. In this new climate, the Pew Charitable Trusts, one of the largest American foundations, resorted to a technicality in the tax code to change its status from a private foundation to a public charity, all the while trumpeting that it was seeking the change to engage openly in advocacy work and that this was the best route to achieve that goal. In 2004, the trust, which had actually distanced itself from its conservative origins and become a pluralistic foundation, received authorization from both the Pennsylvania Attorney General and the IRS for the change—to many observers' amazement. Because its endowment originated from seven different family trusts rather than a single one, the foundation argued successfully that it received its funds from diverse origins and therefore met the basic requirement of a public charity, a status it would easily keep by raising money annually to enlarge its endowment. A large private foundation, which for a long time had insisted on anonymous giving, still closely monitored by heirs of the original donors, successfully manipulated the rules—claiming its several trust funds as the source of its diversity—to become a public charity and lobby.

The only serious limitation that remains to the political activities of nonprofits is their being barred from entering electoral contests. Many cross even that line under the old guise of educational campaigns, and the legal environment is making it easier for them to do so. It is too early to gauge the long-term impact the 2010 Supreme Court decision, *Citizens United v. Federal Election Commission*, will have on nonprofits.[99] In this decision, the court has removed spending limits on corporations and labor unions to fund candidates for public office. This was the outcome of a suit a conservative nonprofit group, which produced a movie during the 2008 presidential primaries attacking then-Senator Hillary Clinton, initiated against the Federal Election Commission.[100] Shortly after the court decision, the fall 2010 campaign for midterm elections generated much new money, some of which donors channeled through nonprofits. The new rules also make it easier for donors to hide their identity, a disturbing fact that has occasioned much debate.

The nonprofit sector has come of age. The Supreme Court's decisions, first allowing churches openly to combine their religious and social work even when using federal funds, and then opening up alternative channels of advocacy work for charities, have made the nonprofit sector the institutional voice of American civil society. By formally declaring churches eligible for federal funds, the court made room for religious belief in a previously secular partnership between nonprofit action and the government. And by giving nonprofit organizations more significant means to lobby, the court put an end to the artificial divide between education and advocacy that had prevailed for so long. The court therefore recognized a level of advocacy, whether religious or political, as a necessary condition of freedom in a strong democracy. Conservatives and liberals, individually and collectively, made nonprofits worthy substitutes for the associations Tocqueville had heralded as engines of American liberty.

CHAPTER 9

American Philanthropy and the World's Communities

During the Cold War, when America's national objective was to combat communism, philanthropic institutions tended to align their activities abroad with those of their government. When finally free from Cold War commitments, they joined an unstable but powerful associational movement that has reshaped civil society in many parts of the world.[1] The collapse of the Soviet Union and the loosening of its grip on its client nations freed voluntary energies in many parts of the world. It reawakened as well the possibilities of a market economy and free associations in places where these had been repressed.[2] American philanthropies therefore saw opportunities to promote capitalism and civil society as engines of democracy.

Whether the task was long-term poverty reduction or humanitarian intervention, philanthropic institutions have assisted in laying the foundations for stable civil societies. They have helped international nongovernmental organizations (INGOs) originating in rich countries reach populations in need, and they have fostered the emergence of indigenous nongovernmental organizations (NGOs) throughout the developing world. This is an important contribution, perhaps on a par with the open-ended philanthropy of a century ago and with the consolidation of the nonprofit sector at midcentury.

The Ethiopian Famine as a New Departure for
International Humanitarian Aid

No case study perfectly illustrates how the humanitarian movement fostered the advent of a global civil society, but the mass philanthropic response to the 1984 Ethiopian famine gives a sense of how the world could mobilize for disaster relief and of Americans' special role in that particular effort. The Ethiopian rescue played a major role in promoting the idea that humanitarianism should cross borders and transcend politics. The French group Doctors Without Borders made the case forcefully, contravening traditional Red Cross policy of respecting an individual nation's prerogatives with their actions in Biafra in 1968; other NGOs reaffirmed cross-border humanitarianism in Laos, Cambodia and Thailand. Some American aid workers had already rebelled against serving as an extension of American propaganda during the Vietnam War (the "shirtsleeve war" of civilian good works, as Vice President Hubert Humphrey called it) and even crossed to the North in ways unthinkable in previous conflicts. But the new efforts for Ethiopia went far beyond such limited displays of independence towards governments in the name of humanitarianism. For American philanthropy, the Ethiopian emergency was the occasion for nonprofits to trump cold war dynamics and act independently from the administration. In joining global efforts to end the famine, philanthropy claimed its independence from foreign policy.

Ethiopian peasants have endured recurrent famines, but that of 1972–74 was especially severe. Merchants and rich landlords hoarded grain from good harvests in parts of the country. Peasants left the land. Students and workers demonstrated against the imperial government in the capital. But Emperor Haile Selassie persisted in denying the reality of the famine even as conditions worsened amidst secessionist wars in Eritrea and peasant revolts that made agricultural activity impossible in northern and southeastern Ethiopia.[3] Although Ethiopia had been a major center of American aid during the early Cold War (see chapter 6), Washington later kept its distance from an increasingly alien regime. The U.S. Congress approved some emergency supplies after much political wrangling, but little was ever delivered to the starving population.

The imperial government's failure to prevent 600,000 deaths led to the military revolution of 1974. A Coordinating Committee of the Armed Forces, Police, and Territorial Army, known as the Derg, took power and eventually elected Major Mengistu Haile Mariam as its chair. His All-Ethiopian Socialist Movement and its Worker's Party of Ethiopia nationalized all land and redistributed it to peasant associations, which were instructed to turn the harvest over to state-sponsored cooperatives.[4]

In reflecting on these events in Ethiopia, Indian economist (and Nobel Prize winner) Amartya Sen showed the deprivation to have been as much the outcome of food withheld as of real scarcity.[5] Sen saw communal development as a means of overcoming the inequity of government distribution, but the U.S. government had no incentive to directly help local Ethiopian communities. Despite disturbing evidence that the socialist regime was guilty of grave human rights violations, a new administration in Washington was briefly open to working with the Ethiopian regime's Relief and Rehabilitation Commission.[6] The U.S. funded road construction, resettlement projects, and early-warning systems for famine, but the revolutionary government was suspicious of U.S. activities, believing that they were covert operations to thwart the revolution. It permitted U.S. humanitarian operations to continue, but it tried to direct those programs towards bolstering its own power. The military government harassed U.S. Agency for International Development (USAID) workers, limited their operations, and failed to provide an accounting for U.S. relief dollars and for those raised through the sale of U.S. food items.[7] Reacting to the collectivization program, political repression, and uncooperative action, the Carter administration rapidly reverted to the older policy of limiting U.S. assistance to immediate famine relief. Wary of doing too much to support the new Provisional Military Administrative Council while other armed groups actively opposed it, U.S. policy had reached an impasse.

The U.S. government continued some humanitarian relief aid but did its best to ensure that it was no longer used for long-term initiatives. In July 1979, President Carter suspended official development assistance to Ethiopia and also opposed multilateral loans from the World Bank and African Development Bank.[8] Soon, no Western aid infrastructure capable of even short-term humanitarian aid was left in Ethiopia. This eventually created conditions that called for a completely new approach from international philanthropy.

The political situation was steadily deteriorating, especially in the embattled provinces of Eritrea, Tigray, and Wollo, and the Derg was able to suppress a Somali-funded secession movement, which emerged in Ogaden in the west, only after receiving large military aid from the Soviet Union.[9] At the same time, the revolutionary government carried out massive population transfers, moving people from drought-affected regions in the north to the more fertile, less densely populated areas of the south and southwest. The motive was in part to depopulate the rebellious North. The populations of entire villages were loaded onto convoys of trucks and buses, escorted by soldiers and local peasant militias. Resettlement involved clearing land for new villages, decimating tree cover and essential vegetation, and devastating wildlife. In addition, northern farmers brought with them their techniques of slash and burn farming, which further damaged the landscape. The ultimate result of the resettlement was a radical reduction in levels of agricultural production. Concentrating rural population in villages in hopes of encouraging a more collectivized society further lessened productivity. Continued warfare and new insurrections in the north, combined with poor rains and harvests, intensified famine conditions and led to the largest campaigns of forced migration ever in African history.[10]

Reluctant to send provisions directly to Ethiopia, the Reagan administration in 1983 channeled only 4,000 tons of badly needed food through Catholic Relief Services, and another 1,500 tons to Ethiopian refugees in Sudan. By comparison, the Soviet Union, which was a food importer itself, donated 9,000 tons of food in June 1983 alone.[11] The U.S. then cut its food assistance commitment to zero for fiscal year 1984 by ending its appropriation to Catholic Relief Services. The administration's difficulties with anti-American rhetoric in multilateral organizations compounded the problem. When a new Ethiopian famine that began in 1983 made headlines in the fall of 1984, tensions between the U.S. government and the U.N. were running high. In 1985 the United States withdrew from UNESCO, where anti-American feelings were also rampant, and cut its aid drastically to the World Bank's International Development Agency, the primary funder of development projects.[12] As a result, what little Western help was given to Ethiopia, which was again experiencing famine, came from the U.N. World Food Program and from the European Community, despite their doubts about the Ethiopian government's willingness to distribute it.

Then events took a turn so dramatic that it unleashed a worldwide humanitarian movement. The BBC filmed the famine, and the world discovered it. In October 1984, viewers in America and many other countries saw their first footage of starving Ethiopians on the evening news. By that time, it was estimated that between 10 and 12 million people (out of a population of 42 million) were starving or on the verge of starvation. This catastrophe coincided with the tenth anniversary of the socialist revolution, which the regime celebrated lavishly in Addis-Ababa, willfully ignoring the human disaster around it.[13] While Ethiopian officials engaged in ceremonial self-congratulation, an estimated 400 million viewers across sixty countries watched the broadcast of the July 1985 Live Aid rock concert held simultaneously in London and Philadelphia to raise money for the famine. Other benefit concerts took place around the world. Michael Jackson's fundraising song "We Are the World" was the number one hit song of 1985.[14]

This intervention to lessen the severity of the Ethiopian famine marked an important moment in the growth of the global humanitarian movement. For Americans, there was a special added dimension. They were knowingly supporting a humanitarian cause in a country the U.S. government had declared off limits. By October 1984, there were only four American agencies left in Ethiopia: the American Friends Service Committee, World Vision, the Mennonite Central Committee, and Catholic Relief Services. Twelve European agencies were also operating, but they were limited in their resources and ability to intervene. But

once the news of the famine broke on the international scene, aid workers rushed to Addis Ababa. Catholic Relief Services and the Lutheran
World Federation, along with local Catholic and Lutheran churches,
organized a new group (Churches Drought Action-Ethiopia) to coordinate the work of all agencies and avoid duplicate overhead costs. By
March of 1985, thirty additional agencies had arrived from different
countries and were working through the new Catholic Relief Services/
Lutheran World Federation unit.[15]

These organizations relied heavily on massive fundraising from all
possible donors: individual governments, international organizations,
and the broad public touched by media reports of the magnitude of the
famine. They distributed 20,000 tons of food to two million people each
month. They raised between $50 and $80 million in six months, an unprecedented total. The average donation was $40.[16] CARE negotiated a
contract with the Ethiopian government to provide 50,000 tons of food
and $10 million in other forms of assistance.[17] INGOs received a wind-
fall of donations that allowed their Ethiopian programs to grow by huge
margins. World Vision's total allocation in 1984 was $7 million. Be-
tween November 1984 and October 1985, it had allocated $25 million
in cash and $40 million in food commodities.[18] American donors, big
and small, embraced the universalistic mission the INGOs promoted
of stopping mass hunger, and in so doing they trumped late Cold War
political divisions.

With the broad American public supporting INGOs in Ethiopia,
the Reagan administration changed course. Responding to public sentiment and the philanthropic activity that signaled it, the administration
approved $45 million for USAID to buy and transport 80,000 metric
tons of food, all of which was to be delivered only to INGOs. Shortly
after, USAID agreed to send an additional 50,000 tons of food, this time
to the Ethiopian government.[19] In the course of the rescue operation,
the Ethiopian government had ceased to be the major intermediary for
American or other foreign help. In 1985, the government handled only
30 percent of all the aid flowing into the country.[20] A similar change
affected other countries where local governments, instead of being the
major beneficiaries of philanthropy, were reduced to the lesser role of

authorizing local indigenous organizations to be grantees of foreign organizations.

With the Ethiopian crisis, American philanthropies thought of short-term aid not as a one-time stopgap measure but as an essential step in a program to support long-term economic and social gains. This put them further at odds with their government, which wanted to make sure that its assistance to a socialist country was devoted exclusively to emergency relief, not to structural development. INGOs received U.S. food from USAID on the condition that they adhere to the distinction between relief and development, but they ignored this requirement. Congressional hearings in 1985 found that Catholic Relief Services had contributed as much as $30 million to agriculture, water, and sanitation projects. USAID argued that that money should have been used instead to defray transportation costs for delivering food relief. Such difficulties were eventually eliminated in 1985 with the passing of the African Relief and Recovery Act, whereby aid for "rehabilitation" was deemed by Congress to be within the law.[21] Ultimately, INGOs were able to carve out a position of independence (at least for a while) from the U.S. government and the Ethiopian government's Relief and Rehabilitation Commission, successfully lobbying for more U.S. aid and taking it upon themselves to organize and execute relief operations in Ethiopia.

The INGOs launched long-term projects for rehabilitation, including irrigation projects; supplying people in camps with seed and tools to re-establish their farms; training local people in basic health/paramedic skills; and, lastly, encouraging wage work within the camps to help keep people active and hopeful. By now, four kinds of nongovernmental relief organizations were operating in Ethiopia: church-based organizations like Catholic Relief Services, Lutheran World Relief, and groups sponsored by Seventh Day Adventists, Baptists, and Presbyterians; non-denominational but religion-inspired agencies like World Vision, Friends of Africa, and Mercy Corps, which had sprung up in the previous decade and were not officially attached to a church; traditional non-sectarian agencies like CARE, Save the Children, and Oxfam; and specific focus agencies, like Technoserve, Women's World Banking, EnterpriseWorks/VITA, and the African-American Labor Conference, many of which dealt in technical assistance and support for entrepreneurial activity.[22] INGO leaders initiated negotiations with the Ethiopian government to set up relief camps, including one in Alamata that was run entirely by World Vision, and one in Korem run by Catholic Relief Services.[23] The INGOs were granted access to the worst suffering rural areas, and they developed a high profile in the media until Mengistu expelled them all in the early 1990s prior to his own demise.

INGOs in Ethiopia were influential providers of welfare and relief services, but their influence was also felt in their support for indigenous NGOs. In 1986, the U.N. General Assembly held a special session to review the Ethiopian drought emergency, and U.N. workshops recognized the growing strength of African NGOs. By the early 1990s, the number of homegrown NGOs in Ethiopia began to outnumber INGOs. At the end of the decade, they made up 72 percent of all NGOs in the country.[24] Similar developments took place in other parts of Africa, and also in Latin America, and in Asia.

Exporting the Textbook: American Democracy in Eastern Europe

American philanthropic organizations operating abroad were thus freeing themselves from Cold War strictures and investing directly in destitute communities even before the collapse of the Berlin Wall in 1989. The subsequent breakup of the Soviet Union in 1991 gave them a new and historic opportunity to export American principles to the many communities that had been directly under Soviet control. Here the prioritiy was not to end starvation but to aid in creating lasting means of generating wealth and civic life. The collapse of Communism and the end of the Cold War coincided with a return of prosperity to the United States. Americans therefore claimed not only the victory of freedom but also that of capitalism over communism. Their faith was renewed in the transforming power of capitalism, which they could now export free from ideological alternatives.

Given these circumstances, what should be the response of American philanthropy? Established American philanthropic institutions had long used their resources to fight communism. Now the old enemy had vanished. Peoples of the former Soviet bloc were looking for alternative models to Marxism. American philanthropies readily settled on two ideas: to promote market mechanisms for the democratization of wealth in place of an economics based on redistribution under state control; and to stimulate associational life to support a strong civil society, independent of the state and respectful of cultural differences. It was a great opportunity to export the American textbook formula: a mix of capitalism and community. Could it work, and how long would it take? That was another issue.

Some important American foundations—making up a small but influential part of the nonprofit sector—vied with the American government, international organizations, and the European Union for a say in rebuilding the former Soviet republics. What these American foundations could spend on such a vast territory was limited. If measured quantitatively in dollars, their contribution was small. In 1990 all American foundations together provided only about "one tenth of what the U.S. government gave through USIA, Department of State, Department of Education, and the National Endowment for Democracy," a Reagan initiative started in 1983 to promote democracy abroad; "one hundredth that of the IMF; one two-hundredth that of the World Bank."[25] But American foundations had their niche. They were independent of congressional appropriations and could act quickly to seed promising new ideas.[26]

Only two years before the Berlin wall came down, Americans had celebrated the bicentennial of their Constitution. Now, various East European countries were rewriting their own constitutions, one after the other, incorporating the language of rights and decentralization, and often adopting principles embodied in the American Constitution. One thinks of the balance of power principles that found their way to Bulgaria and Romania, the first countries to approve new constitutions.[27]

Eastern Europeans were also recovering the tradition of civil societies and advocacy groups that had once flourished within their borders—but had been largely silenced. As Eastern Europeans searched for a conceptual model, they looked to the United States, but also to their immediate neighbors in Western Europe, who were deeply concerned that the democratization of the former Soviet bloc not derail. In the process, Eastern Europeans discovered the writings of Alexis de Tocqueville, and in doing so they entered into dialogue not only with the Americans (who have regarded Tocqueville as their theoretician of civil society) but also with the French, and at the same time they found a narrative that illuminated events unfolding in their own countries. Eastern Europe's revolutionary moment resonated with Tocqueville's story of the collapse of an old regime and the urgent need to rediscover a civil society that had been repeatedly suppressed. Other giants of Western thought also appeared on the East European scene. As one observer remarked, Locke, Hume, and Ferguson came back "with a Polish and Hungarian accent."[28]

Tocqueville's *Democracy in America* was translated into all the East European languages in the 1990s, first in fragments and then in full. A Bulgarian scholar provided a translation of the introduction to *Democracy in America* (taken from the English translation) in 1989, and by the end of the year, the vice president of the Bulgarian republic was presiding over a Tocqueville symposium. Bulgarian intellectuals integrated Tocqueville into the history curriculum at their universities. Polish intellectuals quoted Tocqueville on the difficult apprenticeship of liberty and on complexities involved in exercising newly acquired political rights.[29] East European intellectuals, like Americans before them, highlighted Tocqueville's praise of voluntary associations and his attack on centralization. With Tocqueville, they embraced the idea that liberty, and the responsibilities that go with it, required boundless energy on the part of civil society. In words he might have borrowed from Tocqueville, a Romanian historian wrote in 1990: "This is a world of energy . . . at no point in life can one rest."[30] All this energy of a civil society in the making appealed to American philanthropists, big and small, who eagerly embraced the challenge of building a non-communist world in Eastern Europe.

American foundations had an opportunity now to help invent a flourishing civil society in countries where only a few years previously the state had reigned. In doing so they built on their previous involvement in these countries, where they had funded organizations that bore witness to repression. Helsinki Watch, a private American organization created in 1978 (with Ford Foundation money), monitored implementation of the Helsinki Accords and generated pressure on abusive governments. The organization kept tabs on the countries that had signed the (renewed) 1985 accords: the Soviet Union, Czechoslovakia, Romania, East Germany, Poland, Turkey, Yugoslavia, Hungary, and Bulgaria. Among its achievements was helping to bring about the release of political prisoners and also pressing for a greater awareness of human rights abroad in the U.S. Congress. In 1986, Helsinki Watch focused on Soviet abuses in Afghanistan. In 1988, the organization changed its name to Human Rights Watch. Human Rights Watch, Amnesty International, and Americas Watch, were the most visible agencies.[31] Also important was the International Commission of Jurists, once presided over by Seán McBride, Irish activist turned statesman and 1974 Nobel Peace Prize laureate, and one of the founders of Amnesty International.[32]

After the Berlin Wall came down in 1989, participation in Soviet and East European affairs replaced "watching." American philanthropy reignited old associational networks. Philanthropists also became private diplomats. Already in the early 1980s, under its president David Hamburg's leadership, the Carnegie Corporation had initiated a dialogue on arms control and security issues at the highest level of government, with General Secretary Mikhail Gorbachev, that helped build bridges between the American and Soviet administrations.[33] Now came a massive investment in civil society. At home conservatives were vowing to defund the left (see chapter 8). They changed their tune when working in communist countries. In Eastern Europe, the opposing philanthropic camps acted in concert, regardless of whether they were perceived at home as conservative or liberal. American foundations in the former Soviet Union all wanted the same thing: the mutual strengthening of capitalism and community. They could not predict when capitalism would succeed, but they promoted conversion to a free market economy and fostered managerial training. They simultaneously championed human rights, the rule of law, and the strengthening of civil society. They found a ready audience among the professionals, and intellectuals who made up the middle classes of the fallen socialist regimes, if somewhat less enthusiasm among members of the higher state nomenclatura.[34]

George Soros emerged as the first, most emblematic, and most committed of the foundation leaders. Soros, the richest of Diaspora philanthropists, took an approach towards his native Hungary that was much like Andrew Carnegie's towards his native Scotland a century before. But the stakes were so much higher in Hungary, where Soros had learned firsthand the damage that totalitarian regimes could do. As a young Jewish boy, he had survived the Nazis, and as a man he had fled the communists.

In America, Soros had made the lion's share of his fortune as an unblinking currency speculator. In 1979, he created The Open Society Fund, partly to leave his children some good work to do and partly to enjoy a tax break. But behind what might have been at the time a routine investment in philanthropy on the part of a wealthy American was a larger idea. Ever since Soros had fled totalitarianism, he had reflected on the need for liberty and openness. As a student at the London School of Economics, he had deepened these thoughts in reading Friedrich Hayek's *The Road to Serfdom* and Karl Popper's *The Open Society and Its Enemies*. Both men were his teachers. They had fled Nazi Austria and loomed large in defending the values of freedom against totalitarian regimes. In their fight against economic controls and for an open society, they were an inspiration to Soros much as, a century earlier, Herbert Spencer had been in justifying the gospel of wealth to Carnegie.

In the 1970s, Soros joined the Ford Foundation in backing Helsinki Watch. In the 1980s, he established Popper Fellowships at Columbia and New York University, and helped dissidents travel out of Eastern Europe and develop contacts in the West. In 1985, he opened a Soros Foundation in his native Hungary, which had retained the least repressive regime in the Soviet bloc.

Soros used his funds wisely. Because the Hungarian forint was not convertible, the Soros Foundation initially spent U.S. dollars on imports such as medical equipment, which the hard-pressed communist regime could not afford, and also Xerox machines that were important tools in circulating information. The state hospitals then paid the Soros Foundation in forints for the medical equipment, and the foundation channeled the forints back into cultural projects, buying books for local libraries, funding renovations of small-town churches, and funding research projects in universities.[35]

Soros created other foundations throughout Eastern Europe: Charter 77 for US-Czech relations; Stefan Batory in Poland; and the Open Society Funds in Bulgaria and Romania. He also started a fund in Russia but was constantly harassed by its tax authorities.[36] Despite its genuine renaissance, Russian civil society remained vulnerable to abuses of power in the name of resistance to American intervention.[37] Eventually Soros left Russia and moved some of his resources to African countries. He has been credited as a one-man Marshall Plan, and his influence over Eastern Europe is widely recognized.

There were other foundations on the ground. Those based in Europe focused on education and social welfare, with German foundations concentrating their resources on the former GDR. Soros and the other American foundations were remarkably consistent in exporting the kind of educational, political, and economic programs that mutually reinforced capitalist practices and civic life. The Soros Foundation Hungary, the Rockefeller Brothers Fund, the Ford Foundation, and the Mellon Foundation promoted market economics by funding the International Management Center in Budapest, the first business school in Central Europe modeled after an American one. The John M. Olin Foundation invested in legal issues, such as revising constitutions and improving the practice of law; the Rockefeller Brothers Fund and the Charles Stewart Mott Foundation worked towards establishing a nonprofit sector; the Smith Richardson Foundation committed itself more generally to promoting democratic institutions.[38]

All made a critical effort to nurture local NGOs. They were conscious of living in a historic moment, of providing for the first time assistance to organizations that were not instrumentalities of the government or the party. Board members of these organizations were no longer apparatchiks but community members, professionals, academics, journalists. Some, like Hungarian economist Zsuzsa Ferge, who worked on poverty, did not see the connection the Americans were making between capitalism and community. They objected to the "one size fits all" theories they often heard at the table, but nonetheless it was a new era. Local initiatives were finally tangible.[39]

The emphasis on investment in local initiatives led some American foundations to promote the community foundation, on the model that had been perfected at home since its modest beginnings in Cleveland just before the First World War (see chapter 2). The Charles Stewart Mott Foundation and Soros were key players in this effort to stimulate philanthropy and civil society with modest local resources. "I was very skeptical that volunteerism would ever exist here again," observed Tomáö Krejci, head of the community foundation in the Slovak city of Ústí nad Labem. But Krejci was pleasantly surprised when "people started turning up to donate their time and skills to projects supported by the community foundation and other charitable efforts."[40] Local community foundations worked for the tolerance of minorities, the legal defense of victims, and a burgeoning nonprofit sector.

A political consensus began to emerge on democracy and human rights, but turning these ideas into real economic and social change was more challenging. The more liberal American foundations pushed political pluralism through women's rights, but a women's movement was a hard sell in the East. Lenin was still remembered for saying "equality is not sameness." Minorities also struggled for recognition, and a subset of foundations put a substantial amount of money into minority integration. Ford, Mott, and Soros funded the Autonómia Foundation in Budapest, which was dedicated to ending discrimination against the poor Roma community. "Plowing is not for gypsies," says an old Hungarian proverb, but the foundation's objective was to turn gypsies into small landholders and to help them buy seedlings and elementary tools. The Autonómia Foundation also helped minority entrepreneurs with some loans; the 1993 loan repayment ratio grew by 400 percent compared to 1992, but still only one third of payments due were made. The foundation also provided some of the poor with housing in former Soviet army barracks and cleaned up some dumping grounds to prevent prevailing winds from blowing refuse into residential communities.[41]

Foundations were not the only American philanthropies exporting American ideas. Mass philanthropy participated too, with Diaspora giving playing an important role. For American mass philanthropy, 1989 was the opposite of 1947 in every way. In 1947, Stalin had closed the Soviet Union to Western money. He had denounced the Marshall Plan as American imperialism, saying he wanted no part of it. But the consequences of the Iron Curtain were much greater than foregoing American tax money. Local populations also lost the large amounts coming in from the vast Russian and Eastern European Diaspora in the United States. For the impoverished population of devastated postwar Poland, the rich American was not the U.S. corporate mogul but a brother or an uncle who worked on an assembly line in Detroit and lived in an unassuming home in Hamtramck, the Polish neighborhood of Detroit. In the Michigan winter, his modest balloon-frame house, its small front lawn adorned with a statue of the Virgin Mary, did not look like much. But though unpretentious, the house was stuffed with appliances purchased with the high wages and high benefits the UAW had negotiated with the auto industry. In the immediate postwar, the American worker began sending some of his surplus income as remittances to family members in the old country to help with the rebuilding. Stalin ended this American intrusion.

When the wall came down in 1989, American mass philanthropy was once again available to a vast East European and Russian population, even though only older Americans had personal memories of the old country. Pittsburgh, Pennsylvania, which once counted a great Slavic population in its steel mills, was still home to 2,000 Czech-American families in the late 1980s. Pittsburgh also had the twelfth largest community foundation in the U.S., which administered 325 donor-advised funds. To help with the Czech-American effort, the Heinz Endowment contributed to a "Friends of the Czech Republic Fund." Money flowed again from Pittsburgh to towns and villages in Czechoslovakia, and to many other places once behind the Iron Curtain.

This mode of giving is important in another respect. In appraising American overseas philanthropy, it is customary to point to the low percentage of GNP that Americans direct abroad compared to other wealthy countries. But Americans fare better in these comparative statistics when one adds in estimates and figures of Diaspora philanthropy. Millions of ordinary Americans with family and roots abroad participate in a global movement that the Internet further facilitates.[42]

Completing the Textbook: "Maximum Feasible Participation" Worldwide

In the 1980s, the philanthropic organizations that had for so long entrusted their resources to the governments of developing countries, only to experience bureaucratic bottlenecks and state corruption, decided instead to channel their funds directly to communities.[43] This was a significant move. There was ample evidence that state actors had not performed well, but would local NGOs give a better return on their investment? The only reason the philanthropies had for hoping so was a strong ideological belief in the power of community. That belief became the new orthodoxy in international aid circles as key figures in development like microcredit pioneer Muhammad Yunus and economist Amartya Sen also embraced it.

The experience a few American foundations had acquired in defining the War on Poverty at home was critical in shaping the idea of direct investment in disadvantaged communities. What these foundations pushed for was in essence a worldwide adaptation of "maximum feasible participation" of the poor; in other words, a principle of providing those in need with the assets required to effect their own economic development (chapter 7). The plan was to turn an infinite number of small communities around the globe into instruments of economic progress and human rights.

It is important to remember in this regard the pioneering part played by the Ford Foundation as the initial backer in 1980 of Yunus and his Grameen Bank, both recipients of the 2006 Nobel Peace Prize for launching microcredit in Bangladesh. Yunus returned to Bangladesh from his years as a Fulbright scholar and economics professor in the United States in the early 1970s with some important ideas gleaned from the Civil Rights movement. Chief among them were the program-related investment strategies that the Ford Foundation had developed. At that time, the Ford Foundation renamed its own Governance and Public Policy Division the "Governance and Civil Society Division" to signal the commitment of its president Franklin Thomas (previously the head of the Bedford-Stuyvesant Redevelopment Corporation) to small communities around the world.

Yunus transformed lending to the poor from an unacceptable risk to a reasonable bet. The innovative part of his approach to microlending consisted in extending credit to communities of borrowers rather than individuals, with the loans to be repaid in small weekly installments over the course of a year. Yunus started by making a few loans from his own pocket in the later 1970s. Having developed some contacts at Ford, he worked with the foundation's representative in Bangladesh, and this led to a loan guarantee of $800,000 from the foundation that went a long way towards convincing still-dubious commercial banks to provide capital for his experiment.[44] Yunus tailored his Grameen Bank to conditions in Bangladesh, focusing on local civic organizations, economic development, and social justice. Community solidarity helped ensure that more than 98 percent of the loans were eventually repaid. This initial success convinced banks, which had earlier dismissed Yunus, to join the venture.[45]

Yunus's success led to more cross-fertilization of ideas with American philanthropy. Early on, Ford Foundation officials had Yunus consult with officials from Chicago's ShoreBank, which Ford had helped start in the early 1970s to make loans in the city's low-income neighborhoods. Yunus later advised Governor Bill Clinton on setting up a microlending program in Arkansas.[46] When president, Clinton adopted the idea in setting up his Community Development Financial Institution Fund to revitalize distressed communities in the United States.

Yunus also pioneered in helping women. While the American civil rights movement-era Program Related Investments were geared towards male entrepreneurs, Grameen Bank used microcredit to pursue social justice for Bangladeshi women. Yunus understood that women bore the brunt of poverty and suffered from intense oppression in a society rigidly dominated by men; he also believed that women would use microloans more effectively than men to lift their families and communities out of poverty. Although Yunus faced opposition from angry husbands and even educated bankers who wanted to restrict women's roles in business, within six years, half of his borrowers were women, and today nearly all of Grameen's loans are made to women.[47] Ford continued supporting Grameen through the early 1990s, and the foundation later expanded its microfinancing philanthropy to Mexico and India.[48] Having succeeded so brilliantly in launching microcredit, Yunus has become the advocate for a larger field of nonprofit social enterprises with high social returns. He shares ideas of extending credit to individual entrepreneurs working for the benefit of disadvantaged communities with other American promoters of social entrepreneurship such as Bill Drayton, founder of the now well-established Ashoka foundation, and eBay's Jeff Skoll.[49] With its roots in Bedford-Stuyvesant and later Bangladesh, the practice of microcredit as a means of helping the poor become entrepreneurs is now being promoted around the world by the U.N., the World Bank, and European organizations. Yunus' idea has been so successful, in fact, that it has spurred the emergence of a for-profit microfinance industry that is now in need of significant regulation.[50]

The strategy of underwriting a multitude of indigenous organizations in the developing world instead of working primarily with governments has found its most powerful theoretical expression in Amartya Sen's work following his historical study of famines. Sen has captured the great coming together of market and civil society principles. With his 1999 *Development as Freedom*, where he synthesized much of his earlier work, he joined a long tradition of political economists who underscore the "freedom of exchange" intrinsic to the market as one of "the basic liberties that people have reason to value."[51] Like Yunus, Sen also saw women's agency as a central ingredient in development and social change, but he insisted also on championing their rights. He argued that it is not enough to be concerned about women's ability to engage in economic activity.[52] The degree to which they have social, political, and economic freedom is itself a leading indicator of development.

Sen promoted individual agency and community as the means to rising out of "deprivation." This would be possible only if institutional arrangements guaranteed freedoms rather than hampering individuals with "unfreedoms."[53] Development, then, is not about raising GNP or generating wealth, but about helping to create institutions that give people economic opportunities, political freedom, social facilities (health care and education), transparency (of government and market arrangements), and protective (i.e., social) security. Sen argued that these are not luxuries that must be postponed in order to achieve development, but rather the very elements that constitute development.

Such ideas became salient in international organizations in the second half of the 1980s. At the U.N., commitment to working with local communities translated into a "New Policy Agenda." In 1986, the U.N. established a special division for NGOs. In 1988, it launched a program to provide direct support for the small-scale activities of NGOs and community-based organizations. In the 1990s, the U.N. even shifted its rhetoric from supporting NGOs to building "sustainable partnerships" with civil society. Counting only the organizations operating internationally, there were 1,600 INGOs in 1980, 2,500 in 1990. The number of American-based INGOs jumped from fifty-two in 1970 to more than 400 by 1994.[54] Despite the many failures that have been reported, these organizations have carried out development projects and with them have fostered a degree of community empowerment around the world.

The World Bank also acted on a commitment to civil society. Its Civil Society Unit arose out of the NGO Unit that was established in 1989, partly in an effort to make the bank appear more attuned to local concerns. Bank President James Wolfensohn encouraged frequent consultation with NGOs. By 1996 the World Bank had civil society liaisons in half of its resident missions.[55] The Bank and other regional development banks established over forty investment funds devoted to disbursing small grants to NGOs and community-based organizations in support of infrastructure projects like roads, bridges, and water systems.[56] More often than not, indigenous NGOs have gained World Bank funding only after having been supported (and thus certified) by a small grant from the Ford Foundation. In parts of the world, they have become indispensable to the economy and society. Some observers of Bangladesh have gone as far as saying that indigenous NGOs constitute not a civil society but a "virtual parallel state." In the early 1990s, their programs reached between 10 and 20 percent of the poor population (or between 13 million and 26 million people). American developmental agencies have followed the same path. In 1981, Congress required that USAID channel at least 12 per cent of expenditures through NGOs, a sum raised to 13.5 per cent in 1986.[57]

Critics have been prompt to point out that international organizations cannot arbitrate conflicts among so many stakeholders and are basically powerless if such conflicts should turn into humanitarian tragedies.[58] But whatever the caveats, the shift to helping smaller communities rather than nation states is an established trend of our times. Among American philanthropists, Ted Turner sanctioned the new internationalism in 1997. In a landmark grant to the U.N., he gave $1billion over ten years on condition that it be used for women and children and other humanitarian projects; this at a time when the U.S. government was still withholding its dues. (Reporters pointed to CNN as the epitome of Turner's belief in global networks.) Turner felt that the U.N.'s global mission and the many projects it operated around the world offered the best place to make a difference. He did not want the gift to go towards the U.N.'s operating budget or other bureaucratic costs and proposed instead to use the U.N. to channel money to the many communities in need.[59] Then Secretary-General Kofi Annan launched the U.N. millennium goals, widely publicized in his 2000 address, "We the Peoples: The Role of the United Nations in the 21st Century." Secretary Annan challenged "member states" to work with "the vibrant constellation of new non-state actors" and to tackle together the eradication of extreme poverty, pandemic diseases, and environmental disasters.[60]

Making the Connection between the Global and the Local: The Role of the Gates Foundation

There remained the very large problem of combining the available funding from international organizations, nation states, and global capitalism, and making it available to the many small communities in need but excluded from economic networks. In the language of the United Nations, a U.S. foundation operating abroad is merely another INGO, but in fact large American foundations have been critical agenda setters. The newest and largest of them has been especially important in finding ways to support communities while bypassing local bureaucratic bottlenecks. The foundation that Bill and Melinda Gates created in 2000 with their Microsoft fortune, reinforced by investor Warren Buffett's gift of part of his own fortune to it, is the world's largest philanthropic foundation, today's counterpart to the Rockefeller Foundation in the 1920s and the Ford Foundation in the 1960s.[61]

Very large profits in high-tech industries and on Wall Street have generated a new wave of exceptionally wealthy philanthropists. With this resurgence of extremes of wealth, the turn of the century has been dubbed a second "Gilded Age."[62] The new rich became philanthropists of a new stripe. For a while, they captured the headlines with something they called "venture philanthropy," a concept that they never really defined, except in so far as it meant that endowments were no longer managed conservatively but to maximize profit.[63] Some promoted hosting for-profit and nonprofit activities under the same corporate roof, which they did until the collapse of the NASDAQ and then the larger financial debacle of 2008.

The Bill and Melinda Gates Foundation emerged from this environment, but it adopted more conventional procedures. Bill Gates, arguably the most successful entrepreneur of his generation, is now its head. By investing his foundation's vast resources, Gates has acted as a catalyst bringing together various public and private actors in the arena of global aid. A recent survey indicates that Gates spearheads a larger American trend of giving internationally. The Foundation Center reports the creation of 143 new foundations between 1995, the year the Gates Foundation came into being, and 2008, with international giving growing at a pace faster than overall giving.[64]

With means equal to that of a nation state, and access to a vast network of experts, the Gates Foundation has enormous leverage, hence the importance of following its work. In conversation with other foundations and a cast of influential brokers committed to the millennium goals—Presidents Clinton and Carter, international rock star Bono among entertainment personalities, and others—the Gates Foundation has invested in civil society in remote areas of the world with the hope of eventually turning over control of stable programs to indigenous communities and their governments.[65] Two of its projects—a second green revolution for Africa, and the worldwide fight against HIV/AIDS with special attention to India—will serve to illustrate the profound contributions that this infusion of big-money philanthropy is making in local communities worldwide.

In 2006, the Gates and Rockefeller foundations began collaborating on a second green revolution, this time directed at Africa. It is a partnership between one of America's newest foundations and one of its oldest, which has acquired over the years much expertise in agricultural work. Both are responsive to criticisms that the original green revolution in Asia and Latin America (see chapter 5) fed the continents but harmed small farmers because of its excessive reliance on agribusiness without community participation. The two foundations launched the Alliance for a Green Revolution in Africa (AGRA), designed to increase African farmers' access to seeds, farming and irrigation technologies, and markets and financing. Gates initially committed only $100 million and Rockefeller $50 million.[66] Retiring U.N. Secretary-General Kofi Annan was named the first chairman of the initiative.[67]

AGRA takes a realistic view of the need to work with governments. In its first year of operation, it made more than 10 initial grants to several ministries of agriculture, as well as to prominent African plant breeders, soil health experts, and leaders of agriculture extension programs. In Kenya, for example, AGRA partnered with Equity Bank, the International Fund for Agricultural Development, and the Kenya Ministry of Agriculture to provide loans totaling up to $50 million to 2.5 million farmers and 15,000 rural shops, fertilizer and seed wholesalers, grain traders, and food processors.[68] As part of the program, the Ministry of Agriculture contributes millions of dollars in subsidies to Kenya's most vulnerable farmers. Kofi Annan announced in 2008 that AGRA had launched a new partnership with the U.S. government's Millennium Challenge Corporation, the agency President Bush created to dramati-

cally increase American government aid abroad.[69] Collaboration between the Gates Foundation and the U.S. government has continued
with President Obama's launch of a Global Agriculture and Food Security Program unveiled in April 2010. Four countries—the U.S., Canada,
South Korea, and Spain—are partnering. As the fifth member, the Gates
Foundation is in effect another state.[70]

AGRA's approach consistently emphasizes local small farmers as
the recipients of its aid. Almost three quarters of Africa's land is being
farmed without fertilizers or improved seeds. The program therefore
develops seeds and fertilizers at U.S. and African research centers and
universities that small farmers can afford. It is seeking to create new
supply chains, including the establishment of rural seed shops or ki-
osks to replace government distribution mechanisms.[71] AGRA channels
money to NGOs in Africa, which then recruit and train local merchants
to become agrodealers. Training in becoming a small capitalist includes
basic courses in business and accounting; other assistance includes inducing fertilizer and seed supply companies to distribute their products
to poor farmers on credit with guarantees from the NGO. These local
dealers can then supply surrounding farmers who no longer have to
travel long distances or pay high transport costs to deal directly with
wholesale supply companies. In this way, Gates and Rockefeller money
find its way to local recipients, stimulating market development and
community regeneration. Even though NGOs have proven no more immune to corruption and inefficiencies than government bureaucracies,
and coordination has remained a difficult issue, the expectation nonetheless persists that global philanthropic resources can effectively reach
local communities.[72]

As a major funder of the worldwide fight against HIV/AIDS, Gates
and his foundation operate both on a global level, and as we shall see in
the case of India, at a local level as well. They have helped build multi-
national funding strategies. Bill Gates's announcements to fellow global
capitalists, who meet annually in the ski resort of Davos, Switzerland,
of large gifts to the medical establishment have been widely advertised.
Gates was instrumental in launching the Global Alliance for Vaccines

and Immunizations, designed to fund research with predictable and legally-binding financial commitments from governments against which money can be borrowed on capital markets. Another fund Gates helped launch is the International AIDS Vaccine Initiative in 1996. From its inception, Gates has contributed to the Global Fund United Nations Secretary-General Kofi Annan launched in 2001 at an Organization of African Unity summit in Abuja, Nigeria. The fund, organized as a nonprofit agency in Geneva, promotes partnerships between donor and recipient governments as well as NGOs, businesses, and philanthropic foundations in attacking HIV/AIDS, tuberculosis, and other infectious diseases. Public and private "stakeholders" (government agencies, academic and research interests, civil society organizations) determine the fund's disbursements to various countries.[73]

With other American foundations, especially the Rockefeller and Clinton Foundations, Gates has generated so-called product development partnerships (PDPs), with large pharmaceutical firms.[74] The Rockefeller Foundation, invested in medical research and public health since its inception, was the first to promote PDPs, and the Gates and Clinton Foundations have greatly expanded them. PDPs are essentially non-profit pharmaceutical companies. Two dozen currently focus on diseases that include HIV, tuberculosis, malaria, Dengue fever, hookworm, pneumonia, meningitis, and others. Gates provides about 50 percent of all funding, private philanthropy as a whole 80 percent. President Bill Clinton has not invested a personal fortune (which he does not have) but rather has enlisted wealthy partners around the world—especially the new rich in countries where these diseases are threatening—to contribute to the relevant funds, and he has negotiated drug production agreements and overseen distribution mechanisms for drugs once they have been tested and approved for the market.[75]

It seems natural that the head of Microsoft should direct a big part of his philanthropy to India, a country that he has come to know well and that has provided his company with much talent. But it has not been an easy proposition. The New York Times reported that India was ambivalent toward "a foreigner's bankrolling prevention of an epidemic that officials have sometimes seemed reluctant to acknowledge."[76] The Indian government has indeed substantially downplayed the epidemic, and most of the money it has spent to quell it has come from outside India.

In 1987, India created a National AIDS Control Program and, in 1992 a division within its Ministry of Health called the National Aids Control Organization (NACO), along with a collection of autonomous state AIDS control societies. NACO established blood banks and STD clinics throughout the country. Local Indian NGOs took on the task of HIV awareness and education. In 1999, with funding largely from the World Bank and USAID, NACO enlisted local NGOs to reach out to high-risk groups. These early efforts of the Indian government seemed ineffective to many observers due to discrimination against the victims that is based on the same kinds of prejudices that have hampered relief efforts in other parts of the world.[77] In countries where the epidemic has afflicted over 30 percent of the population, as in Botswana, for example, it is impossible for authorities and ordinary people alike to look the other way. But when the epidemic is still limited to high-risk populations, it is easier to engage in discrimination and ostracize victims, especially in a stratified society like India. The sick and high-risk groups have become the new untouchables.

The segregation of AIDS victims makes it much harder to control the epidemic. As Amartya Sen points out, the fear of retribution drives the gay community underground, where it is much harder for efforts to prevent the spread of the disease to reach.[78] Section 377 of the Indian Penal Code, a leftover of British colonial rule still on the books until July 2009, prescribed ten years in jail as the penalty for sodomy. The law was applied arbitrarily. Policemen used its threat to extort money from wealthy gay men. Arrested gay men reported being beaten "worse than stray dogs," forced to perform oral sex on policemen, and being tortured with electroshocks to the testicles.[79]

In facing this discrimination, the Gates Foundation committed itself to what one might loosely describe as philanthropic vertical integration, that is, the foundation would coordinate all levels of the campaign against HIV/AIDS until such time as the campaign could be entrusted back to the Indian government. As we have seen, the foundation steers global financial flows towards scientific research. At the same time, at least in the case of India, it takes the next step and fosters basic prevention measures such as the distribution of condoms and syringes among the ostracized populations. The foundation has found it helpful to use its leverage not only in major international partnerships, but also on the ground. A century ago, Frederick Gates advised John D. Rockefeller, Sr., to trust grantees with big projects, what he called wholesale philanthropy, and avoid micromanaging or retail giving (see chapter 1). In fighting HIV/AIDS in India, the Gates Foundation is, however, finding that it needs to combine wholesale and retail to achieve the necessary connection between the global forces of capitalism and action at the level of communities.

In 2003, the Bill and Melinda Gates Foundation created a new organization, Avahan, to fight AIDS in India and do so specifically at a grassroots level. Much of Avahan's program consists of efforts to organize prevention campaigns directly, take the sick out of hiding, and sustain community strength through advocacy for open treatment. In establishing Avahan, Bill Gates and his wife Melinda themselves met with small groups of sex workers in India to talk about the spread of the disease and what they could do together to stop it. The Gateses recorded their impression of one such meeting with a dozen sex workers in Chennia, India, who wore for the occasion "their best saris, gold necklaces, and bindis on their foreheads" and talked about "the things they wanted for themselves and their children" as if they came "from any walk of life."[80] The women expressed these hopes even though they were carriers of a deadly disease, as well as subject to recurrent violence at the hands of the police, pimps, and clients alike. Cynics may call this kind of dialogue posturing on the part of very rich Americans. But what is striking instead is the ways in which the Gateses are attempting to open a road that goes as directly as possible from the halls of high global finance, where much of the world's wealth is generated, to the red light districts of Mumbai or to truck stops along Andhra Pradesh highways.

The Avahan organization has all the features of a twenty-first century global enterprise. An international panel of experts on HIV programming, a board of directors, and a World Health Organization evaluation advisory group provide technical advice on measuring results, as do state advisory committees and NGO partners. Avahan has also brought in a number of philanthropic partners in order to evaluate and monitor the success of its programs, including Yale and Duke universities, Family Health International, and Corridors of the University of Manitoba. Locally, Avahan claims to be not an operating organization but a "conduit" to help existing efforts scale up their operations. Nonetheless it is hands-on. From its office in Delhi, Avahan director, former McKinsey & Company executive Ashok Alexander, has worked with Indian authorities to identify key districts where Avahan could intervene.[81] Six Indian states, with a combined population of 300 million, account for 83 percent of the country's HIV infections. In each state, the lead implementing partner takes charge of enlisting local NGOs and recruiting peer outreach workers to educate and raise awareness among high-risk groups.

Alexander has initially committed the bulk of the money not to the Indian government's NACO but to partners of his own choosing. Some are INGOs like the International AIDS/HIV Alliance, Family Health International, Pathfinder, and CARE. A few are indigenous NGOs like the Hindustan Latex Family Planning Promotion Trust (founded in 1992), the India HIV/AIDS Alliance, founded in 1997, and the LEPRA Society (originally the British Empire Leprosy Relief Association). Vasavya Mahila Mandali, a nonprofit Ghandian organization founded in 1969 dedicated to women and child welfare, is the lead partner in Andhra Pradesh. In the same state, Avahan has funded (via CARE) a program named Saksham ("self reliant" in Sanskrit) that builds self-sustaining organizations in the East Godavari District to curb risky behaviors and help victims voice their needs.[82]

Reaching high-risk groups requires an extensive awareness campaign on the part of the Gates Foundation. The office in New Delhi recruits national film celebrities, sports stars, and business leaders to reach millions of people through public service announcements on TV and radio, in movie houses, and on billboards. Then Avahan associates work along 8,000 km of primary truck routes through large tracts of the interior in Andhra Pradesh and Karnataka, to reach a mobile population of two million truckers. The teamsters represent an important bridge population of persons who have sex with both sick and healthy partners. They transmit the diseases to their wives, who pass it on to the next generation through pregnancies, putting a much larger population at risk.

At truck stops, far from the halls of high finance and pharmaceutical PDPs, Avahan associates organize educational meetings through drama, street theatre, entertainment shops, and competitions. In the cities, they concentrate on the red light districts. The network of local NGOs recruits sex workers and turns them into part-time social workers and educators among their peers (and compensates them for lost income). Peers are issued identity cards to show that they are associated with HIV prevention programs, and some police directors have signed these cards to endorse the sex workers' newly earned status. As a by-product of its AIDS prevention campaign, Avahan has thus created a crisis network that can respond to violent incidents against sex workers at the hand of pimps, customers, gang members, and the police. The Hindustan Latex Family Promotion Trust distributes a crisis response card with an 800 number, written in Telegu for Telegu-speaking areas of Southern India. Stopping the violence is a precondition of prevention and treatment.

The sex-workers-turned-health-workers bring others to counseling centers where Avahan-supported groups provide physicians and nurses as well as counselors and also lawyers. When in the village of West Godavari, in the state of Andhra Pradesh, a peer outreach worker employed by the Hindustan Latex Family Planning Promotion Trust was beaten by villagers who thought she was inducing young women into sex work, the local NGO partner approached the village president and the village council to stop the violence, and, in the end, the village opened a drop-in center and joined the AIDS battle. By December 2005, Avahan was supporting 134 grassroots NGOs in 533 Indian towns. They had reached 65 percent of the high-risk population. It is not possible to say how much of AIDS containment in India has been the direct outcome of the Avahan campaign, but there is no doubt as to its visibility and influence.

The Gates Foundation's approach differs from that of other public and private American funders in its emphasis on the pragmatic. Although the U.S. government has been quite generous in joining the battle against HIV/AIDS, especially in Africa, USAID workers are prevented by law from mentioning the possibility of abortion to pregnant women who had contracted the disease.[83] Launched in 2003 by George W. Bush, the President's Emergency Plan for AIDS Relief (PEPFAR) reinstituted this Reagan-era policy, which President Clinton had ended. The consequences are at times surreal. In a one-room AIDS clinic in Haiti, doctors afraid of losing their U.S. government funding if they contravened the gag rule, divided the room into two halves, one for patients helped with Gates Foundation money, and the other for those being served with PEPFAR funds. They marked the chairs accordingly. Patients at Gates chairs could be advised about the use of condoms or, when appropriate, the possibility of an abortion, but not those in PEPFAR chairs.[84] The Obama administration has again rescinded the rule. Similar limitations have affected the private sector. Many of the medical missionaries sent to Africa by American evangelical groups to help HIV/AIDS patients have insisted on preaching abstinence and on distributing medicine only after a prayer. But Gates is independent of American taxpayers' money as well as funding from evangelical sects. His more pragmatic assessment of the spread of diseases gives the global movement its progressive cast.

In the 1980s, it was the mass philanthropic response to the Ethiopian crisis that signaled a new independence from Cold War strictures on the part of INGOs. The Soviet Union collapsed soon after. A large communitarian movement became the primary recipient and generator of private philanthropic international aid. While large foundations have contributed innovative ways of making global funds available to these communities across the world, and of limiting the role of state intermediaries, the turn-of-the-century technological revolution has very much helped mass philanthropy contribute to the same trend.

It is now possible for every citizen willing to spend a little money to respond directly and almost instantly to world emergencies simply by

sitting down at a computer or picking up a cell phone. The great beneficiaries of the new superfast mass philanthropy are the larger charities
and INGOs, for they have the know-how to intervene where needed.
Kosovo in 1999 was the first international crisis to generate significant
online gifts. The trend has since gained momentum at an exponen-
tial rate, with text messaging providing additional speed.[85] Ironically,
the Internet and related high-speed communications, which are the
most impersonal of means, have brought personal financial participation in the global associational revolution within reach of practically
everybody.

To achieve its mission, modern philanthropy has embraced communities around the world and bypassed states. But its means can never
be adequate to its most ambitious goals. The newfound speed in sending
donations and the high creativity of progressive organizations cannot
substitute for state resources in the process of rebuilding after a major
disaster or for making inroads on any of the millennial goals. While
global philanthropy has bet much of its resources on the mutual rein-
forcement of individual agency and community, a strong civil society
only exists in the context of a reliable state. If states have been obstacles
to progress or, as in some cases, collapsed altogether, returning them to
their proper role remains a challenge that global philanthropy cannot
ignore in our new century.

CONCLUSION

As this history has shown, philanthropy in the United States is not simply the consequence of a universal altruistic impulse; it is also a product of the large organizational revolution that American managerial and financial capitalism orchestrated in the last century and a half.[1] Adam Smith made the case for universalism in the opening of his classic *The Theory of Moral Sentiments* by observing: "How selfish soever man may be supposed, there are evidently some principles in his nature, which interest him in the fortune of others, and render their happiness necessary to him, though he derives nothing from it except the pleasure of seeing it."[2] For this Scottish founder of modern political economy, this altruistic vision encompasses "the greatest ruffian, the most hardened violator of the laws of society" as well as the ordinary citizen. That American giving on a large scale reflects altruism, there is no doubt. But Americans of different wealth and culture have turned a universal desire to do good into a distinct brand of philanthropy. They have learned to turn market profits and market methods into a philanthropic engine powerful enough to influence the course of their history.

One way to appreciate the novelty of philanthropy in America is by turning to those pioneer anthropologists who, a century ago, observed giving in small surviving nonmarket societies in order to gain a glimpse of an alternative to profit-making. They generated an influential discourse on giving. Columbia University anthropologist Franz Boas investigated the potlatch among American Indians of the North Pacific coast. Bronislaw Malinowski contributed his studies of free and reciprocal giving (or *kula*) in the Trobriand Islands. Marcel Mauss, in a landmark synthetic essay he wrote in 1923 entitled *The Gift*, portrayed the ritualistic and reciprocal exchange of gifts his colleagues had discovered as the "total social fact" of archaic societies. Mauss went on to contrast this archaic giving with selling in modern market societies. After positing the gift as the main form of economic, social, and cultural exchange in a world very different from ours, Mauss explained that the Greeks and the Romans were first to distinguish between a sale and a gift, and to insist on treating a sale as a contract subject to the rule of law and a gift as a moral obligation.[3] This dichotomy was adopted by Christianity and remained dominant in Western civilization until such time as the Americans invented modern philanthropy.

Americans have come to think of philanthropy not as a gift only, but also as an investment. Late nineteenth-century Americans who made large fortunes were the first to openly combine the ideas of managing the market and giving in a single mechanism geared for social progress. That money needs to be available before it can be given is obvious; the innovation lay in bridging the gap between a transaction in which you act for profit and a gift, in effect merging in various proportions the two activities. Having inherited a critical distinction between profit-making and giving, inscribed in law and custom, they have made the two behaviors organically dependent rather than outcomes of opposite impulses, as Adam Smith implied.[4]

The innovation was not limited to rich philanthropists. Broad participation gave philanthropy its democratic imprint in America. While the wealthy have invested their fortunes in large foundations, Americans of modest means have financed their own institutions of philanthropy from surplus income, also the product of capitalism. These two kinds of institutions both oversee their endowments and manage their activities with techniques learned from for-profit corporations, a distinguishing mark of American philanthropy.

In other words, American philanthropy is not a matter of the rich helping people in need, but of people, rich or not, providing for their own future. American philanthropy contains a very important and motivating element of frank self-interest. Donors themselves gain when their contribution leads to a cure for a common disease or when it provides them access to better cultural amenities.

In attempting to characterize American philanthropy, Alexis de Tocqueville's grasp of the relationship between interest and altruism remains an essential starting point. Tocqueville saw in American life the application of Smith's humanity to market forces. Instead of merely concluding that all human beings have a generous impulse, he uncovered the means Americans have used time and again to turn generosity to their advantage. He labeled the mechanism "self-interest properly understood."

It took Tocqueville some time to establish a positive connection between "self-interest" and collective betterment. In his travels, he at first saw people fending only for themselves everywhere he turned. "Private interest rears its head here constantly, reveals itself openly, and proclaims itself to be a social theory," Tocqueville wrote disparagingly to his friend Ernest de Chabrol from New York in 1831.[5] But he later changed his mind and posited instead an "enlightened love" of oneself that leads Americans to "sacrifice a portion of their time and wealth" to public affairs.[6] Using language inherited from the political philosophy of the eighteenth century, Tocqueville speculated that in America, "interest" had replaced "virtue" as the motivation for working for the common good. Turning self-interest into a benefit for all, Tocqueville argued, was a positive development for civilization because as an impulse, it was in much greater supply than virtue. Tocqueville applied this concept to explain the development of associations in America. Here was a joint enterprise to which people could adhere freely, and help themselves while helping others.

Tocqueville's formulation may be even more applicable to philanthropy, as we have described it in this history, than to associations. Tocqueville could not anticipate it, but mass philanthropy, with its army of volunteers raising money in American neighborhoods year after year to help solve some of the larger problems of the country, is a constant reenactment of self-interest properly understood. Individual Americans return to society some monetary gain with the motivation that it might benefit them in the long run. This same idea can also be applied to American philanthropy abroad. In participating in the vast expansion of American influence in the world, philanthropic institutions have been constrained by Realpolitik, especially in times of war, but they have explicitly invested in global welfare.

Although philanthropy operates on a much smaller scale than government, the resources available to foundations and broadly supported organizations are large enough that continual debate about the proper relationship of government to philanthropy has become a distinctive feature of American society. Generally speaking, the federal government wants to encourage philanthropy, but it also wants to control it, and this has repeatedly led to friction. The government feels most comfortable when philanthropy adheres to "charitable" purposes, an adjective still used in the tax code to characterize philanthropic and nonprofit institutions, not only because it is inherited from their early identification with the church but also because it reflects the lesser range of activities the state is willing to subsidize. The government is less at ease with philanthropy's entry into the realm of policymaking, and has proven most hostile to its efforts at advocacy, seeing its own prerogatives challenged directly. Given the sweeping goals of American philanthropy, this conflict has been played out over and over again.

In accordance with the constitutional separation of church and state, American philanthropy has also largely been ecumenical if not secular. Many Christians have had no trouble supporting a broadly defined philanthropy with aims that may even be at odds with their religious tenets. After John D. Rockefeller III, a liberal Protestant, created the Population Council to promote birth control around the world, Henry Ford II, who had converted to Catholicism when getting married, surprised Ford Foundation officers by authorizing its support.[7] Churches have generally looked to find common cause with secular goals, adapting their activities to the secular philanthropic model, if only to benefit from grants from the U.S. government. Catholic Relief Services and federated Protestant charities have acted not as missions but as humanitarian institutions combining taxpayer money with their own for carrying out modernizing projects in many theaters around the world. Conservative Christians, however, have resisted this trend; Howard Pew, a large donor to evangelical causes, participated in the politics of philanthropy at midcentury with the goal of stemming the secular tide. In his view and that of others since, proselytism and good works need to go hand in hand.

How much of a contribution to American democracy at home and abroad philanthropy is likely to make in the future is of course a matter of speculation. Before the 2008 collapse of financial markets, economists predicted a massive intergenerational transfer of wealth from the baby-boom generation in the coming years, much of it going to philanthropic causes.[8] The amount of giving is now likely to be less. Economic set-backs always generate the fear that philanthropy may dry up or may be inadequate to the challenges faced. This was the case during the Great Depression when President Hoover unsuccessfully called philanthropy to the rescue, and it has been widely feared that the Great Recession might have the same result.

But philanthropy is deeply entrenched in the American political economy because it draws on values that Americans claim for them-selves in otherwise compartmentalized parts of their lives: a commit-ment to profit-making but also to social justice; a respect for individual freedom and a strong sense of community. The routine of philanthropy depends on the exercise of skills in business, organization, law, and out-reach, skills that many Americans train for and in which they excel.

Big-money philanthropy in America has found new leaders, who express little doubt about their ability to deliver. Spearheaded by War-ren Buffett and Bill Gates, forty American billionaires publicly an-nounced on August 2010 that they would give at a minimum half of their fortunes away during their lifetime or after their death.[9] The list is growing. Had the announcement come in the days prior to Tilden and Carnegie, it would have been important for these super-wealthy Ameri-cans to make their donations while alive in order to avoid strictures limiting bequests to narrow goals inappropriate to such large sums. That this is no longer a concern is another sign that there are in fact few re-strictions left on the magnitude of the tasks philanthropists may under-take. But unlike John D. Rockefeller III in the 1970s, who was active in organizing the nonprofit sector as a whole, Buffett and Gates are talking primarily to their peers.

Equally as important as the club of billionaires is to the future of philanthropy are the contributions Americans of modest means chan-nel through mass appeals that have so often worked in sync with large donations in the prosecution of the American Century. In times of emergency, the generosity of Americans always makes the headlines. Witness the outpouring of money following 9-11 or Katrina or the Haiti earthquake. A more difficult question is whether the mass of Americans will recognize, in the consistent and regular giving they have practiced in a civilization of abundance, a trait that continues to define them as Americans. If there is a lesson from the history I have told, it is that philanthropy enlarges democracy when it is an activity in which the many participate.

NOTES

Introduction

1. Wesley C. Mitchell, "The Backward Art of Spending Money," *American Economic Review* 2 (June 1912): 269–81.

2. Anna M. Harkness, Stephen V. Harkness's widow, created the Fund in 1918; Harkness had been a close associate of Rockefeller in the founding of Standard Oil. On Mitchell's appointment, see Guy Alchon, *The Invisible Hand of Planning: Capitalism, Social Science, and the State in the 1920s* (Princeton: Princeton University Press, 1985), 53–59.

3. Andrew Carnegie, *Autobiography of Andrew Carnegie* (Boston: Houghton Mifflin, 1920), 255.

4. Werner Sombart, *Why Is There No Socialism in the United States?* (1906; trans. Patricia M. Hocking and C. T. Husbands, with a foreword by Michael Harrington, White Plains, NY: International Arts and Sciences Press, 1976), 106.

5. Julius Rosenwald, "Principles of Public Giving," *Atlantic Monthly* 143 (May 1929): 601.

6. According to the Bureau of Economic Analysis, in 2009 the nonprofit sector accounted for 5.5 percent of GDP, or $779.1 billion (It was only 2.5 in 1955). In 2005 the nonprofit sector comprised 9.7 percent of the American workforce. In the same year, the sector was estimated to have total assets of $3.4 trillion.

Independent Sector estimates sources of nonprofit revenues for 2008 as follows: 50 percent from dues, fees, charges; 29.4 percent from government contributions; 12.3 percent from private charitable contributions; 8.3 percent from other sources (primarily interest on endowments).

Private charitable giving totaled $303.75 billion in 2009. This was a 3.6 percent decline from 2008, which *Giving USA* notes is "the steepest decline" since *Giving USA* began computing the figure in 1956. Giving broken down by category is as follows: Individual giving: $227.41 billion (75 percent); Charitable bequests: $23.8 billion (8 percent); Corporate gifts (including corporate foundations): $14.1 billion (4 percent); Foundation grants: $38.44 billion (13 percent) [$15.41 billion estimated from family foundations].

The largest recipients by category are as follows: Religion: $100.95 billion (33 percent); Education: $40.1 billion (13 percent); Gifts to "grantmaking, private, community and operating foundations": $31 billion (10 percent); Unallocated giving: $28.59 billion (10 percent); Human services (includes emergency response charities): $27.08 billion (9 percent); Public-society benefit (United Way, Jewish federations, etc.): $22.77 (8 percent); Health: $22.46 billion (7 percent); Arts, culture, humanities: $12.34 billion (4 percent).

2009 and 1987 are the only two years in which giving has not increased in current dollars since 1969. Giving in 2009 totaled 2.1 percent of GDP. Despite the recession that begun in 2008 (at least so far), giving has remained above 2 percent since the mid-1990s.

In 2009 the U.S. spent approximately $667 billion on defense, including $146 billion for overseas operations. The Office of Management and Budget estimates 2009 defense spending at about 4.6 percent of GDP. Using the 2009 dollar figures, the nonprofit sector was nearly 17 percent larger than the Department of Defense budget (including the wars). Measured as a percentage of GDP, the nonprofit sector surpassed defense spending in 1993.

Chapter 1
"For the Improvement of Mankind"

1. But not quite the 31,000 denounced by the Farmer's Alliance; see Merle Curti, Judith Green, and Roderick Nash, "Anatomy of Giving: Millionaires in the Late Nineteenth Century," *American Quarterly* 15 (Autumn 1963): 416–35.

2. Cornell was also in part a government-funded land grant college.

3. John Ensor Harr and Peter J. Johnson, *The Rockefeller Century: Three Generations of America's Greatest Family* (New York: Charles Scribner's Sons, 1988).

4. *Outlook* 86 (July 27, 1907): 648–57; see also George Iles, "The Art of Large Giving," *Century Illustrated Magazine* (March 1897): 76–79.

5. Robert H. Bremner, *American Philanthropy* (Chicago: University of Chicago Press, 1960, revised 1988), 122.

6. Olivier Zunz, *Why the American Century?* (Chicago: University of Chicago Press, 1998), 3–23.

7. Peabody was originally from Massachusetts; the Peabody Museum at Harvard bears his name. In Baltimore, he influenced Johns Hopkins to found his new school; in London, J. P. Morgan apprenticed with him; see Franklin Parker, *George Peabody: A Biography*, with a foreword by Merle Curti (Nashville: Vanderbilt University Press, 1956); Daniel Coit Gilman, "Thirty Years of the Peabody Education Fund," *Atlantic Monthly* 79 (February 1897): 161–66.

8. Howard S. Miller, *The Legal Foundations of American Philanthropy, 1776–1844* (Madison: State Historical Society of Wisconsin, 1961); James J. Fishman, "The Development of Nonprofit Corporation Law and an Agenda For Reform," *Emory Law Journal* 34 (Summer 1985): 61–83.

9. Gareth Jones, *History of the Law of Charity, 1532–1827* (Cambridge: Cambridge University Press, 1969), 23–26, and other sections for a brilliantly concise explanation of British precedents.

10. W. K. Jordan, *Philanthropy in England 1480–1660* (New York: Russell Sage Foundation, 1959), 141–42.

11. *Saltonstall v. Sanders*, 93 Mass. 446, 454 (1865).

12. See Irvin G. Wyllie, "The Search for an American Law of Charity, 1776–1844," *Journal of American History* 46 (September 1959): 206–10.

13. Stanley N. Katz, Barry Sullivan, and C. Paul Beach, "Legal Change and Legal Autonomy: Charitable Trusts in New York, 1777–1893," *Law and History Review* 3 (Spring 1985): 51–89.

14. McGraw's Estate, 111 N.Y. 66; 19 N.E. 233 (1888).

15. James Barr Ames, "The Failure of the 'Tilden Trust,'" *Harvard Law Review* 5 (1891–1892): 389–402; Austin W. Scott, "Charitable Trusts in New York," *New York University Law Review* 26 (April 1951): 251–65; Andrew O'Malley, "The Origins and Failure of Samuel J. Tilden's Charitable Bequest," M.A. thesis, University of Virginia, 2003; Peter Dobkin Hall, *Inventing the Nonprofit Sector and Other Essays on Philanthropy, Voluntarism, and Nonprofit Organizations* (Baltimore: Johns Hopkins University Press, 1992), 185–86.

16. Michael F. Holt, *By One Vote: The Disputed Presidential Election of 1876* (Lawrence: University Press of Kansas, 2008).

17. "Wealth," *North American Review* 148 (June 1889): 660.

18. Limiting assets of "eleemosynary institutions," as charities were technically called, from the Greek *eleēmosynē* and the Latin *eleemosynarius*, or "gift of compassion," and defining bequests too narrowly.

19. Marion R. Fremont-Smith, *Philanthropy and the Business Corporation* (New York: Russell Sage Foundation, 1972), 39–40.

20. Carnegie said of his trustees: "They shall best conform to my wishes by using their own judgment"; quoted in Alan Pifer, *Philanthropy in an Age of Transition* (New York: Foundation Center, 1984), 40.

21. *Knight's Estate*, 159 PA 500 (1894).

22. *People v. Dashaway Association*, 84 Cal. 114 (1890); see also Elias Clark, "The Limitation on Political Activities: A Discordant Note in the Law of Charities," *Virginia Law Review* 46 (April 1960): 448, n. 44.

23. Carl Zollmann, *American Law of Charities* (Milwaukee: Bruce Publishing Co., 1924), 20–46.

24. According to the English barrister the foundation consulted in April 1925, the General Education Board would have stood a better chance of receiving an exemption in Great Britain because it was specifically dedicated to education: "The General Education Board and the Rockefeller Foundation—Opinion," Rockefeller Foundation; Administration—Program and Policy; Record Group 3.1, series 900, box 5, folder 52, Rockefeller Archive Center.

25. See for instance Amos Griswold Warner, *American Charities: A Study in Philanthropy and Economics* (New York: Thomas Y. Crowell & Co., 1894), 8, 20, 180.

26. William Rhinelander Stewart, ed., *The Philanthropic Work of Josephine Shaw Lowell* (New York: Macmillan, 1911).

27. Olivier Zunz, *The Changing Face of Inequality: Urbanization, Industrial Development, and Immigrants in Detroit, 1880–1920* (Chicago: University of Chicago Press, 1982), 259–80.

28. Allan Nevins, *John D. Rockefeller: The Heroic Age of American Enterprise* (New York: Charles Scribner's Sons, 1940) vol. 2, 291; Frederick Taylor Gates, *Chapters in My Life* (New York: Free Press, 1977), 161.

29. Mrs. Sage received 300 "begging letters" a day, wrote Ruth Crocker: *Mrs. Russell Sage: Women's Activism and Philanthropy in Gilded Age and Progressive Era America* (Bloomington: Indiana University Press, 2006), 200; see also William H. Allen, *Modern Philanthropy: A Study of Efficient Appealing and Giving* (New York: Dodd, Mead, & Co., 1912).

30. On Rockefeller, see Gates, *Chapters*, 163; on de Forest, Joan Waugh, *Unsentimental Reformer: The Life of Josephine Shaw Lowell* (Cambridge, MA: Harvard University Press, 1997), 154–55; James J. Hijiya, "Four Ways of Looking at a Philanthropist: A Study of Robert Weeks de Forest," *Proceedings of the American Philosophical Society* 124 (December 1980): 404–18.

31. Paul Krause, *The Battle for Homestead, 1880–1892: Politics, Culture, and Steel* (Pittsburgh, PA: University of Pittsburgh Press, 1992), 238.

32. Theodore Roosevelt, *An Autobiography* (New York: Library of America, 2004 [1913]), 710.

33. See Stanley N. Katz and Barry D. Karl, "The American Private Philanthropic Foundation and the Public Sphere, 1890–1930," *Minerva* 19 (Summer 1981): 249–50.

34. Judith Sealander, *Private Wealth and Public Life: Foundation Philanthropy and the Reshaping of American Social Policy from the Progressive Era to the New Deal* (Baltimore: Johns Hopkins University Press, 1997), 224.

35. Thomas G. Andrews, *Killing for Coal: America's Deadliest Labor War* (Cambridge, MA: Harvard University Press, 2008).

36. See Frederick P. Keppel, *The Foundation: Its Place in American Life* (New York: Macmillan, 1930; reprint, with an introduction by Ellen Condliffe Lagemann, New Brunswick: Transaction Publishers, 1989), 27–29; Merle Curti and Vernon Carstensen, *The University of Wisconsin: A History, 1848–1925* (Madison: University of Wisconsin Press, 1949), vol. 2, 223–32.

37. David Hammack, "American Debates on the Legitimacy of Foundations," in *The Legitimacy of Philanthropic Foundations: United States and European Perspectives*, ed. Kenneth Prewitt, Mattei Dogan, Steven Heydemann, and Stefan Toepler (New York: Russell Sage Foundation, 2006), 55.

38. Keppel, *The Foundation*, xix, 108; Judith Sealander mentions Andrew Carnegie, John D. Rockefeller, Sr., John D. Rockefeller, Jr., Edward Harkness, Olivia Sage, Julius Rosenwald, Elizabeth Milbank Anderson, and Edward Filene as having "very general goals for shaping society"; see her "Curing Evils at Their Source: The Arrival of Scientific Giving," in *Charity, Philanthropy, and Civility in American History*, ed. Lawrence J. Friedman and Mark D. McGarvie (Cambridge: Cambridge University Press, 2003), 223.

39. Merritt Madison Chambers, *Charters of Philanthropies: A Study of Selected Trust Instruments, Charters, By-laws, and Court Decisions* (New York: Carnegie Foundation for the Advancement of Teaching, 1948).

40. Joseph Frazier Wall, *Andrew Carnegie* (Pittsburgh, PA: University of Pittsburgh Press), 828–84.

41. On the national university, see A. Hunter Dupree, *Science in the Federal Government: A History of Policies and Activities* (Baltimore: Johns Hopkins University Press, 1957), 220.

42. Ellen Condliffe Lagemann, *Private Power for the Public Good: A History of the Carnegie Foundation for the Advancement of Teaching* (New York: College Entrance Examination Board, 1983): 159–78; the plan also required that the college admit only students with a four-year high school education; see Abraham Flexner, *Henry S. Pritchett* (New York: Columbia University Press, 1943), 95.

43. As Institute Director Simon Flexner called Gates's dream. See Albert F. Schenkel, *The Rich Man and the Kingdom: John D. Rockefeller Jr., and the Protestant Establishment* (Minneapolis, MN: Fortress Press, 1995), 85.

44. *A Report to the Carnegie Foundation for the Advancement of Teaching*, with an introduction by Henry S. Pritchett (New York: Carnegie Foundation for the Advancement of Teaching, 1910).

45. Donald Fleming, *William H. Welch and the Rise of Modern Medicine* (Baltimore: Johns Hopkins University Press, 1954), 175–79.

46. Steven C. Wheatley, *The Politics of Philanthropy: Abraham Flexner and Medical Education* (Madison: University of Wisconsin Press, 1988), 82.

47. Keppel, *The Foundation*, 58.

48. Eduard C. Lindeman, *Wealth and Culture: A Study of One Hundred Foundations and Community Trusts and Their Operations During the Decade 1921–1930* (New York: Harcourt Brace, 1936; reprint, with an introduction by Richard Magat, New Brunswick: Transaction Publishers, 1988), 9.

49. Dorothy Ross, *The Origins of American Social Science* (New York: Cambridge University Press, 1991), 98–140.

50. Gates, *Chapters*, 91–99.

51. Schenkel, *The Rich Man*, 41.

52. John D. Rockefeller, Sr., *Random Reminiscences of Men and Events* (Salem, NH: Ayer, 1885; reprint, New York: Doubleday, Page & Co., 1909), 148 (page citation is to the reprint edition).

53. Ron Chernow, *Titan: The Life of John D. Rockefeller, Sr.* (New York: Random House, 1998), 298–329.

54. Thomas Wakefield Goodspeed, *A History of the University of Chicago: The First Quarter Century* (Chicago: University of Chicago Press, 1916), 301, 310.

55. *President's Report of the University of Chicago*, Administration, Decennial Publications, First Series, vol. 1 (Chicago: University of Chicago Press, 1903), 519.

56. As Schenkel notes in *The Rich Man* (70), Rockefeller held to a "basic modernist affirmation."

57. See Robert E. Kohler, *Partners in Science: Foundations and Natural Scientists, 1900–1945* (Chicago: University of Chicago Press, 1991), 41–70, on defining scientific policy.

58. Horace Mann Bond, *Negro Education in Alabama: A Study in Cotton and Steel* (Washington, DC: The Associated Publishers, 1939; reprint, with an introduction by Wayne J. Urban and an afterword by Martin Kilson, Tuscaloosa: University of Alabama Press, 1994), 142.

59. James D. Anderson, "Northern Foundations and the Shaping of Southern Black Rural Education," *History of Education Quarterly* 18 (Winter 1978): 379.

60. W.E.B. Du Bois, *Black Reconstruction in America, 1860–1880* (1935; reprint with an introduction by David Levering Lewis (New York: Free Press, 1998), 219.

61. Bond, *Negro Education in Alabama*, 264.

62. Louis D. Rubin, Jr., *Teach the Freeman: The Correspondence of Rutherford B. Hayes and the Slater Fund for Negro Education, 1881–1887*, 2 vols. (Baton Rouge: Louisiana State University Press, 1959).

63. Louis R. Harlan, *Separate and Unequal: Public School Campaigns and Racism in the Southern Seaboard States, 1901–1915* (Chapel Hill: University of North Carolina Press, 1958; reprint, with a new preface by Hugh Hawkins, New York: Atheneum, 1968), 75–101 (page citations are to the reprint edition).

64. Charles William Dabney, *The Public School Problem in the South*. Paper presented at the 1901 Conference for Education in the South, Special Collections, University of Virginia Library.

65. Paul M. Gaston, *The New South Creed: A Study in Southern Mythmaking* (Baton Rouge: Louisiana State University, 1970; reprint, with a new afterword by the author and a new introduction by Robert J. Norrell, Montgomery: NewSouth Books, 2002), 118 (page citation is to the reprint edition).

66. *Proceedings of the Second Capon Springs Conference for Christian Education in the South*, 1899, 76.

67. Harlan, *Separate and Unequal*, 92–93.

68. Schenkel, *The Rich Man*, 75.

69. Charles William Dabney, *Universal Education in the South* (Chapel Hill: University of North Carolina Press, 1936), vol. 2, 534.

70. Dabney, *The Public School Problem*.

71. Anderson, "Northern Foundations," 379. Robert J. Norrell, *Up from History: The Life of Booker T. Washington* (Cambridge, MA: The Belknap Press of Harvard University Press, 2009), 222, 274.

72. John Graham Brooks, *An American Citizen: The Life of William Henry Baldwin, Jr.* (Boston: Houghton Mifflin, 1910), 226.

73. Eric Anderson and Alfred A. Moss, Jr., *Dangerous Donations: Northern Philanthropy and Southern Black Education, 1902–1930* (Columbia: University of Missouri Press, 1999), 75.

74. See Harlan, *Separate and Unequal*, 77–78; James D. Anderson, *The Education of Blacks in the South, 1860–1935* (Chapel Hill: University of North Carolina Press, 1988), 91.

75. Peter M. Ascoli, *Julius Rosenwald: The Man Who Built Sears, Roebuck and Advanced the Cause of Black Education in the South* (Bloomington: Indiana University Press, 2006), 79.

76. Morris Robert Werner, *Julius Rosenwald: The Life of a Practical Humanitarian* (New York: Harper & Brothers Publishers, 1939), 136.

77. Horace Mann Bond, *The Education of the Negro in the American Social Order* (1934; reprint, with a new preface and an additional chapter by the author, New York: Octagon Books, 1966), 134.

78. Ibid., 112–13.

79. Harlan, *Separate and Unequal*, 42.

80. "Until the Southern Negro has a vote and representation on school boards, public control of his education will mean his spiritual and economic death," commented W.E.B. Du Bois, as quoted in Anderson and Moss, *Dangerous Donations*, 205.

81. Anderson and Moss, *Dangerous Donations*, 220.

82. "Memoranda from the Old Man Buttrick," Johns Hopkins Hospital, Baltimore, MD, January 17, 1924, Jackson Davis Papers, Accession 3072, Box 2, 1924, GEB, Special Collections, University of Virginia Library.

83. Jackson Davis to Wycliffe Rose, September 2, 1910, Davis Papers, 3072, 6, 1939; see a photograph of Ms. Randolph in Dabney, *Universal Education*, vol. 2, opposite 446.

84. Davis to Hon. J. D. Eggleston, Jr., Davis Papers, 3072-G, 1, 1911–1915.

85. Davis Papers, 3072, 8, n.d., "Writings on Education."

86. "The Jeanes Visiting Teachers," 19, Davis Papers, 3072-G, 1, 1936, 1954.

87. Davis can be compared to Nathan C. Newbold in North Carolina; see Glenda Elizabeth Gilmore, *Women and the Politics of White Supremacy in North Carolina, 1896–1920* (Chapel Hill: University of North Carolina Press, 1996), 161–62.

88. Jackson Davis, "Discussion of graduate and professional education for Negroes," Southern University Conference, Atlanta, Georgia, October 31, 1939, Davis Papers, 3072, 6, 1929–46, speeches.

89. Edwin R. Embree, *Julius Rosenwald Fund: Review of Two Decades, 1917–1935* (Chicago, 1936), 14; John H. Stanfield, *Philanthropy and Jim Crow in American Social Science* (Westport, CT: Greenwood, 1985), 99.

90. Bond, *The Education of the Negro in the American Social Order*, 141; Mary S. Hoffschwelle, *The Rosenwald Schools of the American South* (Gainesville: University Press of Florida, 2006), 37–38.

91. Hoffschwelle, *Rosenwald Schools*, 231–32, 236–37.

92. Horace Mann Bond and Julia W. Bond, *The Star Creek Papers*, ed. Adam Fairclough, with a foreword by Julian Bond (Athens: University of Georgia Press, 1997), 77.

93. Branch Taylor, *Parting the Waters: America in the King Years, 1954–63* (New York: Simon and Schuster, 1988), 27–68.

94. Joseph F. Kett, *The Pursuit of Knowledge Under Difficulties: From Self-Improvement to Adult Education in America, 1750–1990* (Stanford: Stanford Uni-

versity Press, 1994), 249–50; Judith Sealander notes that this did not prevent congressmen from denouncing Rockefeller, *Private Wealth*, 52.

95. John Ettling, *The Germ of Laziness: Rockefeller Philanthropy and Public Health in the New South* (Cambridge, MA: Harvard University Press, 1981), 4.

96. William A. Link, *A Hard Country and a Lonely Place: Schooling, Society, and Reform in Rural Virginia, 1870–1920* (Chapel Hill: University of North Carolina Press, 1986), 111.

97. Americans had been giving abroad in response to recurrent natural or political disasters, the chronology of which Merle Curti has given us in *American Philanthropy Abroad* (New Brunswick, NJ: Rutgers University Press, 1963).

98. David Nasaw, *Andrew Carnegie* (New York: The Penguin Press, 2006), 786–87.

99. John Farley, *To Cast Out Disease: A History of the International Health Division of the Rockefeller Foundation (1913–1951)* (New York: Oxford University Press, 2004), 34, 47, 61.

Chapter 2
The Coming of Mass Philanthropy

1. Mark Twain, *Roughing It* (New York: Library of America, 1984 [1872]), 761.

2. Merle Curti, *American Philanthropy Abroad* (New Brunswick, NJ: Rutgers University Press, 1963), 82–98, 119–33.

3. Theodore Roosevelt, *An Autobiography* (New York: Library of America, 2004 [1913]), 278.

4. Lilian Brandt, *How Much Shall I Give?* (New York: Frontier Press, 1921), 57.

5. John Ryan, *A Living Wage: Its Ethical and Economic Aspects* (New York: Macmillan, 1906), 140–41; see also Frank Hatch Streightoff, *The Standard of Living Among the Industrial People of America* (New York: Houghton Mifflin, 1911).

6. Mary Wilcox Brown, *The Development of Thrift* (New York: Macmillan, 1899), 7.

7. Margaret F. Byington, *Homestead: The Households of a Mill Town* (New York: Russell Sage Foundation, 1910; reprint, with a new introduction by Samuel P. Hays, Pittsburgh, PA: University Center for International Studies, 1974), 97.

8. Ryan, *A Living Wage*, 145.

9. Michael E. Teller, *The Tuberculosis Movement: A Public Health Campaign in the Progressive Era* (New York: Greenwood Press, 1988), 3.

10. Richard Carter, *The Gentle Legions: National Voluntary Health Organizations in America* (New York: Doubleday & Company, 1961; reprint, New Brunswick, NJ: Transactions Publishers, 1992), 71 (page citation is to the reprint edition).

11. The National Association for the Study and Prevention of Tuberculosis was renamed the National Tuberculosis Association (NTA) in 1918.

12. Scott M. Cutlip, *Fund Raising in the United States: Its Role in America's Philanthropy* (New Brunswick, NJ: Rutgers University Press, 1965), 54–55.

13. Jacob Riis, "The Christmas Stamp," *Outlook,* July 6, 1907, 511.

14. Emily Bissell, "The Story of the Christmas Seal," undated clipping, Bill Frank Collection, box 11, folder 28, Historical Society of Delaware, Wilmington.

15. *Scribner's Dictionary of American History,* "Postal Savings Banks" (New York: Charles Scribner's Sons, 1940), vol. 4, 319.

16. Cutlip, *Fund Raising,* 55.

17. Ibid., 57–58.

18. Nancy Tomes, *The Gospel of Germs: Men, Women, and the Microbe in American Life* (Cambridge, MA: Harvard University Press, 1998), 122; S. Adolphus Knopf, *History of the National Tuberculosis Association, the Anti-Tuberculosis Movement in the United States* (New York: NTA, 1922), 43.

19. Richard K. Means, *A History of Health Education in the United States* (Philadelphia: Lea & Febiger, 1962), 117–23.

20. From $4.72 billion in 1916, personal saving nearly doubled in 1917, then climbed to almost $13 billion in 1918, before falling back to $9.3 billion the following year. See series F 540–51, "National Saving, by Major Saver Groups, in Current Prices: 1897–1945," in *Historical Statistics of the United States: Colonial Times to 1970,* U.S. Bureau of the Census (Washington, DC, 1975).

21. See my essay "Mass Philanthropy as Public Thrift for an Age of Consumption," in *Thrift and Thriving in America: Capitalism and Moral Order from the Puritans to the Present,* ed. Joshua Yates and James Davison Hunter (New York: Oxford University Press, 2011), 335–49.

22. Office of the Messrs. Rockefeller; Medical Interests, Record Group III, Series 2, sub-series k, box 17, Folder 133, Rockefeller Archive Center.

23. C.E.A. Winslow, *The Life of Hermann M. Biggs, M.D., D.Sc., LL.D.: Physician and Statesman of Public Health* (Philadelphia: Lea & Febiger, 1929), 213.

24. Robert Taylor, *Saranac: America's Magic Mountain* (Boston: Houghton Mifflin, 1986), 74.

25. Olivier Zunz, *Making America Corporate, 1870–1920* (Chicago: University of Chicago Press, 1990), 94–96.

26. David Beito, *From Mutual Aid to the Welfare State: Fraternal Societies and Social Services, 1890–1967* (Chapel Hill: University of North Carolina Press, 2000), 162–64.

27. Tomes, *Gospel of Germs,* 128.

28. Teller, *The Tuberculosis Movement,* 33.

29. Knopf, *History of the National Tuberculosis Association,* 31.

30. The BCG vaccine (Bacillus Calmette-Guérin), from the French Institut Pasteur, was first used only in 1921.

31. Richard H. Shryock, *National Tuberculosis Association, 1904–1954: A Study of the Voluntary Health Movement in the United States* (New York: National Tuberculosis Association, 1957), 116.

32. Roderick D. McKenzie, *The Metropolitan Community* (New York: McGraw-Hill, 1933).

33. John Melpolder, "Democratizing Social Welfare Efforts," *The Survey* 37 (December 16, 1916), 304.

34. John R. Seeley et al., *Community Chest: A Case Study in Philanthropy* (Toronto: University of Toronto Press, 1957), 17; Eleanor Brilliant, *The United Way: Dilemmas of Organized Charity* (New York: Columbia University Press, 1990), 19 and 320, notes 6 and 7.

35. Cutlip, *History of Fundraising,* 18, 66–67.

36. Roy Lubove, *The Professional Altruist* (Cambridge, MA: Harvard University Press, 1965), 186.

37. "Unique Attempt to Solve Philanthropy's Big Problem," *New York Times,* April 6, 1913.

38. Peter Dobkin Hall, *Inventing the Nonprofit Sector and Other Essays on Philanthropy, Voluntarism, and Nonprofit Organizations* (Baltimore: Johns Hopkins University Press, 1992), 51.

39. John D. Rockefeller, Sr., *Random Reminiscences of Men and Events* (Salem, NH: Ayer, 1885; reprint, New York: Doubleday, Page & Co., 1909), 155 (page citation is to the reprint edition).

40. Clarke A. Chambers, *Seedtime of Reform: American Social Service and Social Action, 1918–1933* (Minneapolis: University of Minnesota Press, 1963), 91–106; see Harry P. Wareheim, "The Campaign," *Proceedings of the National Conference of Social Work at the Forty-Ninth Annual Session Held in Providence, Rhode Island, June 22–29, 1922* (Chicago: University of Chicago Press, 1922), 410–15.

41. Daniel J. Walkowitz, *Working with Class: Social Workers and the Politics of Middle-Class Identity* (Chapel Hill: University of North Carolina Press, 1999), 29.

42. Leonard P. Ayres, "Progress of the Community Trust Movement: A Beneficent Plan Which Has Acquired Nationwide Scope," *Trust Companies* 48 (1929): 463–64.

43. Raymond Moley, *Realities and Illusions, 1886–1931: The Autobiography of Raymond Moley,* Edited with foreword and epilogue by Frank Freidel (New York: Garland, 1980), 111.

44. As quoted in Nathaniel R. Howard, *Trust for All Time: The Story of the Cleveland Foundation and the Community Trust Movement* (Cleveland, OH: Cleveland Foundation, 1963), 20.

45. Irene Hazard Gerlinger, *Money Raising: How To Do It* (Los Angeles: Suttonhouse, 1938), 3.

46. Ibid.

47. William E. Leuchtenburg, *Herbert Hoover* (New York: Henry Holt and Company, 1999), 25–32.

48. On tax collection in 1913, before the income tax, see George T. Kurian, ed., *A Historical Guide to the U.S. Government* (New York: Oxford University Press, 1998), 324.

49. Curti, *Philanthropy Abroad,* 230–31.

50. Foster Rhea Dulles, *The American Red Cross: A History* (New York: Harper and Brothers, 1950), 104.

51. "How Manchester-by-the-Sea Raised Its Share of the Red Cross Endowment," *American Red Cross Bulletin* 6 (October 1911): 29–33.

52. Mabel Boardman, "A Red Cross Message," in *America to Japan*, ed. Lindsay Russell (New York: G. P. Putnam's Sons, 1915), 60–61.

53. Dulles, *American Red Cross*, 148.

54. Ibid., 151; Cutlip, *Fund Raising*, 117; see also American Red Cross, "World War I Accomplishments of the American Red Cross," American Red Cross Museum; available at http://www.redcross.org/museum/history/ww1a.asp (accessed September 2, 2010).

55. C. Howard Hopkins, *John R. Mott, 1865–1955: A Biography* (Grand Rapids, MI: Eerdmans, 1979), 535–44.

56. As quoted in Lubove, *Professional Altruist*, 189–90.

57. "1919 War Chest: give your share: 60 funds, local and war relief, in one, Dec. 2nd to 9th, 1918," http://books.google.com/books; "Help Fill the War Chest: Humanity Calls You" (Philadelphia: Ketterlinus, ca. 1914–1918); available at http://docsouth.unc.edu/wwi/41913/menu.html (accessed December 29, 2010).

58. Frank A. Vanderlip, "Financing with War Savings Certificates," *Annals of the American Academy of Political and Social Science* 75, no. 164 (January 1918): 33, 36.

59. Charles Gilbert, *American Financing of the War Effort* (Westport, CT: Greenwood, 1970), 139–40.

60. Daniel Holt, "Policing the Margins: Securities Law and the Legitimacy of American Corporate Finance, 1890–1934" (Ph.D. diss., University of Virginia, 2008), chapter 5.

61. Curti, *Philanthropy Abroad*, 245–47.

62. Ibid., 227.

63. Former University of Colorado and Cornell President and former head of National Association for the Study and Prevention of Tuberculosis

64. Curti, *Philanthropy Abroad*, 309

65. Combining seven organizations: the YMCA (primarily) but also the YWCA, the National Catholic War Council, The Jewish Welfare Board, the War Camp Community Board, the American Library Association, and the Salvation Army.

66. Hopkins, *Mott*, 540.

67. Cutlip, *Fund Raising*, 88.

68. Arnaud Marts, *Philanthropy's Role in Civilization: Its Contribution to Human Freedom* (New York: Harper and Brothers, 1953), p. 110.

69. Henry Merritt Wriston, *Report on War Chest Practice* (presented to the Connecticut State Council of Defense, 1918), 67–68.

70. http://www.joycetice.com/military/warchest.htm (accessed September 17, 2010).

71. David L. Lewis, *The Public Image of Henry Ford* (Detroit: Wayne State University Press, 1976): 92, 95.

72. Hopkins, *Mott*, 541.

73. Hopkins, *Mott*, 538.

74. Gerlinger, *Money Raising*, 8.

75. Earl S. Brown, *A History of Switzerland County's Part in the World War* (Connersville, IN: Express Printing, 1919), available as transcribed by Ruth A. Hoggatt on http://myindianahome.net/gen/switz/records/military/WWI/warchest.html (accessed September 4, 2010).

76. Mary Wilcox Brown, *The Development of Thrift* (New York: Macmillan, 1899), 7.

77. *Scribner's Dictionary of American History*, "Thrift Stamps" (New York: Charles Scribner's Sons, 1940), vol. 5, 267.

78. Editorial, *English Journal* 7, (June 1918): 397.

79. May 23, 1918, poster of the local War Chest Fund, available at http://www.joycetice.com/military/libebond.htm (accessed on September 3, 1010).

80. Cutlip, *Fund Raising*, 141

81. Curti, *Philanthropy Abroad*, 254–57.

82. André Tardieu, *Devant l'obstacle: L'Amérique et nous* (Paris: Émile-Paul frères, 1927).

83. John Price Jones, *The American Giver: A Review of American Generosity* (New York: Inter-River Press, 1956), 12.

84. Cutlip, *Fund Raising*, 86–87.

85. In this position, he learned fund raising from Guy Emerson, another former journalist, whom Bishop William Lawrence of the Episcopal Church had trained in his successful effort to raise pensions for ministers; Cutlip, *Fund Raising*, 95.

86. Ibid., 43, 172–75; Richard L. Geiger, *To Advance Knowledge: The Growth of American Research Universities, 1900–1940* (New York: Oxford University Press, 1986), 51.

87. Merle Curti and Roderick Nash, *Philanthropy and the Shaping of American Higher Education* (New Brunswick,, NJ: Rutgers University Press, 1965), 205.

88. Cutlip, *Fund Raising*, 271–80.

89. *Campaign Notes of the American Society for the Control of Cancer* 10, 1927; Tamblyn and Brown, Inc., *Raising Money: New Business to Meet a New Need* (New York: Tamblyn & Brown, 1925).

90. The American City Bureau, *Bureau News*, vol. 1, 1919, American City Bureau files, Indiana University Purdue University at Indianapolis [IUPUI] Archives.

91. With the help of women's organizations, the Museum of Fine Arts in Boston opened its doors in January 1908 to Sunday docent service, *Handbook of the MFA*, 1915, 408. Not only did wealthy women donate large collections (such as suffragist Louisine Havemeyer's gift to the Metropolitan Museum of Art in New York in 1929), but they also helped open up the cultural institutions and made up a large part of their constituency; see Kathleen D. McCarthy, *Women's Culture: American Philanthropy and Art, 1830–1930* (Chicago: University of Chicago Press, 1991), 111–12.

92. Cutlip, *Fund Raising*, 169.

93. In 1935 the American Association of Fund-Raising Counsel was created through the work of nine major fundraising firms: "Minutes of Meeting of the American Association of Fund-Raising Counsel Held at the Advertising Club, New York City, October 21, 1935," IUPUI archives; Arnaud C. Marts, "Evolution of Marts and Lundy, Inc.," typescript, Marts and Lundy Records, 1926–1992, Series I, IUPUI archives.

94. Charles Flint Kellogg, *NAACP: A History of the National Association for the Advancement of Colored People, vol. 1: 1909–1920* (Baltimore: Johns Hopkins University Press, 1967), 107.

95. Raymond Moley, "The Community Trust," *Proceedings of the National Conference of Social Work at the Forty-Eighth Annual Session Held in Milwaukee, Wisconsin, June 22–29, 1921* (Chicago: University of Chicago Press, 1921), 428.

96. David C. Hammack, "Community Foundations: The Delicate Question of Purpose," in *An Agile Servant: Community Leadership by Community Foundations,* ed. Richard Magat (New York: Foundation Center, 1989), 29.

97. C. M. Bookman, "The Community Chest Movement—An Interpretation," *The National Conference of Social Work Annual Proceedings, 51st Annual Session* (Chicago: University of Chicago Press, 1924), 22.

98. Lubove, *Professional Altruist,* 213.

99. Cecile Clare North, *The Community and Social Welfare: A Study in Community Organization* (New York: McGraw-Hill, 1931), 298–99.

100. Chambers, *Seedtime of Reform,* 93.

101. David Sills, *The Volunteers: Means and Ends in a National Organization* (Glencoe, IL: Free Press, 1957), 42–43.

102. David M. Oshinsky, *Polio: An American Story* (New York: Oxford University Press, 2005), 49.

103. Ibid., 68.

104. Nina Gilden Seavey, Jane S. Smith, and Paul Wagner, *A Paralyzing Fear: The Triumph Over Polio in America* (New York: TV Books, 1998), 90.

105. R. J. Prendergast, "Raising the Big Wind," *American Mercury* 13 (April 1928): 464; cited in Lubove, *Professional Altruist,* 215.

106. Stanley Lebergott, *The Americans: An Economic Record* (New York: W.W. Norton & Company, 1984), 342; personal saving between 1922 and 1929 was higher than between 1900 and 1915. Statistics on giving before World War II are spotty, but the trend was upward. For example, in 1919, annual private gifts and grants to higher education totaled $7,584,000. By 1929, this figure stood at $26,172,000. Spending on fraternal organizations (a category that also includes recreation) stood at $140 million in 1914, but this figure had more than doubled to $302 million by 1929. John Price Jones estimated that charitable contributions rose from less than $650 million in 1923 to more than $803 million in 1929: *The American Giver,* table 1. On giving, see U.S. Bureau of the Census, *Historical Statistics of the United States* (2006), vol. 2, 877, table Bg211 ("Higher Education Expenditures, Endowment Income, Receipts, and Voluntary Support, by Sources: 1919–1995; All

Higher Education: Private Gifts and Grants"); vol. 2, 897, table Bg309 ("Voluntary Membership Organizations—Number, Indicators of Economic Significance, Employment, Employee Consumption, Expenditures, and Income, by Source: 1909–2000; Personal Consumption Expenditures for Recreation, Clubs, and Fraternal Organizations"); and vol. 2, 923, table Bg591 ("Philanthropic and Charitable Giving, and Philanthropic Revenue of Nonprofit Organizations: 1900–1997; Charitable Contributions").

107. Alexis de Tocqueville, *Democracy in America*, trans. Arthur Goldhammer (New York: Library of America, 2004 [1835/1840]), 610–16.

108. Brandt, *How Much Shall I Give?*, 56.

109. Bookman, "Community Chest Movement," 22–23.

110. T. N. Carver, "Thrift and the Standard of Living," *Journal of Political Economy* 28 (November 1920): 784–86.

111. Carl Joslyn, "What Can a Man Afford?," *American Economic Review* 11, supp. no. 2 (December 1921): 114.

112. Ellis Lore Kirkpatrick, *The Farmer's Standard of Living* (New York: Century Company, 1929), 192.

113. Ibid., 183.

114. Emily H. Huntington and Mary Gorringe Luck, *Living on a Moderate Income: The Incomes and Expenditures of Street-Car Men's and Clerks' Families in the San Francisco Bay Region* (Berkeley and Los Angeles: University of California Press, 1937), 128–31, 166.

115. Robert Bremner, *American Philanthropy* (Chicago: University of Chicago Press, 1988), 133.

116. Willford Isbell King, *Trends in Philanthropy: A Study in a Typical American City* (New York: National Bureau for Economic Research, 1928), 75.

117. Bremner, *American Philanthropy*, 138.

118. Wesley C. Mitchell, ed., *Recent Social Trends in The United States: Report of the President's Research Committee on Social Trends* (New York: McGraw-Hill, 1933), 1168 and 1219.

119. John Price Jones, "Public Opinion, the Depression, and Fund-Raising," *Public Opinion Quarterly* 1 (January 1937): 142–47.

Chapter 3
The Regulatory Compromise

1. *Jackson v. Wendell Phillips*, 96 Mass. 539, 555 (1867); Gray, in dialogue with British law, is quoting Sir Francis Moore.

2. Ellen Carol DuBois, "Outgrowing the Compact of the Fathers: Equal Rights, Woman Suffrage, and the United States Constitution, 1820–1878," *Journal of American History* 74 (December 1987): 846; see also Elizabeth Griffith, *In Her Own Right: The Life of Elizabeth Cady Stanton* (New York: Oxford University Press, 1984), 92; the gift was to William Lloyd Harrison, Wendell Phillips, Edmund Quincy,

Maria W. Chapman, L. Maria Child, Edmund Jackson, William L. Bowditch, Samuel May, Jr., and Charles K. Whipple; Among the feminists, Wendell Phillips, Lucy Stone (now the wife of Henry Blackwell), and Susan B. Anthony.

3. *Jackson*, 96 Mass. at 565.

4. Ibid. at 555.

5. *George v. Braddock*, 45 N.J. Eq. 757, 766 (1889).

6. Ibid.

7. *Lewis's Estate*, 152 PA 477, 477–80, 25 A. 878 (1893).

8. *Garrison v. Little*, 75 Ill. App. 402, 405–411 (1897).

9. *Collier v. Lindley*, 203 Cal. 641, 266 P. 526, 529 (1928); see also Elias Clark, "The Limitation on Political Activities: A Discordant Note in the Law of Charities," *Virginia Law Review* 46 (April 1960): 448, note 44.

10. John Witte, Jr., "Tax Exemption of Church Property: Historical Anomaly or Valid Constitutional Practice?" *Southern California Law Review* 64 (January 1991): 363–415.

11. Charles W Eliot, "The Exemption from Taxation of Church Property, and the Property of Educational, Literary, and Charitable Institutions." To the Commissioners of the Commonwealth, appointed "to inquire into the expediency of revising and amending the laws of the State relating to taxation and the exemptions therefrom." Cambridge, December 12, 1874. In *American Contributions to Civilization and Other Essays and Addresses* (New York: The Century Co., 1907), 302–303, 323, 335.

12. Clark, "Limitation on Political Activities," 448.

13. Kenneth Liles and Cynthia Blum, "Development of the Federal Tax Treatment of Charities: A Prelude to the Tax Reform Act of 1969," *Law and Contemporary Problems* 39 (Autumn 1975): 6–56; Marion R. Fremont Smith, *Governing Nonprofit Organizations: Federal and State Law and Regulation* (Cambridge, MA: The Belknap Press of Harvard University Press), 56–87.

14. William J. Shultz, *The Taxation of Inheritance* (Boston: Houghton Mifflin), 1926), 109.

15. 55 Cong. Rec. 6,741 (1917).

16. Robert H. Bremner, *American Philanthropy* (Chicago: University of Chicago Press, 1960, revised 1988), 127.

17. Edward Rabin, "Charitable Trusts and Charitable Deductions," *New York University Law Review* 41 (1966): 916.

18. *Treasury Decisions under Internal-Revenue Laws of the United States* 21 (January-December 1919): 285. See also Oliver A. Houck, "On the Limits of Charity: Lobbying, Litigation, and Electoral Politics by Charitable Organizations Under the Internal Revenue Code and Related Laws," *Brooklyn Law Review* 69, 1 (2003–2004): 9.

19. Appeal of Sophia G. Coxe, 5 BTA 261, 262–863 (1926).

20. See John J. Miller, *The Unmaking of Americans: How Multiculturalism Has Undermined the Assimilation Ethic* (New York: Free Press, 1998), 55; and Appeal of Herbert E. Fales, 9 BTA 828, 828–832 (1927).

21. "Deduction from Tax for Gift Clarified," *New York Times*, March 6, 1928.

22. Appeal of Herbert E. Fales.

23. Revenue Act of 1934, Pub. L. No. 73–216, 48 Stat. 680 (1934).

24. See Wayne E. Fuller, *Morality and the Mail in Nineteenth-Century America* (Urbana: University of Illinois Press, 2003), 98–128.

25. Daniel Kevles, *In the Name of Eugenics: Genetics and the Uses of Human Heredity* (New York: Knopf, 1985), 54.

26. *Buck v. Bell*, 274 U.S. 200 (1927).

27. For evidence on the practice of sterilization at the local level and support for it, see "Sterilization of Mental Defectives, 1923 Del. Laws, Vol. 33, Ch. 62, p. 152" in *Directory Relating to and Concerning Welfare Institutions and Laws of the State of Delaware* (Dover: Delaware State Board of Charities, 1932), 11–13.

28. "Anthony Comstock to Charles O. Heydt, December 11, 1899," Office of Mssrs. Rockefeller, Medical Interests, Record Group III, Series 2, Subseries K, Box 17, Folder 131, Rockefeller Archive Center; on John D. Rockefeller, Jr.'s personal gifts, see Ellen Chesler, *Woman of Valor: Margaret Sanger and the Birth Control Movement in America* (New York: Anchor Books, 1993), 277, and an important series of memoranda in Office of Messrs. Rockefeller, Medical Interests, Record Group III 2 K, Box 1, Folder 139, Rockefeller Archive Center.

29. Albert F. Schenkel, *The Rich Man and the Kingdom: John D. Rockefeller, Jr., and the Protestant Establishment* (Minneapolis, MN: Fortress Press, 1995), 87.

30. Chesler, *Woman of Valor*, 72n.

31. Raymond B. Fosdick, *John D. Rockefeller, Jr.: A Portrait* (New York: Harper & Brothers, Publishers, 1956), 386.

32. James Reed, *The Birth Control Movement and American Society: From Private Vice to Public Virtue. With a New Preface on the Relationship between Historical Scholarship and Feminist Issues* (Princeton, NJ: Princeton University Press, 1984), 202.

33. *Slee v. Commissioner*, 15 B.T.A. 710, 713 (1929).

34. *Slee v. Commissioner*, 42 F.2^d 184 (2^d Cir. 1930)].

35. David M. Kennedy, *Birth Control in America: The Career of Margaret Sanger* (New Haven: Yale University Press, 1970), 225.

36. "Birth Control Unit Plans $100,000 Fund," *New York Times*, January 11, 1930.

37. Chesler, *Woman of Valor*, 324.

38. Olivier Zunz, *Why the American Century?* (Chicago: University of Chicago Press, 1998), 25–45.

39. National Economy League, *Brief in Support of the Petition of May 4, 1932 to the President and the Congress for the Elimination of Expenditures of $450,000,000 Per Annum for Veterans of the Spanish-American and World Wars not in Fact Suffering from Disabilities Incurred in Service* (New York, 1932); idem, *Functional Organization Chart, Virginia Branch* (n.p., 1932).

40. "Economy Lobby," *Time Magazine*, January 2, 1933.

41. "Angels of Economy League To Be Bared," *Washington Post*, January 10, 1933.

42. 78 Cong. Rec. 5861 (1934); Liles and Blum, "Development of the Federal Tax Treatment of Charities," 9; Clark, "Limitation on Political Activities," 447, notes 40 and 41.

43. 78 Cong. Rec. 5959 (1934).

44. *George*, 45 N.J. 757; *Taylor v. Hoag*, 273 Pa.194, 200, 116 A.826 (1922).

45. In 1955, the 6th Circuit Court in *Seasongood v. Commissioner*, 227 F.2d 907, declared "substantial" to be above 5 percent of time and effort; see "The Revenue Code and a Charity's Politics," *Yale Law Journal* 73, 4 (March 1964): 674.

46. 78 Cong. Rec. 5861 (1934).

47. Revenue Act of 1934, Pub. L. No. 73–216, 48 Stat. 680 (1934); Houck, "On The Limits of Charity," 12–23.

48. "Charitable," *New York Times*, March 7, 1928.

Chapter 4
The Private Funding of Affairs of State

1. Barry D. Karl, *The Uneasy State: The United States from 1915 to 1945* (Chicago: University of Chicago Press, 1983), 74.

2. Ellis Hawley, "Herbert Hoover, the Commerce Secretariat, and the Vision of an 'Associative State,' 1921–1928," *Journal of American History* 61 (June 1974): 116–40.

3. Gary Dean Best, *The Politics of American Individualism: Herbert Hoover in Transition, 1918–1921* (Westport, CT: Greenwood Press, 1975), 94.

4. David Burner, *Herbert Hoover: A Public Life* (New York: Knopf, 1979), 261.

5. Herbert Hoover, *American Individualism* (Garden City, NY: Doubleday, Page & Co., 1922), 56.

6. Best, *Politics of American Individualism*, 93.

7. James Allen Smith, *The Idea Brokers: Think Tanks and the Rise of the New Policy Elite* (New York: Free Press, 1991), 52–53.

8. "Harding Names 38 on Unemployment," *New York Times*, September 20, 1921.

9. William E. Leuchtenburg, *Herbert Hoover* (New York: Henry Holt and Company, 2009), 51–70; Olivier Zunz, *Why the American Century?* (Chicago: University of Chicago Press, 1998), 42–45.

10. Norton had advised Jerome D. Greene of the Rockefeller Foundation to invite Robert Brookings as a founding trustee of the Institute for Governmental Research; see Smith, *Idea Brokers*, 53.

11. David A. Hounshell, "Industrial Research and Manufacturing Technology," in *Encyclopedia of the United States in the Twentieth Century*, ed. Stanley I. Kutler (New York: Charles Scribner's Sons, 1996), vol. 2, 843.

12. Raymond B. Fosdick, *The Story of the Rockefeller Foundation* (New York: Harper & Brothers, 1952), 159–60, 163; Robert E. Kohler, *Partners in Science: Foundations and Natural Scientists, 1900–1945* (Chicago: University of Chicago Press, 1991), 266.

13. Gail Radford, *Modern Housing for America: Policy Struggles in the New Deal Era* (Chicago: University of Chicago Press, 1996), 50–51.

14. Hawley, "Herbert Hoover, the Commerce Secretariat," 133–34.

15. Donald Critchlow, *The Brookings Institution, 1916–1952: Expertise and the Public Interest in a Democratic Society* (Dekalb, IL: Northern Illinois University Press, 1985), 74.

16. Burner, *Hoover*, 194.

17. Bruce A. Lohof, "Herbert Hoover, Spokesman of Humane Efficiency: The Mississippi Flood of 1927," *American Quarterly*, 22 (Autumn 1970), 690–700.

18. John M. Barry, *Rising Tide: The Great Mississippi Flood of 1927 and How It Changed America* (New York: Simon and Schuster, 1997), 370.

19. Burner, *Hoover*, 193.

20. Robyn Spencer, "Contested Terrain: The Mississippi Flood of 1927 and the Struggle to Control Black Labor," *Journal of Negro History* 79 (Spring 1994): 170–81.

21. Barry, *Rising Tide*, 390.

22. Lohof, "Herbert Hoover, Spokesman of Humane Efficiency," 116.

23. Bruce Lohof, ed., "Herbert Hoover's Mississippi Valley Land Reform Memorandum: A Document," *Arkansas Historical Quarterly* 29 (Summer 1970): 112–18.

24. Burner, *Hoover*, 195–96; Barry, *Rising Tide*, 392.

25. Morris Robert Werner, *Julius Rosenwald: The Life of a Practical Humanitarian* (New York: Harper & Brothers Publishers, 1939), 293.

26. Ibid., 253.

27. Ibid., 254.

28. Ibid., 352–53; Peter M. Ascoli, *Julius Rosenwald: The Man Who Built Sears, Roebuck and Advanced the Cause of Black Education in the American South* (Bloomington: Indiana University Press, 2006), 356–57.

29. "Inaugural Address of Herbert Hoover, March 24, 1929," Herbert Hoover Presidential Library and Museum, http://hoover.archives.gov/info/inauguralspeech.html (accessed September 27, 2010).

30. Barry D. Karl, "Foundations and Public Policy," in *Encyclopedia of the United States in the Twentieth Century*, ed. Kutler, vol. 1, 496b.

31. John M. Glenn, Lilian Brandt, and F. Emerson Andrews, *Russell Sage Foundation, 1907–1946* (New York, 1947), 2: 514–15.

32. *The Nader Study Group Report on Dupont in Delaware: The Company State* (Washington, DC: Center for Study of Responsive Law, 1971).

33. Andrew J. F. Morris, *The Limits of Voluntarism: Charity and Welfare from the New Deal through the Great Society* (Cambridge: Cambridge University Press, 2009), 4.

34. Lammot du Pont to John Raskob, November 18, 1930, in Raskob papers, Acc. 473/678, Hagley Museum and Library [HML].

35. *Work & Relief in Wilmington, Delaware in 1931–1932* (Wilmington: Mayor's Employment and Relief Committee, n.d.) 21, Longwood Mss. Group 10, 1164, HML.

36. Barry John Plimmer, "Voluntarism in Crisis: An Exploration of the Effects of the Great Depression in Delaware, 1929–38" (Ph.D. diss., University of Hull, 1996), 12–13.

37. *Work & Relief, 1931–32*, 21.

38. Plimmer, "Voluntarism in Crisis," 14.

39. "Animals: Doak's Polly," *Time*, December 15, 1930.

40. *Work & Relief*, 13–15.

41. A new fundraising drive called the Block-Aid Campaign was begun: Plimmer, "Voluntarism in Crisis," 24.

42. Nan Elizabeth Woodruff, *As Rare As Rain: Federal Relief in the Great Southern Drought of 1930–31* (Urbana: University of Illinois Press, 1985), 8–9, 18–19, 22, 36, 41.

43. David Hamilton, "Herbert Hoover and the Great Drought of 1930," *Journal of American History* (March 1982): 854.

44. Woodruff, *As Rare As Rain*, 11; "Hoover Names Body To Aid the States in Drought Relief," *New York Times*, August 20, 1930.

45. Hamilton, "Hoover and the Great Drought," 855.

46. Woodruff, *As Rare As Rain*, 29.

47. Ibid., 74–75, 82–85.

48. "Hoover Asks Nation To Give $10,000,000 for Red Cross Aid," *New York Times*, January 14, 1931"; "$25,000,000 Drought Fund Is Declined By Red Cross," *New York Times*, January 29, 1931; "Edison Gives His Birthday Cake for Sale to Aid Relief Fund," *New York Times*, February 14, 1931.

49. Woodruff, *As Rare as Rain*, 84.

50. Walter I. Trattner, *From Poor Law to Welfare State: A History of Social Welfare in America* (New York: Free Press, 1974), 273.

51. Woodruff, *As Rare as Rain*, 87–90.

52. Burner, *Hoover*, 266.

53. Fosdick, *Rockefeller Foundation*, 203, 209; "Rockefellers Add $750,000 for Idle," *New York Times*, November 18, 1931.

54. Glenn, Brandt, and Andrews, *Russell Sage Foundation* 2: 489.

55. David Hammack and Stanton Wheeler, *Social Science in the Making: Essays on the Russell Sage Foundation, 1907–1972* (New York: Russell Sage Foundation, 1994), 47.

56. Robert H. Bremner, *American Philanthropy* (Chicago: University of Chicago Press, 1960, revised 1988), 140.

57. Ibid., 139–142.

58. Woodruff, *As Rare as Rain*, 70.

59. William R. Brock, *Welfare, Democracy, and the New Deal* (Cambridge: Cambridge University Press, 1988), 138–39.

60. Fearing such conflicts, the SSRC had not wanted to join the President's Conference on Unemployment in 1923, see Barry D. Karl, *Charles E. Merriam and the Study of Politics* (Chicago: University of Chicago Press, 1974), 208–209.

61. Josephine Brown, *Public Relief, 1929–1939* (New York: Henry Holt and Co., 1940), 142.

62. Guy Alchon, *The Invisible Hand of Planning: Capitalism, Social Science, and the State in the 1920s* (Princeton, NJ: Princeton University Press, 1985), 168.

63. "Message to the Legislature, Albany, August 28, 1931," in *The Roosevelt Reader: Selected Speeches, Messages, Press Conferences, and Letters of Franklin D. Roosevelt*, ed. Basil Rauch (New York: Rinehart & Co., 1957), 62–64; W. A. Warn, "Roosevelt Asks $20,000,000 For Jobless, Raising Fund By A 50% Income Tax Rise," *New York Times*, August 29, 1931.

64. June Hopkins, *Harry Hopkins: Sudden Hero, Brash Reformer* (New York: St. Martin's Press, 1999), 67–70.

65. Ibid., 91–123.

66. Brock, *Welfare, Democracy*, 24.

67. Ibid., 127.

68. Brown, *Public Relief*, 415.

69. Ibid., 186.

70. Andrew J. F. Morris, "Charity, Therapy and Poverty: Private Social Service in the Era of Public Welfare" (Ph.D. Diss., University of Virginia, 2003), 85.

71. Brown, *Public Relief*, 186.

72. Hopkins, *Hopkins*, 158, 165.

73. Brock, *Welfare, Democracy*, 166.

74. Hopkins, *Hopkins*, 165; see also Brock, *Welfare, Democracy*, 168.

75. Brown, *Public Relief*, 301, quoting Harry Hopkins.

76. Brock, *Welfare, Democracy*, 280.

77. Jeff Singleton, *The American Dole: Unemployment Relief and the Welfare State in the Great Depression* (Westport, CT: Greenwood Press, 1996), 174.

78. Gene D. L. Jones, "The Chicago Catholic Charities, the Great Depression, and Public Monies," *Illinois Historical Journal* 83 (Spring 1990): 25; see also Morris, *Limits of Voluntarism*, 219.

79. Plimmer, "Voluntarism in Crisis," 88–95.

80. Morris, "Charity, Therapy and Poverty," 83.

81. Morris, *The Limits of Voluntarism*, 22.

82. "Review of CWA Activities in the State of Delaware for 1933," 3; Crane Papers, 1416/98, HML.

83. Plimmer, "Voluntarism in Crisis," 43–44.

84. Ibid., 45.

85. *Reports of the Special Commissions to Study the Need for Relief in New Castle, Kent, and Sussex Counties, 1934*, Crane Papers, 1416/99, HML.

86. Plimmer, "Voluntarism in Crisis," 173.

87. "Drought Relief Cash Ample, Says Hopkins," *New York Times*, June 19, 1934; Donald Worster, *Dust Bowl: The Southern Plains in the 1930s* (New York: Oxford University Press, 1979), 113–14.

88. Worster, *Dust Bowl*, 18–20, 28.

89. H.R. 7054, 74th Cong., 1st sess.; Worster, *Dust Bowl*, 212–13.

Chapter 5
From Humanitarianism to Cold War

1. Arthur C. Ringland, "The Organization of Voluntary Foreign Aid: 1939–1953," *Department of State Bulletin* (March 15, 1954): 383.

2. Except the Red Cross, because it already had its own regulations outlined in its congressional charter; Merle Curti, *American Philanthropy Abroad* (New Brunswick, NJ: Rutgers University Press, 1963), 414; Allen W. Dulles, "Cash and Carry Neutrality," *Foreign Affairs* 18 (January 1940): 179–95.

3. Ringland, "Organization of Voluntary Foreign Aid," 384.

4. Curti, *Philanthropy Abroad*, 452–53.

5. Joseph E. Davies, Charles P. Taft, and Charles Warren, *Voluntary War Relief During World War II: A Report to the President by the President's War Relief Control Board* (Washington, DC: GPO, 1946), 5.

6. "Cordell Hull to FDR," March 3, 1941, in *State Department Bulletin* 4 (March 15, 1941), 282.

7. International lawyer Charles Warren replaced the deceased Keppel as board member, executive order 9205, July 25, 1942.

8. Davies et al., *Voluntary War Relief*, 10; Ringland, "Organization of Voluntary Foreign Aid," 385; Curti, *Philanthropy Abroad*, 456; Harold J. Seymour, *Design for Giving: The Story of the National War Fund, Inc., 1943–1947*, with a foreword by Winthrop W. Aldrich (New York: Harper & Brothers, 1947), 1–21, 73.

9. Franklin Roosevelt, "Radio Address of the National War Fund Drive," October 5, 1943, American Presidency Project, http://www.presidency.ucsb.edu/ws/index.php?pid=16322&st=&st1= (accessed October 11, 2010).

10. Davies et al., *Voluntary War Relief*, 11.

11. Ibid., 8.

12. Landrum Bolling, with Craig Smith, *Private Foreign Aid: U.S. Philanthropy for Relief and Development* (Boulder, CO: Westview Press, 1982), 16.

13. Ronald E. Stenning, *Church World Service: Fifty Years of Help and Hope* (New York: Friendship Press, 1996).

14. Davies et al., *Voluntary War Relief*, 11.

15. Curti, *Philanthropy Abroad*, 456

16. Ibid., 526.

17. Allan Nevins, *Herbert H. Lehman and His Era* (New York: Scribner, 1963), 227–33; William I. Hitchcock, *The Bitter Road to Freedom: The Human Cost of Allied Victory in World War II Europe* (New York: Free Press, 2008), 243–46.

18. George Woodbridge, *UNRRA: The History of the United Nations Relief and Rehabilitation Administration* (New York: Columbia University Press, 1950), vol. 2, 20.

19. Nevins, *Lehman*, 243–44.

20. Ibid., 272.

21. Bolling, *Private Foreign Aid*, 155–56; Nevins, *Lehman*, 274.

22. Curti, *Philanthropy Abroad*, 459.

23. The member organizations, many church-sponsored, were American Baptist Relief; American Friends Service Committee; Brethren Service Committee; Church World Service; Committee on Christian Science Wartime Activities of the Mother Church; Congregational Christian Service Committee; International Migration Service; International Rescue and Relief Committee; Labor League for Human Rights, AFL; Lutheran World Relief; Mennonite Central Committee; National CIO Community Services Committee; Russian Children's Welfare Society; Tolstoy Foundation; Unitarian Service Committee; War Relief Services-National Catholic Welfare Conference.

24. There was also ARK, American Relief for Korea, which had private philanthropies on the ground assisting with food and social services.

25. Wallace Campbell, *The History of CARE: A Personal Account* (New York: Praeger, 1990), 15.

26. Curti, *Philanthropy Abroad*, 498–99.

27. Campbell, *History of CARE*, 27.

28. Davies et al, *Voluntary War Relief*, 15.

29. Nevins, 277.

30. Curti, *Philanthropy Abroad*, 484–85.

31. Akira Iriye, *Global Community: The Role of International Organizations in the Making of the Contemporary World* (Berkeley: University of California Press, 2002), 42–43.

32. John Ensor Harr and Peter J. Johnson, *The Rockefeller Century: Three Generations of America's Greatest Family* (New York: Charles Scribner's Sons, 1988): 431–33.

33. Volker R. Berghahn, *America and the Intellectual Cold Wars in Europe: Shepard Stone between Philanthropy, Academy, and Diplomacy* (Princeton, NJ: Princeton University Press, 2001), 143–47.

34. On McCloy, see Alan Brinkley, *Liberalism and Its Discontents* (Cambridge, MA: Harvard University Press, 1998), 177–209; Kai Bird, *The Chairman—John J. McCloy: The Making of the American Establishment* (New York: Simon & Schuster, 1992).

35. On Stone, see Berghahn, *America and the Intellectual Cold Wars in Europe*.

36. Paul G. Hoffman, "Memorandum to the Board of Trustees," 29 January 1951, report 010619, Ford Foundation Archives [FF].

37. Paul G. Hoffman, "To the Trustees of the Ford Foundation," July 13, 1951, report 010619, FF; *Tax-Exempt Foundations: Hearings on H. Res. 561, Before the Select Committee to Investigate Tax-Exempt Foundations and Comparable Organizations*, 82nd Cong. 231 (1952) (statement of Paul G. Hoffman, President and Director, Ford Foundation).

38. Dyke Brown to Rowan Gaither and Joseph M. McDaniel, Jr., "Development of Program I," April 26, 1951, report 010601, FF.

39. The Ford Foundation, *Annual Report for 1951*, December 31, 1951, 13.

40. Ibid.; and Report of the President to the Board of Trustees, April 10, 1951, report 010619, FF; Brown to Gaither and McDaniel, Jr., "Program I," report 010601, FF; Milton Katz to Rowan Gaither and Dyke Brown, "A Reexamination of the Program Categories under Area I," October 26, 1951, report 010619, FF.

41. Richard T. Arndt, *The First Resort of Kings: American Cultural Diplomacy in the Twentieth Century* (Washington, DC: Potomac Books, Inc., 2005), 179, 228.

42. Ibid., 117–18.

43. Ibid., 114.

44. Akira Iriye, "The Role of Philanthropy and Civil Society in U.S. Foreign Relations," in *Philanthropy and Reconciliation: Rebuilding Postwar U.S.-Japan Relations,* ed. Tadashi Yamamoto, Akira Iriye, and Makoto Iokibe (Tokyo and New York: Japan Center for International Exchange, 2006), 51–52.

45. Francis X. Sutton "Draft Manuscript, Ford Foundation History Project, Overseas Development, Part II, August 1984, report 011765, FF.

46. Edwin R. Embree, "Timid Billions," *Harper's Magazine* 198 (March 1949), 33; *Hearings before the Select Committee . . . 1952,* 344, "Statement of Charles Dollard, President, Carnegie Corporation, New York"; see also Morton Keller and Phyllis Keller, *Making Harvard Modern: The Rise of America's University* (New York: Oxford University Press, 2001), 227.

47. Paul G. Hoffman, *Peace Can Be Won* (Garden City, NY: Doubleday and Company, 1951), 151.

48. "Notes on Conference with Walter Bedell Smith, Allen Dulles and others, April 3, 1951," Office of the President, H. Rowan Gaither, Area One, The Establishment of Peace, Group 21, Box 1, Series 1, Folder 1. This explains in part why, in early 1953, the foundation felt comfortable in declining yet another request from Senator Joseph McCarthy for information on its activities. When Hoffman received a request for information from the junior senator from Wisconsin in early 1953, Gaither, who had by then replaced him as president, politely declined the invitation. Office of the President, H. Rowan Gaither, Group 21, Series 6, Box 12, Folder 140, Ford archives.

49. Dyke Brown to Paul G. Hoffman, appendix to "Development of Area I Statement," December 19, 1951, report 010619, FF.

50. Pierre Grémion, *Intelligence de l'anticommunisme: Le Congrès pour la liberté de la culture à Paris, 1950–1975* (Paris: Fayard, 1995); Hugh Wilford, *The Mighty Wurlitzer: How the CIA Played America* (Cambridge: Harvard University Press, 2008), 86.

51. Raymond Aron, *Mémoires. Cinquante ans de réflexion politique* (Paris: Julliard, 1983; reprint, Paris: Presses Pocket, 1990), 330–32 (page citation is to the reprint edition); Wilford, *The Mighty Wurlitzer,* 239.

52. Robert L. Daniel, *American Philanthropy in the Near East, 1820–1960* (Athens: Ohio University Press, 1970), 201.

53. Mary Coburn, "Near East Foundation Progress Report," in *Basic Project Reports* (New York: Near East Foundation, 1933), 8.

54. Daniel, *Philanthropy in the Near East*, 262; Curti, *Philanthropy Abroad*, 610.

55. Raymond B. Fosdick, *The Story of the Rockefeller Foundation* (New York: Harper & Brothers, 1952), 184. The phrase "green revolution" is usually thought to have been coined by United States Agency for International Development administrator William Gaud in 1968; see Nick Cullather, *The Hungry World: America's Cold War Battle Against Poverty in Asia* (Cambridge, MA: Harvard University Press, 2010), 5; Mark Dowie gives the credit to W. H. "Ping" Ferry, who was in charge of public relations for the Ford Foundation at the time of the creation of the International Rice Research Institute in 1960; see his *American Foundations: An Investigative History* (Cambridge, MA: MIT Press, 2001), 112.

56. For a convenient summary, Joel L. Fleishman, *The Foundation, A Great American Secret: How Private Wealth Is Changing the World* (New York: Public Affairs, 2007), 115–24; "Norman Borlaug, Plant Scientist Who Fought Famine, Dies at 95," *New York Times*, September 14, 2009.

57. Ian Martin, "The Ford Foundation in India and Pakistan, 1952–1970," October 8, 1971, 53, report 001970, FF.

58. Darlene Rivas, *Missionary Capitalist: Nelson Rockefeller in Venezuela* (Chapel Hill: University of North Carolina Press, 2002), 38–44; Frank A. Ninkovich, *The Diplomacy of Ideas: U.S. Foreign Policy and Cultural Relations, 1938–1950* (Cambridge: Cambridge University Press, 1981), 36–38, on why Rockefeller could not trust the State Department.

59. Kenneth R. Iverson, "The 'Servicio' in Theory and Practice," *Public Administration Review* 11 (Autumn 1951): 223–28; Rivas, *Missionary Capitalist*, 52–54.

60. Curti, *Philanthropy Abroad*, 576; Bolling, *Private Foreign Aid*, 35–38.

61. The Stanford biologist Paul R. Ehrlich sparked the "zero population growth" movement with *The Population Bomb* (New York: Ballantine Books, 1968).

62. James Reed, *The Birth Control Movement and American Society: From Private Vice to Public Virtue. With a New Preface on the Relationship between Historical Scholarship and Feminist Issues* (Princeton, NJ: Princeton University Press, 1984), 203; Daniel M. Fox, "The Significance of the Milbank Fund for Policy: An Assessment at Its Centennial," *The Milbank Quarterly* 84, 1 (2006): 1–32.

63. Matthew Connelly, *Fatal Misconception: The Struggle to Control World Population* (Cambridge, MA: The Belknap Press of Harvard University Press, 2008).

64. Rivas, *Missionary Capitalist*, 216; when the war ended and Rockefeller left the State Department, he launched, along with a number of former CIAA and IIAA staffers, related nonprofit and for profit agricultural development ventures (in the end unsuccessful) in Latin America under the leadership of Kenneth J. Kadow, the former head of the Department of Horticulture at the University of Delaware. Had it been legal, Rockefeller would have merged the two under a single corporation in an early version of "philanthrocapitalism."

65. Sergei Y. Shenin, *The United States and the Third World: The Origins of Postwar Relations and the Point Four Program* (Huntington, NY: NOVA Science

Publishers, 2000), 10–11; Robert Donovan, *Tumultuous Years: The Presidency of Harry S. Truman, 1949–1953* (New York: W. W. Norton & Company, 1982), 28–29; David Ekbladh, *The Great American Mission: Modernization and the Construction of an American World Order* (Princeton, NJ: Princeton University Press), 97–98.

66. On Rockefeller chairing Truman's IDAB, see Rivas, *Missionary Capitalist*, 173, 185–201.

67. In Walter M. Daniels, ed., *The Point Four Program* (New York: H. Wilson Company, 1951), 12–17.

68. "H. G. Bennett Heads the Point 4 Program," *New York Times*, November 15, 1950. On Ensminger, see Eugene S. Staples, *Forty Years: A Learning Curve. The Ford Foundation Programs in India* (New York: Ford Foundation, 1992), 50; see Sutton, "Draft Manuscript, Ford Foundation History Project," part II.

69. For Hoffman, the prime minister was the one man "upon whom depends the entire question of whether India goes Communist or does not." *Hearings before the Select Committee . . . 1952*, 232.

70. Senate Committee on Foreign Relations, Technical Assistance, S. Rep. No. 85–139, at 299 (1957).

71. Harry S. Taylor, "Oral History with Douglas Ensminger," June 16 and 17, 1976, Truman Presidential Museum and Library, Columbia, Missouri; see also Gary R. Hess, "Waging the Cold War in the Third World: The Foundations and the Challenges of Development," in *Charity, Philanthropy, and Civility in American History*, ed. Lawrence J. Friedman and Mark D. McGarvie (Cambridge: Cambridge University Press, 2003), 319–39.

72. Shenin, *The United States and the Third World*, 92.

73. "Government Utilization of Private Agencies in Technical Assistance," in Senate Committee on Foreign Relations, *Technical Assistance: Final Report of Subcommittee on Technical Assistance Programs*, 85th Congress, 1st Sess. (1957), 306.

74. Edward Kissi, "Famine and the Politics of Food Relief in United States Relations with Ethiopia, 1950–1991" (Ph.D. Diss., Concordia University, 1997).

75. Curti, *Philanthropy Abroad*, 615.

76. Ibid., 612.

77. Morris Robert Werner, *Julius Rosenwald: The Life of a Practical Humanitarian* (New York: Harper & Brothers Publishers, 1939), 98–99.

78. Samuel Halperin, "Ideology or Philanthropy? The Politics of Zionist Fund-Raising," *Western Political Quarterly* 13 (December 1960): 969–70.

79. Yaacov Bar-Siman-Tov, "The Limits of Economic Sanctions: The American-Israeli Case of 1953," *Journal of Contemporary History* 23 (July 1988): 430–31.

80. Michael Beschloss, *Presidential Courage: Brave Leaders and How They Changed America, 1789–1989* (New York: Simon & Schuster, 2007), 210, 214–22.

81. Truman extended de jure recognition in January 1949; see Michael J. Cohen, *Truman and Israel* (Berkeley: University of California Press, 1990), 199–222, 274.

82. Isaac Alteras, *Eisenhower and Israel: U.S.-Israeli Relations, 1953–1960* (Gainesville: University Press of Florida, 1993), 16.

83. Merrill D. Peterson, "*Starving Armenians*": *America and the Armenian Genocide, 1915–1930 and After* (Charlottesville: University of Virginia Press, 2004), 1.

84. "Morgenthau Says U.S. Backs Israel," *New York Times*, October 21, 1948, 8; "Morgenthau Sees Israel Soviet Foe," *New York Times*, November 2, 1948, 15.

85. "Israel Aid Asked by Mrs. Roosevelt; We Must Help All Who Desire Freedom, She Adds—Donates $3,500 to Appeal Fund," *New York Times*, March 2, 1950, 24; Display ads, *New York Times*, April 29 and June 11, 1952.

86. Display ads, *New York Times*, February 15, 1954 and April 16, 1956.

87. "Lehman Asks Help for Jewish Appeal," *New York Times*, April 17, 1950, 20.

88. Samuel Halperin, "Ideology or Philanthropy? The Politics of Zionist Fund-Raising," *Western Political Quarterly* 13 (December 1960): 960; Halperin, *The Political World of American Zionism* (Detroit, MI: Wayne State University Press, 1961), 201.

89. Halperin, *The Political World*, 380.

90. Deborah Dash Moore, *To the Golden Cities: Pursuing the American Jewish Dream in Miami and L.A.* (Cambridge, MA: Harvard University Press), 238–39; Marc Lee Raphael, *A History of the United Jewish Appeal, 1939–1982* (Chico, CA: Scholars Press, 1982), 45.

91. Moore, *Golden Cities*, 83–84.

92. Ibid., 237.

93. Edward S. Shapiro, *A Time for Healing: American Jewry Since World War II* (Baltimore: Johns Hopkins University Press, 1992), 204–205.

94. Raphael, *United Jewish Appeal*, 39–45.

95. Abraham Ben-Zvi, *Decade of Transition: Eisenhower, Kennedy, and the Origins of the American-Israeli Alliance* (New York: Columbia University Press, 1998), 56–57.

96. Irving Spiegel, "U.S. Jews Start $100,000,000 Fund," *New York Times*, December 2, 1956.

97. Spiegel, "$35,100,000 Given to Jewish Appeal," *New York Times*, March 4, 1957.

98. Alteras, *Eisenhower and Israel*, 265; Stephen E. Ambrose, *Eisenhower* (New York: Simon & Schuster, 1984), vol. 2, 386–87.

99. Alteras, *Eisenhower and Israel*, 271.

100. William S. White, "Johnson Warns President Against 'Coercing' Israel," *New York Times*, February 19, 1957; Thomas J. Hamilton, "U.N. Debate Today on Mideast Issue Is Still Uncertain," *New York Times*, February 22, 1957.

101. American Jews formed political institutions to press home their concerns. Created in 1954, the Conference of Presidents of Major Jewish Organizations was an umbrella group of sixteen national groups eager to speak to the White House and State Department with one voice. They included the American Zionist Committee for Public Affairs, B'nai B'rith, Hadassah, Jewish War Veterans, the American Zionist Federation, and the American Jewish Congress. The year 1954 also saw the creation of the American Zionist Committee for Public Affairs (its full title was later

changed to the American Israel Public Affairs Committee, AIPAC). This group, a formal lobby dedicated to supporting Israel, dealt mainly with Congress.

102. Alteras, *Eisenhower and Israel*, 295–98, 300.

103. Aleksandr Fursenko and Timothy Naftali, *Khrushchev's Cold War: The Inside Story of an American Adversary* (New York: W. W. Norton & Company, 2006), 58, 62–65.

Chapter 6
Philanthropy at Midcentury: "Timid Billions"?

1. These figures understate the reality as all surveys until 1960 remained woefully incomplete. See David C. Hammack, "American Debates on the Legitimacy of Foundations," in *The Legitimacy of Philanthropic Foundations: United States and European Perspectives,* ed. Kenneth Prewitt, Mattei Dogan, Steven Heydemann, and Stefan Toepler (New York: Russell Sage Foundation, 2006), 55.

2. Frank G. Dickinson, *The Changing Position of Philanthropy in the American Economy*, with an introduction by Solomon Fabricant (New York: National Bureau of Economic Research, distributed by Columbia University Press, 1970), 4–19.

3. David Cannadine, *Mellon: An American Life* (New York: Alfred A. Knopf, 2006), 547, 598.

4. Ibid., *Mellon*, 345.

5. Paul Mellon, with John Baskett, *Reflections in a Silver Spoon: A Memoir* (New York: William Morrow and Company, 1992), 300; on Mellon and the National Gallery, see Cannadine, *Mellon*, 505–82.

6. John Morton Blum, *Roosevelt and Morgenthau: A Revision and Condensation of "From The Morgenthau Diaries"* (Boston: Houghton Mifflin, 1970), 168–70.

7. Ibid., 170.

8. Ibid., 149.

9. Roy G. Blakey and Gladys C. Blakey, "The Revenue Act of 1935," *American Economic Review* 25 (December 1935): 673–90; William Greenleaf, *From These Beginnings: The Early Philanthropies of Henry and Edsel Ford, 1911–1936* (Detroit, MI: Wayne State University Press, 1964), 181.

10. Greenleaf, *From These Beginnings*, 185–86.

11. Ibid., 187–88.

12. Allan Nevins, *Ford*, vol. 3: *Decline and Rebirth, 1933–1962* (New York: Scribner, 1963), 411.

13. Ibid., 413.

14. Frederick P. Keppel, *The Foundation: Its Place in American Life* (New York: Macmillan, 1930; reprint, with an introduction by Ellen Condliffe Lagemann, New Brunswick, NJ: Transactions Publishers, 1989), xix.

15. Joseph C. Kiger, *Philanthropic Foundations in the Twentieth Century* (Westport, CT: Greenwood Press, 2000), 43; F. Emerson Andrews, *Philanthropic Giving*

(New York: Russell Sage Foundation, 1950), 92; on Ford and universities, Francis X. Sutton, "The Ford Foundation and Columbia: A Paper for the University Seminar on Columbia University, 16 November 1999," unpublished.

16. F. Emerson Andrews, *Corporation Giving* (New York: Russell Sage Foundation, 1952; reprint, with a new introduction by Michael Useem, New Brunswick: Transaction Publishers, 1993).

17. Morrell Heald, *The Social Responsibilities of Business, Company, and Community, 1900–1960* (Cleveland: Press of Case Western Reserve University, 1970), 155–73.

18. Andrews, *Corporation Giving*, 229–35; Heald, *Social Responsibilities*, 265.

19. Heald, *Social Responsibilities*, 218; Merle Curti and Roderick Nash, *Philanthropy and the Shaping of American Higher Education* (New Brunswick, NJ: Rutgers University Press, 1965), 242–43.

20. Arthur W. Page even got involved in the curriculum by encouraging Harvard historians to study individual liberty rather than state functions. His was an unexpected call for a social history from the bottom up in the name of investment in philanthropy, long before the history profession, spurred by 1960s populism, adopted such a program; see Page Papers, 1908–1960, U.S. Mss 51 AF, box 56, Wisconsin Historical Society.

21. Andrews, *Philanthropic Giving*, 234; Dickinson, *Changing Position of Philanthropy*, 22–23.

22. Andrews, *Philanthropic Giving*, 105–10.

23. For example J. K. Lasser, *How Tax Laws Make Giving to Charity Easy* (New York: Funk & Wagnalls Co., 1948); J. K. Lasser Tax Institute and Ralph Wallace, *How to Save Estate and Gift Taxes* (New York: American Research Council, 1955); Beardsley Ruml and Theodore Geiger, eds., *The Manual of Corporate Giving* (Washington, DC: National Planning Association, 1952).

24. Kenneth Liles and Cynthia Blum, "Development of the Federal Tax Treatment of Charities: A Prelude to the Tax Reform Act of 1969," *Law and Contemporary Problems* 39 (Autumn 1975): 31.

25. Andrews, *Philanthropic Giving*, 91.

26. Dickinson, *Changing Position of Philanthropy*, 22–23.

27. Andrews, *Philanthropic Giving*, 50–60.

28. Robert D. Putnam, *Bowling Alone: The Collapse and Revival of American Community* (New York: Simon & Schuster, 2000), 117.

29. John R. Seeley et al., *Community Chest: A Case Study in Philanthropy* (Toronto: University of Toronto Press, 1957; reprint, with a new introduction by Carl Milofsky, New Brunswick, NJ: Transaction Publishers, 1989), 195, 159 (page citations are to the reprint edition).

30. Eleanor Brilliant, *The United Way: Dilemmas of Organized Charity* (New York: Columbia University Press), 32; Andrews, *Philanthropic Giving*, 139; Seeley, *Community Chest*, 27.

31. Seeley, *Community Chest*, 257, 391–92.

32. Brilliant, *United Way*, 30.

33. And about 75 percent by 1954, ibid., 26–27, 323 n. 4.

34. Andrews, *Philanthropic Giving*, 144.

35. *Bulletin of the American Association of Fund Raising Counsel* 93 (November 1957), 1.

36. Edwin R. Embree, "Timid Billions—Are the Foundations Doing Their Job?" *Harper's Magazine* 198 (March 1949), 30, 31, 33.

37. Raymond B. Fosdick, *The Story of the Rockefeller Foundation* (New York: Harper & Brothers, 1952), 100.

38. Andrews, *Philanthropic Giving*, 219.

39. Embree, "Timid Billions," 35.

40. Morton Keller and Phyllis Keller, *Making Harvard Modern: The Rise of America's University* (New York: Oxford University Press, 2001), 182.

41. Robert Bremner, *American Philanthropy* (Chicago: University of Chicago Press, 1960, revised 1988), 160.

42. Seeley, *Community Chest*, 95.

43. Andrew J. F. Morris, *The Limits of Voluntarism: Charity and Welfare from the New Deal through the Great Society* (Cambridge: Cambridge University Press, 2009), 68–69.

44. *Tax-Exempt Foundations: Hearings on H. Res. 561, Before the Select Committee to Investigate Tax-Exempt Foundations and Comparable Organizations,* 82nd Cong. 15–17, 43 (1952) (statement of Ernest V. Hollis, Chief of College Administration in the U.S. Office of Education).

45. David Hammack and Stanton Wheeler, *Social Science in the Making: Essays on the Russell Sage Foundation, 1907–1972* (New York: Russell Sage Foundation, 1994), 81–82. The Carnegie Corporation of New York reported that 73 percent of its grants in 1947–48 involved the social sciences as opposed to only 28 percent in 1945–46, Andrews, *Philanthropic Giving*, 226.

46. Waldemar A. Nielsen, *The Big Foundations* (New York: Columbia University Press, 1972), 107–18.

47. Dwight Macdonald, *The Ford Foundation: The Men and the Millions* (New York: Reynal & Company, 1956; reprint, with a new introduction by Francis X. Sutton, New Brunswick: Transaction Publishers, 1989), 3 (page citation is to the reprint edition).

48. "Report of the Trustees of the Ford Foundation, September 27, 1950," in *Tax-Exempt Foundations: Hearings on H. Res. 561, Before the Select Comm. to Investigate Tax-Exempt Foundations and Comparable Organizations,* 82nd Cong. 206 (1952).

49. Francis X. Sutton, "The Ford Foundation: The Early Years," *Daedalus* 116 (Winter 1987): 41–91; Macdonald, *Ford Foundation*, 10–11.

50. Charles Dollard of the Carnegie Corporation, "Informational Bulletin no. 2, 25 January 1949," Study for the Ford Foundation on Policy and Programs, box 1, folder 2, Ford Foundation Archives [FF].

51. The Study Committee (H. Rowan Gaither, Jr., chairman), *Report of the Study*

for the Ford Foundation on Policy and Program (Detroit: The Ford Foundation, November 1949), 52.

52. "Background on Personnel, December 20, 1948," "Organizational Chart," Study for the Ford Foundation on Policy and Programs, box 3, folder 24; "Release 7.p.m.," December 20, 1948, Study for the Ford Foundation on Policy and Programs, box 1, folder 6, FF.

53. Sutton, "The Early Years," 47.

54. "General Statement (tentative)," Study for the Ford Foundation on Policy and Program, box 3, folder 25, FF.

55. *Report of the Study for the Ford Foundation*, 47.

56. Dollard, "Informational Bulletin no. 2."

57. *Report of the Study for the Ford Foundation*, 19–20; see also Alan R. Raucher, *Paul G. Hoffman: Architect of Foreign Aid* (Lexington: University Press of Kentucky, 1985), 82.

58. *Report of the Study for the Ford Foundation*, 91.

59. Olivier Zunz, *Why the American Century?* (Chicago: University of Chicago Press, 1998), 36–39.

60. Ellen Condliffe Lagemann, *The Politics of Knowledge: The Carnegie Corporation, Philanthropy, and Public Policy* (Chicago: University of Chicago Press, 1989), 141–46, 176–77.

61. Morton Keller and Phyllis Keller, *Making Harvard Modern: The Rise of America's University* (New York: Oxford University Press, 2001), 187.

62. *Report of the Study for the Ford Foundation*, 43–46.

63. Ibid., 20.

64. Macdonald, *Ford Foundation*, 102.

65. Dyke Brown to Ford File, February 9, 1949, Study for the Ford Foundation on Policy and Programs, box 3, folder 25, FF.

66. Peter H. Odegard, "Tentative Report Submitted, 3/5/49," Study for the Ford Foundation on Policy and Programs, box 3, folder 33, FF.

67. The feeling was that "the results of natural sciences *always* produce new social problems, the solution of which is *never* provided by the natural sciences" wrote Bill McPeak to Roman Gaither on May 20, 1949, Study for the Ford Foundation on Policy and Programs, box 3, folder 25, FF.

68. T. Duckett Jones, "Preliminary Form of a Proposed Statement for the Health Division," Study for the Ford Foundation on Policy and Programs, box 3, folder 30, FF; W. G. Beadle, "Statement as Related to the Field of Biology," March 1949, box 3, folder 32.

69. Harry S. Ashmore, *Unseasonable Truths: The Life of Robert Maynard Hutchins* (Boston: Little, Brown and Company, 1989), 314–22.

70. Ralph Engelman, *Public Radio and Television in America: A Political History* (Thousand Oaks, CA: Sage Publications, 1996), 136–39.

71. See Alice O'Connor, "The Politics of Rich and Rich: Postwar Investigations of Foundations and the Rise of the Philanthropic Right," in *American Capitalism: So-*

cial Thought and Political Economy in the Twentieth Century, ed. Nelson Lichtenstein (Philadelphia: University of Pennsylvania Press, 2006), 228–48; Thomas C. Reeves, *Freedom and the Foundation: The Fund for the Republic in the Era of McCarthyism* (New York: Alfred A. Knopf, 1969), 21–39.

72. Raucher, *Paul G. Hoffman,* 98; Sutton, "The Early Years," 73, reports the firing at an earlier date.

73. Sutton, "The Early Years," 83.

74. *Report of the Study for the Ford Foundation on Policy and Program,* vol. 2 (Report on Education): 33, 41.

75. Nielsen, *Big Foundations,* 90; Nancy J. Weiss, *Whitney M. Young, Jr., and the Struggle for Civil Rights* (Princeton, NJ: Princeton University Press, 1989), 91.

76. Captain William H. Stayton to J. Howard Pew, Esq., December 16, 1936, Acc. 1634, box 1, American Liberty League, 1936–37, Hagley Museum and Library [HML].

77. Robert F. Burk, *The Corporate State and the Broker State* (Cambridge, MA: Harvard University Press, 1990), 278–98.

78. Hayek had thought of calling his group the Acton-Tocqueville society, Acc. 1634, box 4, 1944, HML.

79. Trust Agreement, J. Howard Pew Freedom Trust, October 24, 1957, Acc. 2020, Series II, box 1, HML.

80. Norman Vincent Peale to J. Howard Pew, May 2, 1945, Acc. 1634, box 7, G1945, HML.

81. James W. Fifield, Jr., to Howard J. Pew, January 4, 1944, Acc. 1634, box 4, HML.

82. Jasper E. Crane to John Foster Dulles, July 2, 1946, Acc. 1416, box 138, HML.

83. On the community chest and community foundation, Acc. 1416, box 111, and on the United Fund, see the 1946 annual report, 3, Acc. 1416, box 100, HML.

84. Jasper E. Crane to Eugene DuPont, October 25, 1946, Acc. 1416, box 100, HML.

85. A. Dorothy Arthur to Harold Brayman, "Speech by Dr. W.E.B. Du Bois at YWCA Public Affairs Meeting on November 19, 1947," November 21, 1947, Acc. 1416, box 100, HML.

86. Joel R. Gardner, *A History of the Pew Charitable Trusts* (Philadelphia: The Trusts, c. 1991).

87. O'Connor, "Politics of Rich and Rich"; Harry D. Gideonse, "A Congressional Committee's Investigation of the Foundations," *The Journal of Higher Education* 25 (December, 1954): 457–63.

88. *Tax-Exempt Foundations: Hearings on H. Res. 561, Before the Select Committee to Investigate Tax-Exempt Foundations and Comparable Organizations,* 82nd Cong. 569–572 (1952) (statement of John W. Davis, Honorary Trustee of the Carnegie Endowment for International Peace); in 1954 Davis would also side with Oppenheimer when the physicist lost his security clearance.

89. *Tax-Exempt Foundations: Hearings on H. Res. 561, Before the Select Committee to Investigate Tax-Exempt Foundations and Comparable Organizations,* 82nd Cong. 344 (1952) (statement of Charles Dollard, President of the Carnegie Corporation of New York).

90. "Robert M. Hutchins, Long a Leader in Educational Change, Dies at 78," *New York Times,* May 16, 1977.

91. *Tax-Exempt Foundations: Hearings on H. Res. 561, Before the Select Committee to Investigate Tax-Exempt Foundations and Comparable Organizations,* 82nd Cong. 297 (1952) (statement of Robert M. Hutchins, Associate Director of the Ford Foundation).

92. Gideonse, "A Congressional Committee."

93. *Tax-Exempt Foundations: Hearings on H. Res. 217, Before the Special Committee to Investigate Tax-Exempt Foundations and Comparable Organizations,* 83rd Cong. 25 (1954).

94. J. Howard Pew to Honorable B. Carroll Reece, April 14, 1953, Acc. 1634, box 96, Foundations 1953–1954, HML.

95. Alfred Dudley Ward, ed., *Goals of Economic Life* (Harper & Brothers, 1953), viii, acknowledgement to the Foundation on ix.

96. J. Howard Pew to James C. Ingebretsen, April 17, 1953, Acc. 1634, box 96, Foundations 1953–1954, HML.

97. Macdonald, *Ford Foundation,* 69–80.

98. "Report of the Director," *Annual Report Covering the Period from 1 January through 31 December 1957* (New York: The Foundation Library Center, 1958), 5–6.

99. For a detailed account of this episode, see Patrick L. O'Daniel, "More Honored in the Breach: A Historical Perspective of the Permeable IRS Prohibition on Campaigning by Churches," *Boston College Law Review* 42 (July 2001): 733–69.

100. Gardner, *A History of the Pew Charitable Trusts; The Pew Memorial Trust, Annual Report 1979* (Philadelphia: The Glenmede Trust Company).

101. Trust Agreement, J. Howard Pew Freedom Trust, October 24, 1957, Acc. 2020, Series II, box 1, HML.

102. J. Howard Pew, "Faith and Freedom: An Address," n.d. Acc. 2020, Series IV, box 1, HML.

103. Martin E. Marty, *Modern American Religion,* vol. 3: *Under God, Indivisible, 1941–1960* (Chicago: University of Chicago Press, 1996), 153.

104. Billy Graham, *Just as I Am: The Autobiography of Billy Graham* (New York: HarperCollins, 1997), 288.

105. On Israel, J. Howard Pew to Roger Hull (Chairman, executive committee, Billy Graham New York Crusade, Inc.), June 18, 1957, Acc 1634, box 54, HML.

106. Billy Graham to J. Howard Pew, March 28, 1957, Acc. 1634, box 54, HML.

107. Jerry Beavan, Executive Secretary to Billy Graham to J. Howard Pew, May 18, 1957, Acc. 1634, box 54, HML.

108. On Niebuhr against Peale and Graham, see Marty, *Under God, Indivisible,* 346–47, and Richard Wightman Fox, *Reinhold Niebuhr: A Biography* (New York:

Pantheon Books, 1985), 266; on Niebuhr turning Graham down for a meeting, see Graham, *Just as I Am*, 301.

109. Michael C. Jensen, "The Pews of Philadelphia: The Shy Super Rich Behind Sun Oil," *New York Times*, October 10, 1971.

110. Pew to Hull, June 18, 1957.

111. Billy Graham to J. Howard Pew, March 28, 1957, Acc. 1634, box 54, HML.

112. "A Report to the Public," Billy Graham New York Crusade, Inc., December 16, 1957, Acc 1634, box 54, HML.

113. Billy Graham to Sid Richardson, April 27, 1957, Acc. 1634, box 54, HML. On Richardson, Graham, and Eisenhower, see Marty, *Under God, Indivisible*, 305.

Chapter 7
Investing in Civil Rights

1. McGeorge Bundy to The Honorable John W. Gardner, Common Cause, February 19, 1977, Office Files of McGeorge Bundy, Series II, box 15, folder 192, Ford Foundation Archives [FF].

2. David Cannadine, *Mellon: An American Life* (New York: Alfred A. Knopf, 2006), xiii.

3. Ibid., 569.

4. 107 Cong. Rec. 14, 791 (1961) (statement of Rep. Patman).

5. Nancy Beck Young, *Wright Patman: Populism, Liberalism, and the American Dream* (Dallas: Southern Methodist University Press, 2000), 208.

6. Ibid., 209.

7. Waldemar Nielsen, *The Big Foundations* (New York: Columbia University Press, 1972), 17.

8. In "A Short Account of International Student Politics and the Cold War with Particular Reference to the NSA, CIA, etc.," *Ramparts* (March 1967), 29–38, Sol Stern, with the special assistance of Lee Webb, Michael Ansara, and Michael Wood, confirmed that the fake foundations distributing CIA money Patman had identified in his investigation had funded the National Student Organization's activities abroad; see Hugh Wilford, *The Mighty Wurlitzer: How the CIA Played America* (Cambridge, MA: Harvard University Press, 2008), 239.

9. F. Emerson Andrews, *Patman and Foundations: Review and Assessment* (New York: Foundation Center, 1968), 14, 46.

10. Young, *Patman*, 17.

11. Thomas A. Troyer, *The 1969 Foundation Law: Historical Perspective on Its Origins and Underpinnings* (Washington, DC: Council on Foundations, 2000).

12. House Committee on Ways and Means, Written Statements by Interested Individuals and Organizations on Treasury Department Report on Private Foundations, vol. 1, 89th Cong. 14–18 (1965).

13. Ibid., at 46.

14. Ibid.

15. Elias Clark, "The Limitation on Political Activities: A Discordant Note in the Law of Charities," *VA Law Review* 46 (April 1960): 449–50.

16. Jeffrey M. Berry, with David F. Arons, *A Voice for Non Profits* (Washington, DC: Brookings Institution Press, 2003), 75–77.

17. Tom Wolfe, *Radical Chic & Mau-Mauing the Flak Catchers* (1971; reprint, New York: Picador, 2009), 41.

18. Arthur M. Schlesinger, Jr., *Robert Kennedy and His Times* (Boston: Houghton Mifflin, 1978), vol. 1, 300; Hugh Davis Graham, *Civil Rights and the Presidency: Race and Gender in American Politics, 1960–1972* (New York: Oxford University Press, 1992), 37.

19. Boynton v. Virginia, 364 U.S. 454 (1960).

20. Leslie W. Dunbar (interviewee), Jacquelyn Hall, Helen Bresler, Bob Hall, Peggy Dunbar (interviewers), "Interview with Leslie W. Dunbar, December 18, 1978," Interview G-0075, Southern Oral History Program Collection (#4007), University of North Carolina.

21. John Dittmer, *Local People: The Struggle for Civil Rights in Mississippi* (Urbana: University of Illinois Press, 1995), 19–40.

22. Schlesinger, Jr., *Robert Kennedy*, 329.

23. Uncle Paul Mellon, whose *Reflections in a Silver Spoon: A Memoir*, with John Bassett (New York: William Morrow and Company, Inc., 1992), are in part a lament on the psychological trauma brought about by immense wealth, never thought the estrangement even worthy of mention.

24. See Dorothy Height, *Open Wide the Freedom Gates: A Memoir*, with a foreword by Maya Angelou (New York: Public Affairs, 2003), 138–39.

25. "Interview with Leslie W. Dunbar."

26. Gerda Weissmann Klein, *A Passion for Sharing: The Life of Edith Rosenwald Stern* (Chappaqua, NY: Rossell Books), 164–65.

27. "Interview with Leslie W. Dunbar"; Pat Watters and Reece Cleghorn, *Climbing Jacob's Ladder: The Arrival of Negroes in Southern Politics*, with an introduction by Leslie W. Dunbar (New York: Harcourt, Brace & World, Inc., 1967), 49.

28. Leslie W. Dunbar, "The Southern Regional Council," *Annals of the American Academy of Political and Social Science* 357 (January 1965): 108–12.

29. Schlesinger, Jr., *Robert Kennedy*, 315.

30. Watters and Cleghorn, *Climbing Jacob's Ladder*, 48; Paul M. Gaston, *Coming of Age in Utopia: The Odyssey of an Idea* (Montgomery: NewSouth Books, 2010), 297–98.

31. "Interview with Leslie W. Dunbar"; Kathleen Teltsch, "Field Foundation, Civil Rights Pioneer, to Die at 49; Survivors Will Be Legion," *New York Times*, February 19, 1989.

32. "Interview with Leslie W. Dunbar."

33. August Meier and Elliot Rudwick, *CORE: A Study in the Civil Rights Movement* (Urbana: University of Illinois Press, 1975), 174–81.

34. "Stephen Curriers Missing on Flight," *New York Times*, January 19, 1967.

35. "The Foundations as Pioneers," *Time*, January 19, 1968.

36. Daniel P. Moynihan, *Maximum Feasible Misunderstanding: Community Action in the War on Poverty*, with a foreword by Seldon M. Kruger (New York: Free Press, 1969), 42; Kruger uses the phrase "creative federalism" on v.

37. Virginia M. Esposito, ed., *Conscience & Community: The Legacy of Paul Ylvisaker* (New York: Peter Lang, 1999); Charles T. Morrissey, "Interview with Paul Ylvisaker," Ford Foundation Oral History Project, September–October 1973, FF.

38. Gregory K. Raynor, "The Ford Foundation's War on Poverty: Private Philanthropy and Race Relations in New York City, 1948-1968," in *Philanthropic Foundations: New Scholarship, New Possibilities*, ed. Ellen Condliffe Lagemann (Bloomington: Indiana University Press, 1999), 206–207, 210, 216; Moynihan, *Maximum Feasible Misunderstanding*, 43.

39. Raynor, "The Ford Foundation's War on Poverty," 212.

40. Alice O'Connor, *Poverty Knowledge: Social Science, Social Policy, and the Poor in Twentieth-Century U.S. History* (Princeton, NJ: Princeton University Press, 2001), 132.

41. Moynihan, *Maximum Feasible Misunderstanding*, 59.

42. Richard Magat, *The Ford Foundation at Work: Philanthropic Choices, Methods, and Styles* (New York: Plenum Press, 1979), 121.

43. Alice O'Connor, "Community Action, Urban Reform, and the Fight Against Poverty: The Ford Foundation's Gray Areas Program," *Journal of Urban History* 22 (1996): 609–15.

44. Alice O'Connor, "The Ford Foundation and Philanthropic Activism in the 1960s," in *Philanthropic Foundations: New Scholarship*, ed. Lagemann, 183.

45. Moynihan, *Maximum Feasible Misunderstanding*, 128.

46. Jennifer Mittelstadt, *From Welfare to Workfare: The Unintended Consequences of Liberal Reform, 1945-1965* (Chapel Hill: University of North Carolina Press, 2005), 220–21, note 26.

47. Berry, *A Voice for Nonprofits*, 11–12; Martha Derthick, *Uncontrollable Spending for Social Services Grants* (Washington, DC: Brookings Institution, 1975), 8.

48. Alan Pifer, *Philanthropy in an Age of Transition: The Essays of Alan Pifer* (New York: Foundation Center, 1984), 203; Ellen C. Lagemann, *The Politics of Knowledge: The Carnegie Corporation, Philanthropy, and Public Policy* (Middletown, CT: Wesleyan University Press, 1989), 220.

49. Derthick, *Uncontrollable Spending*, 7–14.

50. Steven Rathgeb Smith and Deborah A. Stone, "The Unexpected Consequences of Privatization," in *Remaking the Welfare State*, ed. Michael K. Brown, (Philadelphia: Temple University Press, 1988), 236.

51. Steven Rathgeb Smith and Michael Lipsky, *Nonprofits for Hire: The Welfare State in the Age of Contracting* (Cambridge, MA: Harvard University Press, 1993), 54.

52. Bruce Jacobs, *The Political Economy of Organizational Change: Urban Institutional Response to the War on Poverty* (New York: Academic Press, 1981), 88–89.

53. Derthick, *Uncontrollable Spending*, 2; Smith and Stone, "Unexpected Consequences," 237.

54. Charles T. Morrissey, "Interview with McGeorge Bundy," Ford Foundation Oral History Project, February 1972 and March 1974, FF.

55. Robert Tolles, *Program Related Investments: A Broader Use of Philanthropy* (first draft), Report 006211, 1975, FF; "Interview with McGeorge Bundy."

56. "Statement Attached to Form 4653 Claiming Status as an Operating Foundation," in Grant 700–0231, to Edward C. Sylvester, Jr., President, Cooperative Assistant Fund, FF.

57. Matt Schudel, "Labor, Hill Official Edward Sylvester Dies," *Washington Post*, February 18, 2005.

58. John G. Simon, President, Taconic Foundation, Inc. to Louis Winnick, Deputy Vice President, The Ford Foundation, February 4, 1970, in Grant 700–0231, FF.

59. Tolles, *Program Related Investments*.

60. Ibid.; Schlesinger, Jr., *Robert Kennedy*, 823.

61. Fred C. Shapiro, "McKissick's Message on Black Power Never Changes; The Successor to Floyd McKissick May Not Be So Reasonable," *New York Times*, October 1, 1967; Thomas J. Sugrue, *Sweet Land of Liberty: The Forgotten Struggle for Civil Rights in the North* (New York: Random House, 2008), 340.

62. Internal 1969 Ford Foundation memo, cited in Randall Brentson Cebul, "'From the Ground Up': Community Organizing, White Backlash, the Ford Foundation, and CORE in the 1967 Election of Carl B. Stokes" (M.A. Thesis, University of Virginia, 2008); see also Karen Ferguson, "Organizing the Ghetto: The Ford Foundation, CORE, and White Power in the Black Power Era, 1967–1969," *Journal of Urban History* 34 (2007): 67–100.

63. Cebul, "'From the Ground Up.'"

64. Ibid.; Jennifer de Forest, "The Closing of the Philanthropic Frontier: The Field and Ford Foundations' Funding of the Metropolitan Applied Research Corporation," 2007, unpublished.

65. Estelle Zannes, with assistance by Mary Jean Thomas, *Checkmate in Cleveland: The Rhetoric of Confrontation during the Stokes Years* (Cleveland, OH: Press of Case Western Reserve University, 1972), 57.

66. Bundy claimed that Seth Taft himself, although defeated, counseled the Ford Foundation a year later to renew the grant to CORE, *Tax Reform, 1969: Hearings on the Subject of Tax Reform, Before the House Comm. on Ways and Means*, 91st Cong. 411, pt. 1 (1969).

67. "Head of Foundation Replies to Accuser," *New York Times*, February 21, 1969; on Rooney's politics, see Hendrik Hertzberg, "The Talk of the Town, 'Hurrah,'" *New Yorker*, (September 30, 1972): 34–35.

68. Kai Bird, *The Color of Truth: McGeorge Bundy and William Bundy* (New York: Simon & Schuster, 1998), 387.

69. Ibid., 386.

70. Richard D. Kahlenberg, *Tough Liberal: Albert Shanker and the Battles over Schools, Unions, Race, and Democracy* (New York: Columbia University Press, 2007), 67–124.

71. As quoted in Jerald E. Podair, *The Strike that Changed New York: Blacks, Whites, and the Ocean Hill-Brownsville Crisis* (New Haven, CT: Yale University Press, 2002), 125.

72. John Ensor Harr and Peter J. Johnson, *The Rockefeller Conscience* (New York: Charles Scribner's Sons, 1991), 293.

73. "Statement by McGeorge Bundy, President of the Ford Foundation to the Committee on Ways and Means, U.S. House of Representatives, on Proposals in Treasury Department Report on Private Foundations, February 20, 1969," File 010880, FF.

74. 115 Cong. Rec. 37,200 (1969).

75. *Tax Reform Act of 1969: Hearings on H.R. 13270, Before the Senate Committee on Finance*, 91st Cong. 676, pt. 1 (1969).

76. *Tax Reform Act of 1969: Hearings on H.R. 13270, Before the Senate Committee on Finance*, 91st Cong. 5354, pt. 6 (1969).

77. de Forest, "The Closing of the Philanthropic Frontier."

78. Harr and Johnson, *The Rockefeller Conscience*, 295.

79. Memorandum, in Office of the President, Office Files of McGeorge Bundy, Series II, box 19, folder 242, FF; for similar reasoning, see Pifer, *Philanthropy in an Age of Transition*, 50–51.

80. John P. Frank, "Conflict of Interest and U.S. Supreme Court Justices," *The American Journal of Comparative Law* 18 (Autumn 1970): 744–61; Lucas A. Powe, Jr., *The Warren Court and American Politics* (Cambridge, MA: Belknap Press of Harvard University Press, 2000), 477–81.

81. Laura Kalman, *Abe Fortas: A Biography* (New Haven: Yale University Press, 1990), 366.

82. Troyer, *The 1969 Foundation Law*.

Chapter 8
In Search of a Nonprofit Sector

1. A controversy emerged early on over the strategic meaning of the term "nonprofit sector"; see Barry Karl's review of Walter W. Powell, *The Nonprofit Sector: A Research Handbook* (New Haven, CT: Yale University Press, 1987) in *Science*, May 22, 1987, 984–85, and Peter Dobkin Hall, *Inventing the Nonprofit Sector and Other Essays on Philanthropy, Voluntarism, and Nonprofit Organizations* (Baltimore: Johns Hopkins University Press, 1992), 244.

2. Alexis de Tocqueville, *Democracy in America*, trans. Arthur Goldhammer (New York: Library of America, 2004), 606.

3. This is the question that Robert D. Putnam is asking in *Bowling Alone: The Collapse and Revival of American Community* (New York: Simon & Schuster, 2000).

4. Alan Pifer, *Philanthropy in an Age of Transition* (New York: Foundation Center, 1984), 12.

5. John H. Filer, Chairman, *Giving in America: Toward a Stronger Voluntary Sector*, Report of the Commission on Private Philanthropy and Public Needs (n.p., 1975), 35.

6. Martha Derthick, *Uncontrollable Spending for Social Services Grants* (Washington, DC: The Brookings Institution, 1975), 2; Steven Rathgeb Smith and Deborah A. Stone, "The Unexpected Consequences of Privatization," in *Remaking the Welfare State*, ed. Michael K. Brown (Philadelphia: Temple University Press, 1988), 237.

7. Steven Rathgeb Smith and Michael Lipsky, *Nonprofits for Hire: The Welfare State in the Age of Contracting* (Cambridge, MA: Harvard University Press, 1993), 56.

8. Ibid., 59.

9. Pifer, *Philanthropy in an Age of Transition*, 24.

10. Peter J. Petkas, "The New Federalism: Government Accountability and Private Philanthropy," in *Research Papers Sponsored by The Commission on Private Philanthropy and Public Needs* (n.p.: Department of the Treasury, 1977) vol. 2, 1305–15.

11. Joan Hoff, *Nixon Reconsidered* (New York: Basic Books, 1994), 70; Timothy Conlan, *New Federalism: Intergovernmental Reform From Nixon to Reagan* (Washington DC: The Brookings Institution, 1988), 31.

12. Richard P. Nathan, Paul R. Dommel, Sarah F. Liebschutz, Milton D. Morris, "Monitoring the Block Grant Program for Community Development," *Political Science Quarterly* 92 (Summer 1977), 222.

13. Pifer, *Philanthropy in an Age of Transition*, 13.

14. John Ensor Harr and Peter J. Johnson, *The Rockefeller Conscience* (New York: Charles Scribner's Sons, 1991), 375–76.

15. Eleanor Brilliant, *Private Charity and Public Inquiry: A History of the Filer and Peterson Commissions* (Bloomington: Indiana University Press, 2000), 56–63, 87–98.

16. Ibid., 110.

17. Daniel P. Moynihan, draft speech, Coalition of National Voluntary Organizations, October 4, 1978, MSS46, Convo, Board Packet, Independent Sector records, 1971–1976, Ruth Lilly Special Collections and Archives, University Library, Indiana University Purdue University at Indianapolis [IS].

18. Brilliant, *Private Charity and Public Inquiry*, 114.

19. Filer, *Giving in America*, 93.

20. Ibid., 42–48.

21. Ibid., 20, 35.

22. Ibid., 70–72; Putnam, *Bowling Alone*, 125, fig. 32.

23. Filer, *Giving in America*, 71–73, Putnam, *Bowling Alone*, 65–79.

24. Filer, *Giving in America*, 82.

25. Ibid., 80–85.

26. Colin B. Burke , "Voluntary and nonprofit associations per capita, by region and type of association, and in selected cities: 1840–1990," Table Bg4, and idem, "Foundations, community trusts, and nonprofit organizations—number, endowment income, and grant expenditures, by sector: 1921–1997," Table Bg36 in *Historical Statistics of the United States, Earliest Times to the Present: Millennial Edition*, ed. Susan B. Carter, Scott S. Gartner, Michael R. Haines, et al. (New York: Cambridge University Press, 2006), http://dx.doi.org/10.1017/ISBN-9780511132971.Bg1-250.

27. Filer, *Giving in America*, 79.

28. Harr and Johnson, *The Rockefeller Conscience*, 376, 387.

29. Brilliant, *Private Charity and Public Inquiry*, 130; on the British Charity Commission, see David Owen, *English Philanthropy, 1660–1960* (Cambridge, MA: The Belknap Press of Harvard University Press, 1964), 572–97.

30. Harr and Johnson, *The Rockefeller Conscience*, 387–88.

31. Brilliant, *Private Charity and Public Inquiry*, 131–32.

32. National Committee for Responsive Philanthropy, *Thirty Years: A History from 1976 to 2006* (Washington, DC: NCRP, n.d.).

33. Jon Van Til, *Growing Civil Society: From Nonprofit Sector to Third Space* (Bloomington: Indiana University Press, 2000), 102; Eleanor Brilliant, "Federated Fundraising," in *Philanthropy in America: A Comprehensive Historical Encyclopedia*, ed. Dwight F. Burlingame (Santa Barbara, CA: ABC-Clio, 2004), 152; National Committee for Responsive Philanthropy, *The Workplace Giving Revolution: A Special Report* (Washington, DC, 1987); Emily Barman, *Contesting Communities: The Transformation of Workplace Charity* (Stanford, CA: Stanford University, 2006), 66–68.

34. "United Way Backs Plan to Relax Hold on Drives," *New York Times*, October 12, 1979.

35. Donald P. Baker, "Federal Campaign is Criticized for Shutting Out New Agencies," *Washington Post*, October 12, 1979; "House Panel Asks Major Changes in Charity Campaign," *Washington Post*, December 25, 1979.

36. "The Collaboration of Coalition of National Voluntary Organizations and National Council on Philanthropy, Background Information and Initial Statements by John W. Gardner and Brian O' Connell," MSS 46, Convo, Board Packet, October 4, 1978, IS.

37. John W. Gardner, "Remarks," Charter meeting, Independent Sector, Wednesday, March 5, 1980, MSS 46, Memos to Members, March–June 1980, IS.

38. Ibid.

39. Daniel P. Moynihan, "On Pluralism and the Independent Sector, a Talk at the Charter Meeting of Independent Sector, March 5, 1980," MSS 46, Memos to Members, March-June 1980, IS.

40. Paul F. Bourke, "The Pluralist Reading of James Madison's Tenth Federalist," *Perspectives in American History* 9 (1975): 271–95.

41. Moynihan, draft speech, October 4, 1978.

42. Joel R. Gardner, *A History of the Pew Charitable Trusts* (Philadelphia: The Trusts, c. 1991); there had been a public mention in 1967 of a gift J. N. Pew, Jr., had made to Stanford.

43. Draft of "Philanthropy of Organized Religion: A Nationwide Survey of the Council on Foundations, November 1984, A Special Project of the Council of Foundations." The council successfully applied to the Pew Charitable Trust for funding, Pew Archives, Accession 2020, series XIII, box 5, Hagley Museum and Library [HML].

44. Ibid.

45. Sarah C. Carey, "An Overview of the Philanthropy of Organized Religion and Possible Areas of Collaboration with Foundations," Council on Foundations, October 15, 1982. Pew Archives, Accession 2020, series VI, box 2, HML.

46. The Gallup Organization, "American Volunteer, 1981," Conducted for Independent Sector, MSS46, Surveys, IS.

47. "Patterns of Charitable Giving by Individuals: An Independent Sector Research Report Based on the 1979 Gallup Survey Commissioned by the Coalition of National Voluntary Organizations," MSS 46, Memos to Members, July–December 1980, IS.

48. Brian O'Connell, "Deduction for Nonitemizers Rises to 50%," MSS 46 Brian O'Connell Originals, 1985, IS.

49. Sandford F. Brandt, "Anatomy of a Bill that Couldn't Pass—But Did: The Charitable Contributions Legislation, 1975–1981," MSS 46, CCL History, 1984, IS.

50. Ibid.

51. The program began with a 1975 Yale study entitled "Proposal for a Study of Independent Institutions," by university president Kingman Brewster, law school professor and Taconic Foundation president (see chapter 7) John G. Simon, and political scientist Charles E. Lindblom. Brewster had been working with John D. Rockefeller III on establishing the Filer commission; he was concerned with the strings attached to federal funding on private universities. *Nonprofit Sector,* edited by Powell, is a major outcome of the Yale program marking the boundaries of the new field.

52. Adam Yarmolinsky, "Regulation of Charitable Fund-Raising: The Schaumburg Decision, A Summary Report from Independent Sector," 1980, MSS 46, Memos to Members, March–June 1980, IS.

53. The two most controversial proposals were the Family Assistance Plan and the Child Development Act, both of which were defeated in Congress. Nixon adviser Pat Buchanan was particularly aggravated that federal bureaucracies were so dependent on liberal think tanks. H. R. Halderman ordered White House staff not to use Brookings; see James Allen Smith, *The Idea Brokers: Think Tanks and the Rise of the New Policy Elite* (New York: Free Press, 1991), 196–99.

54. Irving Kristol, "On Corporate Philanthropy," *Wall Street Journal,* March 21, 1977.

55. Lewis F. Powell, Jr., to Eugene B. Sydnor, Jr., Chairman, Education Commit-

tee, U.S. Chamber of Commerce, "Confidential Memorandum: Attack of American Free Enterprise System," August 23, 1971; see John B. Judis, *The Paradox of American Democracy: Elites, Special Interests, and the Betrayal of Public Trust* (New York: Routledge, 2001), 116–17; William E. Simon, *A Time for Truth* (New York: Reader's Digest Press, 1978), 299.

56. Quoted in Alice O'Connor, *Social Science for What? Philanthropy and the Social Question in a World Turned Rightside Up* (New York: Russell Sage Foundation, 2007), 131.

57. Kristol, "On Corporate Philanthropy"; Alice O'Connor, "Financing the Counter Revolution," in *Rightward Bound: Making America Conservative in the 1970s*, ed. Bruce J. Schulman and Julian E. Zelizer (Cambridge, MA: Harvard University Press, 2008), 162.

58. Donald T. Critchlow, *The Conservative Ascendancy: How the GOP Right Made Political History* (Cambridge, MA: Harvard University Press, 2007), 117.

59. Jeffrey M. Berry, with David F. Arons, *A Voice for Non Profits* (Washington, DC: Brookings Institution Press, 2003), 81.

60. Kim Phillips-Fein, "'If Business and the Country Will Be Run Right': The Business Challenge to the Liberal Consensus, 1945–1964," *International Labor and Working-Class History* 72 (2007): 192–215; Smith, *Idea Brokers*, 175.

61. Judis, *Paradox*, 123–24.

62. Kathleen Teltsch "Conservative Unit Gains from Legacy: Olin Foundation Tells of Plan for Education Activity with Founder's 50 Million," *New York Times*, October 2, 1983.

63. Idem, "Fund Selects Head for Study of Public Policy," *New York Times*, September 26, 1985.

64. Karen Rothmyer, "The Mystery Angel of the New Right: How Richard Mellon Scaife Shelled Out a $100 Million To Bring Us the Many Voices of His Conservative Chorus," *Washington Post*, July 12, 1981; Bernard Weinraub, "Foundations Assist Conservative Cause: Institutions Finance Publications, Political Research Groups and Scholars to Spread Ideas," *New York Times*, January 20, 1981.

65. Frederick C. Klein, "MacArthur's Millions: New Foundation Shapes Up as a Big One and One That Will Be Far from Typical," *Wall Street Journal*, April 26, 1979.

66. Jeff Krehely, Meaghan House, and Emily Kernan, "Axis of Ideology: Conservative Foundations and Public Policy (n.p.: National Committee for Responsive Philanthropy, March 2004), 10.

67. Andrew Rich, *Think Tanks, Public Policy, and the Politics of Expertise* (New York: Cambridge University Press, 2004), 53–55

68. Lee Edwards, *The Power of Ideas: The Heritage Foundation at 25 Years* (Ottawa, IL: Jameson Books, 1997), 9; Critchlow, *Conservative Ascendancy*, 128.

69. Smith, *Idea Brokers*, 200; Godfrey Hodgson, *The World Turned Right Side Up: A History of the Conservative Ascendancy in America* (Boston: Houghton Mifflin, 1996), 177–80.

70. Judis, *Paradox*, 124.

71. Ibid., 144–45; Critchlow, *Conservative Ascendancy*, 130.

72. Smith, *Idea Brokers*, 200

73. See especially Steven M. Teles, *The Rise of the Conservative Legal Movement: The Battle for the Control of the Law* (Princeton: Princeton University Press, 2008).

74. Minutes of the Columbia University Seminar on Philanthropy, 19 March 1984.

75. Hodgson, *World Turned Right Side Up*, 176–77; Joseph Crespino, "Civil Rights and the Religious Right," in *Rightward Bound*, 94.

76. Charles L. Heatherly, ed., foreword by Edwin J. Feulner, Jr. (Washington, DC: Heritage Foundation, 1981)

77. Gilbert A. Lewthwaite, "U.S. Withdraws Rules on Lobby Financing," *Baltimore Sun*, March 10, 1983.

78. O'Connor, "Financing the Counter Revolution," 164.

79. Lester M. Salamon, "The Changing Partnership Between the Voluntary Sector and the Welfare State," in *The Future of the Nonprofit Sector: Challenges, Changes, and Policy Considerations,* ed. Virginia A. Hodgkinson and Richard W. Lyman (San Francisco: Jossey-Bass Publishers, 1989) , 45–46.

80. Anne S. Morrison, "The Reagan Economic Program: A Working Paper for Grantmakers," Council on Foundations, Inc., September 1981, MSS 46, Government Relations, Council on Foundations, 1981–1983, IS.

81. Salamon, "Changing Partnership," 49

82. Brian O'Connell, "What Voluntary Activity Can and Can't Do for America," discussion draft, 1989, MSS 46, Publications, IS.

83. "Points of Light Initiative: Community Service as National Policy, June 22, 1989, The White House, MSS 46, Points of Light, 1989–1991, IS.

84. Brian O'Connell, "Sector Chairperson's observations, Independent Sector Membership Meeting, New York City, May 9, 1984, MSS 46, Annual meeting Packet, April 1984, IS.

85. Idem, "What Voluntary Activity Can and Can't Do for America."

86. Marvin Olasky, *The Tragedy of American Compassion* (Washington, DC: Regnery Gateway, 1992), 209.

87. Amy E. Black, Douglas L. Koopman, and David K. Ryden, *Of Little Faith: The Politics of George W. Bush's Faith-Based Initiative* (Washington, DC: Georgetown University Press, 2004), 44–45.

88. Mark Chaves, "Religious Congregations," in *The State of Nonprofit America,* ed. Lester M. Salomon, 288; see also Andrew Walsh, ed., *Can Charitable Choice Work? Covering Religion's Impact on Urban Affairs and Social Services* (Hartford, CT: Pew Program on Religion and News Media and the Greenberg Center for the Study of Religion in Public Life, 2001).

89. Ceci Connolly, "Gore Urges Role for 'Faith-Based' Groups," *Washington Post,* May 25, 1999.

90. Adam Clymer, "Filter Aid to Poor Through Churches, Bush Urges." *New York Times,* July 23, 1999.

91. Ibid.

92. Laura Brown Chisolm, "Sinking the Think-Tanks Upstream: The Use and Misuse of Tax Exemption Law to Address the Use and Misuse of Tax Exempt Organizations by Politicians," *University of Pittsburgh Law Review* 51 (1989), 577–640.

93. Berry and Arons, *Voice for Nonprofits*, 82; Planned Parenthood Federation of America, Inc., "A-122 Lobbying Rules," May 16, 1984, MSS 46, OMB, Organizational Response, 1983–1984, IS.

94. Oliver A. Houck, "On the Limits of Charity: Lobbying, Litigation, and Electoral Politics by Charitable Organizations Under the Internal Revenue Code and Related Laws," *Brooklyn Law Review* 69, 1 (2003–2004): 67.

95. Berry and Arons, *Voice for Nonprofits*, 55.

96. Ibid., 65.

97. See Sheldon D. Pollack, *The Failure of U.S. Tax Policy: Revenue and Politics* (University Park, PA: Penn State Press, 1999), 174–75; *Regan v. Taxation With Representation*, 461 U.S. 540 (1983).

98. Houck, "On the Limits of Charity," 45–46, 66.

99. *Citizens United v. Federal Election Commission*, 130 S. Ct. 876 (2010).

100. Philip Rucker, "The Film That Cracked the Case," *Washington Post*, January 22, 2010.

Chapter 9
American Philanthropy and the World's Communities

1. A "global associational revolution" said Lester M. Salamon in "The Rise of the Nonprofit Sector," *Foreign Affairs* 73 (July–August 1994): 109.

2. See Zi Zhongyun, *The Destiny of Wealth: An Analysis of American Philanthropic Foundations from a Chinese Perspective* (Dayton, OH: Kettering Foundation Press, 2007); the first Chinese edition of this book was published in 2002 under the title *A Good Way to Distribute Wealth (That Is To Spend Money)*. Openness towards civil society institutions remains threatened throughout the world, as Douglas Rutzen and Catherine Shea report in "The Associational Counter-Revolution," *Alliance* 11, 3 (September 2006): 27–28.

3. Edmund J. Keller, "Drought, War, and the Politics of Famine in Ethiopia and Eritrea," *Journal of Modern African Studies* 30 (December 1992): 609–24.

4. Angela Ravens-Roberts, "Famine, Fieldwork, and Performance: Issues and Implications of the Practice of Relief Intervention—A Case Study from Ethiopia, 1984–1988," (Ph.D. diss., University of Minnesota, 2000), 34–37.

5. Amartya Sen, *Poverty and Famines: An Essay on Entitlement and Deprivation* (New York: Oxford University Press, 1980), 1.

6. Steven Varnis, *Reluctant Aid or Aiding the Reluctant?: U.S. Food Aid Policy and Ethiopian Famine Relief* (New Brunswick, NJ: Transaction Publishers, 1990), 41.

7. Hailu Lemma, "Politics of Famine in Ethiopia," *Review of African Political*

Economy 12 (August 1985): 44–58; Joseph Berger, "Eritreans Ask Separate Aid, Saying Rebel Areas Get Little," *New York Times*, November 25, 1984.

8. Opening remarks by Kenneth Hackett of Catholic Relief Services, "The Ethiopian Crisis: Philanthropy in Action," Minutes of the Columbia University Seminar on Philanthropy, May 13, 1985.

9. Varnis, *Reluctant Aid*, 35

10. Ravens-Roberts, "Famine, Fieldwork, and Performance," 37–40; Clifford D. May, "Relations Sour Between Ethiopia and Western Food Donors," *New York Times*, February 18, 1985.

11. Jay Ross, "Famine, War Threaten Thousands in Ethiopia. U.S. Slow to Aid Ethiopia, a Soviet Ally, in Famine," *Washington Post*, June 26, 1983.

12. Stephen Ryan, *The United Nations and International Politics* (New York: St. Martin's Press, 2000), 91–95; Stanley Meisler, *The United Nations: The First Fifty Years* (New York: Atlantic Monthly Press, 1995), 228–38.

13. Edward Kissi, "Beneath International Famine Relief in Ethiopia: The United States, Ethiopia, and the Debate over Relief Aid, Development Assistance, and Human Rights," *African Studies Review* 48 (September 2005), 123.

14. Kurt Jansson, Michael Harris, Angela Penrose, *The Ethiopian Famine: The Story of the Emergency Relief Operation* (London: Zed Books, 1987), 27.

15. Hackett, "The Ethiopian Crisis."

16. Joseph Berger, "Offers of Aid for Stricken Ethiopia Are Pouring in to Relief Agencies. Thousands Offer Aid to Ethiopia Famine Victims," *New York Times*, October 28, 1984.

17. Philip M. Boffey, "Disputes Erupt over Ethiopian Relief Efforts," *New York Times*, November 1, 1984.

18. Peter Davies, president, InterAction, "The Role of U.S. PVOs in the Ethiopian Crisis," Minutes of the Columbia University Seminar on Philanthropy, October 14, 1985.

19. Philip M. Boffey, "US Will Provide $45 Million for Famine Relief in Ethiopia," *New York Times*, October 26, 1984; David E. Sanger, "Agencies Step Up Relief for Ethiopia," *New York Times*, November 3, 1984.

20. Jansson et al., *The Ethiopian Famine*, 23.

21. Varnis, *Reluctant Aid*, 106.

22. Hackett, "The Ethiopian Crisis."

23. Mohammed Amin, "Relief Workers Struggle to Feed Thousands in North Ethiopia," *Washington Post*, October 24, 1984.

24. Marc Lindenberg, *Going Global: Transforming Relief and Development NGOs* (Bloomfield, CT: Kumarian, 2001), 5.

25. Robert P. Beschel, Jr., "The Role of U.S. Foundations in East/Central Europe: Conference Report," and idem, "Foundation Grantmaking Relating to Central Europe and the Soviet Union," The Ford Foundation, The Pew Charitable Trusts and the Rockefeller Brothers Fund, January 11, 1991, Reports 012072 and 012052, Ford Foundation Archives [FF].

26. James M. Goldgeier and Michael McFaul, *Power and Purpose: U.S. Policy Toward Russia after the Cold War* (Washington, DC: The Brookings Institution, 2003), 67, 72–73, 84–85.

27. Joanna Regulska, "Self-Governance or Central Control? Rewriting Constitutions in Central and Eastern Europe," in *Constitution Making in Eastern Europe*, ed. A. E. Dick Howard (Washington, DC: Woodrow Wilson Center Press, 1993), 138–39.

28. Marschall Miklós and Kuti Éva, "Hungary," in *Governance and Civil Society in a Global Age*, ed. Tadashi Yamamoto and Kim Gould Ashizawa (Tokyo: Japan Center for International Exchange, 2001), 179.

29. Vassil Penev, "La notoriété de Tocqueville en Bulgarie," *La Revue Tocqueville/The Tocqueville Review* 18, 1 (1997), 95–96 ; Henryk Wozniakowski, "Anomie polonaise: Entre droit et symbole, entre civisme et patriotisme," *La Revue Tocqueville/The Tocqueville Review* 18, 1 (1997), 127.

30. Alexandru Zub, "Sur les traces de Tocqueville en Roumanie," *La Revue Tocqueville/The Tocqueville Review* 18, 1 (1997), 90.

31. "Soviet and East European Study Group Interim Report for Discussion at the Board Meeting on December 8, 1998," Ford Foundation, Report 016394, FF.

32. Ford Foundation grant to International Commission of Jurists, 1977–1979, Grant Number 07700120, FF; see also Shepard Forman and Kojo Bentsi-Enchill, "International Human Rights Efforts: Human Rights and Governance Program, The Ford Foundation," and Francis X. Sutton, "Poland," prepared for Human Rights, Governance and International Affairs Committee of the Board of Trustees, June 23, 1982, Reports 006622, FF.

33. Other foundations joined the effort, especially the Charles Stewart Mott Foundation and the John D. and Catherine T. MacArthur Foundation; see Joan E. Spero, *The Global Role of U.S. Foundations* (New York: Foundation Center, 2010), 6.

34. Maurice Aymard, "Europe from Division to Reunification: The Eastern European Middle Classes During and After Socialism" in *Social Contracts under Stress: The Middle Classes of America, Europe, and Japan at the Turn of the Century*, ed. Olivier Zunz, Leonard Schoppa, and Nobuhiro Hiwatari (New York: Russell Sage Foundation, 2002), 372, 376.

35. See Michael T. Kaufman, *Soros: The Life of a Messianic Billionaire* (New York: Alfred A. Knopf, 2002).

36. Kevin F. F. Quigley, *For Democracy's Sake: Foundations and Democracy Assistance in Central Europe* (Washington, DC: Woodrow Wilson Center Press, 1997), 87–102.

37. Douglas Rutzen and Catherine Shea report on their monitoring at the International Center for Not-for-Profit Law (ICNL) in "The Associational Counter-Revolution," *Alliance* 11, 3 (September 2006): 27–28.

38. Ibid., 24, 40, 66; Beschel, "The Role of U.S. Foundations in East/Central Europe."

39. Aymard, "Europe from Division to Reunification," 363.

40. Burton Bollag, "Community Foundations Across Eastern Europe Advance 'Step by Step,'" *Chronicle of Philanthropy*, October 18, 2001.

41. Ford Foundation grant to Autonómia Foundation, Budapest, 1990, Grant Number PA900–1516, FF.

42. Carol C. Adelman, "The Privatization of Foreign Aid: Reassessing National Largesse," *Foreign Affairs* 82 (November–December 2003): 9–14.

43. See for example three pamphlets that the New Delhi office of the Ford Foundation published to mark "50 Years of Partnership with India": Manoshi Mitra, *Women, Poverty, and Livelihoods*, 21–23; B. G. Verghese, *Human Resources, Development, and Capacity Building*, 24; Pachampet Sundaram, *From Public Administration to Governance*, 13–26 (New Delhi: The Ford Foundation, 2002).

44. Muhammad Yunus, *Banker to the Poor: Micro-Lending and the Battle Against World Poverty* (New York: Public Affairs, 1999), 112–13, 176, 183–84.

45. "Muhammad Yunus and The Grameen Bank Win the Nobel Peace Prize for 2006," Ford Foundation Press Release, New York, October 17, 2006.

46. Yunus, *Banker to the Poor*, 176–77.

47. Ibid., 71–83.

48. "Muhammad Yunus and The Grameen Bank Win the Nobel Peace Prize for 2006."

49. Muhammad Yunus, *Creating a World Without Poverty: Social Business and the Future of Capitalism* (New York: Public Affairs, 2007), 31. See also David Bornstein and Susan Davis, *Social Entrepreneurship: What Everyone Needs to Know* (New York: Oxford University Press, 2010).

50. "Leave Well Alone; Microfinance," *Economist*, November 20, 2010; Lydia Polgreen and Vikas Bajaj, "Microcredit Is Imperiled in India by Defaults," *New York Times*, November 18, 2010; Muhammad Yunus, "Sacrificing Microcredit for Megaprofits," *New York Times*, January 14, 2011.

51. Amartya Sen, *Development as Freedom* (New York: Anchor Books, 2000), 6.

52. Ibid., 201.

53. Ibid., 33.

54. Lindenberg, *Going Global*, 3; Shepard Forman and Abby Stoddard, "International Assistance," in *The State of Nonprofit America*, ed. Lester M. Salamon (Washington, DC: Brookings Institution Press, 2003), 243.

55. Jude Howell and Jenny Pearce, *Civil Society and Development: A Critical Exploration* (Boulder, CO: Lynn Rienner Publishers, Inc., 2001), 96.

56. Lindenberg, *Going Global*, 11.

57. Gerard Clarke, *Politics of NGO's in Southeast Asia: Participation and Protest in the Philippines* (Florence, KY: Routledge, 1998), 7–8; *Human Development Report* (Oxford: Oxford University Press for the United Nations Development Programme, 1993), 92.

58. William Easterly, *The White Man's Burden: Why the West's Efforts to Aid the Rest Have Done So Much Ill and So Little Good* (London: Penguin Books, 2006).

59. "Ted Turner's Gift"; "Thanks a Billion, Ted," *New York Times*, September 21, 1997.

60. Kofi A. Annan, *We the Peoples: The Role of the United Nations in the 21st Century* (New York: United Nations, 2000), 74; see also Jeffrey D. Sachs, with a foreword by Bono, *The End of Poverty: Economic Possibilities for Our Time* (London: Penguin Books, 2005), 210–11.

61. Bill Gates founded the William H. Gates Foundation in 1994 and the Gates Library Foundation in 1997; the two organizations merged in 2000 into the Bill and Melinda Gates Foundation; Warren Buffett made his pledge in 2006.

62. Louis Uchitelle, "Age of Riches: The Richest of the Rich, Proud of a New Gilded Age," *New York Times,* July 15, 2007.

63. Brock Brower, *The New Philanthropists and the Emergence of Venture Philanthropy* (Washington, DC: The CSIS Press, 2001); Matthew Bishop and Michael Green, *Philanthrocapitalism: How the Rich Can Save the World* (New York: Bloomsbury Press, 2008), 88–97.

64. *International Grantmaking IV: An Update on U.S. Foundation Trends* (New York: Foundation Center, 2008).

65. *Time Magazine* named Bill and Melinda Gates and Bono "Persons of the Year" in December 2005.

66. "Foundations to Invest $150 Million On Africa's Seed Systems," *Africa News,* September 14, 2006.

67. "'Green' Alliance Appoints Kofi Annan as Chair," *Africa News*, June 14, 2007.

68. See http://www.agra-alliance.org.

69. *Philanthropy News Digest*, June 16, 2008; on the Millenium Challenge Corporation, see Carol Lancaster, *George Bush's Foreign Aid: Transformation or Chaos?* (Washington, DC: Center for Global Development, 2008).

70. The new trust fund is administered by the World Bank; see U.S. Treasury Department, Fact Sheet, Thursday, April 22, 2010, Global Agriculture and Food Security Program.

71. "AGRA Takes Certified Seeds to Farmers in War On Hunger," *Africa News,* October 2, 2007.

72. Ann C. Hudock, *NGOs and Civil Society: Democracy by Proxy?* (Cambridge: Polity Press, 1995).

73. Spero, *The Global Role of U.S. Foundations*, 11–16.

74. Stefanie Meredith and Elizabeth Ziemba, "The New Landscape of Product Development Partnerships (PDPs)," in *Health Partnerships Review* (Global Forum for Health Research, Geneva, 2008), 11–16.

75. Bethany McLean and Joan Levinstein, "The Power of Philanthropy," *Fortune* 154 (September 18, 2006); Cecilia Dugger, "Clinton Helps Broker Deal for Medicine to Treat AIDS," *New York Times*, December 1, 2006.

76. Amy Waldman, "Gates Offers India $100 million to Fight AIDS: Plans to Finance 10-Year Program," *New York Times*, November 12, 2002.

77. Gowri Parameswaran, "Stemming the Tide: Successes, Failures, and Lessons Learned in Tamil Nadu, India," *Dialectical Anthropology* 28 (2004): 397–414.

78. Amartya Sen, "Foreword," *AIDS Sutra*, 14.

79. Siddharth Dhanvant Shanghvi, "Hello, Darling," *AIDS Sutra*, 69.

80. Bill and Melinda Gates, "Introduction," *AIDS Sutra*, ix–x.

81. Priya Shetty, "Ashok Alexander: Taking On the Challenge of AIDS in India," *The Lancet* 366 (November 26, 2005): 1843.

82. This account is based on four 2008 internal reports from the Bill and Melinda Gates Foundation's Avahan India AIDS Initiative, "The Power to Tackle Violence: Avahan's Experience with Community Led Crisis Response in India"; "Avahan— The India AIDS Initiative: The Business of HIV Prevention at Scale"; "Use it or Lose it: How Avahan Used Data to Shape Its HIV Prevention Efforts in India"; "Managing HIV Prevention From The Ground Up: Peer Led Outreach at Scale in India."

83. The Reagan administration instituted the Mexico City Policy, also known as the Gag Rule, in 1984; the Clinton administration ended it in January 1993; the Bush administration re-instituted it in January 2001; the Obama administration re-scinded it again in January 2009.

84. Interview with Dr. Rebecca Dillingham, Infectious Diseases and International Health, University of Virginia School of Medicine, April 2010.

85. Nicole Wallace, "Red Cross Sees Jump in Internet Donations," *Chronicle of Philanthropy*, September 9, 1999.

Conclusion

1. Its initial phase is described in Alfred D. Chandler, *The Visible Hand: The Managerial Revolution in American Business* (Cambridge, MA: The Belknap Press of Harvard University Press, 1977); Olivier Zunz, *Making America Corporate, 1870–1920* (Chicago: University of Chicago Press, 1990); and Naomi R. Lamoreaux, *The Great Merger Movement in American Business, 1895–1904* (Cambridge: Cambridge University Press, 1985).

2. Adam Smith, *The Theory of Moral Sentiments* (London, 1759; reprint: Indianapolis, IN: Liberty Fund, 1982), 9.

3. Marcel Mauss, "Essai sur le don. Forme et raison de l'échange dans les sociétés archaïques," *L'année sociologique*, 1923–1924; *Sociologie et anthropologie*, with an introduction by Claude Lévi-Strauss (Paris: Presses Universitaires de France, 1950), 239.

4. Economists Matthew Bishop and Michael Green have emphasized this theme in a recent book they have titled *Philanthrocapitalism: How the Rich Can Save the World* (New York: Bloomsbury Press, 2008).

5. Olivier Zunz, ed. *Alexis de Tocqueville and Gustave de Beaumont in America: Their Friendship and Their Travels*, trans. Arthur Goldhammer (Charlottesville: University of Virginia Press, 2010), 38.

6. Alexis de Tocqueville, *Democracy in America*, trans. Arthur Goldhammer (New York: Library of America, 2004), 611.

7. Oscar Harkavy, *Curbing Population Growth: An Insider's Perspective on the Population Movement* (New York: Plenum Press, 1995), 12.

8. Susan U. Raymond and Mary Beth Martin, *Mapping the New World of American Philanthropy: Causes and Consequences of the Transfer of Wealth* (New York: Wiley, 2007).

9. Announcement at http://www.givingpledge.org; see also Stephanie Strom, "Pledge to Give Away Half Gains Billionaire Adherents," *New York Times*, August 4, 2010.

INDEX

AAFRC (American Association of Fundraising Counsel), 68, 313n93
A&P stores, 202
Abolitionists, bequest to, 78–81, 314–15n2
Abortion, gag rule on, 292
Abrams, Frank, 175
Acheson, Dean, 140, 157
ACLU (American Civil Liberties Union), 257, 260
Adolescent Family Life Act (1983), 257
advertising: Depression-era fundraising via, 123; as educational vs. political, 206–7; specific groups targeted in, 62–63. *See also* mass media
advocacy: conservative initiatives in, 189–200; conservatives and liberal-pluralists as converging in tax rules on, 259–63; education distinguished from, 5, 89–103, 196–97, 206, 228–30; foundation funds for targeting specific elections and candidates, 222–23; giving combined with, 78–85, 314–15n2; liberal initiatives in, 180–89; objectivity vs., 98–99. *See also* politics and political issues
Afghanistan, Soviet abuses in, 274
Africa: Green Revolution in, 285–86; HIV/AIDS campaign in, 288. *See also* Ethiopia
African Americans: attitudes toward charity, 18; displaced in Mississippi flooding, 111, 112, 113–14; educational drive for southern schools for, 30–40; labor conference concerning, 270; NAACP membership drive among, 68–69; school decentralization experiment and, 224; voter registration drive for, 208–11, 222–23. *See also* civil rights; racial segregation
African Development Bank, 267
African Relief and Recovery Act (1985), 270
AFSC. *See* American Friends Service Committee (AFSC)
Agger, Carol, 228–29
AGRA (Alliance for a Green Revolution for Africa), 285–86
agricultural development: Dust Bowl causes and recovery, 120–21, 134–35; extension

agencies and, 40–41; Hoover's land redistribution scheme and, 113–16; northern philanthropic support for southern, 40–41; philanthropic efforts extended abroad, 41–43; post-WWII foreign aid program for, 151–59; rice research and, 157. *See also* farm families; Green Revolution; rural development
Agriculture Department, U.S., 135
AIDS campaigns, 285, 286–92
Aid to Families with Dependent Children program, 215
AIPAC (American Israel Public Affairs Committee), 167, 326–27n101
Alabama, public education spending of, 36
Albania, rural development program in, 152
Alcott, Gordon, 251
Alderman, Edwin, 33–34
Aldrich, Nelson, 21
Aldrich, Winthrop W., 139
Alexander, Ashok, 290
Allen, Harold B., 152
Allen-Bradley Company, 250
All-Ethiopian Socialist Movement, 266
Alliance for a Green Revolution for Africa (AGRA), 285–86
almsgiving, 18. *See also* charity and charities; giving
alternative funds concept, 241
Aluminum Company of America, 171
American Action, 190
American Association of Fundraising Counsel (AAFRC), 68, 313n93
American Association of Social Workers, 126
American Baptist Education Society, 19, 27
American Birth Control League, 91, 94–97
American Cancer Society, 163, 241
American City (magazine), 67–68
American City Bureau (firm), 67–68
American Civil Liberties Union (ACLU), 257, 260
American Council for Nationalities Service, 222
American Council of Learned Societies, 195

351

POLITICS AND SOCIETY IN TWENTIETH-CENTURY AMERICA